ISLAM IN THE SUDAN

ISLAM IN THE SUDAN

J. Spencer Trimingham

FRANK CASS & CO. LTD.
1965

Published by Frank Cass & Co. Ltd.,
10 Woburn Walk, London, W.C.1
by arrangement with
Oxford University Press.

First edition 1949
Second impression 1965

*Printed by Charles Birchall & Sons Ltd.
London and Liverpool.*

PREFACE

THE aim of this survey is to help all who are interested in the Sudanese to understand the significance of Islam in their lives. Whilst it is true that a real understanding of the influences which have moulded, and are moulding, the religious thought and spiritual experience of any Islamic people can only be obtained in actual living contact with their cultural and spiritual life, yet, before that contact can be made, one must have a very considerable general and technical knowledge of Islam as a basis for interpretation. Further, the living religion of the people of any particular region is characterized by such diversity and confusion that the new-comer armed with a general text-book on Islam is hardly prepared for the actual religious scene. My aim has been to try to present the reader with the background upon which to base a genuine understanding of the Sudanese, and pave the way to a living contact. I am not describing theoretical Islam, it must be clearly understood, but the living religion of a particular region. If I were describing Christianity in England to-day I should not be interested primarily in what theologians say Christianity is, but should be concerned about the social conditions in which Christianity has during the centuries been the influencing factor, showing how it has moulded men, and how the character and environment of the people have in their turn moulded the form of their Christianity. This is what I have attempted for the Northern Sudan. I hope that the need for systematization and arrangement has not tended to defeat its own end. At any rate, I have tried to make my presentation sociological as well as Islamic, or, in other words, synthetic as well as specialized.

The question of one's 'approach' to Islam cannot be avoided if we are to determine its meaning to us and others to-day. But in dealing with someone else's religion we need a special approach, for in the words of the modern poet:

> I have spread my dreams under your feet;
> Tread softly, because you tread on my dreams.

I can only offer my presentation hoping that it is sufficiently true to the living Islam of the Sudan to enable the reader to make for himself a real approach.

This book has been written during the war years whilst carrying out administrative duties which had to be placed first. Naturally its composition has been affected by those conditions, by the impossibility of sustained periods of study, and by the inaccessibility of libraries; all these have caused the book I have written to fall short of the ideal of the study I should like to have written. If I were to mention by name all my friends, Sudanese, government officials, and missionaries, who have helped me in so many ways, this preface would read like a directory. But though not mentioned by name I am most grateful to them all, for without their help this book could not have been written. My debt to other writers will be sufficiently clear from the references in the footnotes and if any remain unacknowledged the oversight is unintentional. I am grateful to the Survey Department of the Sudan Government for permission to reproduce the map at the end of the book.

J. S. TRIMINGHAM

June 1946

CONTENTS

Preface v

Introduction ix

1. The Land and the People 1
1. The Land 1
2. The People: 4
(*a*) Nubian-speaking Tribes 7
(*b*) Beja Tribes 10
(*c*) Arabic-speaking Tribes 16
(*d*) Muslim Negroids 31
(*e*) Pagan Tribes of the Southern Sudan 35
(*f*) Languages 35

2. Historical Outline: The Christian Kingdoms to the Arab Conquests 39
1. Sketch of Early History 39
2. Conversion of the Nūba to Christianity 48
3. History of Maqurra 59
4. Arab Penetration and End of the Kingdom of Maqurra . . 67
5. History of 'Alwa 72
6. Causes of the Decay and Eclipse of Christianity in the Sudan . 75

3. History of the Sudan under Muslim Rule . . 81
1. Expansion of the Arab Tribes and Arabization of the Sudanese . 81
2. Nubia and Donqola 83
3. The Sennār Confederation 85
4. Dārfūr and its Conversion 89
5. The Turkiyya 91
6. The Mahdiyya 93
7. The Anglo-Egyptian Sudan 96
8. The Expansion of Islam in the Sudan 98

4. Orthodox Islam 105
1. Introductory: General Characteristics of Sudanese Islam . 105
2. The Islamic Church-State 112
3. The Traditional System in the Sudan 115
4. The Modern Organization of the 'Ulamā' . . . 120
5. The Mosques, their Staff and Congregations . . . 122

5. Beliefs and Practices of Popular Islam . . 126
A. SAINT-WORSHIP:
1. Saints in Islam: Muslim Idea of a Holy Man . . . 126
2. Peculiarities of Saint-worship in the Sudan . . . 129
3. Shrines and the Practices connected with them . . . 141
B. ESCHATOLOGICAL ELEMENTS:
1. Belief in a Mahdī 148
2. Mahdism in the Sudan 150
3. Persistence of Belief in a Mahdī and Mahdism . . . 157

C. ANIMISTIC INFLUENCES IN SUDANESE ISLAM:
1. Islam and Animism 163
2. Non-Islamic Superstitions and Pagan Practices . . 166
3. Pagan Influences on Social and Family Life . . . 179

6. The Religious Orders 187
1. The Development of Ṣūfism in Islam 187
2. The Rise of the Religious Orders 191
3. Introduction of the Orders into the Sudan . . . 195
4. Method of Organization 202
5. Doctrines 206
6. Ritual and Practice 212
7. Qādiriyya 217
8. Shādhiliyya 222
9. Majdhūbiyya 224
10. Sammāniyya 226
11. Idrīsiyya (Aḥmadiyya) and Rashīdiyya . . . 228
12. Mirghaniyya or Khatmiyya 231
13. Ismā'īliyya 235
14. Tijāniyya 236
15. Minor Orders (Sanūsiyya, Zabāl'a, 'Azmiyya, and Egyptian Orders) 239

7. Islam and Pagan Sudan 242
1. Islam in contact with Pagan Sudan: 242
(*a*) Tribes East of the Nile 242
(*b*) The Nūbas and Islamic Penetration . . . 244
(*c*) The Pagan Nilotic Tribes 246
2. Muslim Propaganda amongst Pagans 248

8. Influence of Westernism on the Sudan . . 252
1. Effect of British Occupation 252
2. The Development of Education 254
3. Intellectual and Social Change 257
4. Economic Change 264
5. Women and Social Change 266
6. The Press 268

Index 269

MAPS

1. THE ANGLO-EGYPTIAN SUDAN (GENERAL) . . . at end
2. THE CHRISTIAN KINGDOMS . . . . . *facing* 64

INTRODUCTION

THE subject of this book is the Northern Sūdānī; and the Sūdānī in a particular aspect of his being—the religious. We shall sketch first the background of our study—the folk and their environment.

On the one hand we have the environment with its divisions into mountain and valley, river and plain, climate and rainfall, light and winds, sand and soil. On the other, MAN—the cultivator, immured in his village and its range of cultivation, gregarious but isolated in his community; then the nomad, secluded, restless, independent but not free, rather entombed in the desert with his camel.

Man in social life we know is conditioned by his environment, geographical and human, which determines his way of life and his psychological make-up. It is the land rather than ethnic factors which helps us to explain these people, both settled and nomad—their psychological and social statism. Here there is an intimate solidarity between spirit and nature which has moulded and absorbed alien influences throughout the ages.

There can be no question of absolute determinism. Man acts as well as reacts. The folk are no more determined by the land, for it is passive, than the land is determined by the folk. Man spends himself on his environment, changes *himself* so as to maintain himself in the environment, utilizes it, and so far dominates it in turn. Thus the Baqqāra changed their mode of life from camel to cattle. All the effort comes from man. Nature is contingent, even in the Sudan, and presents infinite possibilities among which the will of man, that is, the master not the cultivator, can choose the one or the other. Thus to-day cotton takes precedence over all other produce.

So plain, however, is each of these half-aspects of life that the one or the other has been insisted on by turns, often to the excessive subordination of the other. But there is constant interplay between spirit and matter, Man and Nature. Whilst the character and destiny of the folk are partly conditioned by the land, since man has to change himself to live in it, they also overcome the land, wrench themselves from it by pain and suffering, and determine their region's place in the world.

There does, however, remain a very profound action of the geographical environment on the folk who live in it, especially in a land as hard as that of the Sudan, which makes the conquest of nature by man seem very small indeed. And when, as on immigrants such as Arabs in the Sudan, the indigenous folk are added to the geographical environment, the combined effect has often been such complete modification that when they have settled they have tended gradually to become fused in type with these indigenous folk.

With both the cultivator and the nomad the monotony and unity of his life are his response to the monotony and unity of the land, whether soil or sand. The *sāqiyas* and *shadūfs* of the Nile banks, the *jizū* of the Buṭāna, the 'cotton soil' of the Jezīra, the pastures of the Baqqāra, explain in great part the life of cultivator or nomad and transmit to him also their qualities and defects. It is because the sand is incarnate in the nomad that he is so independent, but also so stagnant. It is because the soil is incarnate in the cultivator that he is so durable, but also so static. The Mahdiyya convulsion upset the whole tenor of nomadic and sedentary life, yet now the nomad tribes have in the main recovered their former cohesion and the cultivator returned to his cultivation.

Still even this mutual conditioning of the environment and the folk is not sufficient to explain the folk, nor the unity of a cultural region which has now come to share in a common destiny. There is one great external factor which above all has moulded the life of the Northern Sudan. This is the persistent influence of that other great waste lying east of the Red Sea—ARABIA. Arabia has sent her people and their language and religion. It is above all that cultural system, *Islām*, which, after the environment, has most influenced the psychology of the people and fused their religious and social ideas into a unity of outlook which excites our wonder and admiration.

The Sudanese received Islām whole-heartedly, but, through their unique capacity of assimilation, moulded it to their own particular mentality; escaping the formulae of theologians, they sang in it, danced in it, wept in it, brought their own customs, their own festivals into it, paganized it a good deal, but always kept the vivid reality of its inherent unity under the rule of the one God.

To understand the life-apprehensions of the Sudanese then we have to take into account two movements: one due to the life-process of the people in contact with their geographical environment: while the other, Islām, is one which is a universal church and a cultural and social system common to a number of different peoples and resulting from intellectual and religious interaction and synthesis. Only by taking both these movements into account is it possible to understand these people. Our special study is Islām as it exists to-day in the Sudan, accepted and synthesized by the Sudanese with their own psychology and indigenous institutions.

I

The Land and the People

I. THE LAND

1. *Boundaries and Nature of the Country*

THE Arabic expression *Bilād as-Sūdān* literally means 'Land of the Blacks', and so is a vague term which could be applied to most of Africa south of the Ṣaḥārā. The name Sudan, however, is always restricted to that area of sub-Ṣaḥāran Africa stretching from the Atlantic to the Red Sea which has been islamized. It is not the true home of the Negro, but that intermediate zone lying between the Hamitic group of North Africa and the Negro group of Central Africa.

The English, however, use the word Sudan in a still more restricted sense to mean the eastern administrative area called the *Anglo-Egyptian Sudan*, and it is this usage to which the material of the present survey is restricted. We shall sometimes need to speak of the *Western Sudan*—the region containing the basin of the Senegal, the Gambia, the Upper Volta, and the Middle Niger—and the *Central Sudan* including the basin of Lake Chad. *Eastern Sudan* will then refer to the Northern Anglo-Egyptian Sudan.

The Anglo-Egyptian Sudan is a vast country of about a million square miles. It is bounded in the north by Egypt; in the east by the Red Sea, Eritrea, and Abyssinia; in the south by the Uganda Protectorate and the Belgian Congo; and in the west by French Equatorial Africa. There are no natural boundaries to this vast area except the Abyssinian Hills in the east and the Nile–Congo watershed in the west.

2. *Physical Features*

The Nile with its tributaries is the most important feature in the Sudan. The White Nile flowing from Lake Victoria enters the Sudan over rapids; after running through a flat savannah country it flows for several hundred miles through the swamps of the *sudd* (Arab. *sadd*, block), emerging at last into bush country between Malakal and Kosti, then through semi-desert plain until its junction with the Blue Nile at Khartoum. In its course it collects the waters of the Upper Nile, Baḥr al-Ghazāl, Baḥr az-Zarāfa, and the Sōbat to produce a regular supply all the year round. The Blue Nile and the Atbara collect their waters from the Abyssinian mountains and cause the phenomenon known as the Nile flood which produces some 80 per cent. of the total Nile discharge. They bring with them also the mud which forms the cultivable land on the Nile banks. The rise of the Blue Nile begins in June, reaches its maximum in August, and begins to fall in September.

The Nile, however, has never been the highway of migration and civilization. It has five chains of cataracts and long bends which have made the desert routes quicker and cheaper. Transport has therefore been by a combination of both river traffic and desert caravan.

The area through which the Nile flows constitutes one vast plain and is a political and not a distinct geographical or ethnological area. The physical features will be lightly sketched.

Between the coast and the Nile lies the Nubian Desert, and on the west the southern part of the Libyan Desert and the Bayūda Desert. A great part of these areas is almost completely void of vegetation and consists of rocky plains with isolated groups of hills and scored with *kh̲ōrs* and *wādīs*. These desert plains extend nearly as far south as Khartoum. A narrow strip of cultivable land runs along the Nile banks having a settled population of Nubians and Danāqla-'Arabs'.

The Red Sea Hills, which mark the eastern flank of the great Rift valley, is a distinct region and among them are valleys in which there is vegetation. The maritime plain again is distinct from the hills and its period of rainfall is in the winter. After the rains it affords grazing for herds, and crops are cultivated in the beds of the *wādīs*.

To the south of the desert is shrub steppe. It is typical nomad country which produces abundant pasturage for camels and goats at certain times of the year owing to a regular if scanty rainfall. The country enclosed by the Nile, Atbara, and Blue Nile and the line Mafāza–Gedāref–Tomat, known as the Buṭāna, is a rolling plain of 'cotton soil' and its face is scored by *wādīs* and *kh̲ōrs*. It is typical nomad country and in the rains affords excellent grazing though there are stretches of pure sandy waste. The northern portion is shared between the S̲h̲ukriyya and Baṭāḥīn nomad 'Arab' tribes.

South of Khartoum, in Kordofān and the west, there runs a red sand belt of thorny savannah steppe. The grasses here are luxuriant during the rains and the country is dotted with small thorny trees. The gum arabic acacia thrives on this sandy soil. The rainfall is heavy enough to allow cultivation of the staple food *dura* (millet) and to give grazing for large flocks and herds. Here live the settled 'Arab' population of Kordofān, the Baqqāra cattle-breeding Arabs, the pastoral negroid Shilluk, and the pagan Nūba in the hills. Dārfūr in the extreme west is also open steppe country, with extensive tracts of fertile land and a central mountain massif, the Jabal Marra.

The long peninsula formed between the White and Blue Niles, known as the Jezīra, is the great cotton-growing district where there are extensive irrigation works and which is one of the most populous parts of the Sudan.

South of the thorny savannah there come plains of dark soil (*badōb* or cotton soil), of open grassy savannah, bordered by swamp (*sudd*) country, where the pastoral Dinka and Nuer live.

To the south and west of these grassy plains lies the savannah forest where there are the Zande kingdoms of the southern Baḥr al-Ghazāl. There is a gradual transition to the red soil region and actual tropical forest is only found in the extreme south along the banks of streams.

3. *The Climate*

The disunity of this region finds expression in the lack of uniformity in its climate which ranges from the extreme aridity of the northern continuation of the Ṣaḥārā to the long rainy seasons of the equatorial forest in the south. The climate has more influence over the people even than the geographical situation, for it determines the fauna and flora of a region, its fertility and the nature of the crops and therefore the way of life of the people.

The most important distinguishing element in the climate of the Sudan is the distribution of the rainfall, and, owing to its variation, the vegetation belts which vitally affect human and animal life run west-south-west and east-north-east. North of Abū Ḥamad it never rains, but southwards the rainfall increases progressively, through the central region, where it is sufficient for grazing and crops, to the extreme south where the rainy season is long and the rains excessively heavy.

In the Northern and Central Sudan, which is our main interest, there are three seasons. The *ṣaif* (summer) from March to June or July is a season of monotonous uniformity. The heat is intense and reaches its peak in May. By day the air vibrates with it and every green thing is parched. In the middle of the day life is dormant and both men and animals seek the comparative coolness of the houses or the shade of the few trees. There are days of hot parching desert winds and especially dust-storms (*habūb*) which turn the sky to a reddish-brown colour, wither the plants, and try alike both man and beast.

At such times the night brings little relief, but normally towards evening during the *ṣaif* there is a fall in temperature bringing cool breezes and with nightfall the sky fills with stars, the earth is illuminated with a magical moonshine, and life breathes once more.

In June the wind changes to the south, heavy clouds gather, strong winds and *habūbs* oppress, then comes a storm of rain. This is the beginning of the rainy season (*kharīf*). In Kordofān these storms will appear every three or four days. It is the 'time for sowing' (*rashāsh*) and by the end of July, when the heavy rains have set in, the cultivated ground becomes covered with a rank green vegetation. In September there follows a period known as *darat*, harvest season, between the end of the rains and the beginning of the dry winter trade-winds, when the weather is both hot and humid and renders life a burden. With the advent of the dry northerly winds in October winter (*shita*) is regarded as having set in, the harvesting is completed, the sun declining, the breezes refreshing, and the annual vegetation dries up. This season lasts until March.

2. THE PEOPLE

The population has naturally always been sparse in the desert and steppe region, denser in the fertile riverain and southern districts, though never has it been very dense. Before the Mahdiyya convulsion the population was estimated at 8,500,000. In 1905 owing to the massacres, diseases, and famines of the Khalīfa's rule it had fallen to 1,853,000. Since then under a settled rule it has increased considerably and the total in 1944 was about six and a half million.[1]

The population of the Sudan falls naturally into two great classes, a northern Muslim area and a southern pagan area, the so-called Arab and negroid areas. The two areas are not defined by any physical feature, but are very clearly distinct ethnologically and culturally. The Muslim area embraces the peoples of the dry desert and steppe regions of the north who are Arabic-speaking and Islamic. In this region there has been some admixture of Arab blood with that of the original population and the adoption of Islam has fused the peoples so that they are culturally homogeneous, for Islam is not so much a creed as a unified social system. In the west this ethnological area extends

[1] A wide margin of error must be allowed for all official population figures. The earlier ones are mere guesses by Sir R. Wingate and the present-day figures are compiled from the rough estimates of D.C.s. Undoubtedly that terrible three-quarters of a century saved the present Government many of the ever-present dangers of over-population. The Government's reluctance to initiate a Census is unfortunate and makes the work of social survey almost an impossibility.

southwards into the Baḥr al-Ghazāl district amongst negroids and in the east up the Blue Nile into Abyssinia. The central region south of Jebelain on the White Nile together with the Nūba Mountains Area in southern Kordofān has remained negroid in race and culture.

The Southern Sudan, which can hardly be defined by any line of latitude (except that the change is evident on the Nile at 12° N. lat.), on the other hand, is totally different in race and culture, and includes all the heterogeneous dark-skinned pagan peoples of the south. We shall be treating in this survey essentially of the Muslim area lying north of 12° N. and stretching to the Egyptian border. The Southern Sudan will be studied only in so far as it has been affected by Islam.

It is rare to find anything approaching a pure racial type among any of the peoples of the Sudan, for this land has suffered from many vents of racial dispersion. All its people are variations between the pure Caucasian and the pure Negro type. So the black-skinned peoples of the south are usually referred to as Negroids. The term 'Arab' has significance in a linguistic and cultural, rather than in a racial, sense and is used in reference to the result of the recent admixture of the indigenous folk and the Arab tribes who settled in the northern and central regions in the Middle Ages. The Arabs brought with them their language and religion which supplanted the original languages (except among some of the Nubian- and Beja-speaking tribes) and Christianity or Animism.

The Northern Sudan

When the Arabs invaded Nubia they met with a people who were a hybrid type of mixed Caucasian-Negroid stock. This type is preserved in the Ḳanūz, Maḥas, Sukkōt, and Danāqla, which groups live on the banks of the Nile from Old Donqola to Aswān and speak different dialects of a language which is not indigenous to this area and was probably introduced by Negroes at the beginning of the Christian era. These Barābra, as they are called in Egypt, although they have adopted Islam, have maintained themselves as a separate entity and have absorbed the alien Arab and other elements and preserved their own language. South of Nubia were other Hamitic-Negroid groups which suffered greater modification by being arabized through social intermarriage and religious prestige.

In the eastern desert the Arabs met with the nomadic Beja tribesmen (the 'fuzzy'), a race according to Seligman[1] of proto-Egyptian

[1] C. G. Seligman: 'Some Aspects of the Hamitic Problem in the A.-E. Sudan', *J.R.A.I.* xliii, 1913, pp. 595–610.

origin, which was more modified in the north by negroid and armenoid influences than the south, and who were akin to the riverain peoples of Nubia. To-day many of the Beja have an admixture of Arab blood and produce faked Arab pedigrees, but, although Muslims, they have preserved their racial characteristics and language.

Since the Arab conquest there has been a gradual absorption of the Arab by the Nubian in the north and by the Black in central Sudan. The resultant type now call themselves 'Arab', but their claim to the title varies very considerably. A native writer gives a very illuminating statement on this:

> The original autochthonous peoples of the Sudan were the Nūba and the Abyssinians and the Zing (blacks). . . . Every (tribe) that is derived from the Hamag belongs to the Zing group, and every (tribe) that is derived from the Fung belongs to the Nūba group. The tribes of the Arabs who are in the Sudan, other than these (i.e. the Nūba, the Abyssinians, and the Zing), are foreigners, and have merely mixed with the tribes mentioned above and multiplied with them. Some of them have retained the characteristics of the Arabs, and the element of Nūba and Zing that is interspersed among them has adopted Arab characteristics; and on the other hand, there have been some Arabs who have become fused with the Nūba and the Zing and adopted their characteristics; but in each case they know their origin.[1]

The latter statement may be true; they may recognize the native element, but they despise it and only acknowledge the Arab. It is very easy too to mistake the Hamitic for a Semitic physical type, especially when, owing to the tendency of the people themselves through having become Muslims, they desire to claim kinship with Arabs and are culturally 50 per cent. Semitic.

The Sudan has in fact, in the course of history, frequently seen its population submit to profound changes, but by some obscure law it has transformed the immigrants and marked them with its own characteristic imprint. The process can be seen in action in the Sudan to-day. The Fellāta Melle of Kasala are being so changed by their environment that they will eventually be indistinguishable from Beja. They have changed from semi-nomadism to the pure nomadic state, have adopted the *tiffa* (fuzzy head), and their grass hut is inclining in make-up to that of the Haḍenḍiwa.[2]

New-comers to the Sudan then have gradually become absorbed and fused in type with the people amongst whom they have settled. Whilst suffering some modification, the original somatic type, which varied

[1] H. A. MacMichael, *Hist. Arabs in Sudan*, 1922, MS. D. 1, vol. ii, p. 197.
[2] Cf. *S.N.R.* ix (2), pp. 85–6.

according to the latitude and rainfall which have influenced the kind of soil and therefore its cultivation and the type of animals bred, has always tended to reassert itself.

The Arabs have, however, impressed their language and religio-culture on all these peoples, so much so that they have done more to weld the people of the Northern Sudan into one people, if not into one race, than any other influence. At the same time there has been little advance in culture since the needs of the dominant classes and the needs of the masses have been so much alike.

For convenience we will consider the inhabitants of the Northern Sudan under the linguistic headings of Nubian-, Beja-, and Arabic-speakers, followed by a short survey of Muslim Negroids.

(*a*) *The Nubian-speaking Tribes*

The Nubians live along the Nile in Egyptian territory from Aswān to Ḥalfa and in the Sudan in Ḥalfa district and Donqola as far south as Debba where the river swings northwards. The earliest inhabitants of this region were of the same stock as the pre-dynastic Egyptians; but through assimilating successive waves of Negroes they came to speak a Negro language and have become the homogeneous Negroid-Hamitic type represented by the Barābra[1] of to-day.

There are four main tribal groups which differ, within the group limit, in dialect and customs, including the building of houses and the dress and hair-dressing of women:

1. The *Kanūz* (43,000) in Egyptian territory between Aswān and Madig. They get their name from the Banū Kanz who were so influential during the last days of the Christian kingdom of Donqola. South of Madig for a short distance are 5,000 Arabic-speaking Nubians.

2. The *Fidaykiyya* (30,000) occupy villages between Korosko and Wādī Ḥalfa. Scattered amongst them is a small tribe of negroid Barābra, the *Matokiyya*.

3. The *Maḥas* in Sudanese territory from Wādī Ḥalfa to near Donqola. They are called Saidokki. These have retained their local *roṭāna* (Maḥaī or Marīsī) and in the main go to Egypt for their livelihood, but there are many sections settled in village-colonies around

[1] Sing. *Barbarī*. This is derived from the classical βάρβαροι, applied by the Greeks to primitive races and borrowed by the Arabs. The Nubians are known by this term in Egypt, and as Danāqla (sing. Donqolāwī) in the Sudan, for the other tribes are not so well known. They call themselves by their tribal names. Only recently in Egypt have the Nubians begun to call themselves Nūbī. There are, for example, professional guilds called *Nādī'n-Nūbiyyīn*. They object to being called *Barābra*. Many, especially among the Fidaykiyya, claim to have a northern origin (i.e. Turkish, Circassian, or Bosnian) and these call themselves *Kushshāf*.

Khartoum and on the White and Blue Niles who have migrated southwards since the sixteenth century. They now speak Arabic and claim an Arab pedigree. They are mainly cultivators, but have built up a great reputation as fekis, the economy of a whole village often being based on feki-mongering.

4. The *Danāqla*,[1] who live along the Nile from the neighbourhood of Donqola to Debba, possess often strong Hamitic facial characteristics. They are strong and well-built people with, in general, fine features, though sometimes the squat nose and thick lips of the Negro will be seen. They possess considerable originality and are quick at learning languages as a code. In their homeland most men are bilingual, speaking ungrammatical Arabic, but few women know Arabic.

In general the Nubian type exhibits both negroid and Hamitic characteristics. The complexion may vary from a deep mahogany brown to almost black with tumid lips and dolichocephalic head. The hair is generally woolly and frizzled and they can only produce a weak beard.

The Nubians are essentially an agricultural riverain people depending upon the Nile for their livelihood, some as boatmen and fishermen, but mainly as a means of irrigating their land. There are two main methods of irrigation: through inundation after the fall of the Nile when the banks and islands are sown; and artificial, by the *sāqiya* turned by bulls and the *s͟hadūf* raised by man-power.

Their narrow strip of Nile cultivation, however, does not produce enough to cope with the natural growth of its meagre population, therefore the majority of the men spend a considerable part of their lives working in towns of Egypt and the Sudan as cooks, houseboys, gate-keepers, *jallāba* (petty traders), and clerks. Each occupational group is organized into a guild with its own shaikh who levies a tax upon its members and is supposed to be responsible for the good conduct of its members to their employers. After making their pile most are contented to return to their homes as cultivators and live happily for the rest of their lives on *dura* bread.

Whilst the Nubians are so enterprising and ready to travel, at the same time they have an intense spirit of clan and love for their native home and soil. Though bitter enmity between some families exists

[1] The Danāqla-Jaʿaliyyīn group, who live along the Nile from Donqola to Khartoum and have adopted the Arabic language and Arab pedigrees, are almost indistinguishable from the rest of the Danāqla, but will be listed with Arabic-speaking tribes; see H. A. MacMichael, *History*, i, pt. ii, ch. i.

in most villages, usually owing to some dispute as to the ownership of their meagre land, their whole life is conducted communally by the inhabitants of a village, all joining together in joy and sorrow, festivals and mourning. It is this deep communal spirit which, in contrast to the individualist spirit of the Arab, has made possible the encouragement and help of the present government in the provision of communal facilities such as pumping schemes and dispensaries maintained by the group. It is customary to bind children to their home by an early marriage and it often happens that matrilocal marriage conditions arise through their seeking their livelihood 'abroad'.

A large and prosperous section of all the towns in the Sudan are Danāqla. It is they who, together with their Arabic-speaking kinsfolk the Ja'aliyyīn, were the slave-traders and boatmen who opened up the Upper Nile and the Baḥr al-Ghazāl region in the last century. Most of these townsfolk have lost their own language, but yet remain a distinct element of the population, retaining all their old customs and mode of life.

The position of the Nubian women is very low. The symbols of the bridegroom are the sword, the knife, the *kurbāj* (hippo skin whip); and the *kurbāj* certainly does not remain unused. The custom of infibulation is practised, not only upon girls, but upon married women when the husbands go 'abroad'. Divorce is one of the Nubian women's great fears and a great shame. The divorced woman goes back to her family where she becomes a slave to be kicked and knocked about unless someone can be found to take her. The *sharī'a* rule that the man who has the full disposal of children is responsible for his divorced wife's maintenance is disregarded. The Nubian women wear out quickly; they are working from their earliest years and the whole care of the household, husband, children, and animals is upon their shoulders, sometimes even the building of houses when the men are away. Fifty years ago they used to wear a short petticoat reaching to the knee but now wear the standardized tob.

Though the Nubians were once Christians and though some of their customs have a Christian origin, all memory of their former religion has vanished. They are bigoted Muslims, but their Islam lacks intensity unless stimulated by the other than religious traits of such a movement as the Mahdiyya or by their passion for trading. Most of them belong to the Mirghaniyya and Idrīsiyya dervish orders.

Under the Christian kingdom their culture, which inherited the remnants of an Egyptian culture and was stimulated from outside, was fairly highly developed. They used painted pottery and built their houses with arched roofs of sun-dried bricks. Now their houses have flat roofs and they have but few surviving handicrafts such as weaving, palm-leaf plaiting, and pottery; nor does the importation of cheap manufactured articles help to revive them.

(*b*) *The Beja Tribes*

Beja is the name given by Arabic authors[1] to a group of truly Hamitic nomadic tribes who live in the eastern district between the Nile, the Atbara, and the Red Sea, embracing the central plain, the Red Sea Hills, the eastern desert, and the hills south of Tōkar.

Although there has been some admixture of alien blood these tribes constitute a unity in both their somatic and linguistic characteristics. Seligman has shown[2] that there are pronounced physical resemblances between the Beja of to-day and the pre-dynastic Egyptian group. They have a certain amount of Arab blood, for the Rabīʿa settled amongst them in the ninth century A.D., but it has not modified their physical and social characteristics.[3] The northern Beja have been more modified than those of the south by negroid blood. The Beja have adopted Islam and an Arab lineage, but have preserved their original languages, racial characteristics, and customs so that they scarcely differ from the Beja described by Ibn Salīm a thousand years ago.

The account given by Ibn Salīm[4] of the Beja as a pagan nomadic people is substantially true of them to-day except for the introduction of Islam which has powers of calling forth a high degree of fanaticism in certain groups. The general ground of their manners and customs has, however, remained substantially unchanged except in the matter of matrilineal descent. Their customs, especially those connected with milk, class them with most of the Hamitic tribes of East Africa.

The physical features of the typical Beja are that

they are moderately short, slightly built men, with reddish-brown or brown skins in which a greater or less tinge of black may be present. The face is

[1] Their own collective name is Beḍawe, which is also the name of their language. They are mentioned in the inscriptions of Adulis (second century A.D.) as βεγὰ and in the Axumite king's inscription as βουγαειτῶν.

[2] *Journ. Anthr. Inst.*, 1913, xliii. 595–610.

[3] Masʿūdī relates (*Les Prairies d'Or*, iii. 33) that in A.D. 943 Bashīr b. Marwān had under his command 30,000 Beja and only 3,000 of the Rabīʿa, Muḍr, and Yemenites. These Beja were Ḥadāreb coast-dwellers and converts to Islam. This helps to show how the Arab immigrants would soon be absorbed into the indigenous tribes and how the latter would acquire a veneer of Islamic culture. Their powers of assimilation of other nomadic elements is shown by the fact that Ibn Baṭūṭa (about A.D. 1340) found a group of the Awlād Kāhil near Sawākin 'mingled with the Beja and understanding their language' (Cairo, 1939, i. 188). These Arabs could not have been there very long.

[4] Maqrizi, *Khiṭaṭ* (Cairo ed., A.H. 1324), i. 313–19.

usually long and oval, or approaching the oval in shape, the jaw is often lightly built, which, with the presence of a rather pointed chin, may tend to make the upper part of the face appear broader than it really is. The nose is well shaped and thoroughly Caucasian in type and form, except in those individuals, comparatively few in number, in whom Negro influence may be suspected. The hair is usually curly.[1]

The Bishārīn and Haḍenḍiwa as a result of centuries of mountain life are a virile and independent people. The remoter groups are truculent and vindictive. The nomads, especially the women, are very shy of contacts with strangers. The characteristics of those who have been drawn into new sedentary ways of life under the present régime through the development of cotton schemes in the Gash and the Baraka are being modified. The Ammar'ar and Benī 'Āmir are more peaceable and teachable than the northern and hill groups.

Whilst these tribes are nomadic in varying degrees and exhibit the same general characteristics, their social and economic life differs considerably from that of the Arab nomads. This is largely due, on the one hand, to the extreme inhospitability of some of the hills and, on the other, to the comparative fertility of other hills and the plateaux they occupy. In general the Beja tribal organization is looser than that of the Arabs. They exhibit the characteristics of a patriarchal society of which the unit is the family. They are not found making any great organized communal movements like the Arab tribes of Kordofān or the Buṭāna, but wander in small family groups in search of grass, in the case of the Bishārīn because of its sparseness and with others because of the comparative plenty for very small herds. The main tribes are divided into sub-sections (*badana*), each with its own camel brand, territorial limits, and well rights. Under the present government the process of tribal unification is moving forward rapidly.

The devolutionary methods which have been adopted by the present government allow them to use their own methods of dealing with crime. These are based upon a special characteristic of the Beja which favours compromise rather than retribution, compensation rather than revenge. Native courts therefore follow their own customary laws (*sawālif*) and the *sharī'a* does not touch them even in the field of family relationships. The Beja for instance have a deeply rooted belief in the sacredness of land and the inalienability of title to territory and their women can have no share in its inheritance.[2] Tribal judges

[1] *Handbook of the Anglo-Egyptian Sudan*, 1922, p. 206.

[2] Land (*aṣl*, root) is regarded as belonging to the tribe, but family ownership is recognized on two grounds only, original occupation of virgin soil or conquest. This should be compared with the Arab '*amāra* or permanent rights obtained by squatting on and developing someone

also will often refuse to carry out the *sharī'a* law of inheritance where a man's son is a ne'er-do-well. In such cases it is held by someone else to keep as *amāna*. Their customs also contrast with Arab tribal law, though now they are approximating more towards it. Until recently blood-money (*dīya*) was never paid by a Beja. The more truculent preferred revenge; others compromised in some way. Similarly with wounds; if they had not been avenged in the heat of the moment, there was no hankering after the 'eye for an eye' method of the Arab: the inflictor would care for his victim and support his family until he was quite well again and then send him away with an appropriate present such as a sword if the wound had been inflicted by that means.

There are four main tribal units, the Bishārīn, Ammar'ar, Haḍenḍiwa, and Benī 'Āmir.

The *Bishārīn* (15,000), who first emerged as a distinct tribe between A.D. 1000 and A.D. 1400, trace their descent back to an Arab ancestor called Bishār ibn Marwān b. Isḥāq b. Rabī'a, who settled in the mine district in the fourth century A.H. Their habitat to-day stretches from the plains of the Buṭāna northwards into Egyptian territory, covering a large area of 50,000 square miles. In the north are the Aliāb and Hamadorāb sections who have connexions with Egypt through having intermarried with the Aṣḥābāb 'Abābda and trading with Aswān. Their chief wealth is in camels. South of these are the Shantirāb, a wild and unintelligent group living in seclusion in their hills. Then come the Amrāb and the Atbai Umm Naji sections, the latter inhabiting the enormous plains between the hills and the river. They are extremely nomadic but more arabicized through their contact with the Nile. Again there are the Atbara 'Omadiyya groups who are bilingual and have mixed with the Ja'aliyyīn: some are semi-nomadic cultivators and others animal owners.

The tribal organization of the Bishārīn, especially those in the north, is very loose owing to their having to move in small groups in search of grass and through their isolation amongst the hills and waterless deserts. The shaikhs of *badanas* are recognized as such, but the real authority is that of the heads of families.

The *Ammar'ar* (45,000) are of pure Beja stock and Reisner has compared them with the Middle Nubians (C Group). They became a tribal entity about A.D. 1750. Their habitat to-day is along the slopes of the Red Sea Hills and the coastal plain north of Port Sudan.

else's land. Squatting is often allowed by the Beja but it can never give permanent rights because of the theory of tribal ownership.

A hundred years ago they were a very unimportant tribe, but having large herds of sheep and camels which do not thrive in the hills, they secured a footing in the plains and especially in the southern area between Khōr 'Arab and the Atbara. Their infiltrations were at first tolerated by the Hadendiwa and Bishārīn original inhabitants but later there were frictions. Some divisions around Sinkāt are cultivators in and around khōrs and others cultivate cotton at Tōkar and the Gash. This expansion has resulted in a considerable amount of intermarriage with other tribes. The majority are still nomadic at heart and have no permanent houses. They show, however, much less tendency than other Beja to cling to their lands and will settle permanently amongst strangers. Of their general characteristics G. E. R. Sanders writes:

> Their speech is notably free from Arabic modernisms and they are recognized as having the best pronunciation of Beḍawiet. The *tiffa*[1] survives among them to a greater extent than elsewhere. In a fight they are the most redoubtable of all three tribes and are seldom challenged on equal terms by the others. Their general way of living, as is the case with all Beja, habituates them to lack of food and water and induces great endurance. Their better physique enables them with proper food to undertake the sharp effort of portering and other hard manual labour more readily than the others[2]. . . . As companions the Amarar are delightful; quick of perception, with a great sense of humour, and usually a fund of anecdote.[3]

The *Haḍenḍiwa* are to-day the largest, most modified, and most important of the Beḍawiet-speaking tribes. They developed into a tribe from a small hill group who, from A.D. 1600, conquered, intermarried with, or absorbed kindred tribes. One Shaikh Mūsa ibn Ibrāhīm who was *nāẓir* during the Egyptian period (d. 1884) is chiefly responsible for the consolidation of the tribe. Under the present régime its prestige has drawn many more non-Haḍenḍiwa groups into the one nāẓirate and to-day the tribe numbers at least 70,000.

The Haḍenḍiwa live between Atbara and the Red Sea and reach as far south as the borders of Eritrea and Abyssinia. They are nomadic or semi-nomadic groupings of camel-owners and caravan guides. In 1928 they started to cultivate cotton and now some 55 per cent. of the Gash and 25 per cent. of the Tōkar allotments are Haḍenḍiwa. The clan system, in spite of this new economic development, still holds as strongly as ever, and since every *badana* seems to have some members

[1] i.e. fuzzy-head.

[2] The porters whom the traveller will see at Port Sudan are of this tribe.

[3] G. E. R. Sanders, 'The Amarar', *S.N.R.* xviii. 214–15.

working in cotton, their prosperity affects the economy of the whole tribe, even in the remotest hills.

The *Benī ʿĀmir*, most of whom speak the Semitic language Tigré, have been Muslim for about a century.[1] In the Sudan, where they number 30,000, they live partly in Tōkar district, partly near Kasala, and along the Eritrean frontier. The majority of the tribe (60,000) live in Eritrea where most sections acknowledge a hereditary chief, the Diglāl, who lives at Agordat. The Benī ʿĀmir are less wild than the Haḍenḍiwa. Those in the Sudan are cattle-owners in the main, with a few cultivators, whilst those in Eritrea seem to own chiefly camels, though many have taken up cultivation.

The Benī ʿĀmir, with allied groups of Ḥabāb, are especially interesting because of their social organization. The tribe has grown up through the association of distinct elements, in contrast to the Haḍenḍiwa who are a consolidation of closely allied groups. Whilst the other Beja give full equality to all members, the Benī ʿĀmir social organization is based upon a form of caste system caused by Jaʿaliyyīn imposing themselves as rulers upon the original mixed groupings of Tigré and Balaw.[2] The aristocracy, known as the *Nabtāb*, are scattered among the various sections in Eritrea. In the Sudan they are found only among the Hasrī section. The *Nabtāb* may not marry outside their own caste. They are mainly Beḍawiet-speakers who claim a Jaʿalī origin and descent from ʿAbbās, though in appearance they do not differ from the rest of the tribe. The ordinary members of the tribe, descendants of the Balaw and other absorbed elements, are known as *Tigré*, 'clients', originally perhaps 'serfs'. The name probably arose through most of the refugees who became 'clients' coming from the Province of Tigré in Abyssinia. Confusion sometimes arises from the fact that they commonly speak of themselves as 'Arabs' in contrast with the Nabtāb.

The old relationships between a Nabtābī and his Tigré still hold, although the old division of labour has come to an end. Nor, under the present government, can all the privileges of a Nabtābī be exercised, such as the one that a Tigré killed by a Nabtābī cannot be avenged. The foundation of the nobility lies in the holding of the fief. The

[1] Muḥammad ʿUthmān al-Mirghanī initiated his missionary propaganda amongst them in 1817.

[2] According to Lobo there was a kingdom of Muslim Balaw in the sixteenth century situated opposite Sawākin (Legrand, *Relation historique d'Abyssinie*, p. 38). A 'tribe of Balaw who inhabit Tigré and are Muslims' are mentioned in the *Futūḥ al Ḥabasha* (ed. R. Basset, p. 319). The tribe weakened following attacks by the Bilen, the Ibtoy of Keren, and other tribes and split up, the broken-up groupings being absorbed by other tribes.

herds are theoretically the property of the Nabtāb, but they are left with the Tigré as though they were his, subject to the payment of certain dues. For instance, the Nabtābī takes one head of sheep from each flock at the ʿĪd al-Kabīr. He keeps for his use a milch cow from every herd and a milch ewe from every flock which he returns when there is no more milk. He has also to be paid certain marriage dues. The Beja milk taboos hold for a Nabtābī as they do for women; a Nabtābī, like a woman, may not milk.

Other minor tribes are the Ḥalanqa, Arteiqa, Kumailāb (Kasala), Shaiāb (Tōkar area), and the ʿAbābda. The *Ḥalanqa*, who live in Kasala district, were once an important tribe, but as a result of divided allegiance and years of conflict with the Haḍenḍiwa, Abyssinians, and Mahdists they have declined and are now almost sedentary. They are supposed to have come originally from the Serāi in northern Abyssinia and the Beḍawiet they speak is full of words from Amharic, Tigré, and Tebedawi. The *ʿAbābda*,[1] the most northern of Beja, are dispersed mainly in Egyptian territory between the Nile and the Red Sea. A large branch, the Meleikāb, is settled along the edge of Nile cultivation from Korosko to Berber. They are often bilingual, but some speak Arabic only as a result of their being for so long guides and camelmen over the Baṭn al-Ḥajar and through their settlement along the Nile valley. Their old dialect of Beḍawiet is still preserved. It has been suggested that they are to be identified with the Blemmyes of the classical authors.

The Islam of the majority of the Beja cannot be regarded as more than skin deep. None are particularly religious, though like most of the Sudanese they are extremely superstitious and show credulity of any fekis who gain amongst them a reputation for possessing *baraka*. Such men, although they may be aliens, are recognized as arbiters in disputes.[2]

During the Mahdiyya only certain sections of Haḍenḍiwa showed any fanaticism, though religion played little part even in their allegiance. The other tribes either held themselves aloof, or, like the Benī ʿĀmir, resisted the Mahdists until it became expedient to profess Mahdism.

1 ʿAbābda, pl. of ʿIbādī. They claim to be descended from an eponymous ancestor called ʿAbad. The word ʿIbādī also means a Nestorian Christian, cf. *Journ. Asiat.*, 1838, ii. 502; and al Masʿūdī, ed. Sprenger, 247, 251.

2 There are many traditions of fekis coming from outside who, marrying into the tribe, have formed a new clan. The Ḥalanqa have an element, the Zailāʿīn, descended from a feki Aḥmad az-Zailaʿī (from Zailaʿ in Somaliland), who have special privileges in religious matters and a mosque known as Allābsaniāb. Also a section of Ashrāf claiming to be descendants of a feki Ḥamad Basi who came from the Ḥijāz to islamize them.

The majority of the nomads care nothing for the religious orders which play so vital a part in the religious life of the settled population of the Sudan. They were affected a little by the fekis of the Funj period, but to-day all who claim to belong to any order—the more settled or more sophisticated—have through propaganda become Mirghaniyya. The others will sometimes say that their Shaikh is ʿAbd al-Qādir al-Jīlānī, but they know nothing of the teaching and do not *dhikr*. Some groups of Haḍenḍiwa (Tirik, Sharaʿāb, and others around Sawākin) are Majādhīb. The Ḥalanqa have a special *walī* Shaikh ʿAbd Allāh, a pupil of Dafaʿ Allāh al-ʿArakī, whose tomb is at Mekali.

Some of the settled Haḍenḍiwa women are ardent in their religion and strict about prayers and fasting. There are *khalwas* for women and there used to be a *zāwiya* for women at Sawākin where after the Friday midday prayer they would sing *Khatmiyya* songs.

(*c*) *The Arabic-speaking Tribes*

Most of the Arab tribes entered the Sudan from Egypt and their emigration will be considered in the next chapter. The term Arab used as an ethnic term in the Sudan to-day is a vague one, and many of the Nubian and Beja tribes whom we have just considered, as well as some purely negroid tribes such as the Funj, lay claim to an Arab ancestry. Pedigrees cannot be trusted at all because all are so obviously artificial, therefore an 'Arab' of to-day may often be a pure African without a trace of Arab descent.[1]

This process of racial disintegration and reintegration took place not so much through conquest as through two allied movements. Firstly, through the infiltration of Arab tribes with their settling and intermarrying with the indigenous peoples, for, as Sir Arthur Keith has said, 'the Arab has an evolutionary relationship to all surrounding peoples'.[2] An indigenous tribe would come under the control of an Arab chief, other tribes would attach themselves, and the whole would take the name of that chief. Dār Ḥāmid in Kordofān, which is now sedentary, is an example of such a composite tribe.[3] And secondly, through the migration of indigenous tribes as a result of the upheaval caused by the Arab infiltration and the Funj invasion. So we have the

[1] An examination of the pedigrees given in MacMichael's *Hist. of the Arabs in the Sudan* will show how 'dummy ancestors' are inserted to link up a new Arabic-speaking group with a recognized tribe. Cf. quot. p. 83 below of 'Nūba who had become Kawāḥla'.

[2] Introd. to H. Field's *Arabs of Central Iraq*.

[3] Cf. MacMichael, op. cit. i. 256–7. It should be noted that names of tribes on the *jmʿ* root, such as the Jamūʿiyya, Jāmʿi, Jawāmʿa, and Jimīʿāb, show that they are conglomerations.

dispersion of the Hamitic Ja'aliyyīn-Danāqla tribes, many of whom have themselves become modified or even had their Hamitic elements submerged by negroid blood, and of the negroid Nūba-Funj groups.

This dispersion has resulted in a gradual fusion between black and white, aborigine and immigrant, with a general tendency to reproduce the original somatic type, except in the case of certain of the camel-owning nomads who, keeping to their old mode of life, belong more definitely to the Arab race rather than to any other. Even with these nomads the stock has been modified by breeding from black slave women acquired during the Egyptian and Mahdiyya periods. Although these Arab tribes brought Islam with them, they in turn have all adopted much in culture and customs that is distinctively African. The Kabābīsh, for instance, a tribe which is regarded with some truth as very Arab, owes its present constitution to the amalgamation of many Arab and Hamitic elements over a long period and especially after the Mahdiyya convulsion had broken the original tribe to pieces; some of which elements, owing to the number of slaves possessed, had been considerably modified by negroid blood. It has adopted the indigenous Hamitic *jirtiq* marriage customs and the practice of the infibulation of women.

Sir H. A. MacMichael has divided the Arabs of the Sudan into two main groups: the *Ja'aliyyīn-Danāqla* group which includes most of the riverain and Kordofān sedentaries, the chief tribes being the Jawābra, Bedairiyya, Shā'iqiyya, Baṭāḥīn, Jamū'iyya, and Jawām'a. These tribes have only the minutest proportion of Arab blood. They are indistinguishable ethnically and culturally from the *roṭāna*-speaking Danāqla with whom it would be better to class them. Some of these tribes, such as the Kordofān Dawālīb, Jawābra, Bedairiyya, Jawām'a, Shuwaiḥāt, who left the Nile at the time of the rise of the Funj and settled in Kordofān, have themselves become absorbed into negroid races, though they still call themselves Ja'aliyyīn. The Ghōdiāt who also migrated at the same time belonged to the Nūba-Funj racial group, and now call themselves Ja'aliyyīn. Secondly, the *Juhaina* group, who have a more legitimate claim to Arab blood, which includes most of the camel-owning nomads of Kordofān (Kabābīsh, Dār Ḥāmid, Ḥamar), those of the Buṭāna and Jezīra (Shukriyya and Rufā'a), and the cattle-owning Baqqāra.[1]

[1] The number of Arab arrivals has been exaggerated and the Semitic morphological type scarcely exists among the settled peoples. If the Semitic arrivals originally represented as much as 5–10 per cent. of the population, their *somatic* characteristics have been reduced to less than 1–2 per cent. Their *cultural* ascendancy, on the other hand, has so profoundly modified the characteristics of the people amongst whom they settled that culturally they may have

For descriptive purposes the 'Arabs' may be classed into two occupational groups: sedentary and nomad. These classes are not fixed absolutely and there is often a transition from one to another depending upon the settled or unsettled nature of the country. When the central government is strong as at present some nomad tribes tend to become semi-nomadic.[1] For example, the looting Baṭāḥīn tribes of the Buṭāna are now both tenders of herds, sheep, goats, cattle, and camels, and also cultivators of *dura* as a rain crop. The occupations of its members consequently have tended to become specialized. The village of Abū Delēj has developed under the present régime as their permanent centre where their Shaikh or Nāẓir lives. The Rubaṭāb around Abū Ḥamad are also both cultivators and nomads and produce the best dates in the Sudan. The same process has happened with the Shukriyya, Shā'iqiyya, Ḥasāniyya, and the Ḥamar. Some tribal 'sections' in Kordofān were forced to become sedentary owing to the destruction of their herds during the Mahdiyya. The sinking of deep-bore wells, by helping to stabilize life necessities, has also led to settlement. The environment, however, is the real determinant of nomad tribes (both camel and cattle) and sedentary groups.

The nomad and the sedentary are to some extent mutually dependent. The nomad brings his clarified butter, cheese, animals, and hides to the towns or *sūqs* and exchanges them for grain, sugar, dates, cloth, personal ornaments, and perfumes.

The Arabs have no sense of national unity. The tribes have never combined for any purpose except on the one occasion under the Mahdī. Whilst they may have the appearance of a unity through speaking one language there is no deeper sense of co-operation as of patriots of a nation ready to join together for their country's welfare. The Turko-Egyptian Government well understood this and took it into practical account in their methods of rule, so that only special conditions brought about a successful national revolt. This state of

a Semitic element of from 25 to 50 per cent. This Arab cultural ascendancy has led to an exaggeration of the Arab racial element (as in H. A. MacMichael's *History of the Arabs in the Sudan*). The attitude of the government official is to class as Arab any Arabic-speaking African Muslim, thus ignoring the very deep Hamitic element. This is similar to the French use of the word *Arabe*. The word Arab then is a *cultural* rather than an ethnic term. We can class the settled population simply as either Semitized-Hamites or Semitized-Negroes, but more clearly as Semitized-Negroid-Hamites (e.g. Ja'aliyyīn) or Semitized-Hamite-Negroids (e.g. Jawām'a, Jamū'iyya; on the constitution of the latter cf. MacMichael, i. 223).

[1] To call a tribe semi-nomadic usually means that in the *kharīf* part of the tribe remains in villages for the cultivation and the rest follow the flocks. During the rest of the year only old men and women will remain in the villages whilst the rest move continuously seeking pasture.

things also explains the backward condition of the Sudanese before the reoccupation. Each district or tribe lived in and for itself, and had its own petty wars with its neighbours, but had neither interests nor action in common with any other. Whether cultivators or nomads they were, and in the main still are, apart from each other, independent and often at enmity.

A strong class system prevails amongst the Arabic-speaking peoples. Arab blood marks the aristocracy, yet the townsman and cultivator despise the *Aʿrāb* (nomads) of the desert,[1] who have a genuine claim to Arab blood and all despise the southern Negroids as *ʿabīd* (slaves), though many are themselves indistinguishable from Negroes.

When the Arabs entered the Sudan conditions, so far as the raising of crops and herds was concerned, were as they have always been until the period of the recent irrigation schemes. Those Arabs therefore who settled in riverain districts, were absorbed into the indigenous sedentaries, and adopted Nubian customs now present the same somatic characteristics as the Danāqla who retained their language; those who settled farther south were absorbed into the various negroid groupings whom they modified culturally. The nomads, on the other hand, retained most of their racial characteristics and tribal life and organization.

The Sedentary Villagers (*Muzāriʿīn*). These live mostly along the Main Nile, the Blue and White Niles with the Jezīra between them, and on the Kordofān plains. Two groups are distinguished by their method of growing crops. For many (*ahl sawāqi*) the Nile is the centre of their existence both as the means of irrigating their land along its banks and for the maintenance of flocks and herds. Their mode of living is scarcely distinguishable from that of the Danāqla. The Nile, however, is not the sole source of life in the Sudan and there are many villages even in the north which have sufficient rainfall to enable them to maintain a meagre cultural life. South of Khartoum, especially in Kordofān, the people depend mainly upon rain-cultivation.

Although the villagers take pride in their fictitious *nisba* or tribal genealogy, tribal organization is weak or non-existent among them. The Egyptian and Mahdiyya periods considerably weakened or broke up tribal groupings and to-day almost all villages contain members of several different tribes, which may be waves of different migrations or remnants of Mahdist armies. In a village of the Blue Nile Province, for instance, one will find a medley of Rufāʿa, Maḥas, Jaʿaliyyīn,

[1] The settled people use the term for any nomad, comparable to the ancient Egyptian word *Aamu*, for both the Semitic nomads of Asia and the Hamitic Beja between the Nile and the Red Sea.

Danāqla, and others.[1] Communal organization therefore has taken the place of tribal organization, and the process of devolution has tended to be slower with them than with nomad tribes. A beginning was made with village councils of elders to deal with petty cases in 1925. Since then local government development has been rapid, rural administrations operate in country districts, and municipalities or town councils in urban areas.[2] Although there are these racial and tribal differences the system is working with success.

Sometimes, especially where a tribe is in a state of transition from nomadic to settled life, the authority of the *nāẓir* of the tribe and the *'umda* of a group of villages would appear to overlap, but dispute is avoided by means of territorial authority. For instance, if a group of Shukriyya happen to be living in a Haḍenḍiwa district they have to acknowledge the Nāẓir of the Haḍenḍiwa. The present tendency is towards greater amalgamation of quite different tribal groups, as, for instance, that of the Teqale (Muslim) Nūba Local Administration with the nomadic Baqqāra Ḥawāzma of the Eastern Jebels in 1943.

The daily life of the *muzāri'* is concerned with his cultivation on river- or rain-land or the beds of *wādīs*—clearing the ground, sowing, hoeing, and harvesting—from June to November (the *kharīf*), which are his busy months, when the rain-land worker especially works hard under fatiguing conditions in the rain and mud. In the *ṣaif* he has little to do except gossip. The riverain cultivator actually has harder work than those who work on the rain-lands because he has some three crops a year, having both rain-cultivation (*dahara*) and also *sāqiya* (i.e. land irrigation by water-wheels), or *selūka* (*jarf* or foreshore cultivation, irrigated by the falling of the Nile flood). Whether the *muzāri'* works on rain- or riverain-land the exigencies of his environment enslave him and his life is one of dependence. Cleaving to the land with the tenacity of aboriginal inhabitants all that can be cultivated is cultivated by the old methods, and that is the limit of the daily trudge from the village. Few things that matter are beyond the horizons of the village, but everything within those limits enters into his life. Every man and animal is known by sight and the part he plays in the life of the village. The very signs of the sky are of practical importance.

The rural industries are primitive enough for a country which has been in touch with higher cultures. They are limited to supplying the

[1] Cf. MacMichael, op. cit. i. 240.

[2] In 1945 there were five rural district administrations, four town councils, and four municipal councils, constituted by statute with executive powers and independent budgets.

necessary implements for agriculture, boat-building, tanning, weaving wool for tents and ropes, cotton for native cloth (*dammūr*), plaiting straw for mats, trays, and baskets, the making of primitive household utensils and pottery, *ʿanqarībs* (rope bedsteads), silver anklets, bracelets, and leather-work (saddles and saddle-bags, sheathes, satchels, shoes).

In the villages and *ferīqs* there are as a rule no shops, but an important feature of local life is that each district has a certain number of markets (*sūqs*) which are held regularly every week or month in open country and have the name of the day on which they are held. They are held on a traditional site unmarked by any building, determined by such things as accessibility and water-supply. In them peasant and nomad sell their produce and buy anything from an amulet to a camel. The merchants travel from *sūq* to *sūq* with their stock on donkeys and camels. The *ʿumda* is usually present and petty cases are settled. Not only are the *sūqs* the centre of peasant-nomad economic life, but they act as a news service.

All the towns have permanent markets and the economic revolution caused by the British occupation has resulted in many insignificant villages becoming market towns. In the towns industrial activity is concentrated. Each trade forms a kind of guild with its own shaikh who settles minor disputes and treats with the authorities. Each trade is grouped in one street which bears its name and in it articles are both made and sold. Bulk products such as grain, melons, fodder, charcoal, and wood are sold in special places called *malaqa*. Several European products, such as tea, sugar, and cotton goods, have become of primary necessity to the simplest Sūdānī.

It is possible to do that most dangerous of things, generalize about the character of the cultivator, although at the cost of missing important factors, for the living reality is complex. Common factors for any group are social and economic conditions and religion and race, but any selection tends to be limited by the writer's own vision and interest. These people, with the enterprising Nubians, are the most important people of the Sudan so far as planning for the future is concerned, but it must be remembered that the term 'Arab' as applied to them is little more than a linguistic term for they are truly indigenous to the land.

The lives of these people have an element of timelessness. Their needs are so simple[1] and life with them has such a natural harmony that

[1] *Food habits* are simple. Tea is drunk on rising, *ghada* comes between 12 and 2 p.m. and consists of a roll of *kisra* (unleavened millet bread) broken up and dipped into a dish of seasoning called *mulāḥ*. The last meal is *ʿasha* in the evening which is the same as *ghada*. *Dura* is also cooked (*ʿasīda*) and a beer is prepared from it called *merīsa* of which a considerable amount

one feels it is this simple maintenance of a natural rhythm which their life is directed to attain. The dignity and courtesy of all who have not been spoiled by urban life is proverbial. The intelligence of the sedentary Sūdānī is certainly more static than dynamic. That is shown by the way in which the experience of his ancestors is crystallized into succinct proverbs which, appearing persistently in his conversation in relation to the changing circumstances of his narrow life, tend to relieve him of personal thought. He can preserve and repeat, but he cannot create.

An intimate solidarity between spirit and nature has been established in the cultivator's soul through his centuries of slavery to the land which can only be broken by breaking the bond between man and nature. This explains the poverty of his aesthetic spirit and the lack of any living art. He expresses any imaginative power he has in his emotated and disembodied Islam. The Sūdānī is uncultivated, less because he is illiterate, as from this staticness of personality caused by his physical environment and his religion. Yet with all this statism, his love of rhythm and songs, of land and life, show that, if he were freed from his religious inheritance, his intellectual, imaginative, and aesthetic development would be easy.

The comprehension of the cultivators as adults is appallingly slow, though their memory is tenacious; yet one finds many of the children quick, vital, and as intelligent as English children of the same age, until they reach the age of puberty when there is a sudden change. This change is due to two things: their physical precocity, due to the climate—the plant growing too quickly—together with the beginning of sexual experience and the early contraction of venereal disease, for this is so prevalent as to affect 95 per cent. of the population; and secondly to their entering a stagnant mental environment. They start life with endless possibilities but are discouraged by the environment in which they find themselves. If they are taken out of their village environment early enough, they make intelligent and capable officials, engineers, doctors, clerks, and traders, though always the waste of sexual energy results in a slowing up of intellectual energy.

It is not so much the climate, enervating though it is, as the religio-social environment which blunts the personality of the young vital Sūdānī. In other words, it is the crass ignorance, stupidity, superstition, and religious bankruptcy which surrounds him when, after circumcision at about the age of ten, he enters the society of men and

is drunk. Meat is normally eaten only as *Karāma*, that is, at a festival or when a guest is entertained.

sinks into slavery to the *zirāʿa* cultivation with its monotonous repetition of the same acts day after day, for intelligence only develops by new acquisitions. Especially is this evident with girls. The promising school girl is submitted to the shock of the pharaonic circumcision at about the age of eight, and even if her mental life and personality survives this, she marries young, is immured in the *ḥōsh*, and is lost to all deepening and widening influences.

The basis of life is the family, but not the family in any sense that we know it, since Muslim social life makes that impossible. The status of women, polygyny, the easiness of divorce, the keeping of concubines, and the resulting flocks of children lead to the herding of women and children. It is a herd rather than a family into which the Sūdānī is born and this explains many things in his personality. The family is herded into a *ḥōsh*, which, among the riverain and urban populations, is a compound of one, two, or more flat-roofed *jālūṣ* houses, and among the Jezīra and Kordofān cultivators a compound of thatched *tukls* surrounded by a thorn fence.[1] The *ḥōsh* is shared in patriarchal fashion with sons and their wives, servants, and perhaps slaves, for though the legal status of slavery has been abolished, it exists to some extent in fact,[2] the whole being under the control of a *ḥabōba* (grandmother) who rules the women and children forcibly, conserves traditions, resists all innovations, and is the terror of the whole household. The

[1] One should note the control exercised by the geography upon the house. Mud houses prevail along the Nile banks. In the savannah regions the normal dwelling is the cylindrical *quṭṭiyya* (the so-called *tukl*) made of a slender framework of poles with a thatched roof, adopted or rather absorbed by the sedentary 'Arab' population from the blacks. The *quṭṭiyya* is surrounded by a thorn fence within which the flocks and herds are penned at night. They also use the *rākūba*, a box-shaped shelter made of poles and covered with straw. It is good for the hot weather since it allows the wind to blow through, but is useless in the rains. The Beja have a haycock-shaped hut, made of matting woven from the leaves of the *dōm*-palm stretched over long curved sticks. The camel-owning Arabs retain their tents of woollen blankets or camel or goats' hair matting (*shuqāq*, *shobaka*); east of the Nile of palm matting (*burūsh*). The Baqqāra houses (*shukkāb*) are cylindrical in shape, constructed of strong matting held in place by ropes, and can be rolled up quickly when moving. They also make rough shelters of bark from the *sunṭ*, and since many are semi-nomadic make rough huts of *dukhn* stalks (*qaṣab*).

[2] Lord Kitchener's *Memorandum to Mudirs*, 1899, still governs the official attitude to slavery: 'Slavery is not recognised in the Sudan, but as long as service is willingly rendered by servants to masters, it is unnecessary to interfere in the conditions existing between them. Where, however, any individual is subjected to cruel treatment and his or her liberty interfered with, the accused can be tried on such charges, which are offences against the law, and in serious cases of cruelty, the severest sentences should be imposed.' About 1928, 6,000 *muwalladīn* slaves of the Baqqāra were registered, only one-third of whom accepted freedom papers. They preferred the security of slavery to having to use their own initiative in the fight for existence. This is not an argument for domestic slavery, but rather is an illustration of the truth of the ancient Greek proverb, 'The day of enslavement deprives Man of half of his Manhood' (*Odyssey*, xvii, ll. 322–3).

women are not excessively secluded except among well-to-do families where, after the age of twelve, the girl is confined to the mother's *ḥōsh* until she is transferred to similar seclusion in her husband's *ḥōsh*. Respectable women do not go out alone or unveiled, for the leaving of the head uncovered is the sign of a slave or of slave-origin. The position of the woman in the family varies according to the racial-class group to which she belongs; she may be the mistress of the house or its slave. The real curse of Islamic family life is not polygyny but the easiness of divorce. In general, they are well treated by the men within the restrictions imposed by Islam and local customs, but the prevailing relationship is one of distrust, suspicion, and deceit. The cousin (*bint ʿamm*), owing to her relationship and the influence of the family, must be well treated and can rarely be divorced except for childlessness. If her husband treats her brutally, she goes off to her parents' *ḥōsh* and imposes conditions for her return—a new *tōb* perhaps or a pair of ear-rings. Still she must observe the proper respect of custom due to him—walk behind him and eat only when he has finished. He never calls her by her name but '*yā mara*' (woman!), or '*yā bitt*' (girl!). He refers to her as *umm awlādī* (the mother of my children), or *al ʿaila* (the family). He must delude himself that he is the master, affect to despise her, and will rarely show her any expressions of tenderness. The older he is the more exacting he becomes.

The system is such that the women are kept in complete ignorance of almost everything except household duties and *nikāḥ*-lore. Sexual matters form the chief topic of their conversation, yet sexual delinquencies are severely punished, often in a proud family by a quietly arranged murder. This contrasts with the laxity of the Baqqāra and Beja.

In character the women differ so widely through their mixed blood that it is impossible to generalize. In early life, in spite of the limitations of their surroundings, they are bright, lovable, affectionate, and often surprisingly intelligent. But they are soon stunted on the sand of African Islamic life. After marriage they show great powers of uncomplaining endurance—all their hardships and life's calamities are attributed to God's will. To the Sudanese women in truth apply the Prophet's words, 'to wait patiently for relief is an act of devotion'; but their immovable patience and slavery to custom truly enslave their menfolk. Through the inertia of the Sudan and Islam they can accept their chains calmly, they are part of life as they know it, and they will tell you with great enjoyment '*niḥna bahāyim*'—'we are cattle'. To any woman probably the height of her happiness is the intrigue enjoyed during the months of planning for the marriage of her daughter.

The prevailing emotional background of their lives is the thraldom of fear. Their fears are of two kinds. Genuine fears such as that of failure to produce sons or of losing her physical attractiveness to her '*rājil*' with consequent divorce or second wife, or fear of spiteful tongues, especially those of the *ḥabōbāt*. Secondly, fears of the unknown, of the unseen world of *jinn* and spirits innumerable, of the casting of the evil eye on herself or her children; fears which her religion cannot dispel.

In her religion it is the social element which predominates—the Friday rendezvous at the cemetery and the occasional *ziyāra* to a saint's tomb. Orthodox religion does not enter into her daily life: her creed is a maze of superstition and folk-lore; though when she becomes a *ḥabōba* she may begin to tell a rosary, fast in Ramaḍān, and sometimes go on pilgrimage, thereby bringing great merit on the whole family.

The nomad tribes differ very considerably from the *muzāriʿīn* and this is accounted for by the radical difference of the influences of pastoral and settled life more than blood, for many groups and some tribes of Arab nomads (e.g. the Kawāḥla and Kināna) are predominantly Hamitic in blood. The desert has a unifying effect upon races that were originally distinct and their peculiarities have disappeared through their uniform environment.

The nomad tribes fall into two distinct groups determined by the land influencing the mode of life and type of animals bred. These are the *Ahl Ibl* (or *Jamāla* or *Bādiya*), camel-people, and the *Baqqāra*, cattle-people. The former, roaming over wide stretches of sparsely inhabited land varying little from that of Arabia, kept free from alien influences, were scarcely changed by their environment though they have adopted certain native customs.[1] The Baqqāra, on the other hand, have been considerably modified in their characteristics through greater intermarriage with Negroids and change in their mode of life.

(*a*) The *Ahl Ibl* are divided into two main groups, all living between the 18th and 13th degrees of latitude. There are those who range west of the Main Nile, who during the *ṣaif* (dry season) are around the line of lat. 14° N. and during the *kharīf* (rainy season) move north and north-west to the fresh grass and the pools caused by the rains; and, secondly, those who range east of the Blue Nile, who tend in the dry

[1] One tribe, the Rashā'ida, who occupy a widely scattered area in Kasala district, emigrated from Arabia in 1846 and are indistinguishable from an Arabian tribe, retaining the dress and dialect of their former home. They refuse to obey any common shaikh and at one time under the present government constituted a difficult administrative problem. Now they are adapting themselves to the new conditions.

season to be near the Nile or well-centres and move east and north-east in the rains to the Buṭāna or Blue Nile Province.

The outstanding feature of Arab nomad life is its rigid conformity to the annual cycle of the steppe climate and its method of government. The unit is the tribe (*qabīla*), which in theory consists of a group of families connected by varying degrees of blood relationship. There is, however, not a single tribe in the Sudan which is truly homogeneous, often several being grouped together under one name; the true and permanent element in the system always being the family or clan. The tribe is ruled by a *shaikh*, or *nāẓir* in Sudan Government language, who is really a *primus inter pares*, his office not being hereditary in principle but usually so in practice. The eldest son does not necessarily succeed; a father sometimes nominates a younger son if he seems better fitted for the position or if the elder son had a slave mother. The central government also has often interfered in the choice of a successor or deposed a shaikh who was not ruling his tribe well.

The shaikh of a tribe unites legislative, executive, and judicial powers[1] in his own person, limited only by the central government. Under him are the shaikhs of 'sections' (*k͟has͟ham buyūt*). The devolutionary policy that the present government has adopted since 1922 has been that of supporting the authority of the shaikhs and of avoiding all apparent interference with tribal life. This has invariably meant strengthening the power of the shaikh, for the power given to him to act as judge has enhanced his executive authority, but the independence of some tribes has naturally weakened under a strong central government. The unity of any single tribe is a fluctuating one, because its prestige depends so much on that of the shaikh and, therefore, changes of allegiance of sub-sections often take place. The government has, however, given new life to some tribes by the amalgamation of disintegrated elements, e.g. the Ḥamar in Kordofān. Many of the tribes have preserved their old customs such as the *naḥās*, the tribal war-drum, as the symbol of the chief authority of the shaikh to which is attached superstitious reverence and an elaborate ceremonial,[2] and the ceremonials observed in moving from one camping-ground to another.

[1] The sentences of the shaikh's court are given according to the unwritten customary law (*'āda*, custom; *'urf*, what is commonly accepted; or *qānūn*), not the *s͟harī'a*, for all possible complications of desert justice have arisen ages ago. The shaikh's courts are conducted with care upon well-established formalities, and the sessions are public and open to all-comers.

[2] The *naḥās* consists of a group of three or more copper drums, called the 'bull', the 'cow', and the rest 'calves'. It seems to be indigenous and not to have been introduced by the Arabs. It is beaten on three occasions: (1) as a summons to war, (2) at a tribal festival, (3) at the death of the shaikh or an important member of his family. The government often presents *naḥās* to reconstituted or amalgamated tribes.

The nomad, born and bred under hard conditions, lives in a life-rhythm of constant adaptation to natural conditions and can support life only because the camel and goat can extract a living from the dry steppe regions; so over vast areas, where forage is almost invisibly scanty, keeping within a few days' limit of watering-places, wander little herds of animals, and their milk, flesh, hides, and hair constitute the economic foundation of the nomad's life. Each tribe has its recognized grazing-range (*dīra*, class. *dā'ira*) with its possession of wells and watering-places. These are jealously guarded and no other tribe may water or graze within them except by committing acts of trespass. Only recently has the long-standing feud between the Kabābīsh and Kawāḥla over grazing rights been settled. Their self-maintenance tribal movements are strictly conditioned by the changes in the seasons. Whilst it is still mid-winter permanent summer quarters (*damar*) are chosen near some watering-place at a well or river. They stay there until the rain clouds first appear when the herds move off southwards seeking fresh grass. The tents and women are left behind at the *damar*, but when the rains are regular baggage camels are sent back to move the camp. This move (called the *nushūgh*) is the happiest time of the nomad's life.

As regards physical characteristics where there has been no great admixture of Negro blood, their features are of a Hamitic type like the Beja rather than Arab. The face is oval, the carriage erect, they shave their hair and do not 'dress' it like the Beja. Their skin colour varies considerably but few have the brownish complexion of the Beja.

The climate and country, conditioning the way of life, account for the extreme individualism and narrowness of outlook which is the characteristic of the nomad. There are no half-tones in the desert or its people. The nomad has been forced to live in isolation with his family and in a state of tension with his neighbours concerning the necessities of life—water and pasturage. He possesses both the qualities and defects of individualism. Solitude has forced him to rely on himself alone and heightened his natural qualities: realism, determination, and dignity. The meagreness of life has led him both to a flamboyant generosity and extreme rapacity. He is by turns good-natured and contentious, courageous and distrustful, faithful and untruthful. There is boasting, jealousy, and rivalry between men of the same tribes and families, often leading to crimes of jealousy and violence. The system of blood-money (*diyya*) is found amongst all nomads, whether Arab or Beja, and is usually paid by the whole tribe. He has developed a queer sense of humour and a capacity to turn most situations within his limited sphere into profit for himself. The clan system and his mode of life has never enabled the nomad to develop regular authority or a stable society, as Ibn Khaldūn says, 'life for them is nomadism and conquest. This is the complete opposite of settlement which leads to civilization. . . . They have no concern for good laws, the restraint of crime, or public security. Their only concern is what they can take of the property of others by pillage and levying toll.'[1] The nomad's so-called freedom too is a myth. Although free of fears of the dark and the spacious which afflict the cultivator, he is just as conditioned by his environment. Even his social life binds him hand and foot, enslaved as he is by social inhibitions, exposed to and afraid of public opinion, and tied by customary law.

Indifferent in their religion and careless of religious observances, the camel nomads are much less fanatical than the cultivators and show a much more tolerant spirit and open-mindedness. Relics of the old star-worship are found in many of their customs, and the lunar calendar still plays its part in desert life. Of their philosophy of life Doughty's words remain as true for the *badū* of the Sudan as of Arabia, 'These Ishmaelites have a natural musing conscience of the good and evil, more than other men; but none observe them less in all their dealings with mankind.'[2]

The nomad is usually monogamous from necessity, but the shaikh has up to four wives along with many other black women; for marriage is a means of increasing his relations and so his influence. The women have considerable influence and enjoy great liberty. Although a man usually marries his paternal cousin as his first wife, marriages are often the result of personal inclination, but a father will rarely consent to give his daughter to one he regards as his social inferior.

(*b*) The *Baqqāra*[3] is a generic term applied to those tribes who breed cattle (*baqar*). This practice was adopted from the blacks by Juhaina tribes who penetrated south of lat. 13° N. to the region where camels cannot live because of the fly. In the strange camel-less environment of pasture-land to which they had come, these lost children of the desert sought to adapt their manner of life to their new circumstances. From being herdsmen of camels, they became herdsmen of cattle. Just as they had formerly raided the camel-herds of their Arab neighbours,

[1] *Muqaddama* (Cairo ed.), pp. 149–50.

[2] *Arabia Deserta*, i. 264.

[3] On the Baqqāra see G. D. Lampen in *The Anglo-Egyptian Sudan from Within*, pp. 130 ff., and *S.N.R.* xvi. 97 ff.

so they raided the cattle-herds of their new black neighbours to restock the newly acquired pasture-land where their camels had died. But that was not all. They found still another local livestock in the sedentary black population of these lands which they also raided to perform the menial tasks of home and field and plain, and whose women also served to keep their own diminishing social body restocked.

These tribes occupy a strip of country which extends from the left bank of the White Nile to Lake Chad, covering in the Anglo-Egyptian Sudan the plains of Kordofān and Dārfūr as far south as the Baḥr al-ʿArab. The majority live in French Sudan. In the dry season they move their cattle to the southern grazing-grounds and hunt the elephant and giraffe for meat, skins, and ivory. In the old days they hunted slaves, for they were some of the worst of the slave-raiders.[1] The suppression of the trade considerably upset their economy and made their lives much more drab. When the rains come and the cotton soil becomes swampy, to escape the fly they move their flocks and cattle to the higher sandy land northwards along lat. 12° and 13° N. The Ḥawāzma tribe spend the whole year in the plains of the Nūba Mountains area. Most of the tribes have some sections which are sedentary. These were forced to do some cultivation, owing to the destruction of their herds during the Mahdiyya in order to exist and acquire money to buy more cattle. Some of them, mainly immigrants and slaves, owing to the fall in cattle prices and the imposition of the poll tax, have remained sedentaries living in villages. Some of the eastern tribes are beginning to cultivate cotton. Their main money-earning occupation to-day is the carrying trade, followed by the sale of cattle and sheep. Though they own many horses, their carrying is done wholly upon bulls, which can carry large loads from between 200 to 300 lb.

The tribes[2] are large, but they overlap very considerably and have only assumed their present tribal definitions within the last hundred years. Each tribe is under a *nāẓir*, under whom as lieutenants are *ʿumdas* or heads of sections. The relations of the *nāẓir* also have authority as his *manadīb* (representatives) which authority sometimes conflicts with that of the *ʿumdas*.

The Baqqāra all claim to be Juhaina, but have been considerably modified through Negro and Fellāta blood whilst their former Arab

[1] They still hanker after the practice and they were discovered in 1928 carrying on a traffic in Berta slaves from Abyssinia.

[2] The main tribes in Dārfūr are the Rizaiqāt, Habbāniyya, Maʿāliyya, Taʿāisha, and Banū Ḥalba; in Kordofān, Awlād Ḥamaid, Ḥawāzma, Messīriyya, and the Ḥumr; on the White Nile, Jimʿ, Dār Muḥārib, Aḥamda and Shankhāb, and the Selaim and Taʿāisha (Jebelain).

cultural characteristics have changed through their lacking the mobility which the camel-owner possesses, which meant intermarriage with Negroids. Some, such as the Awlād Ḥamaid, are almost wholly negroid, though they may have acquired some other elements through marriage with other tribes. The best and least modified Baqqāra are to be found in Kordofān. Many other tribes, especially in Dārfūr, look negroid rather than Arab. G. D. Lampen writes, 'The men have usually thick lips and snub noses, and the women are short in stature and have often very short hair, and the prevailing colour everywhere is dark rather than light.'[1] On the other hand, the Jimʿ of the White Nile are Hamitic of Nubian Jaʿalī stock who immigrated to Kordofān and, becoming cattle-raisers, acquired typical Baqqāra customs such as their mode of hair-dressing and dances.

The Baqqāra have a very distinctive dialect and their customs differ through being cut off from other Arab tribes. They are the most war-like Arabs in the Sudan, employing guerrilla tactics for they are excellent horsemen, and also most fanatical, in contrast to the religious indifference of the camel-nomads. This fanaticism is probably due to their Negro blood—the mixed Arab-Negro usually being fanatical. They are easily moved by fekis and will follow one as a leader. They have kept their independent spirit and pride of race but lost some of the characteristic Arab individualism. They are extremely ignorant and short-sighted, except on matters connected with cattle. Their life, in contrast to that of their northern brethren, is easy, lacking all stimulus, and consequently they are idle and mentally lethargic. Through living near the marshes many are diseased. In the *ferīq* (cattle-camp) they spend their time idly in conversation whilst the women and slaves do all the work. Conversation is a fine art, and they possess a very rich language for its expression, but the subject-matter is trivial, being confined to gossip and scandal, with diversions into personal reminiscences and tribal history. Their women enjoy greater freedom even than the northern nomads. They wear much jewellery and amber. Their chief recreations are going to the market and the dance which they have adopted from the blacks, and which they perform to the chanting of songs composed by their tribal poetess (*ḥakkāma*) who is a very important figure in tribal life.

There is considerable variation between the marriage customs of the Baqqāra and camel-nomads. The Baqqāra bridegroom does not wear special ornaments and dress, though some of these customs are now being introduced.

[1] Op. cit., p. 131.

(*d*) *Muslim Negroids*

Many negroid groups situated mainly in the Central and Western Sudan have become Muslim, but most of them have retained their own languages and customs. Many are on the border-line between paganism and Islam. These need to be considered shortly.

(I) In the Eastern Sudan there are large colonies of FALLĀTA. This term is used loosely in the Sudan to mean any West African. They are mainly Hausa, Fulbe, Kanūri, and Borqū.[1] These were originally pilgrims who, during the nineteenth century, on their return from Mecca, have settled permanently in the Sudan and many of whom now use Arabic. They can be classified into three groups. (1) Pilgrims passing through the Sudan, including the many colonies on the pilgrim routes. The main route is through Dārfūr to El-Obeyd, from where the majority now take the train. Since they have to earn money on the way the whole pilgrimage takes from four to seven years. (2) Large permanent colonies, especially in Kasala and Sennār districts, many of which have resulted from the settlement of large groups of West Africans disbanded from the Khalīfa's armies in depopulated districts between Sennār and Sinja. There is a large colony near Sennār under Mai Wurno, son of the ex-Sultan of Sokoto, and another under Mai Aḥmad, ex-Amīr of Misau. Omdurman, too, has a colony and a large floating population of pilgrims, most of whom belong to the casual labour market. Colonies grow up around most government stations because of labour needs, whilst the Jezīra irrigation scheme would be unworkable without them. (3) Two nomadic cattle-owning clans (ʿIkka and ʿIbba) with a *dār* of their own in southern Dārfūr, who have been there at least two hundred years and now speak Arabic.

In general the Fallāta are shy and distrustful, thrifty and industrious, dissimulative and fanatical, being easily affected by fekis. They are despised and disliked by the Arabs, but are used by them for manual labour and as feki-exorcists, for which they have a high reputation. There is a legend current in the Sudan to reinforce their magical powers which says that they are descended from a chameleon.

(II) In Dār Funj, the district south of the Jezīra between White

[1] To Sudanese they are also known as *Takārīr* (sing. *Takrūrī*, really the name of a tribe) or simply *Nās al-gharb*—westerners. The Fulbe are called Falāta by the Kanūri, and Fulānī by the Hausa. In 1925 Mr. Latham of the Nigerian Government made a survey of the Nigerians in the Sudan and estimated their number at 80,000; of these 40,000 were permanently settled, 15,000 settling, and 25,000 in transit. There is no estimate for other westerners.

and Blue Niles, there are so-called FUNJ (Fuñ) groups, who are groups of semi-arabicized Negroids belonging to no definite ethnic unit. The Arabs call them *Hamaj* (*Ar.* uncivilized or aborigines), but they call themselves by the names of the various hills they inhabit (Gule, Moya, &c.). They are probably one of the races whom the Funj conquered. The *nāẓir* of the district bears the title of *mānjil* and considers himself a descendant of the Hamaj kings of Sennār. The majority speak Arabic and profess Islam, but they have retained their original language and pagan customs. They live next to sedentary agriculturalist groups which have remained pagan—the *Berta*, *Ingessana*,[1] *Jebelāwīn*, with the *Burūn* and the *Khoma* farther south.

(III) The non-Arab inhabitants of Dārfūr can be classed into the following groups:

1. The TIBBU (*Tūbū*) or northern Negroid-Hamites of the eastern Ṣaḥārā. These are the semi-nomadic *Zaghāwa*, a turbulent people, now speaking Arabic, who live on hills (e.g. al ʿAṭshān) of northern Dārfūr and are closely connected with the nomadic *Quraʿān* (or Dazāgada) and *Bedāyāt* of the Ennedi highlands, most of whom belong to French Equatorial Africa, but often raid into the Eastern Sudan. They are nominal, though fanatical, Muslims, much afflicted by fekis (called by the Zaghāwa *hogi* and by the Bedāyāt *heki*), but retaining fetishist superstitions and customs contrary to Islamic Law.

2. Sedentary indigenous races; comprising the FŪR inhabiting Jebel Marra and the country west of it, the MAṢĀLĪT between the Fūr and Wadā'i, and the DĀJO in central Dārfūr. These are all sedentaries living in villages and growing *dukhn* or *dura* according to the type of soil.

The FŪR (Fūrakang) are important historically. They are a negro race inhabiting the Jebel Marra range. H. A. MacMichael says of them:

The Fūr in general, with the exception of the Kungāra branch, are socially, physically, and intellectually inferior to the average of the tribes who are their neighbours to the east and north. But it is the Kungāra whose virility has preserved to the race the predominance which was gained some three centuries ago by their ancestors, and this superiority of the Kungāra is evidently due to an Arab strain which they have acquired. They are, generally speaking, a

[1] Arabic name for the people of the Tabi Hills in Dār Funj. The people of Kukur (one of these hills) have, however, been in contact for a considerable time with the Arab pastoralists, who with their flocks wander about the plains, and the Islamic feasts of Ramaḍān and Bairam have been incorporated into the Kukur ceremonial system. At Kukur, too, the Muslim recessed grave has been adopted. (Cf. Seligman, *Pagan Tribes*, p. 437.)

people of better physique and higher intelligence, and in their habits more cleanly, than the common Fūr, and they are much better Muhammedans.[1]

The native administration of the Fūr proved difficult owing to the rivalries of tribal chiefs until the administration in 1930 recognized the hereditary position of the *Maqdūms* (or viceroys) as presidents of inter-tribal courts. The Zalangei, a homogeneous Fūr unit, are administered directly by *Sharṭā'is* who are hereditary sub-chiefs under whom are tribal elders (*damāliq*).

The Fūr are nominally Muslims, but the memorization of the Qur'ān is a magical rite and they retain a full paraphernalia of local malignant spirits inhabiting snakes, stones, and trees, who are placated by magical rites.[2]

The Maṣālīṭ, inhabiting the *dār* of that name in the extreme west, has its own Sulṭān, Muḥammad Baḥr ad-Dīn Abū Bakr and the Sudan Government official is known as the 'Resident'.[3] It is the only complete example of a native administration in the Sudan, with its own budget, system of officials, police force, and courts. H. A. MacMichael says of the *Maṣālīṭ* that they 'are more than half negroes, with the slightest Arab leaven. They are a warlike people of fairly good physique and intelligence, but they are regarded askance by the Dārfūr and Kordofān tribes owing to the power of metamorphosis, chiefly into hyaenas, which they are believed to possess.'[4] They became nominally Muslims within fairly recent times and cannibalism was only suppressed about 1890 under Sulṭān Abukr Ismā'īl. Modern Mahdism has spread rapidly amongst the Maṣālīṭ who are potentially fanatical and Islam now means to them devotion to the person of 'Abd ar-Raḥmān ibn al-Mahdī.[5] Those in the north are rapidly becoming arabicized and their language contains a large proportion of Arabic words.

The Dājo are one of the oldest races of Dārfūr. They live in the central region, in Dār Misairiyya and on the north-west boundary of the Nūba area. They have a hereditary sultan and live by cultivation and breeding cattle.

1 Op. cit. i. 91.

2 On Fūr life and customs see H. A. MacMichael, op. cit. i. 91–114.

3 This Sultanate rose to power during the Mahdiyya and achieved independence from 'Alī Dīnār in 1905 after a number of wars. There was fighting with the French in 1910, and peace was made with the secession of part of the country to the French. The Sulṭān's dominion was occupied by the Sudan Government in 1920 following the Anglo-French Convention of 1919.

4 *Hist.* i. 87. At Tūnīsī (*Voyage au Darfour*, pp. 355–6) recounts that all the Fūrians believed that the Maṣālīṭ can transform themselves into hyenas, cats, and dogs.

5 The Sulṭān Endoka (*c.* 1910) forsook Mahdism for the Tijāniyya, but his brothers and all the fekis in the *Dār* are Mahdists.

3. Immigrants such as the semi-nomadic Mīdōb of the hill mass of that name some 200 miles in circumference. They have villages at the foot of the hills, but most of the time are away with their sheep and goats. They are negroid with a Hamitic strain claiming kinship with and speaking a language akin to that of the Barābra; the Bertī a sedentary tribe of mixed origin who live in the Tagābo hills south-west of Jebel Mīdōb and the sandy land east of Al Fāshar; the Birqed a fairly large tribe living between Jebel Ḥaraiz and the Dār Rizaiqāt, the Baiqo, the Mīma, and the nomadic cattle-raising Fallāta.

(IV) The Nūba of southern Kordofan, though pagan in the main, are important in this survey because of their geographical situation. Nūba is a general term used in Kordofān for any black pagan. They are aboriginal tribes inhabiting the isolated hills and ranges of the southern Kordofān plain, and are surrounded and interpenetrated by Muslims. They are not a homogeneous group for they are the back-wash of many African tribes who have sought refuge in the hills, so they differ profoundly in physical type, language, and culture.[1] Though they number over 300,000 or 72 per cent. of the population of the area (1921), a hurried journey through the country tends to give the impression that the Nūba is a rare specimen, the plains being occupied by negroid-looking Baqqāra and settled black 'Arabs'. They are simple agricultural groups, possessing few cattle, working hard to provide the millet, sesame, and other crops for their yearly needs. They are excessively strong, cheerful, of great independence of mind, and vigorous tribal traditions. They live in autonomous groups under the control of tribal priests (*kujūrs*), some of whom have both temporal and spiritual powers, though other tribes have a *mek* (leader) who exercises temporal authority. Their religion, which is the cult of the Ancestral Spirit, plays a vital part in their lives, for their whole social structure is based on it. Most groups of these people have maintained their paganism in spite of continual Muslim pressure which has driven them from the plains into their hill strongholds. Under the present régime they are coming more and more under peaceful Arab cultural influence.

[1] Cf. Hillelson, *S.N.R.* xiii. 144: 'Recent Arabs and Europeans applied the name "Nuba" to the negroid hillmen of Kordofān. This led to an unfortunate confusion, in so far as the impression was created that the negroes thus designated by a common name are a more or less homogeneous people. The linguistic evidence suggests that there are three distinct stocks: (1) Speakers of Hill Nubian, (2) Speakers of Sudanic languages, and (3) Speakers of Pre-fix languages, and it is only in reference to the first group that the name "Nuba" is historically justified; in the case of the other two it is a misnomer.'

(e) *Pagan Tribes of the Southern Sudan*

South of the curved Baqqāra migrational strip live the great negro pagan tribes, living in no ordered world, having no common language, and no conception of political and cultural unity.

Professor Seligman[1] divides these tribes into four great sub-racial units:

1. *The Dolichocephals* (Long Heads): in whom there is a Hamitic element:

(a) *The Nilotes*—Shilluk, Nuēr, and Dinka. They are tall, long-legged, and very dark-skinned. They despise clothing and Muslim or European culture. They are all pastoral, living in an atmosphere of cattle, and spend half the year out of their villages with their cattle.

(b) *The Nilo-Hamites*—the true Bāri and various Latuko-, Didenga-, and Turkana-speaking tribes who are chiefly herdsmen but also good agriculturalists. They have a culture very different from the Nilotes. To-day they seem to be in a state of transition from pastoral to agricultural modes of life as the result of having lost most of their cattle.

2. *The Mesaticephals* (Broad Heads):

(a) *The Funj-Nūba* peoples already mentioned.

(b) The *South-western Group*—Azande and tribes of the Ironstone plateau, Bongo-Mittu, and kindred groups. They are in complete contrast to the two groups of Nilotes and Nilo-Hamites in physical appearance, temperament, and culture, being medium headed, of medium stature, and copper-coloured. They are cheerful and sociable and have shown themselves readily adaptable to changing conditions of life. They are essentially agricultural and have no cattle, but are keen hunters.

(f) *Languages*

NUBIAN is the language spoken by the Barābra, a Hamitic type akin to the Sōmālī who live on the Nile banks, between the first and fourth cataracts. There are four dialects: Kenzī-Mattokki, Sukkōtī, Maḥasī, and Donqolāwī. Kenzī and Donqolāwī, though geographically farther apart, seem to be closely allied. Kenzī is spoken from Shellāl to Korosko, Sukkōtī south of that, Maḥasī from Wādī Ḥalfa to Ḥannek, and Donqolāwī from Kerma to Ambiqōl.

[1] *Pagan Tribes of the Nilotic Sudan*, ch. i, upon which the notes which follow are based.

Dialects cognate to these exist along negroid Nūba of certain hills in the north of the Nūba Mountains area[1] and in Dārfūr.[2] One thing is certain, Nubian cannot be indigenous to the Nile valley. It has no connexion with the language of the Meroitic inscriptions of this region which lasted to within the period of the Christian kingdoms. We know further that Nubian was the language of the early Christian Church in Nubia, but we do not know clearly the events which brought about this change of language.

Zyhlarz[3] thinks that Nubian was introduced into the Nile valley from southern Kordofān by the Nuba in the third century B.C. If so, then Nubian and Meroitic must have existed side by side in the Island of Meroë. It is possible that Nubian was the spoken tongue and Meroitic remained as the priestly and official language until the downfall of the kingdom in A.D. 350. Another view is that Meroitic remained the language of the country until Nubian was introduced by the Nūba from Kordofān during the invasion of the fourth century A.D. This is more likely in view of the fact that there are so few Meroitic words in Nubian.

The written language was developed, replacing Greek, with the union of the northern kingdoms and the Arab invasion (A.D. 641). There are texts of the Middle Ages (eighth and ninth centuries) written in Greek characters, with the addition of signs borrowed from Demotic and using one dialectal form like the modern Maḥasī. This shows that the language has evolved little during this period, although Arabic does provide some 30 per cent. of the modern Barābra vocabulary.

Few of the scholars who have studied Nubian think alike on its classification. It has been associated on grammatical grounds with Dinka and Shilluk. Westermann[4] and Meinhof[5] included it in the Sudanic language family. G. W. Murray's view[6] is that the basis of the language is Sudanic on which waves of Hamitic influence have

[1] Hugeirat, Abū Ganuk, Tabaq, Shifr, Kasha, Karko, Kunit (or Kujuria), Fanda, Wali, Dilling, Ghulfān (two hill-groups), Debri, Habila, Kaderu, Daier (except Sidra), to which groups only of the people of the Nūba Mountains is the name Nūba correctly due. These Nubian dialects differ from those of the north, but the resemblances are too marked for there to be any doubt about their having a common origin.

[2] Jabals Mīdōb (a form of Hill-Nubian) and Birqed—a third type of Nubian called by Zyhlarz South-west Nubian.

[3] 'Zur Stellung des Darfur-Nubischen', *W.Z.K.M.* xxxv. 1928. See also S. Hillelson's study of Zyhlarz's pamphlet in *S.N.R.* xiii. 137 ff.

[4] *Die Sudansprachen.*

[5] 'Eine Studienfahrt nach Kordofan', Abhandlungen d. Hamb. Kolonialinstituts, xxxv. 1916.

[6] *An English-Nubian Comparative Dictionary*, 1923, Intro.

been superimposed. Reinisch[1] regards it as a connecting link between Sudanic and Hamitic. L. Homburger[2] claims it as definitely Hamitic. Among the Arabs, Nubian or any other non-Arabic language is known as *roṭāna* (jargon).

Tu Beḍāwie is spoken by the majority of the nomad Beja of the Red Sea Hills from Egypt to Kasala. There are five main dialects: ʿAbābda, Ḥalanqa, Ammār'ar, Bis͟hārīn, and Haḍenḍiwa. The latter is the principal dialect of the language. Beḍāwie is the most widely spoken of the Hamitic languages[3] and owing to contact with Arabic a fair number of Arabic roots and grammatical forms have been introduced.

Tigré is a Semitic language, akin to the Tigriña of Eritrea, and is the modern representative of the ancient Geʿez. It has not been so strongly influenced by Amharic as Tigriña. Geʿez is more closely related to Sabian than Arabic, and Tigré may be regarded as a representative of an older Semitic stock than Arabic. It is spoken by many groups of the Benī ʿĀmir and the Ḥabāb. Locally it is known as K͟hasa from the name of the largest sub-section of the Benī ʿĀmir.

Arabic is spoken over a very large area of the Northern Sudan and is the symbol and preserver of the cultural unity of the region. The literary language is the classical of the whole Arabic-speaking world used only in writing, lectures, and conferences. It is never the language of conversation. The term Sudan Arabic is given by Europeans to a κοινή which is spoken and understood over the whole area, for it has a recognizable individuality which distinguishes it from Syrian, Egyptian, or any other dialect. There are, however, a large variety of sub-dialects, differing considerably, though mainly in vocabulary and idiomatic usage. They are difficult to classify because they have not been studied and one group tends to grade into another.[4] The following main dialect groups of the sedentary population can be distinguished: (1) *Northern*: Northern province; (2) *Central*: Omdurman, the Jezīra, and the country east of the Blue Nile; (3) *Western*: White Nile, Kordofān, and Dārfūr.[5]

[1] *Die sprachliche Stellung des Nuba*, Vienna, 1911.

[2] L. Homburger, 'La Morphologie nubienne et l'égyptien', *Journ. Asiat.*, 1931, pp. 249–79.

[3] Cf. Meinhof, *Die Sprachen der Hamiten*, 1912, on its relationship to the other Hamitic languages.

[4] S. Hillelson's *Sudan Arabic Texts* (1935) provides excellent dialect material and the Introduction deals with grammatical and phonetic features peculiar to the various dialects.

[5] The dialect of the Baqqāra tribes of Kordofān and Dārfūr differs considerably in vocabulary, idiom, and even grammar, with many onomatopoeic words, owing perhaps to the influence of Sudanic languages. The other nomadic tribes of the Sudan also have their own

The urban dialect of Omdurman, freed from all purely tribal and local features, evolving rapidly, sensitive to external influence, literary and political, is becoming increasingly a recognizable standard for Sūdānī Arabic and is the common medium of communication between speakers in the towns who may have been brought up under the influence of a local dialect. Formed as it has been through the agglomeration of people from all over the Sudan there is a family resemblance between it and most other dialects. The villagers, who constitute the majority of the population, will naturally never give up their local dialects, but these will be modified in time and to-day some approach to the *κοινή* is used by village headmen and others in touch with the wider world.

Although surrounded by African languages and although intermarriage has been such that few are of pure Arab blood, the dialects of the Sudan are surprisingly free from external corruption. They have imposed themselves on Nubian which has so little influenced it that the only borrowings from it are a few agricultural and irrigation terms.[1] But naturally they have been modified through rubbing against each other and other influences, and it is only of certain groups of the camel nomads, such as the Kabābīsh, that the words of d'Escayrac de Lauture hold good:

> Leur langue altérée un peu par le temps, accrue de quelques mots empruntés aux vocabulaires des nègres, est cependant encore la langue du Hedjaz plus harmonieuse, plus concise, plus énergique, plus grammaticale et plus arabe que les jargons parlés en Égypte ou dans le Gharb.[2]

dialects which have not been studied and cannot therefore be classified. There are even dialects within some of the tribes (e.g. the Kabābīsh), owing to the amalgamation of different elements.

[1] A few words have been borrowed from the Beja; e.g. *ʿanqarīb*, rope-bedstead, from *angare*; *marfaʿīn* (marʿafīb), hyena from *mirʾfi*; *baʿshōm*, fox, from *b ashi*.

[2] *Mémoire sur le Soudan*, 1856, p. 43.

2

Historical Outline: The Christian Kingdoms to the Arab Conquests

I. SKETCH OF EARLY HISTORY

THE internal history of the Sudanese peoples is unpreserved. All that has come down to us are those contacts of the Sudanese with other nations, especially the Egyptians, Byzantines, and Muslims, which have been preserved in inscriptions and writings, an increasing amount of internal archaeological evidence, and the traditions of the people themselves, which are especially valuable for the central area for the last four hundred years. As a background to such evidence we should picture a vast country of pagans, broken up into innumerable tribes speaking different languages, of migrations, wars, and raids for cattle, women, and slaves, with their attendant evils of the destruction of crops, the burning of huts, the enslavement of tribes, and the terrors of pestilence and famine.

The earliest name of this country known to us is the vague Egyptian term *Ta-Neḥesu*, which, like the Arabic *Bilād as-Sūdān*, means the 'Land of the Blacks'. The later Egyptian name was *Kash*, which, like the classical *Ethiopia* (later appropriated by the Abyssinians), was given to the unknown and vaguely defined region lying to the south of Egypt, comprising the Nile Valley region, south of S͟hellāl, to the juncture of the Niles, and including the eastern area to the Red Sea. The name Nubia, as representing the northern part of this region, did not appear until Roman times, though we shall need to use that term to distinguish the area between the first cataract (Aswān) and the third (Ḥannek).

Our earliest picture of the Sudan takes us well back some five thousand years beyond the beginnings of the first dynasty in Egypt, and shows us Egypt south of the Delta and Nubia inhabited by a single race possessing a homogeneous Hamitic culture. These are the so-called pre-dynastic people who much resembled the Beja of to-day. They had their own arts and crafts, were acquainted with copper and cultivated the ground along the river. Naturally, being a desert steppe region with periodic variations in climate, it has been affected by periods of racial dispersion. A thousand years later tribes of Negroes of a short, broad-headed type, who do not now exist in the Sudan, moved northwards into Nubia and introduced a characteristic African culture, which, however, soon came to embody many local Hamitic features. At the same time Libyans from the west began settling in Nubia, and by about 2000 B.C. these various Hamites and Negroes had fused into one hybrid but homogeneous people much like the Barābra inhabiting the same area to-day, and a characteristic Nubian civilization had developed.

Another influx of Negroes of a different type came soon afterwards, These were tall, strong men resembling certain of the Nūba tribes of southern Kordofān. They advanced northwards sweeping all before them and destroyed the forts and watering-stations which the Pharaohs had erected in the Donqola region. This invasion was felt by the Egyptians to be a direct menace to their trade-routes and even to imperil the very existence of their state whose centre was at Thebes and therefore had to be taken seriously. The Pharaohs sent southwards a series of expeditions, in the third of which (1879 B.C.) Senusret III finally beat the Negroes back. Subsequently he rebuilt the forts and reorganized the southern region on a permanent basis. The policy of punitive expeditions having proved unworkable, the Pharaohs were not content with political annexation, but adopted a policy of assimilating the country culturally. An Egyptian colony was established at Kerma, which became the administrative centre of the area until it was destroyed by fire about 1600 B.C.

In the time of Aahmes I (XVIIIth Dynasty) who expelled the Hyksos, the country was divided into two vice-royalties, Wawat in the north and Kash (the Biblical Kush, comprising Donqola and Ḥalfa provinces, with a varying southern boundary) in the south. Military or trading expeditions were sent into Kordofān and Sennar.

The most important and continuous of the external cultural influences on Nubia was that of the Egyptians. The Egyptians had, through a series of crises, become completely differentiated from the southerners in culture at the time of the foundation of the United Kingdom (*c.* 3400 B.C.), and a large area of Nubia was annexed to act as a buffer, though fully incorporated into the Egyptian state. The attitude of the Pharaohs to Nubia was to regard it purely as a dependency which possessed important trade-routes producing for them slaves and gold, but they egyptianized it very thoroughly and filled it with Egyptian immigrants who developed an urban civilization entirely based on that of Egypt, though influenced by local customs and the physical environment. The majority of the Nubians remained uncivilized peasants and herdsmen, but owing to the settled conditions the riverain district from Aswān to Semna became fairly populous. Under the new Empire many towns were founded and magnificent temples built, each of which was 'a centre of propaganda, a community of scribes learned in Egyptian medicine, law, and religion, and of artisans trained in every ancient craft'.[1] Taxes were collected, the trade in ivory, slaves, ebony, and spices developed, and the mines of the eastern desert were worked for gold and emeralds.

In the eastern district we should not forget the influence of the Beja nomads, a Hamitic-speaking race, resembling the pre-dynastic Egyptians of Upper Egypt, which has infiltrated continually into surrounding regions where it has been absorbed, yet has persisted in its own deserts throughout the centuries almost unmodified to this day.[2]

Kingdom of Napata (750–300 B.C.)

About 947 B.C. a Libyan family, who had settled in Egypt and intermarried with the Theban royal family, assumed the royal power, founding the XXIInd Dynasty under Shashank. Other pastoral Libyans[3] from the west (the *Temehu*) entered Nubia and eventually founded a monarchy with its capital at Napata, near Jabal Barkal. The priests of Amon then brought great prestige to the city by transferring themselves with their god from Thebes to Napata. This led the Nubian King Kashta (*c.* 750 B.C.), who had the title of King of Kash, to attempt the political unification of the whole Egyptian world. He himself conquered Upper Egypt as far as Thebes. His successor Piānkhī (744–710 B.C.) almost completed the unification when he pushed into the Nile Delta, attacked and defeated the Saïtes, and levied tribute on the whole of Egypt. He installed a branch of the royal family at Meroë (near Kabushiyya).

The next ruler, Shabaka (710–700 B.C.), not only ruled the whole of Egypt, but sent an expedition under Tirhākā, son of Piānkhī, to assist Hezekiah, King of Judea, and allied states against the Assyrian Sennacherib. After his death Tirhākā continued the war with the Assyrians, but was defeated in 670 B.C. and Egypt was invaded. Tanutamon, who followed, reoccupied Egypt for a time, but was expelled by the foreign Asshurbanipal and the local Saïtes of the Delta

[1] Reisner, *S.N.R.* i. 236.

[2] Cf. Seligman, 'The Hamitic Problem in the Anglo-Egyptian Sudan', *J.R.A.I.* xliii (1913), 593–705; G. W. Murray, 'The Northern Beja', *J.R.A.I.* lvii (1927), 39–53.

[3] Eduard Meyer (*Geschichte des Altertums*, ii. 52) thinks they were not Libyans but descendants of Hrihor, the High Priest of Amon who established the Theban theocracy *c.* 1075 B.C.

and *c.* 661–654 B.C. was back in Napata with the frontier at Aswān. From that time the dynasty ruled over Ethiopia alone, the northern border of which then lay near Philae and the southern towards the *sudd* region.[1] The short period of Ethiopian political expansion and entry into the events of the great world was now ended, but whilst Egypt became subject to successive alien conquerors, Ethiopia remained an independent Egyptaic civilized power until the arrival of the Nūba in the third century A.D.

By this time Egyptian influence had brought into existence a derived, but independent, Nubian culture. It remained strongly Egyptian in its characteristics, for during its most brilliant period its kings were also Pharaohs of Egypt and brought up skilled Egyptian architects and craftsmen to build and decorate their temples and public buildings. They used a script derived from the Egyptian to write their native language, worshipped Egyptian gods besides their own, and buried their kings in pyramids. Napata, as we have seen, became an important centre of the Amonite theocracy and Theban culture. The state was theocratic, the king himself being forced to abdicate at the command of Amon who then installed a new ruler. The material power of Napata was based on the control of the gold-mines and trade-routes between Egypt and the southern supplies of slaves and ivory. When the contact with Egypt was broken after 661 B.C., the foreign culture also declined and became purely imitative with few original elements. At the same time it remained true to old Egyptian ideas longer than Egypt itself, forming a barrier impassable, first to Christianity, and then, when it did eventually accept Christianity, to Islam.

Kingdom of Meroë (300 B.C.–A.D. 350)

We have said that during the period when the kings of Napata were Pharaohs of Egypt, their power was spreading southwards and they settled a branch of the royal family at Meroë, near the foot of the Sixth Cataract, as ruler of the 'Island of Meroë', the country enclosed by the Atbara and the Blue and White Niles. In course of time Meroë gained more and more influence, becoming an important trade centre, not only because of the north and south route along the Nile, for there is a fairly long stretch of navigable river, but also for the west-to-east caravan-route to the Red Sea ports. The city thus occupied a position of strategic importance, being more fertile and better situated than

[1] Reisner, *S.N.R.* ii. 65, has shown that the people of Jebel Mōya (Sennār District) had direct trade connexions with Napata.

Napata for the administration of the country and the maintenance of its frontiers, whilst it was in closer touch with the fertile productive south. Further, when the Napata gold-mines became exhausted, that city became more and more a religious and administrative capital, until eventually, about 300 B.C., the king at Meroë claimed the supreme authority. For a time there were two kingdoms, but in 225 B.C. Ergamene, King of Meroë, gained the supremacy and from then (except from 100 to 25 B.C.) Ethiopian rule was centred at Meroë.

The great days of the Meroitic kingdom were contemporaneous with that of the Ptolemaic dynasty in Egypt (332–30 B.C.) and Hellenistic and Roman influences show themselves in the culture of the highly civilized capital, Meroë. Napata, like the post-imperial Thebes, was compensated for the loss of its political power by continuing as the ecclesiastical and cultural centre of the kingdom, until the time of the Ptolemies, when there was a cultural revival in Meroë. As Reisner writes:

> The temples of Napata with their endowed bodies of priests and craftsmen educated in the learning of Egypt remained the cultural centre of the kingdom, while Meroe became the centre of material wealth and political power. . . . It was not until a generation or so after the death of Nastasen that the rulers of Meroe introduced a revival of learning and art under the influence of Ptolemaic Egypt and made their capital for the first time the cultural centre of Ethiopia.[1]

But contact with the north gradually diminished, the knowledge and use of Egyptian died out, and a new cursive script, the Meroitic, appeared. The kingdom was only vaguely known to the Greeks and Romans. The ruling class at Meroë was, no doubt, like that of northern Ethiopia, Hamitic with a strong negroid element; but the bulk of the population of the island of Meroë, through continuous pressure from the west and south, had become predominantly negroid. They were a primitive, half-sedentary, half-nomadic people, living by the cultivation of millet and cotton and by hunting.

During this period the term *Noubai* first appears. The earliest mention of this people is in Eratosthenes (276–196 B.C.), quoted by Strabo:

> On the left of River Nile Nubians (Noubai) dwell in Libya, a great people, beginning at Meroë and reaching the bends of the river. They are not subject to the Ethiopians, but independent, being divided into several kingdoms.[2]

[1] *S.N.R.* ii. 61.
[2] Strabo, *Geography*, Bk. vii.

Here the Noubai are clearly distinguished from Libyans and Ethiopians and were at this time a separate element dwelling alongside the original people.

During the first century A.D. the Roman historians speak of queens of Ethiopia called 'Candace'.[1] Prof. F. Ll. Griffith has shown that this word is a title meaning simply 'queen', and that a number of Candaces ruled as regents during the minority of their sons.

When the Romans arrived at Syene (Aswān), the first historical Candace attacked the Roman garrison there and captured it (25 B.C.). Petronius, the Prefect of Egypt, therefore marched into Nubia, attacked and sacked Napata, and sent a thousand slaves home to Caesar. This Candace is supposed to have been the Amon Tarit, co-Pharaoh of Netek Amon, who has left numerous monuments in Nubia as far up the river as Nāqa, north-east of Khartoum. Meroë remained an independent kingdom, though Nero contemplated its invasion and, about A.D. 65, sent southwards a small exploratory expedition which, with the help of local chiefs, penetrated up the Nile as far as the *sudd* region. They reported that a Candace was reigning at Meroë, but that the country was too poor to be worth invading. They mentioned also that the region north of Meroë was decentralized and that forty-five petty princes were reigning between Aswān and Meroë. The Romans from A.D. 54 left the Nubians masters of the country from Primis (Ibrīm) southwards. No evidence exists to show that any Candaces reigned after the first century A.D., the records giving only kings of Meroë.

From the first to the fourth century the kingdom of Meroë declined in power, due, as we shall see, mainly to the arrival of the Nūba from the south-west. The unsettled condition of Egypt and the seizure of the Dodekaschoinos region, south of Philae, by the Blemmyes[2] caused a slackening off in the trade with that country and the economic

[1] Cf. Acts viii. 27; Strabo, *Geography*, Bk. xxii.

[2] In A.D. 253/4 a Blemmy prince, Pa-smun, son of Paesi, set up an inscription at Philae in which he called himself 'the great ambassador to Rome' of his King Tereramani (cf. Woolley and McIver, *Karanog*, iii. 90). From that time the Blemmyes occupied northern Nubia and raided Roman territory regularly. Julius Aemilianus defeated them in A.D. 261, but they were soon raiding the Thebaid again and occupied Coptos and Ptolemais. Aurelian threw them out again in A.D. 274, but two years later, supported by Narses, they once more took possession of the Thebaid. Procopius records that Diocletian (A.D. 284–305) settled some Nobatae from 'the city of Oasis' (Kharga?) along a tract of the Nile, 'for in this way he thought that they would no longer harass the country about Oasis'. He also 'decreed that to them and to the Blemyes a fixed sum of gold should be given every year with the stipulation that they should no longer plunder the land of the Romans. And they receive this gold even up to my time (A.D. 545), but none the less they overrun the country there' (*De Bello Persico*, Loeb. ed. p. 187).

decline which followed weakened the central authority in Meroë, which could not control effectively the border regions of the kingdom.

About A.D. 350, at the time when the Axumite kingdom was at the height of its power, its first Christian king, Aeizanes (ʿĒzānā), made a predatory expedition against the Nūba in the 'Island of Meroë'. He defeated them, as he records in an Ethiopic inscription,[1] on the Takkāzē (Atbara), burnt their towns, 'both those built of bricks and those built of reeds', and burned their stores of corn and cotton, then attacked Kāsū (Meroë), which was probably all that was left of the kingdom, and also ʿAlwa (near the modern Khartoum).

The effect of this invasion was far-reaching for it ended the rule of the Meroitic dynasty and the country henceforward was linked up with the south rather than the north. The native Meroitic script disappeared and also the characteristic Meroitic painted pottery, whilst Nubian took the place of Meroitic as the spoken language.

What had actually taken place in Meroë? Linguistic evidence leads to the conclusion that the name *Noubai* originally belonged to Negroids of Kordofān and that the *Noubai* of the north were immigrants from the south-west who, through partial conquest and settlement, changed the language of the people. After the break up of the kingdom, Meroitic remained for a short time the priestly language, but declined as a spoken language, and Nubian, the language of the vigorous recent immigrants, became dominant.

In the Axumite king's inscription recording his invasion of A.D. 350, the Nōbā and the Meroites are clearly distinguished, though they were apparently living side by side. The towns of the Nōbā, he says, were grass huts; they also had some brick towns captured from the Meroites.

It seems then that before A.D. 350 tribes of Nūbas from Kordofān and the Jezīra[2] invaded Meroë, captured some towns, and settled at first as a distinct separate element from the existing population. They adopted some elements of the Meroitic religion and in time must have inter-married with the Meroitic Ethiopians.

The fall of the Meroitic Kingdom was probably due chiefly to the arrival of these immigrants, although it is possible that the new arrivals, apart from the Hamitic ruling class, may have been akin to the general Meroitic population. The trade of Meroë with Egypt declined owing to the economic crisis Egypt was passing through. The Blemmyes,

[1] Littmann, *Deutsche Aksum Expedition*, iv. 33; translated by Budge, *History of Ethiopia*, pp. 255–8.

[2] These are Zyhlarz's *Group B*; see his article 'Zur Stellung des Darfur-Nubischen', *W.Z.K.M.* xxxv, 1928, and S. Hillelson, 'Nubian Origins' (*S.N.R.*, 1930, pp. 137–48).

too, owing to the weakness of both countries, had intensified their perennial raids into Meroë and Roman Egypt, thus imperilling the trade-routes. Finally, the invasion of Aeizanes destroyed the dynasty and broke up the kingdom.

Aeizanes' inscription mentions *Red Nōbā* farther north:

And after that I sent the army of Halên, and the army of Laken down the Sêdâ (Nile north of the junction with the Atbara) against the towns of the Nôbâ which are made of reeds . . . and my peoples arrived at the frontier of the Red Nôbâ and they returned safe and sound.[1]

The term 'Red' would lead one to suppose that they were the original Hamitic population or colonies of Blemmyes, for in northern Nubia the original population were still comparatively undisturbed, whereas in Meroë the two peoples were living side by side. On the other hand, they may be the Noubai mentioned by Eratosthenes as occupying Upper Nubia from Meroë to 'the bends of the river'.

From the Fall of Meroë to Justinian I

In the fifth century the Nūba are mentioned as being on the border of Egypt in the appeal of Appion, Bishop of Syene (Aswān), to the Emperor Theodosius II (A.D. 425–50) asking him to instruct the military authorities to protect the churches at Philae which had been raided by the *Blemmyes* and the *Annoubádes*. This shows that the Noubades were now in lower Nubia, south of Ibrīm. Some of the Blemmyes were settled along the Nile from Ibrīm to Philae[2] and had adopted certain Egyptian deities.

The appeal of Appion was followed by a campaign of the General Maximinus, in A.D. 451, against an alliance of Blemmyes and the Noubades, whom he defeated and compelled to agree to a treaty, one clause of which fixed a truce for a hundred years; whilst another stipulated that Blemmyes and Noubades should be allowed, according to their ancient custom, to enter the Island of Philae, to visit the Temple of Isis, and take away her statue for their own religious festivals for a specified time.[3]

About the middle of the sixth century idol worship was suppressed in the Island of Philae by Justinian I (527–65), and the Blemmyes

[1] Budge, *History of Ethiopia*, pp. 255–8.

[2] MacMichael (*Hist. of the Arabs in the Sudan*, i. 37) writes: 'Olympiodorus actually visited their country between 407 and 425 A.D.: he specifies Primis (Ibrīm, 60 to 70 miles below Ḥalfa) as their last city on the Nile; and the inscription of Silko, who warred with them in the sixth century, corroborates this.'

[3] Priscus, *Fragmenta*, in *Historici Graeci Minores*, edit. L. Dindorfius, Lipsiae, 1870, p. 332.

were driven from the stretch of the river they occupied from Primis to Syene by Silko, the first Christian king of the Nobades. Procopius, who died about A.D. 565, says:

> From the city of Auxomis to the Aegyptian boundaries of the Roman domain, where the city called Elephantine is situated, is a journey of thirty days for an unencumbered traveller. Within that space many nations are settled, and among them the Blemyes and the Nobatae, who are very large nations. But the Blemyes dwell in the central portion of the country, while the Nobatae possess the territory about the River Nile. . . .[1]
>
> . . . Both these nations, the Blemyes and the Nobatae, believe in all the gods in which the Greeks believe, and they also reverence Isis and Osiris, and not least of all Priapus. But the Blemyes are accustomed also to sacrifice human beings to the sun. These sanctuaries in Philae were kept by these barbarians even up to my time, but the Emperor Justinian decided to tear them down. Accordingly Narses . . . tore down the sanctuaries at the emperor's order, and put the priests under guard and sent the statues to Byzantium.[2]

Silko records his victories over the Blemmyes in a Greek inscription which he set up in the Temple of Talmis (Kalābsha) which begins, 'I Silko am Chieftain of the Nobadae and of all the Ethiopians.[3] I came to Talmis and to Taphis. Once, twice, I fought with the Blemmyes, and God gave me the victory after the three. I conquered them once and for all and made myself master of their cities. . . .'[4] There may well have been a connexion between these two events, for previously when the Nubians worshipped idols the two peoples had been allied and both worshipped at the Philae sanctuary.

After Silko's victory the Blemmyes are no longer heard of on the Nile itself. They were either assimilated or joined their fellows in the eastern deserts. The Nubian kingdoms now extended down the Nile northwards to just south of Philae.

Archaeological evidence also records the appearance in Lower Nubia during the fifth and sixth centuries of a 'new and distinctly non-Egyptian type of grave'[5] which is of a primitive kind. These people are called by Reisner the 'X-group'. Their culture was predominantly

[1] Procopius, *De Bello Persico* (Loeb ed., transl. H. B. Dewing), p. 185.

[2] Procopius, op. cit., pp. 187–9. The Temple of Isis at Philae was first completed in the reign of Nectanebos (360–342 B.C.)

[3] The title is difficult to justify since the Makoritae and Alodaei were not subject to him, but the distinction he makes between the Nobadae and the Ethiopians shows that the Nubians were still a distinct element from the rest of the population.

[4] Budge, *The Egyptian Sudan*, ii. 308. Silko is supposed to be a Christian because he ascribes his victory to God and refers to the gods of the Blemmyes as 'idols' (*ὤμοσάν μοι τὰ εἴδωλα αὐτῶν*).

[5] Reisner, *Arch. Survey of Nubia*, 1907–8, p. 345.

Meroitic, but with a strong negroid element which seems to show that they were immigrants coalescing with the Meroites.[1]

The problem of how the Nubians got to this region is by no means settled. Zyhlarz's view is that the Nōbā of Aeizanes' inscription (Group B) spread northwards and joined their brethren, the Red Nōbā (Group A), on the conversion of the north to Christianity. But it is probable that groups moved up north before that time. They found the process of change to the Nubian language already far advanced and soon the Nubian element became strong enough to spread farther up the Nile valley and rule the local Hamitic population, although in time they were absorbed into it. This would account for the wide difference in physical characters between the hill Nūba of Kordofān and the Nubians of the Nile valley.[2]

2. CONVERSION OF THE NUBA TO CHRISTIANITY

When Christianity came to the Sudan the people of the north were Hamites coalescing with Negroes. They were more Hamitic in the north, though possessing a considerable negroid element, which increased in strength southwards until it became dominant in the Island of Meroë. South of Meroë, on the White Nile and Sobat, were the negroid Shilluk tribes, and over the deserts and hills in the east and north-east as far as the Red Sea coast roamed the Hamitic Beja.

The immigrant Nūbas at the time of the Axumite invasion were still distinct from the Meroitic Ethiopians, but now they were coalescing with the indigenous population, which adopted the Nubian

[1] Firth writes: 'The steady increase in the amount of X-group material southwards, and its Ethiopian character, are in favour of its representing a late Ethiopian culture, pushed into the Roman area from that direction. . . . The X-group people were Sudanese in type and culture, and the pottery has many similarities with the latest Meroitic pottery' (*Arch. Surv. Nub.*, 1908–9, pp. 40–1). The anatomical reports of the Survey show that 'The X-group people were strongly negroid aliens who had suddenly made their way north into Nubia, bringing with them a mode of burial and a type of pottery which Dr. Reisner has declared to be distinctly non-Egyptian' (Elliot Smith and Derry, *Arch. Surv. Nub.*, Bull. 5, Cairo (1910), 12).

[2] Among the Nūba of the Nile a definite Hamitic type predominates, whilst the hill Nūba are negroid. Seligman (*J.R.A.I.* xliii, 1913, 610–25) therefore built up a theory which has been adopted by MacMichael (*Hist.*, vol. i, i. 2) that Danāqla traders penetrated into the Nūba hills within comparatively recent times and imposed their language upon the Negroids. This theory is scarcely tenable. From the differences between the dialects of the hill Nūba and the riverain Nubians, which exhibit distinct independent features, no theory of borrowing will hold, and their separation must have taken place in early times. Nor is there any evidence, as Seligman admits (loc. cit. 620), that the hill Nūba have been influenced culturally by the Danāqla. The influx of Nūba into the Hamitic population of this northern region was not sufficient to modify seriously their racial and cultural characteristics. On this question see S. Hillelson, 'Nubian Origins', *S.N.R.*, 1930, pp. 137–48.

language, and, though we find the people worshipping the ancient Meroitic gods, they were also practising primitive African rites. The north, however, had been for a long period under Hellenistic influence and the country was ruled by many petty chiefs, some of whom aped the Byzantine state and used Greek as the written language of court and commerce. Nubian was not reduced to writing until the Christian period.

When the first Christian missionaries arrived in the Sudan they found three kingdoms, Nubia, Maqurra, and Alodia, to whom the petty chiefs paid such allegiance as accorded with their overlords' ability to enforce it.

Christianity was introduced into the Sudan in the sixth century as a definite missionary endeavour of the Church of Egypt and was the first contact of Christianity with the Negro race.[1] Our main source for the history of this period is the *Ecclesiastical History* of a contemporary writer, John of Amida (d. 586), Monophysite Bishop of Ephesus.[2]

Christianity had spread rapidly in Egypt where its development had been unique. The Egyptians accepted and assimilated its essential genius in such a way that it deeply influenced their inner religious life. At the same time they moulded it to suit many of their own conceptions so that their form of the religion came to express their nationalism in a way which had been denied to them in the political sphere. This is shown in a number of ways.[3] Firstly, their own language, Coptic,

[1] Eusebius's statement (*Vit. Constantini*, i. 8) that Christianity penetrated to the Ethiopians and Blemmyes in the reign of Constantine (313–17) in fact refers to the kingdom of Axum and nomadic Beja tribes, and arises out of the ambiguity of the word Ethiopia which has been taken sometimes in a broader, sometimes in a narrower, sense. Christianity was first introduced into Axum from Egypt by merchants through the commercial and maritime relations which existed between the two countries. Origen's (185–254) remark 'we are not told that the Gospel has been preached among *all* the Ethiopians' (*Comment. Matt.* xxiv. 9) implies that it had been preached somewhere in this region. But the shipwrecked Frumentius and Aedesius were the real founders of the Church of Axum, though we know they were helped by these early Christians and Greek merchants. A first-hand account of the conversion obtained from Aedesius is given by Rufinus (*Eccl. Hist.* i. 9). Frumentius was consecrated Bishop by St. Athanasius in A.D. 330, and within his lifetime Axum was officially converted and the religion was spreading into other parts of Abyssinia. The Sudan, however, scarcely seems to have been influenced from Axum, where the religion was still very localized, and after the invasion of Aeizanes about A.D. 350, the break up of the Meroitic kingdom, and the expansion of the Beja, the Sudan was in turmoil and friendly relationships between its princes and Axum were severed.

[2] John of Ephesus, *Ecclesiastical History*, Part III, transl. R. Payne Smith (1860), pp. 250–9, 315–27; abridged in *Mich. Syr.* ii. 265–7, 348. See also P. Kraus, *Die Anfänge des Christentums in Nubien*, 1930; J. Maspero, *Hist. des Patriarches d'Alexandrie*, 1923, pp. 233–6, 286–90; J. Maspero, 'Théodore de Philai', *Rev. de l'hist. des rel.* lix. 299–317.

[3] Cf. Bonet-Maury, *L'Islamisme et le Christianisme en Afrique*, pp. 37 ff.

was utilized as the vehicle of the Christian message from an early date. Compare this with the North African Numidian Church which used Latin and failed to survive the Islamic conquest. The scriptures were translated even into the dialects of Upper and Lower Egypt and of the Western Oasis. When the Egyptian Church became nationalistic Coptic was also used in worship. Secondly, the constitution of the Church, which dates from the time of the persecutions, was unusual in organization and discipline. The bishop, for example, was elected by the universal suffrage of the church members and until the time of Jerome was regarded simply as the head of the priests (*primus inter pares*). Thirdly, the ascetic aspect of the faith, monasticism and anchoritism, developed to a morbid degree. Fourthly, a remarkable 'Catechistical School' had developed at Alexandria, associated with the great names of Clement, Athanasius, Cyril, and especially Origen. Its aim was the instruction of the proselytes who left the Serapeum imbued with Greek Philosophy. This was the first Christian theological college, and it taught not only the life and teaching of Christ, but showed the agreement of His teaching with that of the philosophers, recognizing the elements of truth in the other religions, and used the methods of the Platonic school. It was this school which sent out missionaries who carried Christianity to pagan tribes in Lydia, Phrygia, Sinai, Arabic Felix, the Thebaid, and Upper Egypt. Finally, Egypt became a centre of the Monophysite reaction against the Hellenistic tendencies of Christianity, into which was concentrated all the passion of the Egyptians for religious independence.

By the reign of Constantine the majority of the population had become Christian, and by the middle of the fifth century non-Christian influences were disappearing rapidly. Idol-worship lingered longest in the Island of Philae on the Egyptian-Nubian border. The Roman authorities allowed it to remain so long from motives of policy, because of the veneration the Nubians and the Blemmyes had for its temples, and its abolition would probably have caused trouble with these turbulent peoples. A treaty, as we have seen, had been signed between the Romans and these two nations which allowed the continuance of worship at the temples of Isis. In A.D. 525 there was a bishop resident on the Island alongside the heathen temples, but pagan worship there was not finally suppressed until the Emperor could count on a favourable reaction in Nubia.

The Egyptian navigator, Cosmas Indicopleustes, writing about 537–47, says, 'among the Nubians and the Garamantes . . . there are everywhere churches of the Christians, and bishops, martyrs, monks and recluses, where the Gospel of Christ is proclaimed'.[1] However exaggerated this statement may be it shows that there were Christians among the Nubians during the first half of the sixth century. We know too that Christians fled from the persecutions of Decius, Valerian, Diocletian, and others to Upper Egypt, where Coptic nationalism had gained its strongest hold, and some of them may have entered Nubia. The commercial and cultural relations between Egypt and Nubia, which, in spite of continuous raiding, were never broken, could hardly have failed to bring Christians to the latter country. But it seems clear from the famous edict of Theodosius I, which counts the Nubians as pagans, and such writers as Priscus and Procopius, who speak of them as worshipping Isis and Osiris, that Christianity had not been accepted by them in any great numbers before the reign of Justinian I (527–65).

John of Ephesus writes:

> Among the clergy in attendance upon pope Theodosius,[2] was a presbyter named Julianus, an old man of great worth, who conceived an earnest spiritual desire to christianize the wandering people who dwell on the eastern borders of the Thebais beyond Egypt, and who are not only not subject to the authority of the Roman empire, but even receive a subsidy on condition that they do not enter nor pillage Egypt. The blessed Julianus, therefore, being full of anxiety for this people, went and spoke about them to the late queen Theodora, in the hope of awakening in her a similar desire for their conversion; and as the queen was fervent in zeal for God, she received the proposal with joy, and promised to do everything in her power for the conversion of these tribes from the errors of idolatry.[3]

The Empress mentioned his desire to do missionary work to Justinian, who decided as protector of the Orthodox Church and for political reasons that this long-delayed task of the Church should be undertaken immediately. He had no desire, however, to see a missionary of Theodosius converting the Nubians to Monophysitism[4] and

[1] *The Christian Topography*, ed. McCrindal, Hakluyt Society, 1897, p. 120. The Garamantes in the classical period were a widely spread nomad tribe extending from Phazania (Fezzān) as far as Nubia. John of Biclarum says that they concluded a treaty of peace with the Empire, and were converted to Christianity in the third year of Justin II (A.D. 569), the same year as the Maccuritae whose country they bordered: 'Garamantes per legatos paci Romanae rei publicae et fidei Christianae sociari desiderantes poscunt, qui statim utrumque impetrant' (ed. Mommsen, xi. 212).

[2] Theodosius was Patriarch of Alexandria 536–66 and was at this time in exile in Constantinople.

[3] John of Ephesus, op. cit., p. 251.

[4] It is scarcely possible to understand the history of the conversion of the Nubians to Christianity without some reference to the controversies within the Church. Justinian himself supported the Council of Chalcedon, but his wife, Theodora, was a Monophysite, and was

therefore 'determined to write to the bishops of his own side in the Thebais, with orders for them to proceed thither and instruct them, and plant among them the name of the synod'.[1] He sent ambassadors to them immediately with gifts of gold and baptismal robes, and ordered the Duke of the Thebais to escort them to the territories of the Nobadae.

The Empress was very annoyed by his precipitancy and determined to outwit him. She sent off Julian with a mandatary of her court with letters to the Duke of the Thebais in which she wrote:

> In as much as both his majesty and myself have purposed to send an embassy to the people of the Nobadae, and I am now despatching a blessed man named Julian; and further my will is, that my ambassador should arrive at the aforesaid people before his majesty's; be warned, that, if you permit his ambassador to arrive there before mine, and do not hinder him by various pretexts until mine shall have reached you, and have passed through your province, and arrived at his destination, your life shall answer for it; for I will immediately send and take off your head.[2]

Theodora was far more feared than Justinian and the Duke had no difficulty in detaining the imperial delegation with specious evasions as to the difficulty of getting together the guides and large caravan necessary for travelling into the barbarous south. When, however, Julian and his company arrived they 'found horses and guides in waiting, and the same day, without loss of time, under a show of doing it by violence, they laid hands upon them, and were the first to proceed'.[3] The Duke was very disturbed by this occurrence and excused himself to the Emperor's ambassador:

> Lo! when I had made my preparations, and was desirous of sending you onward, ambassadors from the queen arrived, and fell upon me with violence, and took away the beasts of burden I had got ready, and have passed onward. And I am too well acquainted with the fear in which the queen is held, to

in the habit of altering or supplementing Justinian's measures, with the result that imperial policy was at times somewhat inconsistent. Justinian had called on the Egyptian Patriarch Theodosius to give public adherence to the Chalcedonian formula, but he had refused, therefore Justinian chose another Patriarch named Paul (A.D. 541). The Egyptians, however, would not recognize him, and from this time until the Arab conquest (A.D. 639) there were two Patriarchs in Egypt, the Melkite (i.e. imperialist) who occupied the throne in Alexandria, but whose authority over the people was a dead letter, being recognized only by the remnants of the Byzantine Church; and the Monophysite, Theodosius and his successors, who lived at the monastery of Nitria (now Wādī'n Naṭrūn where a group of monasteries still exist). It was from Nitria that Theodosius pushed out his missionary expeditions, so that, as Mrs. Butler writes, 'religious strife in the north became religious zeal in the south' (*The Church in Egypt*, i. 330).

[1] John of Ephesus, op. cit., pp. 251–2.

[2] Ibid., p. 252.

[3] Ibid., p. 253.

venture to oppose them. But abide still with me, until I can make fresh preparations for you, and then you shall also go in peace.[1]

The legate we are told was very annoyed and cursed him thoroughly, but did not at the time realize the intrigue.

In the meantime Julian arrived at the Nubian frontier about A.D. 543. The king had been officially informed of the arrival of an imperial embassy and sent a detachment to escort them to Pakharas (Faras, the capital, north of Wādī Ḥalfa). On their arrival the ambassador presented his credentials and gifts, and 'immediately with joy they yielded themselves up, and utterly abjured the error of their forefathers and confessed the God of the Christians, saying, "that He is the one true God and there is no other beside him"'.[2]

Julian then gave to the king and his nobles teaching in Christianity and took the opportunity of warning them against the 'errors' of the Emperor's party. When, therefore, the other ambassador arrived:

he also gave the King the letters and presents, and began to inform and tell him, according to his instructions as follows: 'The King of the Romans has sent us to you, that in case of your becoming Christians, you may cleave to the church and those who govern it, and not be led astray after those who have been expelled from it.' And when the King of the Nobadae and his princes heard these things, they answered them, saying, 'The honourable present which the King of the Romans has sent us we accept, and will also ourselves send him a present. But his faith we will not accept: for if we consent to become Christians, we shall walk after the example of pope Theodosius, who, because he was not willing to accept the wicked faith of the King, was driven away by him and expelled from his church. If, therefore, we abandon our heathenism and errors, we cannot consent to fall into the wicked faith professed by the King.'[3]

After all this intrigue Julian set to work more earnestly. He used to relate how he sat day after day in caverns full of water from nine o'clock to four in the afternoon, baptizing the people who thronged to join the new faith. He apparently found the strain and heat too much, and returned to Constantinople after two years to report to Theodora,

[1] Ibid., p. 253.

[2] Ibid., p. 254. The formula bears a remarkable resemblance to the Muslim *shahāda*, 'lā ilāha illā'llāh'. Abū Ṣāliḥ at a later date (1208) writes from hearsay: 'It is said that the Nubians formerly worshipped the stars, and that the first of them who was converted to the knowledge of the truth and the religion of the law of Christ was Baḥriyyā, son of the king's sister, who was learned in the science of the sphere and was wise and skilful. When he was converted to the religion of Christ, all the blacks of Nubia followed him, and he built for them many churches throughout the land of Nubia, and many monasteries, which are still flourishing, and some of them are at a distance from the river and some upon its banks' (*The Churches and Monasteries of Egypt*, ed. Evetts and Butler, pp. 265–6).

[3] Ibid., pp. 254–5.

leaving behind Theodore, Bishop of Thebais, who was also an old man, to maintain and consolidate his work.[1] Theodore had to leave in A.D. 551 to attend to his own diocese, and the Nubians were left without guidance for eighteen years, until the exiled Theodosius realized that this mass conversion was not enough, 'for on the very day of his departure from this world (566 A.D.) he had them in his memory, and especially because the blessed Julian, their teacher, had died but a very short time before, and also because her late majesty, the queen Theodora, had given orders that the excellent Longinus should be made bishop there'.[2] Immediately after Theodosius' death Longinus was consecrated bishop, but he had considerable difficulty in getting away from Constantinople owing to the opposition of the Melkites. He was arrested on the boat on which he had embarked and detained for three years, but eventually, after disguising himself and putting on a wig, 'for he was very bald', he succeeded in getting away.

On his arrival in Nubia (569) he was joyfully received and 'immediately he began to instruct them afresh, and enlighten them, and teach them. And next he built them a church, and ordained clergy, and taught them the order of divine service, and all the ordinances of Christianity.'[3] Then he got the king to send an ambassador to the Emperor, Justin II, with presents. This ambassador, our chronicler, John of Ephesus, actually met, and he relates how highly he praised Longinus, saying: 'Though we were Christians in name, yet we did not really know what Christianity was until Longinus came to us.'[4]

Longinus stayed in Nubia on this first visit for about five years. In 575 he was invited to Egypt in connexion with the abortive attempt to elect a Monophysite patriarch. The king and nobles did their best to persuade him to stay, saying, 'once again, as before your arrival, we shall be left like orphans without a father',[5] but finally they let him go, providing him with the means for his journey to Philae, where he met the eighty-year-old Theodore, from whence he travelled to Alexandria where he quickly got himself into trouble.

Longinus, however, was not done with this region, and he has still another great achievement to his credit—the conversion of Alodia.

In the Northern Sudan were three kingdoms, apart from the great Beja tribes. Nubia, in which Longinus was working, was in the Lands of the Nobadae (Syriac, Nābadōs); far to the south with their capital at Sōba, near the modern Khartoum, were 'the people whom

[1] On Theodore see J. Maspero, 'La Vie de Théodore de Philae', *Rev. Hist. Rel.* lix. 303–4.
[2] John of Ephesus, op. cit., p. 256.
[3] Ibid., p. 257. [4] Ibid., pp. 257–8. [5] Ibid., pp. 257–8.

the Greeks call Alodaei';[1] whilst 'between the Nobadae and the Alodaei is a country inhabited by another people called the Makoritae'.[2] This contiguity of the Nobadae to the southern and western Hamitic and negroid tribes was of vital importance for the spread of the Gospel into the heart of Africa.

The King of Alodia heard of what was happening in Nubia, and desired the same sort of influence in his kingdom. He therefore sent a petition to the King of the Nobadae, Awarfīūla,[3] asking him to permit Longinus to come and evangelize Alodia. This was about 578 when Longinus had left the country. But the King of the Nobadae sent ambassadors to him in Egypt who persuaded him to agree to return and visit Alodia. However, when the Melkites heard of this the Patriarch Peter deposed him[4] and sent a copy of the deposition to the king, whose reception of the bearers was uncompromising, 'We will not receive anyone but our spiritual father, who begot us again by a spiritual birth.'[5]

When the bishop had returned to Nubia in A.D. 580, the King of Alodia sent another embassy asking for Longinus. The Melkites heard of this and sent two bishops and others to Alodia with orders saying that since Longinus had been deposed and was unable to baptize and ordain legally, these two bishops would instruct them in the right path. But the King of Alodia would not receive them, saying:

> We know not who you are, nor can we receive you, nor be baptized by you: but we will receive him who baptized the Nobadae, and by him will we be baptized. And as for what you say of him, we do not listen to it: for we see that you are his enemies, and speak thus of him from envy. Depart, therefore, from our land, that you die not miserably.[6]

The reception of a second invitation to Alodia convinced Longinus 'that the conversion of that kingdom was the good purpose of the grace of God. The Lord therefore stirred up the spirit of Longinus to go to

1 Ibid., p. 315. Copt. ⲁⲗⲱⲟⲇⲓⲁ, Gk. Ἀλῶος. It has been traced as far back as the fourth century B.C. in the *Il(t)* of the Stela of Nastasen (328–308 B.C.), and is mentioned in the inscription of ʿĀzānā (A.D. 350) as a city built of bricks. A temple there (later converted into a church) dates from Meroitic days. We shall call this country *Alodia* during the Byzantine period and after the Arab conquest of Egypt by the Arabic name *ʿAlwa* for which a seventh-century form *Αλωα* gives some authority. Alodia probably extended from Kabūshiyya to Sennār.

2 Ibid., p. 319.

3 He was probably the successor of Silko. In 559 we hear of a king called Eirpanome (cf. Maspero, loc. cit., p. 306), who may have been this Awarfīūla or another intermediate king.

4 Longinus had consecrated a patriarch of his party secretly, but when the Alexandrians heard of it they chose another patriarch, Peter IV, who took all measures against Paul of Antioch and Longinus.

5 John of Ephesus, op. cit., p. 317.

6 Ibid., p. 318.

them.' The Nubians were disappointed at his departure so soon after his return, but prepared a large caravan and sent with him nobles and men well acquainted with the desert routes, for his journey was not so simple as it seemed. He had other difficulties to contend with than those involved in an arduous journey through the desert amongst wild peoples, as the King of the Nobadae wrote later to Theodore of Alexandria:

> But because of the wicked devices of him who dwells between us (i.e. between the Nobadae and the Alodaei), I mean the King of the Makoritae, I sent my saintly father (Longinus) to the King of the Blemyes, that he might conduct him thither by routes farther inland; but the Makorite heard also of this, and set people on the look out in all the passes of his kingdom, both in the mountains and in the plains, and as far as the sea of weeds (the Red Sea), wishing to lay hands on my father, and put a stop to the good work of God, as my father has written hither to tell me.[1]

This journey to the Blue Nile took Longinus two hundred days. He could not travel by the shorter route up the main Nile because of the opposition of the Makoritae, and the King of the Nobades had to arrange for him to go through the country of the nomad Blemmyes by dangerous and unfrequented desert routes through the Red Sea Hills, during which he and his companions endured many hardships. 'Not only did we become ill ourselves', he wrote, 'and despaired of our safety, but also the animals that were with us died, not being able to bear the heat, and the thirst in the mountains, and the unwholesomeness of the water, so that we lost no less than seventeen camels.'[2]

We would naturally suppose that the King of the Makoritae was still pagan. But it has been suggested that the deputation of the Emperor Justinian whom Theodora outwitted may have penetrated to Makoria after their failure with the Nobades.[3] John, Abbot of Biclarum (d. 610), a Catholic writer, says that the *Maccurritae* were converted in the third year of Justin II (569, the same year as the Garamantes), and that they sent a deputation to Constantinople in 573 taking gifts of elephants and a giraffe as a token of friendship.[4] If they

[1] John of Ephesus, op. cit., p. 325.

[2] Ibid., p. 322. This letter was forwarded by the King of the Nobades to Alexandria where John of Ephesus must have copied it.

[3] Cf. Kraus, *Die Anfänge des Christentums in Nubien*, 1930; and Kirwan, 'Christianity and the Ḳura'ān', *J. Eg. Arch.* xx. 201–3.

[4] The two passages are as follows: Anno III Justini imp. (569), 'Maccurritarum gens his temporibus Christi fidem recepit'; Anno VII (573) 'Legati gentis Maccurritarum Constantinopolim veniunt dentes elephantinos et camelopardam Iustino principi munera offerentes sibi cum Romanis amicitias collocant.' *Chronica Joannis abbatis monasterii Biclarensis*, ed. Th. Mommsen in *Monumenta Germaniae Historica: Auctores Antiquissimi*,

were Christians the ease with which the Melkites were able to send two bishops to Alodia is accounted for.

After all their trials Longinus and his companions fell in with a royal escort led by a prince called Aitikiyā (or Itika) which had been sent to meet them, and escorted them to the Blue Nile. The bishop, in his letter to the King of the Nobades, goes on:

And on our arrival at the river's bank, we went on board a vessel; and the King hearing of our arrival rejoiced, and came out in person to meet us and received us with great joy. And by the grace of God we taught him, and have baptized him and his nobles and all his family; and the work of God grows daily.[1]

He then goes on, and this shows that Christian influence was in Alodia before his mission arrived,

but inasmuch as there are certain Abyssinians, who have fallen into the malady of the fancy of Julianus[2] and say, that Christ suffered in a body not capable of pain, or of death, we have told them what is the correct belief, and have required them to anathematize this heresy in writing, and have received those persons upon their presenting their recantation.[3]

The King of Alodia took the occasion of the forwarding of Longinus's letter to Alexandria, through the King of the Nobadae, to write to the latter, saluting him as a brother in spirit since he has now become a Christian, thanking him for his help and asking for Church equipment:

Thy love is remembered by us, my lord, our brother Orfiulo, because thou hast now shown thyself my true kinsman, and that not only in the body, but also in the spirit, in having sent hither our common spiritual father, who has shown me the way of truth, and of the true light of Christ our God, and has baptized me, and my nobles, and all my family. And in everything the work of Christ is multiplied, and I have hope in the holy God, and am desirous

1894, xi. 212–13. The location of the Makoritae of John of Ephesus is quite definite. The problem is whether the Maccurritae of John of Biclarum, who may be identified with the nomadic *Μακκοῦραι* of Ptolemy (*Geog.* iv. 2. 19), are different peoples or branches of the same tribe. If the latter, then the Makoritae of the Sudan may well have been influenced by the conversion of the Garamantes and Maccurritae of the Ṣaḥāra, for desert trade-routes ran from Kordofān and Donqola to Waddān and Fezzān.

[1] John of Ephesus, op. cit., pp. 322–3.

[2] Julianus of Halicarnassus (sixth century) was a Monophysite leader who held the Phantasiast heresy that our Lord's body was incorruptible. This heresy caused a schism in the Egyptian Church on the death of Timothy III in 536. In the year of his death (565) Justinian adopted this heresy. This shows that Christianity had penetrated to Alodia before the arrival of Longinus, it confirms that the way had already been prepared for him, and explains the invitation of the king.

[3] John of Ephesus, op. cit., p. 323.

moreover of doing thy pleasure, and driving thy enemies from thy land.[1] For he is not thy enemy alone, but also mine: for thy land is my land, and thy people my people. Let not thy courage therefore fail, but be manful and take courage: for it is impossible for me to be careless of thee and thy land, especially now that I have become a Christian, by the help of my father, the holy father Longinus. As we have need, however, of church furniture, get some ready for us: for I feel certain that thou wilt send me these things with carefulness, and I will make thee an answer: but on the day on which I was keeping festival I did not wish to write, lest my letters should fail. Be not anxious then, but encourage thyself, and play the man: for Christ is with us.[2]

John of Ephesus concludes his narrative of the conversion of the Alodaei by informing us that it took place in A.D. 580.[3] The unfortunate political rivalries within the Egyptian Church, through the partisan bias of the writers, have obscured for us much of the history of the conversion of the Sudan. The Melkites did all they could to thwart the work of Longinus, but the kingdoms of Nobadia and Alodia remained faithful to the Monophysite Church of Egypt and were to render it valuable service in the future.

During Longinus's ministry many temples in both kingdoms were converted into churches,[4] other churches were founded, and by the end of the sixth century the Sudanese of the three kingdoms were united by a common religion. We have no evidence of any forcible conversions and the religion seems to have been accepted whole-heartedly by these peoples, though obviously the conversion of the kings and nobles made it wise to adopt the official religion. The nomad Beja of the eastern desert remained pagan in the main,[5] but, with that exception,

[1] The Nobadae seem to be at war with the Makoritae.

[2] John of Ephesus, op. cit., pp. 320–1.

[3] Ibid., p. 326.

[4] Pope Gregory in his instructions to the Abbot Mellitus, whom he had sent to Britain, told him to destroy the idols, but preserve the temples for Christian worship, 'that so the people might more willingly renounce their errors, resorting to the worship of the one true God in their accustomed places'.

[5] The influence of Christianity upon the nomadic Beja tribes roaming between the Nile and Red Sea was very slight and affected mainly those of the Red Sea coast. Eusebius (*Vit. Constant.* i. 8) speaks of its penetration amongst the (coastal) Blemmyes in the reign of Constantine. In A.D. 700 a Coptic bishop, Barnabas, was appointed to the port of ʿAidhāb to minister to seamen and merchants. He lived at Qifṭ but from time to time sent a priest and a deacon to ʿAidhāb (*Pat. Or.* iii. 499 f.). There was a great movement of Beja expansion at the beginning of the eighth century which almost brought the kingdom of Axum to an end. Christianity, however, survived in the highlands of Tigrai, and a new kingdom emerged whose main sphere of influence was to the south, but which influenced the coastal and southernmost Beja. The Muslims at first would not make any treaty with the Beja who raided into Upper Egypt because they were pagans. When they did so it was from motives of expediency. Al-Yaʿqūbī (A.D. 872; *History*, edit. Houtsma, 1883, i. 217–19) mentions five Beja kingdoms between the Nile and the Red Sea, of which the people of one, the Baqlīn, called God *al-zabjīr*, probably a corruption of the Abyssinian Christian name for God, *egzīʾabeḥēr*. In his *Kitāb-*

at the time of the Arab invasion Christianity was professed throughout north-east Africa as far as the southern frontier of the Axumite kingdom.

We know almost nothing of the further history of these Christian kingdoms until the Arab invasion of Egypt in A.D. 639. The capital of Nubia was at first at Balāña but, after the introduction of Christianity, it was transferred to Faras nearby. The language of the country, Nubian, through the influence of Christianity became a written language and therefore the official, as well as the spoken, language of Nubia. When next they emerge in history, Nobadia and Makuria were united into one kingdom with Donqola, its capital, dominating the trade-routes into Africa.

3. HISTORY OF MAQURRA

It is improbable that there can have been any important contact between Arabs and Nubians before the conquest of Egypt. Arab tribes undoubtedly crossed the Red Sea, but they would soon be lost in the vast spaces of the Sudan and absorbed into the nomadic Beja tribes.

In A.D. 639, seven years after the Prophet's death, following the conquest of Palestine and Syria, the Muslim general ʿAmr ibn al ʿĀṣi invaded Egypt, and the conquest was completed when Alexandria

al-Buldān (ed. de Goeje, 1892, pp. 336–7) he writes, 'the religion of the Zanāfaja is like that of the Ḥadāriba. They have no revealed law, but worship an idol which they call *Ḥaḥākhū*.' The presence of Muslims at the mines brought in more Muslim influence. Masʿūdī (A.D. 935) says that the Ḥadrāba (i.e. Ḥadāreb) tribe alone were Muslims and the rest were pagans venerating an idol (*Murūj*, ed. Meynard and Courteille, 1863, iii. 34). Abū Isḥāq al-Istakhrī (*masālik al mamālik*, written about A.D. 911) writes of the Beja as idolaters. Muṭahhar b. Ṭāhir al-Maqdisī writing in A.D. 966 mentions a Christian Beja tribe called Nasriyya which Huart amends to Bishariyya (*Le livre de la création*, edit. and transl. C. Huart, iv. 69). Al Idrīsī, who completed his book in 1154, writing of the Balīyūn (Balaw), says, 'They are Jacobite Christians and so are all the people of Nubia and Abyssinia and the majority of the Beja' (*Description de l'Afrique et de l'Espagne*, R. Dozy and M. J. de Goeje, 1866, text, p. 27). Yāqūṭ (1179–1229) says that Sawākin was peopled by blacks of the Beja race who were Christians (*Geographisches Wörterbuch*, ed. Wüstenfeld, iii. 182). Ibn Saʿīd (1214–87) says that after the Abyssinians 'come the Beja, a people partly Christian, partly Muslim, who possess the Island of Sawākin in the Sea of Suez' (quoted by Ibn Khaldūn, *Hist. des Berbères*, transl. de Slane, 1854, ii. 109). Ibn Baṭūṭa's references (Cairo ed. 1939, i. 43, 188) give the impression that both ʿAidhāb and Sawākin in A.D. 1330–40 were Muslim towns. Maqrīzī (1366–1442) describes the Beja as pagan with the exception of the Ḥadāreb who 'had become Muslim though their faith was weak' (*Khiṭaṭ*, i. 315). It is fairly clear that the nomadic Beja as a whole remained pagan, though some few in the coastal districts or adjoining the Christian kingdoms came under Christian influence. After the rise of the Funj they were incorporated into the loosely knit Confederation. The real movement towards Islam commenced at the beginning of the seventeenth century when Jamūʿiyya, under Makk Ghanam, occupied part of the present Hadendiwa country and influenced the Beja groups amongst whom they lived.

fell in A.D. 641. Before the end of that year the whole country was in the hand of the Arabs. Their success was due less to military force than to the hatred between the Monophysites and the Melkites. The majority of the Coptic Monophysite population welcomed the invaders as their liberators from the authority of the Melkite Patriarch and the persecutions of the Roman Emperor Heraclius. Michael the Syrian writes: 'It was no little advantage for us to be delivered from the cruelty of the Romans, from their malice, from their anger, from their cruel zeal against us and to find ourselves at peace.'[1] ʿAmr gave them the usual terms, guaranteeing their religious freedom and protection for themselves and their property on condition of payment of a personal tax (*jizya*). He also summoned the Patriarch Benjaman and other bishops from exile and reinstated them in their offices. Egypt for some centuries was regarded by the Caliphate as a Christian country with a Muslim army of occupation.

The information to be derived from Arab authors on the first clashes of the Muslim armies with the Nubians (A.H. 20/21) is somewhat confusing.[2] It is fairly clear, however, that small parties of raiders were first sent out against the Nubians, probably with no thought of a definitive conquest. These raiders were all defeated by the Nubians and forced to retire discomforted. This statement of Ibn ʿAbd al-Ḥakam (d. A.D. 871) is about as near as we can get to the truth:

ʿAmr b. el-ʿĀṣī sent out also (ʿUqba b.) Nāfiʿ b. ʿAbd el-Qais el-Fihrī with a company, and their horsemen entered Nubia in repeated summer incursions, like those which the Greeks were accustomed to make. This went on until the time when ʿAmr was removed from the command over Egypt, and was succeeded by ʿAbd Allāh ibn Abī Sarḥ, who made terms with the natives.[3]

The Nubians, encouraged by their success, continued raiding over the border and laying waste the nearer section of Upper Egypt. ʿAbd Allāh b. Saʿd b. Abī Sarḥ, after he had succeeded ʿAmr as *amīr* of Egypt in A.H. 25 (A.D. 646/7), determined to put an end to this and in A.D. 651/2 led a well-equipped expedition into Nubia. He was able to penetrate as far as Donqola and laid siege to the town, bombarding

[1] *Chronique de Michel le Syrien*, trans. Chabot (1905), iii. 413.

[2] Cf. Ibn ʿAbd al-Ḥakam (d. A.D. 871), 'The Mohammedan Conquest of Egypt', transl. C. C. Torrey in *Yale Biblical and Semitic Studies*, 1901, pp. 284, 307–10; Al-Balādhurī (d. A.D. 892), *Futūḥ al-Buldān*, ed. de Goeje (1866), pp. 236 ff.; Yaʿqūbī, *Taʾrīkh*, ed. Houtsma (1883), pp. 179 ff.; Maqrīzī, *Khiṭaṭ* (Cairo, A.H. 1324), i. 323.

[3] Ibn ʿAbd al-Ḥakam, loc. cit., p. 284; see also Yaʿqūbī, *Taʾrīkh*, ii. 179–80. According to Maqrīzī (*Khiṭaṭ*, i. 323) it was ʿAbd Allāh ibn Saʿd who was sent by ʿAmr with 20,000 soldiers against the Nūba and stayed there until recalled.

it with catapults and ruining the cathedral; whereupon the King Qalīdūrūn sued for an armistice. ʿAbd Allāh was only too pleased to agree because his forces had suffered heavily. The Arab historians are in agreement that the Nubians were excellent archers, for they were given the nickname of *rumāt al-ḥadaq* (pupil-smiters). Therefore ʿAbdallāh finally made a treaty of peace with them, not being able to subdue them. It was in regard to this battle that the poet said:

> 'My eyes ne'er saw another fight like Damqula,
> With rushing horses loaded down with coats of mail.'[1]

The king came out to meet ʿAbd Allāh who 'gave him an honourable and courteous reception and concluded peace with him on a yearly payment (*baqṭ*) of three hundred and sixty slaves, promising him a present of grain when he complained of the dearth of grain in his country'.[2] The treaty ran as follows:

This is a treaty granted by the *Amīr* ʿAbd Allāh ibn Saʿd ibn Abī Sarḥ to the Chief of the Nūba and to all the people of his dominion, a covenant binding upon the Nūba, both great and small, from the frontier of Aswān to that of ʿAlwa.

ʿAbd Allāh ibn Saʿd ensures security and armistice between them and the neighbouring Muslims in Ṣaʿīd (Upper Egypt), together with other Muslims or clients (*Ahl-adh-Dhimma*).

You people of the Nubian race shall be secure under the safeguard of Allāh and His apostle, Muḥammad the Prophet. We shall neither attack you, nor wage war against you, nor make raids upon you, as long as you observe the conditions arranged between us and you. You may enter our land as travellers not as settlers. We may enter your land as travellers not settlers. It is your duty to protect those Muslims or their allies who put up in your land or travel there until they depart. You shall restore to the land of Islam every run-away slave of the Muslims who have fled to you, you must not take possession of him, nor prevent nor thwart a Muslim who comes to take him and must help him until he goes. You shall take care of the mosque which the Muslims have built in the square of your city and not prevent any from praying there; you shall keep it swept and illuminate it and respect it.

Every year you shall pay three hundred and sixty head of slaves to the chief of the Muslims. They shall be of the medium type of slaves of your land, free from bodily defects, both male and female, neither extremely old men, nor old women, nor children under age. These you shall hand over to the Governor of Aswān.

[1] Ibn ʿAbd al-Ḥakam, loc. cit., pp. 307–8.

[2] Maqrīzī, *Khiṭaṭ*, i. 323. Maqrīzī's material is quoted from a book entitled 'Nubia, Maqurra, ʿAlwa, the Beja and the Nile', by ʿAbd Allāh b. Salīm al-Aswānī, which has not come down to us. Ibn Salīm was sent as ambassador by Jawhar, General of the Fāṭimid Khalīfa, Muʿizz, in A.D. 969, to invite George of Nubia to pay the *baqṭ* to him as new ruler of Egypt, and embrace Islam.

No Muslim shall be obliged to repel an enemy who attacks you or defend you against him from the frontier of ʿAlwa to that of Aswān. If you give refuge to a slave of a Muslim, or kill a Muslim or ally, or attempt to ruin the mosque which the Muslims have built in your city, or withhold any of the three hundred and sixty head of slaves, then this truce and security shall be cancelled and we and you shall return to hostility until God judges between us, and He is the best of all judges.

Upon these conditions we are bound by the covenant of God and His pledge and that of His apostle the Prophet Muḥammad; and you stand pledged to us by those you hold most holy in your faith, by the Messiah, the Apostles and all those you venerate in your religion and community; God be the witness between us and you.

Written by ʿUmar ibn Sharḥabīl in Ramaḍān, A.H. 31 (A.D. 652).[1]

This treaty is interesting. First, it shows that the Muslims had no thought of annexation and agreed to the neighbourhood of a non-Muslim state; although the clause stipulating the building of a mosque at Donqola and the arrangements for trading activities did lay the foundation for later Arab penetration of the country.

Secondly, it remained in force for six hundred years until the Fāṭimid period. The reason being that it was rather a treaty of mutual toleration and a trade agreement than a tribute to an overlord, for the Nubians had not been defeated.[2] The very word *baqṭ* is new.[3] At the time of its payment the Nubians are said to have courteously handed over forty additional slaves as a present and received in return a large gift of wheat, barley, wine, horses, and materials, which at a later period certainly exceeded the amount of the whole of the *baqṭ*.[4]

[1] Maqrīzī, *Khiṭaṭ*, i. 323–4.

[2] The accounts of this compact are confusing. It is clear that the *baqṭ* was no tribute. Ibn ʿAbd al-Ḥakam (d. A.D. 871), whose tradition goes back to Abū Ḥabīb, one of these Nubian slaves, says 'the terms which ʿAbd Allāh made with them were these: The Muslims were not to attack them, nor they the Muslims; Nubia was to pay to the Muslims so and so many slaves every year, and the Muslims were to pay the Nubians yearly so and so much wheat and lentils. Ibn Abī Ḥabīb says, moreover, that they (the Nubians) had no compact of any kind with the Egyptians; but simply this agreement, for mutual protection, with the Muslims' (loc. cit., pp. 307–8). He then quotes a shaikh of Egypt who gives the terms of agreement much as they are in Maqrīzī.

[3] C. H. Becker suggests that the word *baqṭ* is derived from Lat. *pactum* (*Enc. Is.* ii. 6), but it probably comes from the ancient Egyptian *bak*, 'tribute in kind' (cf. note in Caetani, *Annali dell' Islam*, iv. 521).

[4] Maqrīzī, *Khiṭaṭ*, i. 324. This is shown by an event about A.D. 847 when the Nubians became lax in payment and the return supply of gifts also stopped. Fairaqi, the son of the King Zakarīya, son of Yaḥnis, was sent to the Khalīfa Muʿtaṣim in Baghdād to report. He was well treated, but the investigation proved that the gifts received by the Nubians were greater than the amount of tribute paid. The gifts were therefore cut down, but Fairaqi was successful in getting a large draft upon the Egyptian treasury to be payable when the tribute was received (Maqrīzī, *Khiṭaṭ*, i. 325). An account from Christian sources is given in the *Chronique de*

Thirdly, the treaty laid the foundation of the slave-trade which was to become such a feature of later rule—a very different thing from ordinary domestic slavery.[1]

Now for a long period the relations between the two countries were restricted and peaceful, except for occasional raids and the withholding of the *baqṭ* from time to time. The Muslim interest in the country south of Aswān was confined to the export of slaves and later the exploitation of the many mines in the Beja country, of which Al-ʿAllāqī on the eastern bank of the Nile near the village of Qubbān was the chief.

We shall concern ourselves mainly with what little is known of the internal history and conditions of the kingdom.

We see from the treaty, which refers to the 'Chief of the Nubians and of all the people of his dominion . . . from the frontier of Aswān to that of 'Alwa', that the two kingdoms of Maqurra and Nubia were now united under one king.[2] Al-Yaʿqūbī, who wrote in A.D. 891, says:

> The Nūba have become two kingdoms. The first is the kingdom which they call Maqurra. They inhabit both the east and west banks of the Nile. The capital of their kingdom is Dunqula. It is they who made peace with the Muslims and pay them the *baqṭ*. Their land is a land of palms, fruit gardens and cultivation. The extent of their land is equal to a two months' journey. The other Nubian kingdom, which they call ʿAlwa, is much more dangerous than Maqurra. Its capital is called Sōba. They have an extensive country equal to a three months' journey and in it the Nile branches out into a number of tributaries.[3]

Michel le Syrien (trans. Chabot, 1905, iii, pp. 90–4). This states that Muʿtaṣim sent an envoy to the Nubians to inquire after the *baqṭ*. He found that Zakarīya was not of royal blood, but ruling as regent during the minority of his son George, who was king by matrilineal descent. George was sent to Baghdād where he was delayed owing to the rebellion of a tax-farmer in Nubia who had become a Muslim.

[1] This was not the only traffic in slaves. Ibn Salīm writes of Bukharās (i.e. Faras), capital of the province of Marīs, 'this district has a governor appointed by the King of the Nūbas (i.e. the King of Maqurra), who is known as the Lord of the Mountain. He is one of their greatest governors on account of his governorship bordering on the territory of the Muslims. Whenever any Muslim travels to Nubia either trading or with a present to the Governor or his Chief, the Governor receives it all and rewards him with slaves; for no one, whether Muslim or not, is ever permitted to have an audience with the King' (Al-Maqrīzī, op. cit. i. 307–8). Especially after Ibn Tulūn founded black regiments the export of slaves increased. The other main export was gold. In exchange, Egypt sent cereals, textiles, and such things as beads, combs, and other small goods.

[2] We do not know when the union took place for there is no evidence to support the suggestion of L. P. Kirwan (*J. Eg. Arch.* xxi. 57–62) that it took place as a result of the Arab threat for the challenge was not very severe. That challenge, however, did cause the Nubians to write their own language and to strengthen their Christianity as a nationalist cult over against Islam.

[3] *Ta'rīkh*, ed. Houtsma, i. 217.

The northern portion of Maqurra, that is, Nubia proper, was known as Marīs.[1] Ibn Salīm says, 'The Nūba and the Maqurra are two peoples, speaking two languages, both living on the Nile. The Nūba are no other than the people of Marīs who neighbour the Muslim region. . . . The Nūba and the Maqurra were at enmity before their conversion to Christianity.'[2] But, as we have seen, Maqurra was used as a general term for the united kingdom from the Egyptian frontier to that of ʿAlwa.

The Maqurrians, if they were Melkites, certainly became Monophysite after the Arab invasion of Egypt. Eutycheus tells us that the Melkites in Egypt remained without a patriarch for the space of ninety-seven years, from the caliphate of ʿUmar ibn al-Khaṭṭāb to that of Hishām ibn ʿAbd al-Malik. During this time the Monophysites took possession of all the churches which belonged to the Melkites and established in them bishops of their sect. Therefore when 'the people of the Nūba sent to them to ask for bishops, they sent them Jacobite bishops; so the Nūba became from that time Jacobites'.[3]

Marīs was governed by an official 'appointed by the King of the Nūba, known as the Lord of the Mountain,[4] on account of his governorship being near to Muslim territory'.[5] The northern district of Marīs between the first and second cataracts was an open district. Ibn Salīm writes:

> At this village[6] is a garrisoned post which is the gateway to the land of the Nūba. From it to the first cataracts of Nubia (i.e. Wādī Ḥalfa) is a ten days' journey. It is a district open to the Muslims who have property in the nearer part and trade in the districts beyond where some of them are domiciled. None of them can speak Arabic correctly.[7]

South of Wādī Ḥalfa was a 'closed district'; it was the duty of the Lord of the Mountain to see that no unauthorized person passed south

[1] In Coptic it is called 'the south region', i.e. Upper Egypt, but it is usually called ⲛⲟⲃⲁⲇⲓⲁ in Graeco-Coptic documents and it is with this that the Arabic Nūbā(tu) is connected. Faras (Cpt. ⲡⲁⲭⲱⲣⲁⲥ; Ar. Bahkarās) was the capital of Marīs. Cf. Griffith, 'Pakhoras–Bakharās–Faras', *J. Eg. Arch.* xi. 259 ff.

[2] Maqrīzī, op. cit. i. 309.

[3] *Patr. Gr.* iii. 1122–3. Cf. Letronne, *Annals*, ii. 386; Wüstenfeld, *Macrizi's Geschichte der Copten*, 1847, p. 22.

[4] *Ṣāḥib al-Jabal*, probably an abbreviation for *jabal al-janādil*, mountain of the cataracts; cf. Idrīsī, *Description de l'Afrique* . . . , ed. Dozy and de Goeje, text, p. 20.

[5] Maqrīzī, op. cit. i. 307–8. The Lord of the Mountain resided at Ibrīm in the time of Abū Ṣāliḥ (p. 266). Ibn Salīm (i. 307) simply writes, 'In this region is 'Najrāsh, capital of al-Marīs, the Castle of Ibrīm and another castle', and says that the Lord of the Mountain resided in this region.

[6] Al-Qaṣr, one mile (or five) south of Philae.

[7] Op. cit. i. 307. These people must have been Nubian Muslims.

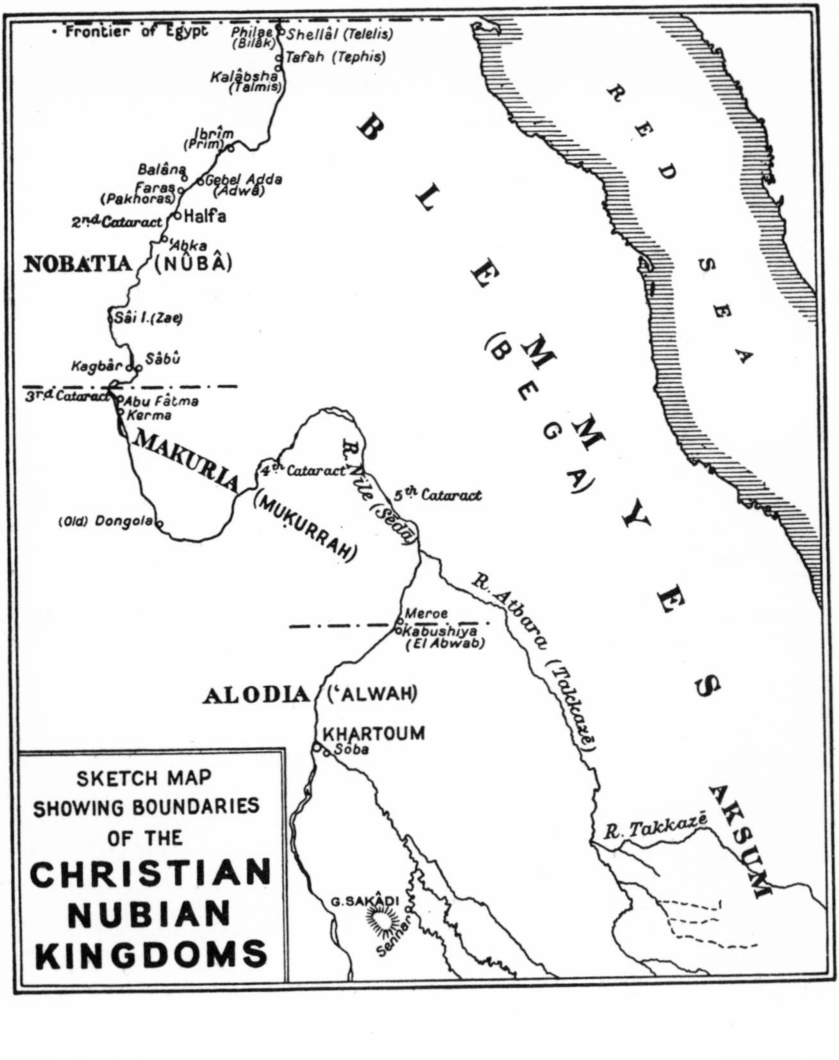

Frontier of Egypt
Philae (Bilâk)
Shellâl (Telelis)
Tafah (Tephis)
Kalâbsha (Talmis)
Ibrîm (Prim)
Balâna
Faras (Pakhoras)
Gebel Adda (Adwa)
2nd Cataract
Halfa
'Abka
NOBATIA (NÛBÂ)
Sâi I. (Zae)
Kagbâr
Sâbû
3rd Cataract
Abu Fâtma
Kerma
MAKURIA (MUKURRAH)
(Old) Dongola
4th Cataract
R. Nile (Sêdâ)
5th Cataract
BLEMMYES (BEGA)
RED SEA
R. Atbara (Takkazê)
Meroe
Kabushiya (El Abwab)
ALODIA ('ALWAH)
KHARTOUM
Soba
R. Takkazê
AKSUM
G. SAKÂDI
Sennar
SKETCH MAP SHOWING BOUNDARIES OF THE CHRISTIAN NUBIAN KINGDOMS

of the second cataract and the policy of isolation seems to have been strictly kept:

At the beginning of the cataracts of the country of the Nūba lies a village called Taqwā (Wādī Ḥalfa) on level ground where the Nubians' boats ascending from Al-Qaṣr on the borders of their country, stop. No boats are allowed to pass this place, nor is any Muslim or any other allowed to ascend the river further except by permission of their Lord of the Mountain.[1]

Masʿūdī tells us that when he was writing his book at Fusṭāṭ in 332/943 he was informed that the hereditary King of Donqola was Kubrā, son of Surūr, and that the southern kingdom of ʿAlwa was under his suzerainty.[2] But he must have been misinformed for there is no other evidence to support his statement. Al-Idrīsī says that the Nubian King carried the hereditary title of *Kāsil* (or *Kāmil*).[3]

The country was very prosperous at this time if one may judge from Ibn Salīm's eyewitness account of what he saw in A.D. 969. Speaking of the Donqola region he writes:

Nowhere on the Nile have I seen such wide banks. I estimated that the river flows from east to west for a five days' journey. Islands break it up between which flow streams through a fertile land where are villages adjoining one another with good buildings and pigeon houses, cattle and flocks, which supply most of the provisions for their towns. Of its birds are the Naqīṭ, the Nūbī, the parrot and other lovely birds. Most of the palaces of their Chief are in this province. I was once, says Ibn Salim, with him and we passed through narrow canals in the shade of the trees growing on both banks. It is said that the crocodiles never harm people there and I have seen people swimming across many of these streams. Then comes Safad Baqal, a district of narrow banks, resembling the first part of their country, except that in it are lovely islands and at a distance of less than two days journey about thirty villages with beautiful buildings, churches, monasteries and many palm trees, vines, gardens, fields and large pastures in which graze handsome and well-bred camels. Their Chief visits here frequently, because on the south it borders on their capital city of Donqola.[4]

Marīs and Maqurra had distinct languages.[5] These were probably two dialects and one of them developed into a written language, which is closely related to the modern dialect of the Fijadija-Maḥas region,[6] probably soon after the Arab invasion of Egypt. It has been suggested that this development was in order to strengthen their independence,

[1] Maqrīzī, op. cit. i. 308.

[2] Masʿūdī, *Les Prairies d'Or* (Meynard and Courteille), 1863, ii. 32.

[3] *Description* . . . , ed. Dozy and de Goeje, text, p. 19.

[4] Maqrīzī, op. cit. i. 309.

[5] Ibid. i. 309; quoted above, p. 64.

[6] Cf. F. Ll. Griffith, *The Nubian Texts of the Christian Period*, Berlin, 1913, pp. 5–6, 68.

but since all the writings which survive are intended for the common people it may have been a natural process of the Christian influence. The whole of the Bible was probably not translated, but fragments of a lectionary in Nubian have been discovered.[1] The Greek alphabet was adopted, with additions from the Coptic and perhaps the Meroitic alphabets. The Nubian writings which survive to-day comprise a lectionary, the 'Nicene Canons', homilies and edifying narratives, obviously translated from Greek and not from Coptic. The earliest dates from the eighth century and the latest the fourteenth century. Inscriptions on church walls in Greek are more common than Nubian inscriptions and perhaps indicate that Greek was the official language of the country.

The following inscription from a gravestone is very typical:

> God of spirits and of all flesh, who didst bring death to nought and trample down Hades and didst give life to the world, give rest to the soul of Angelosko in a place of light, in a place of refreshment, from which pain and grief and lamentation have fled away; every sin committed either in word or deed or thought forgive as Thou art good and dost love men, because there is no man who shall live and not sin, for Thou art alone, Thou art without sin and Thy justice is eternal justice. Lord, Thy word is the Truth, for Thou art the rest of Thine own (servants, Give rest to) Thy servant Angelosko Komatiekhon. And to Thee we sing glory, to Father and Son and Holy Ghost now and for ever and for ages of ages. Amen.??? The years of his life are 69.[2]

Their liturgy and prayers, according to Abū Ṣāliḥ, were also in Greek, for when Christianity was introduced the Egyptian liturgy had not been translated into Coptic, and Greek during the Hellenic period had been the language of the Nubian court.[3] Coptic books also circulated in the Sudan, since the country was full of Coptic monks and priests, who of course kept the church in dependence upon Egypt. Some Nubians are mentioned in the records of the Palestine Pilgrims' Text Society as visiting Jerusalem between A.D. 1180 and 1480.[4]

J. W. Crowfoot describes the typical church in Nubia as

> a small basilica with entrances from the north and south aisles, a stairway to the roof at the south-west corner and a small room of unknown use at the north-west corner, and at the east end three internal apses, often with a narrow passage behind the central apse connecting the prothesis with the diaconicon:

[1] Cf. Griffith, op. cit., pp. 24–41.

[2] J. W. Crowfoot, 'Five Greek Inscriptions from Nubia', *J. Eg. Arch.* xiii. 229. The Christian inscriptions from Nubia are discussed by Junker, *Zeitschr. f. äg. Spr.* lx.

[3] Abū Ṣāliḥ, op. cit., p. 272.

[4] The various references are brought together by J. W. Crowfoot, 'Christian Nubia', *J. Eg. Arch.* xiii. 148–9.

remains of seats round the central apse, of a screen corresponding to the modern iconostasis, of an altar and an ambo, have been found in some churches. This is the type which with slight variants is found in Lower Nubia, in Donqola province at Wādī Ghazāli and Gebel Bakhīt, for example, and in the far south at Segadi.[1]

4. ARAB PENETRATION AND END OF THE KINGDOM OF MAQURRA

The kingdom of Maqurra lasted for seven hundred years and its fall was due to both internal and external causes. These will be discussed later.

As we have seen, one of the duties of the Lord of the Mountain was to ensure that no unauthorized person penetrated to the region above Wādī Ḥalfa. Traders only were allowed into Maqurra and they would not be Arabs. Muslims were allowed to enter and even settle in the border area and this region became a place of refuge for Arabs who found things too hot for them in Egypt.

Whilst Egypt remained under Arab control the relationships between Muslims and Nubians were happy, friction only being caused by the occasional withholding of the *baqṭ*. However, with the rise of non-Arab rulers in Egypt their relationship began to change. Ibn Ṭūlūn in A.D. 869 sent punitive expeditions, composed mainly of nomad Arabs living in Upper Egypt, against the Nubians and Beja.[2] These Arabs, who were mainly Rabīʿa and Juhaina, settled in the country, some amongst the Nubians near Aswān, and others with the Beja. The attraction of the Beja country for the Arabs was freedom from the growing restrictions of Egyptian rule and the exploitation of the gold-mines at Al-ʿAllāqī. At first there was friction, but the Arabs gradually intermarried with the Nubians and Beja and acquired control.[3] Both the Nubians and Beja retained their languages, racial

[1] J. W. Crowfoot, op. cit. xiii. 144. For photographs and plans of churches see Mileham, *Churches in Lower Nubia*, 1910; and Somers Clarke, *Christian Antiquities in the Nile Valley*, 1912.

[2] The Arabs had soon come into contact with these restless tribes. ʿAbd Allāh b. Saʿd saw some specimens on the Nile bank as he was returning from his Donqola expedition and after inquiries thought them too insignificant to be worth negotiating with. The Beja continued their raids into Muslim Egypt as before and ʿUbaid Allāh b. al-Ḥabḥāb (governor of Afrīqiya, A.H. 116–23) is said to have made a treaty with them similar to that with the Nubians (Ibn ʿAbd al-Ḥakem, loc. cit., pp. 309–10). In A.D. 831, during the Caliphate of Al-Ma'mūn, an expedition was sent against them, after which the treaty was reaffirmed with their King Kanūn, but made little difference to Beja habits (Maqrīzī, *Khiṭaṭ*, i. 316).

[3] After describing a defeat of the Beja by the Muslims followed by a visit of the Beja prince to Mutawakkil at Baghdād in A.H. 241 (A.D. 855/6), Ibn Salīm writes: 'When the Muslims increased at the mines and intermingled with the Beja their evil doings decreased. After searching many found gold dust, and the news spread and people of many lands repaired

characteristics, and customs, and the Arabs were so absorbed that they became indigenous. The Nubian Kenūz of to-day, who live from Aswān to Korosko, are the result of the absorption of the section of the Rabīʿa which settled near Aswān with the Nubians of that district. Kanz-ad-Dawla was an hereditary title given by the Fāṭimid Khalīfa al-Ḥākim in A.D. 1020 to Abū Makarram Hibat-Allāh, Shaikh of the Rabīʿa and *amīr* of Aswān, whence they are known to the Muslim historians as the Banū Kanz. This tribe was in practically complete control of Upper Egypt during the Mamlūk period and played an important part in the events leading to the fall of the Christian kingdom. Another Beja group, the ʿAbābda, were influenced more thoroughly and are now Arabic-speaking.

The substitution of ʿAyyūbid rule for that of the Fāṭimids was accepted quietly by the Egyptians, but the black soldiers of the Fāṭimids, who had been banished to Upper Egypt, smouldered in rebellion, pillaged the country, and attacked Aswān. Ṣalāḥ-ad-Dīn sent his brother Shams-ad-Dawla Ṭūrān Shāh against them in 1172; after defeating them he attacked Nubia, probably because Nubians had helped or sheltered the rebels. He sacked Ibrīm and pillaged the church of which Abū Ṣāliḥ gives an account soon after when it had been restored:

In the land of Nūbia is the city of Ibrīm, the residence of the Lord of the Mountain, all the inhabitants of which are of the province of Marīs; it is enclosed within a wall. Here there is a large and beautiful church, finely planned, and named after Our Lady, the pure Virgin Mary. Above it there is a high dome, upon which rises a high cross.[1]

Shams-ad-Dawla established a Kurdish garrison in Ibrīm, but it was able to hold it for scarcely two years and the kingdom of Maqurra still remained intact. The following year Kanz-ad-Dawla led a mixed Nubian-Arab force into Egypt, but was defeated, captured, and put to death. Shams-ad-Dawla had been asked by Ṣalāḥ-ad-Dīn to report

there, amongst whom was Abū ʿAbd ar-Raḥmān b. ʿAbdallāh b. ʿAbd al-Ḥamīd al-ʿUmarī after his war against the Nūba in the year 255 (A.D. 868/9). He had with him the Rabīʿa and the Juhaina and other Arabs. As a result of their coming civilization increased among the Beja so that the caravans which brought provisions from Aswān consisted of 60,000 camels, apart from what the traders carried from Al-Qulzum to ʿAidhāb. The Beja inclined to the Rabīʿa and intermarried with them. It is related that the priests of the Beja, before any of them became Muslims, had told them their gods ordered them to obey both the Rabīʿa and Kanūn, which they did. When ʿUmarī was killed and the Rabīʿa took possession of the islands (of the Beja), and the Beja became friendly with them, the Rabīʿa drove away the Arabs who opposed them. The Rabīʿa married the daughters of the Beja chiefs and because of that their raids against the (other) Muslims stopped' (Maqrīzī, op. cit. i. 317–18).

[1] Abū Ṣāliḥ, op. cit., p. 266.

on the advantages of Nubia as a retreat for himself in case he got into difficulties with his overlord Nūr-ad-Dīn, but he was not impressed by what he saw of it, nor by the report of an envoy he sent to Donqola, and reported unfavourably. The Egyptian rulers still had no thought of annexation.[1]

The kingdom of Maqurra was comparatively unaffected by these raids. As we have seen, the Nubian policy was to leave the northern region open, but rigidly to exclude Muslims from passing into Maqurra proper except for trading purposes. Of the flourishing condition of Donqola at the beginning of the thirteenth century Abū Ṣāliḥ writes:

> Here is the throne of the King. It is a large city on the banks of the blessed Nile, and contains many churches and large houses and wide streets. The King's house is lofty, with several domes built of red brick, and resembles the buildings in Al-ʿIrāq; and this novelty was introduced by Raphael, who was King of Nubia in the year 392 of the Arabs (A.D. 1002).[2]

A decided change in the Egyptian policy came with the rise of the 'Slave-Dynasty' of the Baḥrī (Turkish) Mamlūks in A.D. 1250. Under the rule of this military oligarchy, Egypt enjoyed a period of great prosperity and expansion. The bedouins proved a nuisance to such a régime, so that their emigration southwards received every encouragement. The most famous Sulṭān, Rukn-ad-Dīn Baibars I (A.D. 1260–77), in his attempt to guarantee the safety of Egypt, intervened actively in the affairs of the kingdom of Maqurra, under the pretext of championship of Nubian pretenders who wished to gain the throne. In A.D. 1272 King David refused the *baqṭ* and made numerous incursions into Upper Egypt. Baibars then sent expeditions into the country in A.D. 1275 and 1276 and a formal treaty was made with one of the pretenders called Shakanda, in return for services rendered, which in effect made the district of Marīs a protectorate.[3]

1 Al-ʿUmarī, *Masālik al-Abṣār*, tr. Gaudefroy-Demombynes, 1927, pp. 47–8.

2 Abū Ṣāliḥ, op. cit., p. 265.

3 Maqrīzī, op. cit. i. 326. An-Nuwairī has preserved the oath taken by the king, which, he says, is the most solemn they possess (cf. Quatremère, *Histoire des Sultans Mamlouks*, 1837, p. 129). It begins, 'By God and the Truth of the Holy Trinity, by the pure Gospel, the pure Virgin, Mother of the Light, by the baptism, the prophets sent by God, apostles, saints and righteous martyrs. May I deny the Messiah (if I keep not this oath) as Judas denied Him and say against Him what the Jews say and believe as they believe; and be like Judas who pierced the Messiah with a lance. I affirm from this very time and hour the utmost sincerity of my intentions towards the Sulṭān, Rukn-ad-Dunya wa'd-Dīn Baibars, and that I will use my influence and power to gain his approval. As long as I remain his *nā'ib* I will not curtail the yearly tribute agreed upon of half the revenue of the country as it was collected by the kings of the Nūba.' The two provinces nearest Aswān (Al-ʿAlī and Al-Jabal) were to be handed over to the Sulṭān and also a yearly tribute of three elephants, three giraffes, five female panthers, and other objects was stipulated.

Maqrīzī says the Muslims stipulated that the Nubians 'should pay the *jizya* of one *dīnār* in cash for each adult male as long as they remained Christians'.[1] Churches were demolished, chiefs taken as hostages, and everything of value carried off. Sawākin on the Red Sea was taken in A.D. 1266.

Many years of internal troubles and disorder now ensued. Qalā'ūn, who took control of Egypt after the death of Baibars (1277), had the definite objective of the occupation of Donqola and sent two expeditions (1287 and 1289) to establish a pretender, son of the King's sister, on the throne as puppet king. The Mamlūk troops systematically devastated the country by burning villages, destroying water-wheels, and carrying away their captives as slaves, though only at the cost of heavy losses. After each expedition, and the second was a full-scale invasion, the King Shamamūn turned out the Mamlūk garrison and the pretender and regained his throne. In 1290 he sent an ambassador to Qalā'ūn offering an augmented *baqṭ* if he would leave him alone. Qalā'ūn was ready to agree because his expeditions had led to anarchy in Upper Egypt and he was just preparing to attack Acre. These ruthless expeditions, although they failed in their immediate objective, brought complete internal anarchy in Donqola.

In 1315 and 1316 other expeditions were sent south by An-Nāṣir Muḥammad b. Qalā'ūn, the second of which captured the King Kerembes and replaced him on the throne by 'Abd Allāh ibn Sanbū, nephew of King Dā'ūd, who was apparently a Muslim. He was killed by the then Kanz-ad-Dawla, who had himself proclaimed king by the Nubians. Under him and his successors, though the Sulṭān tried to turn him out a number of times, Nubia was really an independent Muslim state.[2]

In A.D. 1365/6 Egypt once more interfered on account of unrest fostered in Upper Egypt by the Banū Kanz, Banū Ja'd, and 'Ikrima. Donqola was now in ruins and had been abandoned by its inhabitants,

[1] Maqrīzī, op. cit. i. 326. This shows that the majority of the people were still Christians. The principles in waging *jihād* (Holy War) are that the conquered people must first be invited to embrace Islam. If they refuse they must choose between (1) submitting to Muslim rule, i.e. becoming *dhimmīs* and paying the *jizya* (poll-tax) and *kharāj* (land-tax); or (2) to fight, when they may be killed or made into slaves. If they become Muslims then they become full citizens of the commonwealth. If they become *dhimmīs*, they are not citizens of the Muslim state, but their lives, property, and religion are assured to them. A *dhimmī*, however, must be of the *ahl-ul-kitāb* (i.e. Jews, Christians, Magians, or Sabeans). In the case of pagans the choice is limited to Islam or death.

[2] This is true, in spite of the fact that Ibn Faḍl Allāh al-'Umarī says, 'the King of Dongola is a subject of the ruler of Egypt; he pays him an annual tribute, and in his country they recite the *Khutba* in the name of the Khalīfa and the ruler of Egypt' (*ta'rīf bi'l-muṣṭalaḥ ash-sharīf*, p. 29).

and the king had taken up his residence at Daw. Nearly all these raids from Egypt, however, were confined to northern Nubia and no serious attempt was made, owing to the power of the Banū Kanz, to turn Maqurra into a dependency of Egypt.

The majority of the population were still Christian,[1] but now that the country was opened up Arab immigration became a flood and the tribes poured southwards to the richer lands beyond the inhospitable Nubian stretch which had up till now acted as a barrier. This immigration was seldom undertaken by organized masses with a definite territorial aim, but by separate tribes or sections with an ill-defined aim of living their nomadic life in the environment best suited to it. The Sudan offered them many opportunities which were closed to them in Egypt with its narrow limits and lack of rain. Much of the country was admirably suited for the pastoral life, and since it had no rigidly organized government such as Egypt enjoyed under the despotic rule of Mamlūk Sulṭāns, they were free to live it as they liked. The Arabs, having no racial prejudices, intermarried freely with the indigenous inhabitants. Further, the succession of the tribal leader's son by a Nubian woman may have been secured by their making use of the matrilinear system prevailing amongst the Nubians and Beja.[2] The power of the Nubian princes was thus gradually weakened or rather absorbed. After the first attacks to obtain *Lebensraum*, the mingling of the peoples could proceed smoothly. With this process also went the gradual conversion of the people to Islam. Ibn Khaldūn describes the process as follows:

And with the conversion of the Nūbians the payment of tribute ceased. Then the tribes of the Guhayna Arabs spread over their country and settled in it and filled it with rapine and disorder. At first the kings of the Nūba attempted to repulse them, but they failed: then they won them over by giving them their daughters in marriage. Thus was their Kingdom disintegrated. and it passed to certain of the sons of Guhayna on account of their mothers

[1] Al-ʿUmarī, writing between 1342 and 1349, says of Nubia, 'les religions de ces populations font partie du christianisme . . . le roi de ce pays est actuellement un musulman, de la famille des Oūlād Kanz ed Dawla' (*Masālik al-abṣār fī mamālik al-amṣār*, trans. Gaudefroy-Demombynes, 1927, pp. 48–9).

[2] The Arabs did not have the same effect upon the nomadic Beja as upon the Nubians. Undoubtedly a matrilinear system once existed amongst them, the present social status of women strongly suggests it, and Ibn Salīm and Masʿūdī (*Les Prairies d'Or*, iii. 33) speak of the Arabs marrying the daughters of Beja chiefs and strengthening the Beja against the Nūba, but it is doubtful if this alone enabled the Arabs to acquire any share in the land. Ibn Baṭūṭa wrote in 1350 of the Beja that 'their women do not share in inheritance' (Cairo ed. 1939, i. 42–3), and to-day one of the strongest Beja customs is that of the unalienability of title to territory so that women cannot inherit land. In this case it was the Arabs who were absorbed into the Beja tribes who retained their own language and social customs.

(*sc.* being Nūba of the blood-royal), *according to the custom of the infidels as to the succession of the sister or the sister's son.* So their kingdom fell to pieces and the Aʿrāb (nomad Arabs) of Guhayna took possession of it. But their rule showed none of the marks of statesmanship, because of the inherent weakness of a system which is opposed to discipline and the subordination of one to another. Consequently they are still divided up into parties, and there is no vestige of authority in their land, but they remain nomads following the rainfall like the Aʿrāb of Arabia.[1]

This shows that the Arabs did not overwhelm the country by numbers but, by infiltration and by the dethroning of the royal houses, they broke up the cultural and religious life of the kingdom. The Arabs moved on after destroying the Nubian political life, for they had now an enormous territory to spread themselves over. The Banū Kanz and ʿIkrima remained in northern Nubia where they were already fully settled, whilst the other tribes, mainly Juhaina and Fezāra, poured southwards. They did not, however, have complete freedom of expansion to the richer lands in the south owing to the continued existence of the Christian kingdom of ʿAlwa.

5. THE KINGDOM OF ʿALWA

ʿAlwa extended from Kabūshiyya, probably as far south as Sennār. Ibn Salīm writes: 'At the beginning of the country of ʿAlwa are villages on the eastern shore of the Nile called Al-Abwāb, "the Gates" (modern Kabūshiyya). Over this region is a governor known as *Ar-Raḥrāḥ*, subordinate to the ruler of ʿAlwa.'[2] This country was independent of the kingdom of Maqurra and was distinct from it culturally. Greek was used only as the ecclesiastical language and possibly for a time after its conversion also at court. The few inscriptions that have been found at Sōba show that their own language was related to that of Nubia, but of an independent development.[3] ʿAlwa was linked up with Egyptian Coptic culture through its official religion, Christianity, but it was more vitally connected with the races of the Southern Sudan, not only because Sōba, its capital, was a great market for slaves, but also in race and culture. Al-Masʿūdī writes: 'Beyond ʿAlwa is a great tribe of blacks called Kunna (?) who are naked like the Zinj.'[4] ʿAlwa also had a cultural influence on the south where it introduced iron, though not the art of extracting the ore.

[1] Quoted from MacMichael, op. cit. i. 138–9.

[2] Maqrīzī, op. cit. i. 310.

[3] Griffith, F. Ll., *Nubian Texts of the Christian Period*, p. 5. One of these is dated A.D. 897.

[4] Masʿūdī, op. cit. ii. 383.

The pottery too from Christian sites shows no trace of Byzantine influence and resembles that of the Southern Sudan to-day.

'Alwa had an hereditary kingship whose seat was at Sōba, near modern Khartoum. Ibn Salīm gives an interesting account:

Sōba, the capital of 'Alwa, lies to the east of the big island between the White and Green Niles, and the northern part is near their confluence. East of it is the river which dries up and whose bed is then inhabited. It contains fine buildings, extensive monasteries, churches full of gold, and gardens. It has a lodging-house (*ribāṭ*) where a number of Muslims lodge.[1] The ruler of 'Alwa is richer than the ruler of Maqurra and has a greater army and more cavalry. His country is more fertile and more extensive. There are few date trees and vineyards. The commonmost type of grain is the white *dura*, which is like rice and from which they make their *kisra* and *merīsa*.[2] They have plenty of meat owing to the quantity of cattle and pastures that are so extensive that it takes days to reach the mountains. They possess noble horses and the tawny pure-bred Arabian camels. Their religion is Jacobite Christianity and their bishops are appointed by the Patriarch of Alexandria, like those of the Nūba. Their books are in Greek, which they interpret in their own language. Their understanding is inferior to that of the Nūba. Their king enslaves whom he wishes of his subjects, whether they have committed a crime or not; they do not object to this, but prostrate themselves before him and do not disobey in spite of the illtreatment they are suffering, but call out 'Long live the King, may his will be done!' The king wears a crown of gold, for gold is abundant in his dominion. . . . I have seen many people and races of the people above mentioned. Most of them acknowledge the Almighty Creator, but approach Him through the sun, moon, and stars. Some of them do not know God, but worship the sun and fire; whilst others worship whatever appeals to them in the way of trees or animals.[3]

It seems that Christianity, being first adopted by the king and nobles, became the state religion. Although it spread as far south as Jabal Saqadī in the Sennār district, it was never truly the religion of the people who remained mainly animistic.[4]

Later, in A.D. 1208, Abū Ṣāliḥ wrote an account of 'Alwa at the time when the kingdom was at the height of its power and prosperity:

[1] This shows the sphere of Muslim trading activities. Al-Ya'qūbī, writing still earlier (A.D. 891), speaks of Muslims frequenting Sōba: 'Now he who directs himself from Al-'Allāqī to the country of the Nūba which is called 'Alwa must make a thirty days' journey, first to Kabāw (Kabār, Kabān?), then to a place called Al-Abwāb, then to the capital city of 'Alwa called Sōba, where the King lives and which Muslims frequent in order to get information about the source of the Nile' (*Kitāb al-buldān*, ed. de Goeje, pp. 335–6).

[2] *Merīsa* is the sweet beer made from millet which is still so popular in the Sudan. *Kisra* is a thin cake of unleavened millet bread, baked on an iron plate (*dōka*) and eaten with a sauce made of ladies' fingers or other vegetables and seasoned with herbs.

[3] Maqrīzī, op. cit. i. 311–12.

[4] Cf. Crowfoot, 'Christian Nubia', *J. Eg. Arch.* xiii. 147.

Here there are troops and a large kingdom with wide districts, in which there are four hundred churches. The town lies to the east of the large island between the two rivers, the White Nile and the Green Nile. All its inhabitants are Jacobite Christians. Around it there are monasteries, some at a distance from the stream and some upon its banks. In the town there is a very large and spacious church, skilfully planned and constructed, and larger than all the other churches in the country; it is called the Church of Manbalī. The crops of this country depend upon the rise of the Nile, and upon the rain.[1]

The kingdom of Donqola had fallen at the beginning of the fourteenth century and the great rush of Arab immigration southwards had started, but though cut off from outside influences, still ʿAlwa survived. The Arab tribes were all separate units who rarely combined and no single tribe was powerful enough to attack it, whilst the Egyptian Mamlūk government had no thought even of holding Donqola. Some tribes were moving around the outskirts of the kingdom for Ibn Khaldūn speaks of sub-tribes of the Juhaina 'close to the Abyssinians',[2] probably in the southern Jezīra. The kingdom split up and internecine warfare took place, with the Arab tribes ever moving their flocks further into the country. In 1474 Arabic-speaking people developed the cosmopolitan town of Arbajī. Eventually Arab tribes completely overran the Jezīra and dominated its population.

The actual fall of ʿAlwa in A.D. 1504 is generally supposed to have been caused by the alliance of the Qawāsma section of the Rufāʿa with a negroid tribe, the Funj, who suddenly appear from the south. But the only evidence for this alliance is the Funj Chronicle,[3] and A. J. Arkell[4] has produced a case against its value as a record of the first two

[1] Abū Ṣāliḥ, op. cit., pp. 263–4. Little is now left of the city of Sōba since Khartoum was built by the Egyptians from its remains.

[2] *Hist. des Berbères*, trad. de Slane (1852), i. 10.

[3] This book is summarized by H. A. MacMichael (*Hist.* ii. 354–434). The account runs: 'Know that the reign of ʿUmāra Dunqas began by his gathering people around him and they went on increasing and he was staying with them in Jebel Mōya, situated west of Sennār. There came to him ʿAbd Allāh Jammāʿ of the Qawāsma Arabs, who was the father of the Shaikh ʿAjīb al-Kāfūtī, ancestor of the Awlād ʿAjīb. The Funj decided to make war on the Kings of Sōba and Qerrī. Therefore ʿUmāra and ʿAbd Allāh Jammāʿ set off with their army, fought the Kings of Sōba and Qerrī and defeated them and slew them. Thereupon they agreed together that ʿUmāra should be King in place of the King of 'Alwa, that is to say Sōba, since he was the greater and that ʿAbd Allāh Jammāʿ should be in place of the King of Qerrī. So he (ʿAbd Allāh) went and demarkated the city of Qerrī, which lies by Jabal ar-Rawyān on the east bank and placed there the throne of his kingdom. Likewise ʿUmāra demarkated the city of Sennār where before him there lived a woman called Sinnār. There he placed the seat of his kingdom. That was in the year A.H. 910 (1504 A.D.). ʿUmāra and ʿAbd Allāh continued to be like brothers, but the rank of ʿUmāra took precedence over the rank of ʿAbd Allāh if they were together in the same place. But when they were apart ʿAbd Allāh was treated exactly like ʿUmāra.' *Manuscript*, pp. 2–3.

[4] 'Fung origins', *S.N.R.*, 1932, pp. 201 ff.

hundred years of the Funj kingdom. Bruce's account, which is earlier than the chronicle, runs:

In the year 1504, a black nation, hitherto unknown, inhabiting the western banks of the Bahar el Abiad, in about latitude 13°, made a descent, in a multitude of canoes, or boats, upon the Arab provinces, and in a battle near Herbagi, they defeated Wed Ageeb, and forced him to capitulation, by which the Arabs were to pay their conquerors, in the beginning, one half of their stock, and every subsequent year one-half of the increase, which was to be levied at the time of their passing into the sands to avoid the fly. Upon this condition, the Arabs were to enjoy their former possessions unmolested, and Wed Ageeb his place and dignity, that he might always be ready to use coercion in favour of the conquerors, in case any of the distant Arabs refused payment; and he thus became as it were their lieutenant. This race of negroes is in their own country called Shillok.[1]

Many are the theories as to the origin of the Funj. It has been suggested,[2] on the basis of Bruce, that they were a band of Shilluk who descended the White Nile, and finding ʿAlwa overrun, aided the indigenous people to whom they were allied in race and culture against the Arabs, but in their own interests, so that they assumed political ascendancy. In the *Ṭabaqāt* of Wad Ḍaif Allāh we read: 'When the Funj first conquered the Arabs they levied the soldiers provisions on the tribes, each tribe having to supply so many pails of milk and others to provide bread.'[3]

If any vestige of the kingdom remained it undoubtedly ended about this time with the rise of the Funj. Christianity still lingered on, but was completely extinguished under the Funj kingdom and Abyssinia was left the sole Christian kingdom in Africa.

6. CAUSES OF THE DECAY AND ECLIPSE OF CHRISTIANITY IN THE SUDAN

(i) *Reasons for the slow spread of Islam*

Islam spread into the Sudan far more slowly than one would have expected, for Islam in the early days possessed an irresistible power of political expansion. This was due less perhaps to the slowing down of the conquest as to the unattractiveness of the land where this barbaric Christianity was ensconced. The treaty of ʿAbd Allāh ibn Saʿd shows that he had no thought of annexation, but simply wished to ensure tranquillity on the southern border of Egypt. The Arabs too seemed

[1] Bruce, *Travels* (ed. 2), vi. 370–1. Bruce was in Sennar in 1772.
[2] Cf. Arkell, loc. cit., pp. 246–7.
[3] *Ṭabaqāt*, Wad Ḍaif Allāh, (M) 21, (S) 23.

to regard the First Cataract at Aswān as the obvious border, and Nubia was not attractive except as a supplier of slaves, which they had provided for by the *baqṭ* and the stipulation that Muslim traders should be allowed to operate in the country.

Further, the Nubians were of an independent character which made them retain their political independence, their language, and their faith. Nor were they oppressed, as the Monophysite Copts were by the Emperor,[1] and did not want relieving of their rulers. So Christianity lasted in almost complete isolation at a low cultural level in Nubia for seven hundred years and its disappearance was due less to external than to internal causes.

(ii) *Underlying causes leading to the decay of Christianity*

The chief causes of the gains of Islam arose from weaknesses in the Christian communities themselves. The Church in the Sudan always remained exotic and never became indigenous in the sense that Islam is to-day. Christianity came as a new cult, weakly grafted on to the regressive pre-Ptolemaic culture of the country, without revolutionizing the lives of either the nobles or the masses. The cult was intimately associated with foreigners and foreign culture. All the bishops and many of the clergy were Egyptians and there was no system of devolution of authority. Nor did any truly independent theological schools develop, their function being filled by the monasteries which were packed with Coptic monks. Owing to this dependence upon Egyptian Monophysitism, when at a later date relations with Alexandria were severed through political causes, no fresh supply of clergy was available. In the reign of Al-Ḥākim relations were cut between Donqola and Alexandria, through his refusal to allow the biennial letter to be written,[2] and when, under the Mamlūks, the Coptic Church suffered great loss of prestige, it was unable to exert any effective influence on the southern lands. Further, the liturgy was in Greek and since people can only worship truly in their own language, worship became mere

[1] To the Copts the Arab invasion came as a relief. Abū Ṣāliḥ writes (Evetts and Butler, op. cit., pp. 230–1): 'This was the period during which the Emperor oppressed the orthodox (i.e. Monophysite) people, and required them to conform to his creed, which was contrary to the truth. From these two men (i.e. Heraclius and Maqauqas-Cyrus, Patriarch of Egypt) the Christians suffered great persecution, yet they would not deny their faith. But in their time the Ḥanifite nation appeared, and humbled the Romans, and slew many of them; and took possession of the whole of the land of Egypt. Thus the Jacobite Christians were freed from the tyranny (of the Romans).'

[2] The patriarchs used to write two letters each year to the Kings of Abyssinia and Nubia. Zacharias (1004–32) was the last to do so, being forbidden by Al-Ḥākim; cf. Abū Ṣāliḥ, op. cit., p. 290.

form and naturally animistic beliefs persisted. The life and will of a people cannot be expressed through a foreign language and a foreign hierarchy and therefore spiritual life sunk to a very low ebb and no movement for reform sprang up. The Sudan had only been in touch with Monophysite Alexandria and no other churches took any interest in these barbaric Christians.[1]

After Donqola was overrun by the Arabs the kingdom of ʿAlwa was left completely without guidance. We get an illuminating insight into the state of its Christianity from the writings of the Portuguese Alvarez who travelled in Abyssinia in the years 1520–7, just after the end of the kingdom of Sōba.

Towards the north, these Bellonos[2] border upon a people who are called Nubiis; and they say that these had been Christians and ruled from Rome. I heard from a man, a Syrian, a native of Tripoli of Syria, and his name is John of Syria . . . that he had been to this country, and that there are in it a hundred and fifty churches, which still contain crucifixes and effigies of our Lady, and other effigies painted on the walls, and all old: and the people of this country are neither Christians, Moors, nor Jews; and that they live in the desire to become Christians. These churches are all in old ancient castles which are throughout the country; and as many castles there are, so many churches. While we were in the country of the Prester John there came six men from that country as ambassadors to the Prester himself, begging of him to send them priests and friars to teach them. He did not choose to send them; and it was said that he said to them that he had his Abima (Abūna, i.e. Metropolitan) from the country of the Moors, that is to say from the Patriarch of Alexandria, who is under the rule of the Moors; how then could he give priests and friars since another gave them. And so they returned. They say that in ancient times these people had everything from Rome, and that it is a very long time ago that a bishop died, whom they got from Rome, and on account of the wars of the Moors they could not get another, and so they lost all their clergy and their Christianity.[3]

Again, Christianity from the beginning was the state religion and never seems to have revolutionized the life of the people, for any Church that is vital to the life of a country must act with sufficient measure of independence to secure its spiritual freedom. This was especially true of the southern kingdom where the king and nobility received Christianity as linking them on with a higher culture. The

[1] The Roman Church made some abortive attempts to penetrate into the Sudan in the thirteenth and fourteenth centuries (cf. du Caillaud, 'Les Tentatives des Franciscains au moyen âge pour pénétrer en Haute-Éthiopie', *Bull. Soc. Géogr. de Paris*, 1896, pp. 212–32).

[2] These are probably Balaw in the region of Qallabāt.

[3] Stanley of Alderley, *Narrative of the Portuguese Embassy to Abyssinia*, by Father Francesco Alvarez, London, 1881, pp. 351–2.

people accepted it nominally, but still retained their animism, so that Ibn Salīm speaks of them as worshipping God, but associating natural objects with Him. In the Sudan also it never cost a man anything to accept Christianity. The Church was not founded on the blood of martyrs because there was never any danger of persecution. So there were no indigenous saints to which to link their saint-practices.

There is no reason to suppose that the mass of the rural population ever were Christians, and Christianity probably only existed in the principal towns and larger villages. That the religion of the masses was animistic is evident from the complete disappearance of purely Christian elements and the retention of the underlying animism in their Islam. These people would then have no difficulty in accepting a religion which so far as they were concerned consisted of the *shahāda*, leaving them free to live as before and practise their old customs, short of actual worship of idols and natural objects.

The Monophysite Church in the Sudan, as in Abyssinia, had become the bulwark of Nubian nationality and sharply differentiated from the static primitive culture of the people; therefore when the rulers became Muslims the whole structure collapsed. As a national institution the Church was narrow in outlook and poverty-stricken in spiritual power. Further, being simply the religious department of the state, it could not possibly create an independent public opinion against national evils such as the slave-trade, which sapped the strength and vitality of the kingdoms; for though domestic slavery might have been tolerated, the slave-trade could not. The Church certainly tolerated the trade and perhaps, as in Abyssinia, profited by it.

Sudanese Christianity also failed utterly to respond to the challenge of the impact of the young and vigorous Islamic religion on its border, which, by isolating the region, caused its Christianity to relapse to the pre-Christian level.

Finally, Christianity, like Islam after it, was conditioned by the effect of the climate, which causes a lack of energy and a weakness of moral resistance. Only vital Christianity, truly developing an indigenous cult, constantly stimulated from outside, could have resisted the onslaught of a religion peculiarly adaptable to Africans.

These are the deep and underlying causes of the decay of Christianity. Whilst Christianity was a living force among them the natural independence of the people caused them to resist Islam, but once it became formal they yielded to the strong Islamic influence surrounding them. The Nubians needed expression for their spiritual aspirations and it was natural that they should turn to the ardent faith which thrust itself upon them, contact with which enriched their region by providing the foundation for a cultural unity.

(iii) *The Immediate Causes*

Some Muslim propaganda was undoubtedly at work in Maqurra and ʿAlwa before they fell for there was a mosque in Donqola and a Muslim lodging-house in Sōba, whilst the Muslim trader is normally a propagandist, but there is no evidence of it being very strong and the drift of the people to Islam was not due to missionary propaganda. Traders might have prepared the way, but Christianity had still the attraction of being the state religion and Islam did not come as a higher cultural influence. In fact what degree of culture Nubia possessed disappeared after the invasion, for nomad Arabs are by no means a civilizing factor. The immediate causes of the fall of the kingdoms were both internal and external.

Internal dissensions in Nubia became acute during the Baḥrite period and gave Baibars opportunity for interference. Self-interest at this time was the only motive of the Christian rulers. Public security was weak, for the collection of slaves for tribute meant constant raiding and led to internal anarchy, so that good government became impossible. Nor did Nubia have the almost impregnable natural protection the neighbouring Monophysite Abyssinia possessed in her highland fastness, though the northern deserts and the poverty of the Sudan did not make it very attractive except to nomads.

The actual downfall of the kingdom of Maqurra was caused by the infiltration and settling of Arab tribes, who gradually intermarried with the Nubians, secured the succession of their sons through the matrilinear system, and undermined what central authority still existed; by the rise of the arabicized Nubian tribe of the Banū Kanz, which differed from other new-comers by its complete identification with Nubian life; and through the internal devastation wrought by the direct interference of the Baḥrite Mamlūks in the affairs of Nubia. The downfall of ʿAlwa also occurred mainly through the immigration of Arab and other riverain tribes, followed by the Negroid–Funj invasion from the south. After the break up of the kingdom, Christianity began to disappear rapidly through the absorption of the inhabitants into the Arab tribal system and the cultural ascendancy of Islam, until now all that is left of these once flourishing Christian kingdoms are the ruins of many churches.[1]

[1] Remains of red brick churches of the ʿAlwa kingdom exist at Sōba, Rūdis, Elti, Kutrānj, Kasemba, Bronko, Ḥaṣṣa Ḥaiṣa, Kāmlīn, Arbaji, and Sennār on the Blue Nile and at Qaṭaina on the White Nile.

After the actual downfall of the kingdoms there followed the political domination of the people by Muslims and so suppression of the natives by people of a differing and powerful belief. There would be the usual social discrimination against Christians and pagans together with the possibility of getting free of these by adopting Islam and allying themselves with Arab tribes. Finally, and far more important, there was the attraction of the seductive power which Islam exercises upon any African people rendered spiritually homeless, especially through its power of assimilation of indigenous practices.

The disappearance of the Church from the Sudan was a very heavy loss to African Christianity. The Church had established itself strongly, deeply influenced social, political, and intellectual life, and offered a powerful rampart to the penetration of Islam into the regions of the Upper Nile. Its fall offers an instance of the grave dangers of the Church being simply the religious institution of the state.

But its disappearance had still graver consequences. Sir Richmond Palmer writes of the effect of the fall of Donqola upon the central Sudan:

> It may be said that up to the close of the fourteenth century, the influence of the Christian Dongola Kingdom was the predominant Eastern Sudanese influence apart from ideas derived from Egypt or fire-worship. From the Red Sea to Lake Chad, it was primarily the collapse of the Christian Dongola Kingdom about A.D. 1320, and the corresponding rise of the Kanem Muslim Kingdom under Hajj Ibrahim about the same date, that settled the religious complexion these regions have maintained till the present day.[1]

We are justified in maintaining then that the fall of Donqola was perhaps the most important single factor influencing the rapid spread of Islam in Africa. From then until modern times the Muslims had no rivals in the spread of their religion throughout the continent.

[1] *The Bornu Sahara and Sudan*, 1936, p. 4.

3

The Sudan under Muslim Rule

I. EXPANSION OF THE ARAB TRIBES AND ARABIZATION OF THE SUDANESE

THE bedouin tribes who poured south after the fall of the Christian kingdom all settled south of Nubia. They followed the line of the Nile through Donqola, where a few stayed, but the country was not very attractive and could not hold many nomads, also the eastern desert was occupied with the war-like Beja and some earlier Arab immigrants, so they moved south along the Main and White Niles until they reached the steppe region, then spread out south-west into Kordofān and south-east up the Atbara and Blue Nile into the Buṭāna and later the Jezīra. Some of the groups who now constitute the Kabābīsh went into the enormous western desert area which was mainly unoccupied except for the nomadic Tibbu. Far more flowed into the Kordofān land of steppes and pasture eminently suitable for camel-breeding which was inhabited by the Nūba and there began to develop the Arab-Negroid race who now inhabit Kordofān. The Jezīra tribes came in with the Funj, though they had been moving around and gradually penetrating the land for some time previously. The Arab-Hamite ʿAbdullāb, whose centre was at Qerri, seem to have settled the Khawālda around Awatib and Kabūshiyya, the Jaʿaliyyīn around Shendi, and the Jamūʿa on the White Nile. The Rufāʿ traversed the Jezīra and were subject to the Funj.

The tribes that are now Baqqāra entered the Sudan by the Nile route and turned west from Donqola until they penetrated what is now French Sudan. Some who were expelled from there, it is said for the murder of the son of the Sultan of Bulāla, settled in Dārfūr in the reign of the Sultan Ḥasan, from whence some tribes drifted eastwards.[1]

These Arab tribes were only small groups. Large tribes such as the Ḥamar and Kabābīsh only formed themselves in the eighteenth or nineteenth centuries when they were joined by other mixed groups.

No doubt these tribes met with some opposition, they made treaties with the powerful black conquerors from the south, but their nomadic

[1] The Sulaim traditions say they were led west by one Abū Tamānya who had married a daughter of the 'Black Sultan', and the Dār Muḥārib recount that their chief at the time of their arrival was Wad as-Sōda (son of the black woman), obviously the result of an Arab-Black union.

habits and ability to intermarry gave them *Lebensraum* in a country not very thickly populated. Many soon succumbed to the advantages of a settled life and were absorbed.

At the same time there was a general movement of Hamitic-Nubian tribes (e.g. Ja'aliyyīn) south and south-west into Kordofān. This movement has often been regarded as being that of Arab tribes, though the number of Arabs who entered the country was comparatively few.[1] Among the tribes that moved to Kordofān were the Jawām'a, Bedairiyya, and Shuwaiḥāt, who were probably already modified, but where they mingled so much with the Nūba that they became almost negroid in their characteristics. In the eighteenth century the Bedairiyya, for instance, still spoke a *roṭāna*. Other indigenous tribes (such as the sedentary Ghōdiāt and the Baqqāra Awlād Ḥamaid) who moved westwards, appear to have belonged to the 'Funj-Nūba' groupings.

During these centuries there was a process of cultural revolution, caused by the arabization and islamization of the people. Two parallel processes are apparent in the arabization of the Sudan: one linguistic and cultural, by which the people of the land acquired Arabic as their language and certain Islamic cultural conceptions and became connected with the Arab tribal system; and the other racial, by which the incoming Arab stock was absorbed in varying degrees by the people of the land, so that to-day a modicum of Arab blood flows in their veins. The cultural arabization of the people was the more profound because it also meant their islamization. The other process it would be more correct to call the indigenization of the Arabs, though, undoubtedly, Arab blood has modified the racial characteristics of the Hamitic and negroid tribes to a greater or lesser degree.[2]

[1] Some of the Egyptian tribes such as the Rabī' and Juhaina were genuine Arabs, but the Arab origin of many of the others is suspect (cf. *Revue du Monde Musulmane*, lvii. 87).

[2] The usual genealogical tree is in this form:

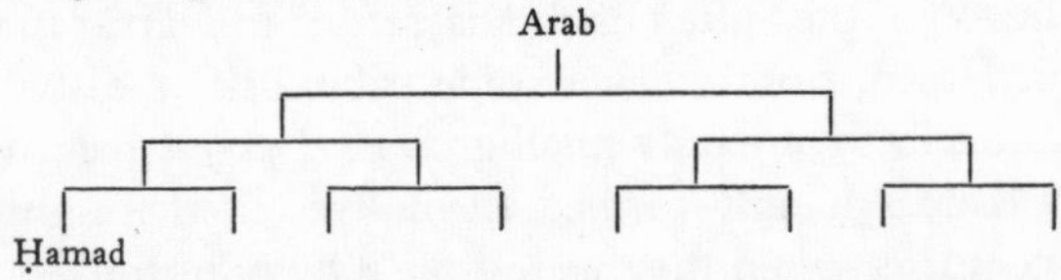

When we invert it and trace Ḥamad back to his great-grandparents, the artificiality of the Arab genealogy is apparent and we may get a *sharīf* with an ancestry like this:

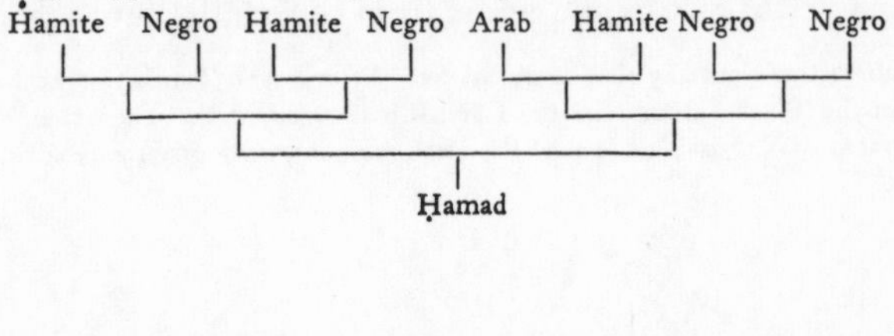

The following description by J. W. Crowfoot of the Tagalle Nubas gives some idea of the process at an early stage:

In some of the eastern hills, Tagalle for example, the people have been Mohammadan for a generation or two, they wear clothes, they speak a good deal of Arabic and some of them pretend to Arab pedigrees, they have given up keeping pigs, they talk with contempt of the 'Naked Nuba'. Such Mohammedan culture as they have adopted, circumcision and wedding rites, the practice of infibulation and so forth, comes from the riverain tribes or from the Kinãna and Kawãḥla settled in their midst, not, curious as it may seem, from the Baggãra tribes with whom they have been in much longer contact. The Arab tribes accept them as Mohammadans and brothers while smiling at their pretensions, and I have heard a Kaḥli at Kollogi describe the inhabitants of a neighbouring hill as 'Nūba who had become Kawãḥla'. In reality, these eastern Nūba are beginning the same metamorphosis which most of our Arabs' African ancestors began a few centuries ago, and the change, which is not complete in the latter case yet, has not gone very far with the Nuba.[1]

The Sudanese offered little resistance to this process of cultural arabization. But though they accepted so much, they remodelled it considerably and preserved not only a foundational Sudanese racial element, but their own nationality in their customs, and, in the case of the Nubians and Beja, their language.

Of the Arab immigrants only a few of the nomadic camel-owning tribes retained their racial integrity. But indigenous tribal institutions in general broke down and the people were forced to adopt the Arab tribal system, though indigenous systems still survived in the Funj kingdom and Dãrfūr. By the time of the Egyptian conquest the Arab tribal system was almost universal. The Funj did not exercise direct rule, so that nominal allegiance to them made no real difference to tribal authority. The cohesion of individual tribes was inconstant, depending on variable factors such as climatic conditions, the personality of the shaikh, a weak shaikh resulting in the transference of border elements, or marriage relationship, or the rise to power of a raiding tribe like the Shã'iqiyya.

The almost universal adoption of the Arabic language is not surprising when one considers its adoption by the intensely conservative Coptic *fallãḥīn*—what is surprising is that the Nubians and Beja preserved their languages.

2. NUBIA AND DONQOLA

After the year A.D. 1366, when the Banū Kanz pillaged Aswãn and suffered so severely for it that they revolted again (1385) and

[1] J. W. Crowfoot, 'Further Notes on Pottery', *S.N.R.* viii. 125.

captured and held Aswān, Egypt did not interfere in Nubian affairs for a long time. The Banū Kanz remained in independent possession of Aswān, the district north and south of it, and the desert of ʿAydhāb.[1] They had so identified themselves with things Nubian that they came to speak the local dialect, though the Nubians became Muslims.

In A.D. 1517 Salīm I of Turkey defeated the Burjī Mamlūks in Egypt and that country became an Ottoman dependency. His generals extended his rule down to the Third Cataract over the Sukkōt and Maḥas in 1520 and garrisoned the country at Aswān, Ibrīm, and Sāy with Bosnian mercenaries under officials of Turkish or Bosnian origin called *Kāshifs*. These northerners, most of whom settled and intermarried with the Nubians, whom the Sudanese called Ghuzz (Turk. *Oghuz*), governed the country for three hundred years. From these Ghuzz many of the Barābra claim to be descended. The central government had no really effective control beyond Aswān when the Howāra Berbers regained control of Upper Egypt in the eighteenth century; and the Ghuzz were quite independent, except for having to send to Cairo a tribute of slaves and dried dates collected from the Barābra. The second Kāshif, Ibn Janbalān, repulsed a Funj attack (*c.* 1520–30) at Ḥannek so severely that they never ventured into Nubia again. At the time of the 1820 conquest the power belonged to three Kāshifs who were brothers whom Burckhardt calls 'the Governors of Nubia'.[2]

In Donqola, south of the Kāshif sphere of influence, the Nubians had split up under many petty *makks* under the overlordship of the Funj. There was a Berber supremacy in the north under the Jawābrā[3] who had been driven into Donqola by the Ghuzz. South of these were the Bedairiyya mekships, from Taiti to the Shā'iqiyya at Jebel Daiqa. Then came the Shā'iqiyya groups centred at Merowe.

The Danāqla and Jaʿaliyyīn became the chief merchants and slave-traders in the Sudan, but the main trade-route at this time was not through Aswān, but through Shendī to Sawākin. The slaves, chiefly children, came mainly from Dār Fartīt, Dār Runga, the Middle Shārī, and the Banda country through Dārfūr,[4] until these countries

[1] Cf. Al-Qalqashandī, *Subḥ al-Aʿshā fī ṣināʿat al-inshā'*, viii. 5–8. They lost Aswān in A.D. 1412 to the Howāra Berbers who had been their allies when it was captured, and who became the dominant power in Upper Egypt until A.D. 1813, when they were defeated by Ibrāhīm Pāshā.

[2] Burckhardt, *Travels in Nubia*, p. 135. Cf. Shuqair, *Ta'rikh as-Sūdān*, ii. 109.

[3] A branch of the Zanātiyya, living from the Third Cataract to Taiti with their headquarters at Arqo. They are said to derive their name from Jābir al-Anṣārī.

[4] Cf. Burckhardt, *Travels*, p. 324.

became almost denuded of easily obtainable human game. This source was utilized because the fighting tribes of the Upper Nile swamps and Dār Nūba strongly resisted the raiders. The age-long connexion of the Sudan with Egypt through trade, cultural influence, and religion thus dwindled during this period almost to nothing.

3. THE SENNĀR CONFEDERATION

The kingdom of Sennār, which is known in the Sudan as the Black Sultanate,[1] was founded by some black raiders who seem to have allied themselves with the indigenous inhabitants of the Jezīra, whom the Funj called Hamaj, against infiltrating Arab tribes, and gained an ascendancy both over them and the Arabs. The word Funj seems to be a political term denoting an aristocracy at Sennār and other centres and does not necessarily relate to any one race or culture. Their maintenance of a standing army of blacks is one of the factors which show that the Funj were a small dominant minority with non-nomadic antecedents. The first Funj king, ʿAmāra Dūnqas (1504–34) recognized ʿAbd Allāh Jammāʿ as his viceroy over all the Arab tribes in the Nile valley. This ʿAbd Allāh was shaikh over a small section of the Rufāʿa which may well have aided ʿAmāra in his bid for supremacy. He founded a dynasty called ʿAbdullāb which ruled from Qerri.

The Funj and their non-Arab subjects were pagans. ʿAmāra Dūnqas is stated[2] to have joined Islam for political reasons. The story is that after Salīm, Sulṭān of Turkey, conquered Egypt in 1517, he sent an expedition into Nubia to help the Gharbiyya Berbers (1520), and also established bases at Sawākin and Maṣawwaʿ, thus threatening the independence of the Beja and Abyssinia. ʿAmāra took alarm at this as a threat against his own kingdom and sent a message stating that if Salīm was thinking of taking the *jihād* against him, he should know that he and his people were Arabs and true believers. As proof of this he sent genealogical tables drawn up by one As-Samarkandī, who is responsible for most of the fictitious genealogies in the Sudan, to prove that the Funj belonged to the Banī Umayya.

This is an unlikely story, for soon after Salīm's Ghuzz took possession of Nubia as far as the Third Cataract, the Funj sought to dispute its possession and sent an expedition against them. The Funj were defeated so severely that they never again tried conclusions with the Ghuzz.

[1] *As-salṭana' z-zarqā'*, literally 'the Blue Sultanate'; compare *An-Nīlu'l-azraq*, 'The Black Nile', always translated as 'The Blue Nile'.

[2] Shuqair, op. cit. ii. 73–4.

Bruce says 'at the establishing of this monarchy, the King and the whole nation of Shillook, were Pagans. They were soon after converted to Mahometism, for the sake of trading with Cairo, and took the name of Fungi, which they interpret sometimes lords, or conquerors, and, at other times, free citizens.'[1]

It is natural for any African raiding tribe to join Islam and their subjects would soon follow. The Funj encouraged professional holy men from over the Red Sea to visit and settle in their kingdom, and it is these men who are responsible for the islamization of the riverain and Jezīra tribes. The condition of the Jezīra under the Funj was a real mixture of pagan Africa with Arabo-Muslim elements. There were Nūba *kujūrs* at the Sennār court and Bruce, when writing of the licensed regicide or *sīd al-qōm*, says:

his place of birth was in a village of Fazuclo, and it appeared to me that he was still a Pagan. He was constantly attended by Nuban priests, powerful conjurors and sorcerers, if you believed him. I often conversed with these in great freedom, when it happened they understood Arabic, and from them I learned many particulars concerning the situation of the inland part of the country, especially that vast ridge of mountains, Dyre and Tegla,[2] which run into the heart of Africa to the westward, whence they say anciently they came.[3]

The people probably spoke various Hamaj-Nūba languages, for Bruce says that Arabic was general only in the upper classes.

The Funj dominated a very wide territory which in the time of its greatest prosperity (the reign of Bādī II 'Abū Diqn', 1642–77) extended from the Third Cataract to Fāzōghlī on the Blue Nile, and from the Red Sea to Kordofān. This kingdom was a loosely knit confederation, rather than a state. There was no centralization of authority and no common institutions. Only the land between the two Niles was directly under Sennār, for the Funj retained regional rulers as tributary kings and allowed all indigenous institutions to continue. Bruce writes that they make

the prince of the state they have conquered their lieutenant in the government of his own country afterwards. Such was the case with Donqola, whose Mek they continue; also with Wed Ageeb, prince of the Arabs, whom they subdued; and such was the case with Fazuclo, Wed Aboud, Jibbel Moia, and other petty states, all of which they conquered, but did not change their prince.[4]

He also tells[5] us that when 'Abd al-Qādir I conquered the districts of Jebels Mōya and Segadī (*c.* 1536), he had the conquered kings circumcised and degraded by being sold as slaves in the market-place, but re-

[1] Bruce, op. cit. vi. 371–2.
[2] Daier and Teqali in the Nuba Mountains.
[3] Bruce, op. cit. vi. 373–4.
[4] Ibid. vi. 391.
[5] Ibid. 385–6.

established their authority with the obligation of paying a light tribute. Their pagan life went on as before. The same happened when they annexed the Nūba Jebels of Teqalī and Daier at the end of the seventeenth century.

The Sennār overlord exercised his authority through retaining the right of choosing his vassal's successor from his family and the exaction of tribute. The tie therefore was very weak and his vassal frequently refused to pay tribute. The Sennār *Makk*, however, maintained a large standing army of Nūba slaves (14,000 foot and 1,800 horse in Bruce's time) and during the palmy days of the kingdom was able to maintain his overlordship. In 1610, for instance, the ʿAbdullāb viceroy revolted and was defeated and killed; but the Funj king nominated his son Al-ʿAjail in his place.

The Funj gave these tributary kings the title of *Mānjil* (or *Mānjilak*). After the death of a *Mānjil*, candidates came to Sennār and intrigued. When one was chosen the king invested him with the *kakar* or chair of state, the *tāqiyya umm qarnain* or head-dress shaped like two horns, an *ʿimma* (turban), a sword, and sometimes a gold-chain (*haikalī*).[1]

The ʿAbdullāb, as overlord of the 'Arab' tribes north of Arbajī,[2] appointed his own subordinate chiefs and invested them with the *tāqiyya*. Shuqair writes:

> If one of these *makks* died the whole tribe meet together, choose a *makk* to be over them and bring him to the shaikh (ʿAjīb). Then the shaikh shaves his head, crowns him with the *tāqiyya* having two horns stuffed with cotton,[3] and seats him on the chair called *kakar*. He then addresses him by the title '*makk*',[4] saying, 'blessing be on you' and the *makk* kisses his hand and prays for him. Then the shaikh orders the *naḥās* (tribal drum) to be beaten, thus publishing his appointment as *makk* over his people.[5]

[1] These were not symbols peculiar to *mānjils* for they were often given as a mark of honour and religious shaikhs were sometimes invested with the *kukur* and *ʿimma* (cf. *Ṭab.* M. 79–80, 143), but not the *tāqiyya* except in the case of Ḥasan wad Ḥasūna (M. 47).

[2] The ʿAbdullāb, who enforced his authority with a standing army of horsemen, levied a tribute which the nomads found irksome. One result of this was the migration of the eastern tribes into Kordofān, and another the settling of nomads who intermarried with the Hamitic or Negroid-Hamite tribes who thereby developed Arab pride of race. By 'Arab' tribes seems to be meant all Arabic-speaking tribes north of Arbajī and also Nubian and perhaps Beja tribes.

[3] Abū Ṣāliḥ (op. cit. [fo. 94a], 260) writes of Bujarās the capital of the ancient region of Marīs, 'there is the dwelling place of Jausār, who wore the turban and the two horns and the golden bracelet'.

[4] *Makk*, plural *mukūk*, is a title and not the equivalent of Arabic, *malik*.

[5] Shuqair, op. cit. ii. 100–1. The *naḥās* (cf. p. 26, n. 2 above) as the emblem of chieftainship is to-day central in tribal ceremonies.

The Funj, however, exercised direct rule in the Jezīra itself over all the tribes, including the Arabs. There was a *wazīr* and relatives of the *makk* also had authority as *arābīb* (sing. *arbāb*). In the time of Bruce the law still survived that a king might 'be lawfully put to death by his own subjects or slaves, upon a council being held by the great officers, if they decree that it is not for the advantage of the state that he be suffered to reign any longer'.[1] The master of the king's household, called *sīd al-qōm*, had the duty of killing him.

The Funj supremacy was brought to an end by the rise to power of Muḥammad Abū Likailik Kamtūr (d. 1776). Muḥammad was a *Hamaj*; in other words, he belonged to one of the indigenous groups whom the Funj conquered. He was instrumental in the defeat of the Abyssinians in 1744, and rallied the Funj after they were defeated in Kordofān by the Muṣabaʿāt, so that defeat was turned into victory. He returned to Sennār to depose King Bādī IV and replace him by a puppet king. The subsequent history of the Likailik supremacy as hereditary viziers is one of internal dissensions, decline, and civil war until the Turkish invasion of 1821 when they surrendered without fighting.

The ʿAbdullāb were completely independent of Sennār from 1770, but the sphere of their control was very limited for the Shā'iqiyya became independent early in the eighteenth century and dominated all the north until the Mamlūks arrived in Donqola after the 1811 massacre.

In 1820 the Funj possessed nothing on the right bank of the White and Main Niles and merely nominal suzerainty on the east bank of the Main Nile. They were in control of the Jezīra as far as Abyssinia and as far south as the Shilluk village of Al-Ais (Kāwa) on the White Nile.

The *Shā'iqiyya* were a nomadic tribe of probable Beja origin[2] who inhabited the country around the Nile from Jebel Daiqa (S. Donqola) to the Fourth Cataract, and came into prominence at the end of the seventeenth century. They were subject to the ʿAbdullāb overlord and their own tradition says[3] that about 1690, after the famine 'Umm

[1] Bruce, op. cit. vi. 372–3. Cf. parallels in custom of ancient Meroë (Diodorus, Bk. III, chap. vi) and Nilotic Shilluk and Dinka (Seligman, *Pagan Tribes*, pp. 90–2, 197–8).

[2] Ibn Salīm (Maqrīzī, *Khiṭaṭ*, i. 309), in writing of this stretch of the Nile in 969, says: 'Beja people, called Zanāfaj live here, who emigrated in ancient times into the country of the Nūba and settled there. They pasture alone by themselves, have their own language and are not mixed with the Nūba, nor do they live in villages; but they have a chief appointed by the Nūba.' The names of the sub-tribes of the Shā'iqiyya all end in the Beja termination *-āb*. The Shā'iqiyya are also said to have some Circassian blood in them.

[3] Cf. oral tradition quoted by Nicholls, *The Shaikiya*, pp. 10–14, and biography in *Ṭabaqāt* of Āʿsir b. ʿAbd-ar-Raḥmān (MacMichael, op. cit. ii. 266–7, 304–5).

Laḥm', a Shā'iqī shaikh 'Uthmān wad Ḥamad, after defeating his overlord, obtained from him a guarantee of Shā'iqī independence. What is clear is that in the middle of the eighteenth century the Shā'iqiyya had overrun the Nubian mekships of Ad-Dufār, Donqola, Al-Khandaq, and Arqū, and had stopped paying tribute to the 'Abdullāb. At the close of the century they dominated the Nile valley from the Ghuzz country to Ḥalfāya, near the confluence of the Niles. Essentially a nomadic and raiding tribe, though they had settled strongholds in their own country, where their chiefs resided, they did not govern, but lived at the expense of the riverain tribes. The whole Nile valley lived in terror of them, and they are responsible for another Danāqla-Ja'aliyyīn dispersion. The Shā'iqī tribes themselves lived in a state of mutual tension, but were able to put aside their private quarrels to unite against a common foe. This ability to unite, together with their warlike prowess and the weakness of the other kingdoms, enabled them to dominate the other tribes.

Their power was challenged in the north at the beginning of the nineteenth century when Mamlūks, fleeing from Muḥammad 'Alī's massacres of 1811, settled in Donqola, drove the Shā'iqiyya out of their stronghold Marāgha (new Donqola) and protected the Danāqla. The Mamlūks and Shā'iqiyya lived in a state of mutual hostility until Muḥammad 'Alī began his conquest of the Sudan in 1820, when the Mamlūks fled southwards and disappeared from history. The Shā'iqiyya united to resist the invader and fought courageously, but armed as they were with lances, were defeated by the well-armed Egyptians. They suffered severely from the invaders, but unable to exist as cultivators, enlisted in the army as irregulars and served their new masters faithfully.

4. DĀRFŪR AND ITS CONVERSION

Dārfūr consists of a large upland steppe plateau broken by isolated hills and a central massif, Jebel Marra. The main ethnic elements are Negro and Hamitic. At some unknown date before the twelfth century a race of blacks, the Dājo, came from the east, dominated the centre and founded a monarchy.[1] Later, in the fourteenth century, some Berber or Nubian people, the Tunjur,[2] began to emigrate there; if

[1] It is suggested, in view of linguistic affinities between the Dājo and the peoples of Kaduqli jebels, that they came from Dār Nūba. The problem of Dājo origins is discussed in *S.N.R.* viii. 59 and xv. 151 ff. The Dājo were not all absorbed and there are a number of their settlements in Dārfūr. They are a very decadent debased type.

[2] MacMichael, op. cit. i. 66, 169, suggests from their own tradition that they were 'an ancient pre-Arab tribe from Nubia. From certain customs that survive among them one

Berber, they had been moved probably by Banī Hilāl pressure in North Africa. The Tunjur gained gradually in power and dominated the blacks. Soon they began to lose their individuality by intermarriage with them and the resultant composite race of aboriginals, Dājo and Tunjur, which also had some Arab blood, is called the Fūr. To-day there remain only a few scattered villages of the Tunjur.

The Tunjur extended their rule over Wadā'ī in the west and formed a barrier to the expansion of Islam into these regions. The history of Tunjur rule is completely obscure until the fifteenth century when the last Tunjur ruler, Shāu Dorshīd, was expelled by his half-brother Dāli or Dalīl Baḥr who was mainly Fūr in blood, and was the first of the Fūr dynasty called the Kēra.[1] This man is still famous for the law he gave the country (the Book of Dāli) which became the basis of the law of the country under a dynasty which lasted until 1916.

Although Islam entered the country with the Tunjur—one of the early rulers, Aḥmad al-Ma'qūr, was a Muslim—it had no effect at all on the life of the country, whose people worshipped stones and trees. The first Fūr ruler to become a Muslim was Sulaimān Solong (1596–1637) who conquered the plains, welded the tribes together into one political unit, and founded a dynasty ruling from Turra[2] which extended its rule over Kordofān. An important landmark of the eighteenth century was the opening of a line of wells from Al-Fāsher eastwards to the Kāga hills which considerably facilitated commerce with the east. Dārfūr was thus brought more into touch with eastern Islamic centres and there began the process of islamization. Sulaimān introduced fekis from the east to instruct the people in Islam.[3] The process was accelerated by Sulaimān's grandson, Aḥmad Bokkor. This Sultan tried to bring some measure of civilization to the country by making it conform more to the idea of a Muslim state, and the state in fact lasted in the same form until 1916. He established elements of

would infer that they were Christians at the date of their migration from the west.' The customs referred to are those of making the sign of the Cross at various ceremonies. The Cross motif is, however, fairly common outside Christianity.

[1] The Tunjur remained in power in Wadā'ī until A.D. 1635 when King Dā'ūd was overthrown by 'Abd al-Karīm al Jāmi', the founder of the first Islamic dynasty of that country, with the co-operation of Arab allies.

[2] Turra is between Marra and Sī. Al Fāsher became the capital in the reign of 'Abd ar Raḥmān ar Rashīd (1785–99).

[3] Sir H. A. MacMichael writes, 'When, in 1916, I visited Turra in Gebal Marra, the seat of the ancient Fūr Kingdom and the burial place of its Sultans since the time of Sulaymān Solong, I found established there a small colony of Gawāma'a "*fukarā*" who claimed descent from an ancestor Idrīs, who had been "brought by Sulayman Solong from the river seven generations ago for the sake of religion." They had ever since been guardians of the royal tombs and "Imāms" of the local mosque' (*Hist.* i. 198).

foreign population from Baqirmi and Bornū, encouraged traders, founded mosques and schools and introduced fire-arms. The people then began gradually to adopt Islam as they were brought into touch with a wider world through traders and fekis. Whilst they have adopted the external practices of Islam, the background of their religious life to this day remains mainly animistic.

The external connexions of Dārfūr have always been with the Wadā'ī-Bornū group rather than the east, and Kordofān was soon lost after the death of Sulaimān. It came again under the Fūr when Sulṭān wad Aḥmad Bukr (1768–87) overran it and remained in their control until the Egyptian conquest. No attempt will be made here to treat of the history of the kingdom of Dārfūr which is a tangle of competitions for the throne, intestinal struggles, and fights with Wadā'ī.[1]

Dārfūr remained the dominating power in the west until the conquest of Muḥammad 'Alī. Muḥammad Bey the Daftardār penetrated the country in 1821, but met with so strong a resistance that he was forced to withdraw. The Sulṭāns of Dārfūr then sought to preserve their independence by isolating their state, forbidding all white people to enter the country, and paying some tribute to Constantinople. But when the time was ripe the Egyptian Government followed up their conquest of Kordofān. From Baḥr al-Ghazāl, Zubair Pāshā penetrated into Dārfūr on an order from the Egyptian Government, being supported in the north by Ismā'īl Pāshā. In 1874 the Sulṭān Ibrāhīm was killed in the struggle with Zubair and Al Fāsher sacked. The Egyptians took over the government until Slatin's surrender to the Mahdists in 1883, but pretenders to the throne continued to maintain themselves in the more inaccessible parts of the country, and before the battle of Omdurmān, Dārfūr was again under a native sulṭān, 'Alī Dīnār Zakariyya.

5. THE TURKIYYA

After the Turkish conquest of Nubia (1518), Egyptian influence over the Sudan almost disappeared. The revival of it came through the imperialist ambitions of Muḥammad 'Alī (d. 1849), the great stadtholder of Egypt, which were to change the destinies of the Sudanese peoples.

The Sudan before the Egyptian conquest, being split up into a number of mekships, wreckage of the Funj Empire, was an easy prey to any invader who thought its annexation worth while. Muḥammad

[1] At-Tūnīsī, *Voyage au Darfour* (1845), gives a valuable account of the customs of the Darfurians and of the political system under the Sultanate.

ʿAlī's principal reasons for its conquest were economic. He thought it to be well populated for the hunting of slaves and to be rich in mineral wealth. He needed slave-recruits for his army and money after his many wars. He also needed an outlet for the large standing army he retained and he possessed an inborn love of conquest which played its part.

Donqola was first annexed (1820), then the country was invaded with two armies: one, under his son Ismāʿīl, took the eastern bank of the Nile as far as Sennār, dealing with the Shā'iqiyya and the Jaʿaliyyīn on the way; the other, under Muḥammad Bey the Daftardār, took the route through the Bayūda Desert to Kordofān where he defeated the Muṣabaʿāt. The occupation was simple, little opposition was met, and little blood was shed in actual fighting, though the exactions of the armies and the reprisals taken afterwards were particularly revolting.

At the time of Muḥammad ʿAlī's death (1849), Egyptian power extended as far south as Kodok, whilst eastwards it included all the Beja lands as far as Kasala and Tōkar districts on the Abyssinian border. The country was organized only for exploitation, direct rule was not administered, and Khartoum, the new capital (1830), had become the central mart of a vast slave-trade. Ivory- and slave-raiders pushed on beyond Egyptian occupied territory and established new centres in the south. The population became discontented and the Khedive Saʿīd (1854–63) issued proclamations abolishing slavery. His functionaries made it a complete dead letter and from 1860 especially slave-raiding by companies of 'Khartoumers', mainly Danāqla-Jaʿaliyyīn centred in chains of stations along the rivers, increased so much that the south was devastated. Sir Samuel Baker writes in 1872 of a southern region:

> It is impossible to describe the change that has taken place since I last visited this country. It was then a perfect garden, thickly populated and producing all that man would desire. The villages were numerous, groves of plantains fringed the steep cliff on the river bank, and the natives were neatly dressed in the bark cloth of the country. The scene has changed! All is wilderness. The population has fled. Not a village is to be seen. This is the certain result of the settlement of Khartoum traders. They kidnap the women and children for slaves, and plunder and destroy wherever they set their foot.[1]

Slave-traders, such as Zubair Pāshā, had become dangerously independent rulers and the Khedive appointed European Governors of Equatoria (Baker, 1870–3 and Gordon, 1874–9) to check their power and try to enforce the anti-slavery decrees. The actual allevia-

[1] Quoted from *The Life of Gordon* by D. C. Boulger, p. 142.

tion was only temporary, but the work of Gordon especially came like a breath of new life to the suffering peoples, opening up for them the vision of better things as a possibility, even though they did not know how to attain them.

The whole Egyptian administration was rotten to the core, and, at the deposition of the Khedive Ismāʿīl in 1879, his vast Sudan possessions were in a state of utter misery through misgovernment and exploitation. Many travellers have given a depressing picture of Egyptian rule in the Sudan—of people governed by force and paralysed by heavy taxation, of the spread of fly areas, the ruination of provinces, the disintegration of pagan tribal communities, their constant alarms, flights, migrations, and the rupture of family ties.

The basic reason for this state of affairs was that the whole economic and social welfare of the Sudan, and to a large extent of Egypt, had come to depend upon slavery. The country was worthless to Egypt, in spite of Muḥammad ʿAlī's ambitions, except for the slave-trade, therefore Egyptian rule was based on it. Such a system, based on greed and sanctioned by Islam, had no consideration for the welfare of the people. The suffering masses themselves, reared in a tradition of fatalism, passively accepted the new order. Religion alone could give the needed impulse to concentrate all this submerged feeling into active expression. But now the time was at hand when religion at last was to provide the necessary stimulus to which the economic and political conditions determined the response.

6. THE MAHDIYYA

Such was the position in 1881 with the field set, as in fact it had been for some time, for a barbarian counter-attack which was to unite the heterogeneous races of the Sudan together to sweep the representatives of the imperfectly westernized Egypto-Ottoman Power out of the country.

One Muḥammad Aḥmad (1843–85), a Donqolāwī, the son of a boat-builder, was the symbol and leader of this revolt which was to establish the theocracy. He had the usual *khalwa* education in Berber and Kereri, then went to Khartoum where he took the *ṭarīqa* from Shaikh Muḥammad Sharīf, khalīfa of the Sammāniyya (in 1861), and from the khalīfa of the Idrīsiyya at Qerri. His zeal and devotion quickly gained him recognition, and after seven years' novitiate he was appointed a teaching shaikh of the Sammāniyya with his own flag and power to admit others. He retired soon afterwards (1871) to Abā Island on the White Nile, where he built a *khalwa*, and began to gather pupils around him, amongst them ʿAlī Wad Ḥilu who was to become his second khalīfa.

He had become discontented with the worldliness of religious leaders such as Muḥammad Sharīf. His outspokenness led to a quarrel between him and his master and his expulsion from the *ṭarīqa*,[1] whereupon he attached himself to a rival Sammānī, Shaikh al-Qurashī of Mesallamiyya, who had taken the *ṭarīqa* from Shaikh aṭ-Ṭayyib, the founder of the order. On Shaikh al-Qurashī's death, Muḥammad Aḥmad succeeded him as khalīfa (1880).

Muḥammad Aḥmad, being closely in touch with the people, for he used to travel around spreading his *ṭarīqa*, was oppressed by their sufferings. He was conscious that their underlying fanaticism was only awaiting the coming of a saviour. Subjecting himself to religious austerities, trying to live out of the world in the Ṣūfī dreamland of fantasy, visions, and ecstasies, all the time this world of reality was pressing on him, burdening him, until suddenly out of the conflict the revelation came to him that *he* was that awaited deliverer—*al-mahdī al-muntaẓar*. This revelation was undoubtedly based on a religious experience in which he genuinely believed, although he was to suffer the fate of most religious reformers and, his vision becoming mixed up with political and social ideas, to practise deliberate deception and use unworthy means.

Convinced of his call, he began in March 1881 to initiate others into the secret of his mission, binding them to one loyalty above all tribal ties, to God through himself, to the *jihād* against the infidel Turk 'to purify the world from wantonness and corruption'. At an early stage he bound certain Baqqāra chiefs to him by a *baiʿa* or oath of allegiance, including ʿAbd Allāh at-Taʿaishī, who was to become his successor.[2] Muḥammad Sharīf had informed Ra'ūf Pāshā, the Governor-General, of what was happening. He at first took no notice, but when Muḥammad Aḥmad proclaimed himself openly as Mahdī (August 1881), a small expedition was sent against him at Abā. After defeating this the Mahdī emigrated to the hill of Qadīr in Kordofān which he made the centre of his propaganda, from where he sent

[1] Muḥammad Sharīf himself told Naʿūm Shuqair (*Ta'rīkh as-Sūdān*, iii. 116–18) that the reason for the expulsion was that Muḥammad Aḥmad revealed his mission to him in 1878 and asked him to become his *wazīr*. Muḥammad Sharīf rejected his claims and held a conference at Abā attended by tribal *nāẓirs* and *qāḍīs* to try to convince him of his errors. He refused to recant and was rejected from the *ṭarīqa*. The Mahdī's followers deny this story.

[2] ʿAbd Allāh had urged Zubair Pāsha to proclaim himself the Mahdī (Slatin, *Fire and Sword*, p. 127; Shuqair, op. cit. iii. 71–2) and a writer in Al-Muqtaṭaf (xxiv. 1905, 5) suggested that it was he who incited Muḥammad Aḥmad to announce himself.

out his emissaries, carrying letters and proclamations announcing the arrival of the Mahdī and the initiation of a new world order. He published his visions of interviews with the Prophet, al-Khiḍr, Gabriel, and the *Aqṭāb*, and poured out summonses to 'emigrate' to join his standard and swear allegiance.

We are not concerned with any detailed description of the Mahdī's successes and the failure of the government measures against him owing to their misunderstanding of the nature and motive-force of the revolt. As a result of his successes the revolt became general. In 1883 El Obeyd fell and Hicks's army was annihilated. The British Government, now in control of Egypt which it had just saved from civil war, decided upon the abandonment of the Sudan and sent General Gordon to perform the task, impossible in its double form, of withdrawing the garrison and leaving behind a form of orderly government.[1] Gordon asked for the old slave-trader, Zubair Pāsha, who was exiled in Egypt, to be sent to the Sudan to reorganize the government, and when his request was refused, determined to hold out himself in the hope that the British Government would send an expedition. Khartoum was besieged and Gordon was killed when it fell on 26 January 1885.

Gordon's death, by eventually giving to the Sudanese what was in effect British instead of Egyptian rule, was the greatest service he rendered to the people he loved, for it cannot be denied that the inspiration of his life of service and his death has given to others the faith and inspiration to follow in the tracks he had blazed.

After the fall of Khartoum the Mahdī set to work to organize his empire, but he did not survive Gordon very long for he died in June of the same year. ʿAbd Allāh at-Taʿaishī succeeded him by right of a proclamation of the Mahdī which ends:

> The Khalīfa ʿAbd Allāh is the Commander of the Faithful, and is my Khalīfa and agent in all religious matters. Therefore I leave off as I have begun—believe in him, obey his orders, never doubt what he says, but give all your confidence to him and trust him in all your affairs. May God be with you all, Amen.[2]

The Khalīfa was a man of great strength of character and prepared to carry on the religio-political programme of the Mahdī. But this he could only do if he maintained the unity of the Mahdiyya and under his rule centrifugal forces such as tribal jealousy often outweighed this essential unity of devotion and aim. He purposed to attack Egypt, but

[1] See B. M. Allen, *Gordon and the Sudan*, 1931, chaps. vi and vii, for a discussion of Gordon's instructions.

[2] Naʿūm Shuqair, *Ta'rīkh*, iii. 173.

internal revolts in Dārfūr and Kordofān prevented him until 1889, when his expedition was defeated at Toski which ended his dreams of world conquest. To consolidate his rule he had to crush the riverain Danāqla, Jaʿaliyyīn, and the Jezīra tribes who had been the Mahdī's chief followers; and to induce his own tribe and other Baqqāra by bribes and force to emigrate to Omdurmān, where, being without their beloved herds, they supported themselves by plundering others. This artificial transplantation of nomads into sedentary lands where their function was parasitic upset the whole structure of society and marked the beginning of the end of the Mahdiyya. The Mahdī's amīrs were disgraced, with the exception of 'Osmān Diqna who held the personal allegiance of many of the Hadendiwa. Thus began the years of tyranny and oppression which have left an indelible imprint upon the minds of the Sudanese. The whole country suffered terribly through oppression and constant warfare, with their still more devastating allies, disease and famine. Whole tribes were decimated and a large part of the country went out of cultivation.

After the fall of Khartoum the British Government had adopted a policy of temporary non-interference with the Sudan, but in 1896 this policy was reversed, the following mixed reasons being contributory: (1) fears about the designs of France on the south, (2) the end of the British training of the Egyptian army, (3) the growth of the imperialistic spirit, (4) an appeal by the Italian ambassador to relieve pressure on Italian forces in Eritrea, and (5) the desire to satisfy a certain spirit of idealism which remembered the death of Gordon by delivering the country from tyranny.

The reconquest began in 1896 and was completed in 1898 with the Battle of Omdurmān and the death of the Khalīfa the following year. So a new political creation, the Anglo-Egyptian Sudan, came into being.

7. THE ANGLO-EGYPTIAN SUDAN

Little need be said about the history and material progress of the Sudan under British rule for that would be to get out of proportion a phase of history which, though unique, can be only transitory.[1] Britain could not after the reconquest hand the Sudan back to Egyptian rule owing to Egypt's past record of misgovernment, nor could she annex it herself because of possible international complica-

[1] Reference may be made to Sir H. A. MacMichael's *The Anglo-Egyptian Sudan* (1934), a Fabian pamphlet, *The Sudan: The Road Ahead* (1945), and significant cultural changes will be dealt with in Chapter VIII, 'The influence of Westernism on the Sudan'.

tions and Egypt's special interest in the Nile waters; hence to satisfy political exigencies and assure the Sudanese of good government a *Condominium* of Great Britain and Egypt was created. This is little more than a political connexion. Britain, by right of conquest and from a sense of trusteeship of the Sudanese lacking in the Egyptians, took on the main burden of administration and the Sudan Government as constituted has had almost complete autonomy free from interference by either the British Foreign Office or the Egyptian Government. This Condominium still exists and was confirmed by the Anglo-Egyptian Treaty of 1936 which stated 'that the primary aim of their administration in the Sudan must be the welfare of the Sudanese'. Egypt was allowed by the Treaty to maintain a force in the Sudan, yet her real role in the modern Sudan, through her political link, has been that of Islamic cultural reinforcement, for the Sudanese have no desire to be ruled by Egyptians.

Britain's attitude as *de facto* governor of the Sudan has been that of trusteeship of the Sudanese peoples who were unable to govern themselves. She has conscientiously placed what she conceived to be their interests first. This has involved the political unification of the Muslim north, training the Sudanese to take an increasing share in administration, and thus fostering their development towards eventual partnership in government.

Under British rule the land has changed out of all recognition. Hostility has been transformed into trust, poverty to sufficiency, and oppression to freedom. In view of the wide racial divergencies and tribal constitution of the country, internal security has been surprisingly well maintained. Slave-raiding was soon suppressed and inter-tribal warfare diminished almost to nothing. Dārfūr was annexed in 1916 after the suppression of the revolt of the Sulṭān 'Alī Dīnār, who had been recognized by the Sudan Government after the Battle of Omdurmān as an independent sovereign, subject to the payment of an annual tribute. The Province has, however, never been truly assimilated into the structure of the Eastern Sudan.

Systems of administration, jurisdiction, and education have been instituted. 'Indirect rule' was substituted for the 'direct rule' of the early administrators. Through the tribal system nomads were given an increasing share in administering their own affairs and local authorities have been given administrative functions in rural and urban areas. The great majority (79 per cent. at the end of 1946) of the clerical staff of the government are now Sudanese.

A steady economic and material development of the country has been maintained in spite of the country's meagre resources. Owing to measures for the encouragement of the cultivators, crop experiments, and irrigation schemes, the area of cultivable land has been widely extended. Food supply has increased and fear of famine dispelled. The population which was about two million in 1900 had risen to approximately six and a half million in 1945. Towns have been developed, villages reinhabited, and nomad tribes reconstituted. Sanitation, preventive medicine, and research have improved health.

This policy of trusteeship has succeeded firstly, because of the quality of the British personnel who, unimaginative and disinterested, have shown a deep spirit of responsibility and devotion; and acquired an *esprit de corps* which place them on a level with the highest achievements of history in the rule of a foreign governing class; and secondly, because the Sudan has been free from complicated internal political problems and white settlement. The trusteeship policy has during the war years been evolving towards a policy of partnership, leading towards eventual self-government. The formation of the Governor-General's Advisory Council for the Northern Sudan in June 1944, whilst it offers as yet little share to the Sudanese in central administration, provides an admirable basis for development towards a closer co-operation between the representatives of the Condominium and the leaders of the Sudanese in the common care for country and people.[1]

8. THE EXPANSION OF ISLAM IN THE SUDAN

After the first irresistible impulse of the Islamic conquest had spread the Arab armies over the Mediterranean littoral, its energies abated and further progress into Africa was stopped, in the east, by the Nubian kingdom, in the west, by the greater attractiveness of Spain, the Berber insurrections, and the quarrels of the Moghrabin emirs. Strong pagan tribes, like the nomadic Qura'ān of the Tibesti, also blocked their progress. 'Uqba b. Nāfi' in his exploratory raids just missed discovering the rich savannah region in the Central Sudan. The second phase of conquest in Africa began in the eleventh century with the irruption from the east of the nomadic Banī Hilāl and Banī Sulaim, the conversion of

[1] Since this was written a further stage towards self-government has been announced: 'The Governor-General has announced to the Northern Sudan Advisory Council that a twenty-year plan to prepare Sudanese for the highest government posts is being launched. Education will be developed so that Sudanese may qualify for the highest posts as soon as possible' (*The Times*, 30 May 1945). Since then it has been decided to form an Executive Council of whose twelve members six will be Sudanese chosen from the members of a Legislative Council which will have a majority of elected members.

the Berbers, and the conquests of the Murābiṭīn in the Senegal, with the result that the whole of North Africa and the Sahara came under Muslim rule. Warrior tribes take to Islam easily because, with its doctrine of *jihād*, it is a means to domination. These nomadic warrior tribes now trekked south and conquered and intermarried with the pagans. This led to the rise in the Western Sudan of such powerful hybrid African kingdoms as the Songhai, Bornū, and Malle.[1]

Islam spread into Eastern Sudan, as we have seen, in the fourteenth century when the fall of the Christian kingdom of Maqurra left most of its northern and central regions open to Muslim penetration. So the two streams met. Traders from Nubia penetrated as far as Nigeria whilst Berber and West Sudan propaganda spread eastward. Bornū and Wadā'i became linked with Dārfūr and Kordofān. But it was the western tribes which did far more for the spread of Islam in pagan Africa than those of the east. The eastern stream could join with the western but could not extend south of Sennār, for though the kingdoms of Donqola and ʿAlwa were islamized, further advance was stopped to the south-east by the Abyssinian Christian fastness, and to the south by the difficulty of penetrating the *sudd* region and the virile resistance of the Nilotic tribes.

The Arab tribes who gained control of the Eastern Sudan, we have said, were not moved by religious zeal, but by the urge to wander in search of pasture, by the spirit of greed and the desire to escape from Mamlūk rule. The nomad Arab, who is rarely fanatical and completely devoid of missionary zeal, makes no attempt at proselytization. The spread of Islam was mainly through penetration, intermarriage, a strategic policy of winning chiefs and group leaders (which includes forcible measures), trade, and the appropriation of slaves. As in the early days of the primary Islamic conquest, conversion to Islam connected the convert with the Arab tribal system as a client.

An anecdote of Ibn Salīm's, which gives a picture of a Muslim missionary at work, shows that there was some direct missionary activity amongst pagans in the fifteenth century. Ibn Salīm, relating his conversation at the Court of Maqurra with a pagan from a country

[1] Eastern influence affected the Central Sudan in the eleventh century because 'it was from Egypt that Islam spread into Kanem, a kingdom on the N. and N.E. of Lake Chad, which shortly after the adoption of Islam rose to be a state of considerable importance and extended its sway over the tribes of the Eastern Sudan to the borders of Egypt and Nubia; the first Muslim king of Kanem is said to have reigned either towards the close of the 11th or first half of the 12th century' (Becker, *Geschichte des östlichen Sudans*, pp. 162–3, quoted by T. W. Arnold, *Preaching of Islam*, p. 320). In the fifteenth century the capital of the kingdom of Kanem was transferred to Bornū, west of Lake Chad, amongst the Negro So.

a three months' journey from the Nile, questioned him about his religion. He answered:

My Lord and thy Lord is God and the Lord of the universe and of mankind; all are one. When asked where He lived he answered, 'in heaven alone'. He related that when the rains tarried or plagues and pestilence afflicted them or their cattle, they ascended the mountain to pray to God, who granted their prayers immediately, and fulfilled their needs before they descended. He then asked the man whether God had ever sent them a prophet. He replied 'No'; whereupon he related to him the missions of Moses, Jesus and Muhammad (God's mercy and peace be with them) and the miracles they were allowed to perform. The man then replied, 'if they have really done this, then they are true.'[1]

It is a quality of Islam to have almost continuously, though with greatly varying intensity and always as a purely secondary task, evoked missionary activities among its adherents. But it must be emphasized that the people who spread Islam in Africa were always African, and chiefly Hamites, whatever Arab blood they had in them. Most of the Central Sudanese Muslim kingdoms (Wadā'i, Bornū, Dārfūr, Teqali, &c.) were founded by some Arabic-speaking Hamitic feki who arrived to propagate trade and Islam. Islam was African in Africa.

The Islam of the Funj and the nomad Arabs was largely nominal. The Funj had proclaimed themselves Muslims from motives of political expediency, although they did invite 'holy men' in from outside and assured them a welcome. The Danāqla and northern tribes knew no more of Islam than the *shahāda* until in the fourteenth century A.D. the Rikābī Shaikh, Ghulām Allāh ibn 'Aid, whose father came from Yaman, founded a seat of learning in Donqola, 'which, when he arrived there, was utterly sunk in error owing to the lack of learned men'.[2] This was developed by his descendants, the four sons of Jābir, who, in the sixteenth century, founded *khalwas* in Shā'iqī country and acquired considerable influence.

In the Funj kingdom itself the first reformer was Maḥmūd al-'Arakī who came from Egypt and settled on the White Nile. But the interesting thing about the foreigners who most influenced the Eastern Sudan was that most of them were from the Ḥijāz. The pilgrimage also took many Sudanese to the holy cities and these on their return set up as fekis.[3] Though unlearned, the activity of these fekis from their *zāwiya*-centres fermented internal missionary activity leading to the

[1] Maqrīzī, op. cit. i. 312.
[2] MacMichael's MS. D. 5 (*d*), *History*, ii. 342.
[3] Some of the Funj kings encouraged their fekis to go on *ḥajj* by paying their expenses (cf. account of Al-Muḍawwi in *Ṭab.* M. 30–1).

revival of Islam in Nubia and Sennār and also the conversion of the Beja and negroid pagan tribes who had been incorporated into the Funj Confederation. Some fekis travelled farther afield into the Central Sudan.[1] The influence of these missionaries, however, was not strong enough to affect the Shilluk along the White Nile, the majority of the Nūba in Kordofān, and the Ingessana, Burūn, and Khoma south of the Funj, all of which are still pagan.

Another important element in the spread of Islam during the Funj régime was the migration of groups of Maḥas and their settlement on the Blue Nile at Tūtī, Ḥalfāya, ʿAilafūn, Kutrānj, Kāmlīn, and many other places. These Maḥas, claiming to be Arab *anṣār*, quickly adopted the Arabic language, the traditional training in jurisprudence and a mystical succession, and set up as miracle-working feki-families, deeply influencing the life of the indigenous tribes in the Funj Confederation.

The most important result of the Ḥijāzian influence was the introduction of the religious orders, the Qādiriyya and the Shādhiliyya, whose mystical teaching was then in a degenerate but popularized form. These orders when established in the Sudan were not centralized and all religious authority was canalized into the hands of the various teaching shaikhs. Sudanese Islam thus became 'cellular', in the literal as well as the metaphorical sense, the *zāwiya* being the nucleus of the embryonic Islamic civilization in a pagan environment. So saint-worship became the most powerful religious influence in the Sudan and a hagiography developed in which Sudanese saints eclipsed the most exalted figures in Islam. Pagan rites and social customs were incorporated with complete freedom. The people remained animistic under Islamic forms for a long time and the islamization of the peoples outside the Funj sphere of influence remained dormant until after the Egyptian conquest.[2]

Dārfūr has always been linked up more with the Central Sudan than the east and from the fourteenth century to the sixteenth, as we have seen, was under the control of the pagan Tunjur who also ruled Wadā'i. It was gradually and partially converted to Islam under the

[1] Such were Muḥammad b. ʿAdlān who went to Bornū and Hausaland, Abū Surūr al-Faḍlī, Sh. Idrīs and Abū Zaid who worked in Dārfūr and Borqū.

[2] Bruce in 1772, whilst speaking of the Arabs as 'intolerant bigots', says of the blacks of Sennār that they 'trouble themselves very little with the detail of the Mahometan religion, which they embraced merely for the sake of personal freedom and advantages in trade; but they are Pagans in their hearts and in their practices, Mahometans in their conversation only. As for the sons of these, they are pagans like their fathers, unless some Fakīr, or Arab saint, takes pains to instruct and teach them to read; otherwise the whole of their religion consists in the confession of faith' (op. cit. vi. 389–90).

dynasty founded by Sulaimān Solong in 1596, one of whose Sulṭāns, Teherāb, conquered Kordofān in the eighteenth century and converted a Nūba tribe called the Koldāji. No schools of learning, however, developed in Dārfūr, such as those on the Niles in the east and Timbuktoo, Kano, and Katsena in the west, and the religion of the people was for long a rather nominal islamized paganism.

The great advance of Islam into central Africa dates from the beginning of the nineteenth century. It was partly due to the renewed activity of militant dervish orders with their cult of the saints, but mainly to the actual conquest and subjugation of pagans, such as the Fulānī domination in Nigeria. Other causes were the activity of the Muslim traders, always Arab-Hamite or Hamitic-Negroid, working with complete freedom from competition; sometimes the appearance of a Mahdī helped; but the most important factor was the social advantages the African gains by belonging to the Islamic social system, with its freedom from colour prejudice, privilege of brotherhood, and consciousness of belonging to a great social system.

The actual missionary awakening was the result of events outside Africa—the growth of Wahhābism and the re-awakening of the dervish orders. Direct influences on the Eastern Sudan mainly go back to one man, Aḥmad Ibn Idrīs, who sent out missionaries from Mecca in the early nineteenth century. These men established their orders in the Sudan and their propagation not only profoundly influenced Sūdānī religious life, but caused some expansion into pagan areas. The influence of the orders in proselytization has often been overemphasized; they were sometimes active missionaries, especially during the very early period of the conquest, but their real contribution was their value in facilitating the psychic assimilation of Islam by Africans.

This awakening took place during the Egyptian period and proselytization went along with the conquest and opening up of the country. Nubians in particular carried on missionary work as an appendage to the slave-trade throughout the whole of pagan Sudan. Pallme, who travelled in Kordofān 1837–9, writes:

> I found the greatest number of Fakeers among the Dongolavi, who are also the most rigid observers of the Mahommedan religion, with one single exception, that they are very fond of brandy. They do not follow agricultural pursuits, but are merchants, brokers, &c. . . . The majority of them are hypocrites, and indeed it is better to avoid them altogether.[1]

Not every Muslim is a missionary, but, in Africa, provided it does not involve personal danger, work of some kind for the conversion of

[1] I. Pallme, *Travels in Kordofan*, 1844. p. 186.

pagans to Islam tends to go on naturally because its propagation promotes trading activities. A better influence than the traders was that of the fekis belonging to the dervish orders, for these would form Muslim centres of worship in the midst of a pagan population, gaining a welcome first as writers of amulets and then as schoolmasters who through Arabic linked the people on to a new and wider life.

Pallme mentions one genuine missionary, Shaikh Badawi, whom he met in El-Obeyd:

> He is a pious man and anything but a hypocrite, hence he is beloved and enjoys the good opinion of all men. He settles disputes, and gives friendly advice to all who come to ask for it, knows no partiality, and in no instance receives a present. . . . As far as his religion is concerned he is a rigid Mahommedan, and defends his opinions and articles of faith with the greatest zeal; but I never heard him speak with contempt of the Christian or of any other religion, as the Derweeshes frequently do. . . . In short, he is a Mahommedan missionary. He has made thousands of proselytes among the heathen negroes, for he strolls about during the greater part of the year in the mountains, endeavouring to disseminate el Islam. He also defends his faith according to the letter of the Koran, sword in hand, and has even lost a son in the fight for the good cause. The Fakeers are very much afraid of him, and take care not to play their pranks in his vicinity; he also feels a thorough contempt for them.[1]

This Shaikh Badawi showed great sympathy with the oppressed population under Turko-Egyptian rule. 'You call yourself Muslims,' he said to the Egyptians, 'God alone knows the truth, but to me you are only the oppressors of my country.'[2] Muḥammad ʿAlī tried to take him, but he kept out of the way in the Nūba hills.

The slave-trade and army recruitment, however, were the most influential agents in the propagation of Islam, because, by breaking up the centres of pagan life, the pagan population tended to recede and the broken up de-tribalized elements were absorbed into Islam. In the south-western Baḥr al-Ghazāl the slavers produced complete tribal disintegration and various groups of '*Fartīt*' (i.e. slaves; such as Kresh, which seem to be debris of Banda origin) became Muslim as a result of their occupation of the country. It is surprising that the neighbouring Wahhābī movement did not influence the Sudan more in the direction of reforming beliefs and holy war.

During the Mahdiyya the work of proselytization received a new impulse and the breaking up of negroid cultural units continued. But the Nilotic tribes strongly resisted Mahdist appeals by force and the great mass of the people south of 10° lat. remain pagan.

[1] Pallme, op. cit., pp. 189–90.

[2] Peney, *Revue d'Ethnographie*, i. 492.

As a result of this dark three-quarters of a century, through the 'trade', disease, famine, and war, many tribes like the Bāri and the Mittu were almost decimated;[1] others, such as the inland Dinka and Nuēr, were saved by the nature of their country; the Zande kingdoms were too strong to be attacked; whilst others, like the Shilluk and the Nūba, resisted the Mahdist troops and, though most of the Shilluk were finally subdued, they, together with the Nūba, many of whom such as the Nyamang were never conquered, preserved their identity.

With everything in its favour, Islam did not spread as rapidly as might have been expected during the Egyptian and Mahdiyya periods. Against the influences in its favour we have to set the brutalities of the Egyptian conquest and the Khalīfa's rule, the inhuman cruelties of the slave-trade, the treacheries of the Muslim traders in spreading venereal diseases, the difficulties in penetrating the *sudd* region, and the natural resistance of the negroid tribes to Islam, for animism is very conservative and Islam plays havoc with pagan institutions. Again in Africa, the strict letter of the Islamic law had to be relaxed in dealing with pagans. The people could not be forced to join Islam by forces so far from their base. Also according to Islamic law a Muslim cannot be sold as a slave, and although this would not weigh with the Egyptians it may have aided in discouraging proselytizing activities among tribes still unraided. This of course did not count during the Mahdiyya whose leaders tried to fulfil the letter of the law whenever their forces were strong enough. But masses of pagans who had been forced to islamize reverted when Mahdist forces weakened.

These causes blocked Islam very considerably in the Eastern Sudan as contrasted with the rapidity of its expansion during the same period in the west.[2] Islam has done nothing whatever to impress itself on the Nilotic and other Eastern Sudan tribes, its spread being almost solely due to conquest and the slave-trade.

Since the British occupation the advance of Islam amongst pagans continues only very slowly, the agents being traders, fekis, and native functionaries. This advance will be discussed more fully in a later chapter.

[1] Lord Cromer writes (*Modern Egypt*, p. 889): 'Prior to 1882, the district lying along the banks of the rivers Rahad and Dinder contained upwards of 800 villages. When Sir Reginald Wingate visited this district in 1902, "not a village remained".'

[2] It should be mentioned that in the west Sudan also the wars and oppression of such conquerors as Al-Ḥājj 'Umar and Samory, together with the war-like energies of the Tijāniyya, caused a hatred of Islam which assumed for them something of the form of a national movement. Cf. Arnold, op. cit., p. 333.

4

Orthodox Islam

I. INTRODUCTORY—CHARACTERISTICS OF SUDANESE ISLAM

OUR object is to try to understand the religion of the Sūdānī Muslim. A new-comer to the Sudan, having read some standard text-book on Islam, tends to take it for granted that the religion of the people is that of the Qur'ān and the law. The mosque is usually the most prominent object he sees and this makes him fail to understand that this is not the only, nor the most important, centre and symbol of their religion. A far more significant symbol of faith scattered about the Sudan in greater profusion than the mosque is the whitewashed domed tomb of a saint. The one may be regarded as the symbol of the system and the other of a living faith. We shall therefore not need to know more of the system than is necessary to understand the faith.

Before we turn to the essential characteristics of Sudanese Islam a few general remarks are necessary.

The study of Islam in any region is not a question of tabulating its fundamental dogmas and practices and thinking that there we have the essence of Islam in Muslim life, but on the contrary, a realization of what Islam really is in Muslim life, what demands it makes in practice rather than in theory, and then seeing how men's personalities have been moulded by the system and getting down to what really constitutes their understanding of God and man. The study of theoretical Islam is for us secondary to the study of what it is creating now in human life and experience.

The Islamic creed appears so simple on the surface that one would not expect to find any great diversity of regional development. But, in fact, Islam is not so much a creed as a social system, a living organism embracing all races and every side of life, which has moulded and adapted itself everywhere to regional conditions.

The origin and historical development of the Islamic system has been obscured through the ecclesiastical coloration of the Islamic tradition and the reader of an introductory text-book tends to get the impression that Muḥammad, the Prophet of Arabia, to whom all tradition goes back, created it. In fact the only original element in Islam is the Prophet Muḥammad himself who, linking himself on to the prophetic tradition of Judaism and Christianity, proclaimed himself essentially the Prophet of the Arabs and became a successful political leader in Arabia. But this was not all. His rise and the political unification which he and his successors imposed on Arabia coincided with forces which caused a new Semitic migration in the seventh century. That migration, as it spread the barbarian nomad war-bands with his creed as their unifying war-cry over Byzantine Egypt and Syria and the Sassanian Empire, gradually took over, along with the administrative and economic systems of the conquered countries, much of their religious and cultural outlook on life. The migrant Arabs, few in number and culturally inferior to the conquered, brought something new and vital—a unifying motive-force without which the exodus would never have succeeded. This was the original prophetic element of Muḥammad embodied in a book, the Qur'ān, and the groundwork in his own successful career for the identification of Church and State. This individual element which gave Islam its recognizable character was absorbed by the masses of converts as a vitalizing element into their Hellenistic-oriental civilization and quickly became its unifying factor. These converts, on the other hand, gave the new prophetic creed, Islam, a world outlook which infused religion into everything in life—a conception of life as foreign to the religiously indifferent nomad Arab of the seventh century as it is to-day.[1] So the prophetic religion Islam became the syncretistic system it is to-day, distinct alike from Muḥammad's conception and the oriental civilization which absorbed it; a new thing in fact arising out of their interaction and synthesis.

The religion of Muslim peoples everywhere is full of non-Islamic customs and superstitions which it has absorbed, but these in no way weaken its religious-social solidarity. As a system it had an extraordinary internal power of assimilating foreign elements which enriched its original naïve concepts, yet at the same time of retaining its own inner will to power, organic unity, and world-outlook.

Its dogmatic development shows the stamp of Hellenistic ideas; its judicial systemization reveals the influence of Roman Law; its political organization under the ʿAbbāsid Khalifate shows the usage of the political ideas of Persia and its mysticism the appropriation of the current ideas of neo-Platonism and Hinduism. But, in each of these spheres, Islam shows its aptitude for

[1] It must be clearly understood that the spread of the Islamic religious system is not to be equated with the spread of Islamic political domination. That system did not then exist and, under the Umayyads, Islam was almost the tribal religion of the dominant minority. The system began to develop under the ʿAbbāsids and at their fall in A.D. 1273 it was fully developed.

organic assimilation and for remodelling foreign elements so that they reveal themselves as such only to the penetrating analysis of a critical investigation.[1]

This quotation refers to Islam's assimilation of elements of highly developed systems, but we must go farther. What about its contact, firstly with those strata of superstitious belief underlying all these oriental systems, and secondly with pure animism in Arabia, Africa, and other animistic regions? All this—the real religion of the people—provided it did not efface the essential individuality of Islam, was absorbed, too, and is a most important factor helping us to understand the hold Islam exercises over the masses. Of the Islamic system, apart from those elements indispensable for the maintenance of its distinctiveness, each people adopted those elements which harmonized most with its national character and ways of life. Whilst all Muslim peoples learn to reverence the *sharīʿa* as the divine law and symbol of the system, their lives are ruled by their own indigenous *ʿāda* or customary law. This process of mutual assimilation has meant that Islam has become practically indigenous in each country into which it has spread. The Qur'ānic, 'thus have we made of you an "intermediary" community' (ii. 137), well illustrates the position of Islam in the religious, cultural, and geographical spheres.

These two factors—the possession of a distinct individuality and the solidarity of a vast social system, together with its power of becoming indigenous by the assimilation or resetting of elements of other cultures—explain the enormous strength of Islam and the tenacity of the grip it holds over its adherents.

An important clue to the understanding of Muslims which arises out of this is that their religious and social life forms a natural whole. Muslims place extreme emphasis on the externals of religion and make no important ethical demands. They have a unified and attainable religious-social code of behaviour. They do not live, as Christians do, in a state of tension, feeling that their lives fall short of their religious standard. Therefore no strain is put on them. Their religious life is wholly a matter of behaviour and conformity. Social customs, though pagan in origin, all alike take on religious and Islamic sanctions. Nobody is wholly conscious of what elements are distinctly religious and Muslim, and what are merely social and pagan, identified with Islam by no logical implication. The result of this is that Islam is a vast complex system but only secondarily a motive power within.

Now let us turn to the religion of the Sudanese. In the Sudan the

[1] Goldziher, *Le Dogme et la loi de l'Islam*, pp. 2–3.

process of assimilation, moving with the imperceptibility of a natural process, has been, on the one hand, the transference of Islamic culture, in which purely religious factors were less decisive than the system; and, on the other, the absorption of the religious elements of regional animistic culture, clothing them in Islamic forms and moulds and directing them all to the one world-outlook. A gradual process of mutual assimilation therefore took place, the animistic elements deriving greater tenacity through absorption into the Islamic system.

Certain factors helped to make this process so easy. We have already shown that in this once 'Christian' country, ignorance of the faith, neglect of the priesthood, animistic beliefs, and the worship of saints, all contributed after the collapse of the state to render the country an easy prey to Islam. Islam came to an uncivilized land where nothing internal in the desires of the people contributed to help it develop along higher levels.

Islam itself was degenerate and, having evolved a popular type of mysticism, was full of superstition and hagiology when it was first taught by the fekis of the Funj kingdom. These men were trained, on the one hand, unimaginatively in the Mālikiyya *madhhab*, which meant that orthodox Islam had no influence on life; and, on the other, profoundly influenced by the degenerate Ṣūfism of the dervish orders. Thus, among people with no cultural background, these men had full opportunity to pander to the anthropolatry and superstitions of the masses and to incorporate it in their very persons. The inaccessibility and unstable political condition of the land kept it out of touch with other Islamic centres, except the Ḥijāz, which were themselves stagnant at this period. This isolation did not lead to the development of schools of learning or any native culture which might have set limits to extravagances. In this way the Islam that developed was strongly imbued with African tendencies and its characteristic elements were emotionalism and superstition.

The Sudan also provided a fertile ground for the development of certain eschatological beliefs current in Islamic countries which formed a revolutionary undercurrent, and when given certain political and economic conditions, were to burst out into a great conflagration of Mahdist fanaticism.

Whilst taking all this assimilation into account we should remember that, since Islam is a theocratic social system embracing the whole of life, we should avoid the mistake of calling the animistic Muslim of the Northern Sudan an animist with but a veneer of Islam, assuming that his inner life is unaffected by Islam. This is true of but a few groups, such as certain negroid groups of Dārfūr and Dār Funj. The arabicized Hamite or Negroid of the Northern Sudan is a genuine and uncompromising Muslim, narrow in his outlook, proud of his religion, convinced of its superiority over all others, and attached to it by a passionate loyalty. The inconsistency in which the average Sūdānī Muslim seems to be placed is only apparent and not real. His outlook on life is truly Islamic and not animistic, for Islam fosters in its adherents a world-outlook foreign to the animist.

Whilst the *sharī'a* as the Law of God holds together this syncretistic system, and in spite of the outward respect for and defence of the Qur'ān, the Traditions, and the obligatory rites and duties, orthodox Islam has no real power over the hearts of the people. The orthodox conception of the relationship of God and man is such an abstraction of truths from their place in life in which alone man deals with them, that it is quite natural that the underlying strata of magic and superstition should break through in emotional methods of devotion and in the cult of the saints to provide the people with intermediaries with God and thus give them a living religion. The outstanding feature of their religious life, we shall show, is that fullness of life is sought through passionate devotion to a holy person who possesses *baraka* (supernatural power). He may be living or dead but is always idealized. Their devotion to the saints is a magical attitude, never involving a change of heart, but rather the transference of power.

We are given an index as to where faith is really placed when we observe to whom people turn in times of trouble and danger. We shall find that the Sudanese repose a faith in saints and superstitious practices which they do not place in the creed they profess.

Life for the Sudanese is so desperately limited and poor, and this yearning to avail themselves of the means at their disposal is so strong, that we cannot wonder that the cult of the saints, superstition and magic have such a hold. The God of orthodox Islam is so exalted and unapproachable that He is only made accessible by the saints who act as His intermediaries. The system, Islam, has reorientated popular beliefs, built them into its own pattern of life and so it has assured their stability and continuity. It is impossible to suppose that the agricultural masses will ever be so influenced by Westernism as to lose their belief in them.

One thing must be said, and that is, that whilst the religious life of the masses is a thing of thraldom to the unknown, whilst it is a blending of gross materialism and fervent devotion, yet it has truly redeeming aspects. In their pathetic devotion to the saints, in their ecstasy at the *dhikr*, their deeper yearnings shine through and bring illumination to lives chained to a hard land and a sterile religion.

In an account of the religion of the Sudan we must take account, not only of the differences of race, but of the observable truth that each group stamps what it acquires, in the religious field as in any other, with its own way of feeling and understanding, according to its aptitude to assimilate it. Naturally there must be variations between the type of Islam practised by inhabitants of different regions, races, and occupational groups in a country with the vastness and disunity of the Sudan. The fusion of Arab and Ḥamite in the north and of Arab and Negro in the central Sudan has led to an infinite number of local variations in superstitions. This increases the natural difficulty of describing the living religion of the people and the following groupings of the population should be kept in mind although we shall not be studying them regionally:

1. *Riverain sedentaries*: (*a*) Roṭāna-speaking Nubians. (*b*) Arabic-speaking Ja'aliyyīn-Danāqla.
2. *Rain-land sedentaries*: Jezīra, Kordofān, &c.
3. *Pastoral-nomads*: (*a*) Arabs, (i) Ahl Ibil; (ii) Baqqāra. (*b*) Beja.
4. *Negroids*: (*a*) Funj Area. (*b*) Dārfūr Province.

We will indicate the main types of religious life which will be found in most parts of the Sudan—three limited groups and the masses.

The Masses. The first group may be called 'the ignorant masses'. These are the people, together with their leaders the feki-class, with whom we are most concerned. The masses observe as well as they can the five fundamental laws of Islam—faith in one God, prayer, fasting, alms-giving, and pilgrimage—in their ignorance these at least they know. They are turned to ritual prayer as a religious duty, but express their inner yearnings in *dhikr* exercises, for they are a race of emotional believers. They can never be regarded as truly orthodox, their orthodoxy being chiefly a question of trite phrases. Magic sways them more than the law and religious ecstasy more than formal prayer. Their leaders are the fekis and shaikhs of the religious orders for whom they have a superstitious veneration. Their religious ideas are based on the wildest possible stories derived from the teaching of the orders about the lives of the prophets and saints. To them the sacred, the *baraka*, the unseen, the supernatural and their appearances are very real. The spirit-world, both harmful and good, is ever present with them. The cult of the saints, both alive or dead, is their religion. They visit their tombs, lay bare their inner desires before them, and implore their aid in time of need. The curse of their lives is the world of harmful spirits which bring disease and death, distress and calamity upon individuals, families, and whole village communities. They rely on the professional feki-exorcist to drive these out. Their social and family life, the whole drama from birth to death, with its festivals, whilst apparently governed by the laws of Islam, is bound up with the underlying strata of animism and almost all practices connected with them are of pagan origin. These ideas and practices again vary according to race, tribe, or region, for Islam won its way by making compromises with the forms of religion which it encountered. That is why the popular religion of the masses is an obstacle to progress. So the educated, whilst clinging to the Islamic system, look upon religion as a matter of ignorance and superstition, something suitable for the *ḥabōbāt*, but not a real inner power in the life of an intelligent man. The religion of the masses, with all its redeeming features, yet stands largely for the things that obstruct rather than for forces which promote life. Whilst the administrator or the missionary must always be sympathetic if he is to understand, he cannot look to such popular Islam as a power with which he can co-operate to build up a new life in Islam.

The Feki-class. These are the religious leaders of the masses, and occupy a unique and distinct position as individuals or as families as the inheritors of the mysterious power (*baraka*) of some famous ancestor. They are religious in the Islamic sense and are always connected with a dervish order, though their mysticism is but vague superstition with no clear-cut features.

It is to his feki that the Sūdānī turns in his trouble, from him that he seeks protection from the unknown peril or evil spirits. To his influence both the extreme orthodox and the modern effendi are alike opposed.

The Conservative Muslim. Most Sudanese are regarded as orthodox but there are a few who are assertively orthodox and steeped in the Qur'ān and Traditions. These prove their orthodoxy by turning away from all modernistic ideas, finding satisfaction in the mechanical formulae of scholastic theology. Only that is good, they believe, which conforms with the standards of the past. Faith to them is blind dogged assent to fixed doctrines; it has nothing to do with the heart, mind, and will. Their morality similarly is the blind performance of fixed duties. They possess that uncompromising narrowness of outlook which is the speciality of this class everywhere and divide mankind into *kāfirīn* (unbelievers) and *mu'minīn* (believers). Still their ideas are clothed with all kinds of weird fancies which are an integral part of Islam. They will find great enjoyment, for instance, in discussing into which heaven

Sayyidnā ʿĪsā ascended or the functions of the nineteen guardians of hell (Qur'ān, lxxiv. 30). For all their dislike of the pseudo-mysticism of the dervish orders and especially the reverence of the masses for their shaikhs, they are by no means uninfluenced by Ṣūfism and an orthodox Ṣūfī classic will often be found in their hands. Our zealously orthodox Muslim usually belongs to the middle class; he may hold a religious post, or be the teacher of a *khalwa*, or a respectable shopkeeper.

The Effendiyya are those who have received a western education and have clerical and technical occupations. They are loyal Muslims in the main even though their outlook on life differs widely from the preceding groups. They are loyal because Islam is the system into which they were born and outside which they would be at sea. At the same time they are up against aspects of the system which they find cramping and against which they struggle in vain. They have lost faith in the religious aspects of Islam, yet show no intelligence in religious matters, more in matters which the western system of education stresses. Too modern to have any vital connexion with popular or orthodox religion, they dabble in a rationalized Islam, yet will visit a feki for guidance in life's crises. In the essentials of the spiritual life they are so vague and uncertain that one cannot tell what they really think and believe. Mocking the superstitions of the masses, they all continue to wear their amulets. Criticizing the faith of their fathers, they yet attend Friday prayers largely for the sake of appearances, for they have a social position to maintain. Their neighbours know that they do not normally pray nor keep the fast, but they are forced to observe most family and social customs and are expected to take their place at religious festivals. They take a great interest in political and social problems, but usually fail to understand them because their environment does not enable them to visualize them in their right setting.

The influence of the effendi must be taken into account in the modern Sudan, but is apt to be exaggerated. He is too self-interested to desire the progress of the masses and his revolt lacks sincerity. At home his influence is negligible because his womenfolk are invariably ignorant and it is amusing to see what little impression his wisdom has upon the *ḥabōbāt*.

2. THE ISLAMIC CHURCH-STATE

Some knowledge of Orthodox Islam is necessary in order to understand, in the first place, something of the totalitarian character of Islam, the meaning of the Muslim Church-State, and the place that conception plays in the lives of all Muslims whom the *sharī'a* touches; and, in the second, the legal system of Islam, which in practice only affects private and family life, and the traditional system of education.

We have already stated that the first stage on the path to understanding Islam is to rid oneself of the idea that Islam simply involves a peculiar religious attitude of mind and the performance of specific practices; whereas in fact Islam is a highly developed social system with clearly defined principles about its organization and the relationship of its members held together by a particular attitude to the supernatural.

The founder of Islam had no conception of such a complete system. He accepted the old pre-Islamic way of life as a matter of course and his legislative innovations were called forth by the opportunist need to regulate practice wherever it conflicted with his conception of himself and his mission. When he died neither Islamic law nor doctrine was fixed. It was, however, his conception of a theocracy which resulted in the course of time, as the system developed, under the influence of oriental civilizations, in the identification of the state as an integral part of the divine revelation.

This theocratic state claimed to be the only power entitled to rule the world, and this claim was the basis of constitutional government. So the world was conceived of as divided into two camps: *dār-al-islām* (home of Islam) and *dār-al-ḥarb* (home of war). Muslims call themselves the *Jamā'a* or the *Umma*, the 'Community', thought of as a religious, social, and political unit, ruled by God through His Prophet. Such an *Umma* could only be ruled by divine law (*sharī'a*).

In theory this is as true now as it was then, because without it Islam would disintegrate; but as soon as Islam spread beyond Arabia, the Muslim governments were faced with facts which they were forced to take into account through having to rule civilized non-Arab populations, some of which became Muslim, some not. As a background to the study of Sudanese Islam we are less interested in the non-Muslim native population (*dhimmīs*) who were regarded as wards of the state, as with the alien peoples who had embraced Islam and formed the bulk of Muslims and retained their own social customs. In time there ceased to be one Muslim state and everywhere regional rulers sprang up. Thus in practice two codes of law appeared: One was the eternal *sharī'a*, the canon law of Islam, which is the revealed law of God through the Qur'ān, supplemented by the *sunna* or usage of the Prophet, developed and codified by analogical reasoning (*qiyās*) and confirmed by *ijmā'* or catholic consent. The other was the regional

ʿāda based on local custom, which varied in every land and was regulated and backed by the will of the rulers. Between these two codes or rather fields of law the boundary was always the same. The *sharīʿa*, though universal in theory, ruled only the Muslim's personal and family life (marriage, divorce, children, inheritance), and certain obligations to God, such as *ṣalāt*, and to his fellows. The local code and the arbitrary will of the ruler covered everything else—civil, criminal, commercial, war, and taxation laws.

This was a necessary division forced on all administrators, but has never been fully accepted by the theologians, though the Canonists had to recognize the practical impossibility of enforcing the *sharīʿa* under existing conditions. The *sharīʿa* became the symbol of the group solidarity of Islam and it has often been the cause of risings against the administrators. Hence, and this is important, for it operates with European administrators as well as Muslim, the unwillingness of administrators often to take many perfectly rational actions which they are afraid will raise against them the theologians and the masses whom they can so easily inflame.

So we get three elements which have always to be taken into account in the Muslim state: (1) the *canonists*, impregnably blocked behind their moribund system of divine law; (2) the *administrators*, recognizing the law in theory, faced with practical situations for which they must legislate, yet never fully independent executives because of fear of the *ʿulamā*; (3) the *masses*, living according to an entirely different standard of personal religion, law, and morality from that of the *sharīʿa*, yet reverencing it and therefore easily stirred by the cry 'Islam in danger'.

Knowledge of the *sharīʿa* was obtained in the first place from the Qur'ān. But since revelation in Islam was limited and fossilized in the Qur'ān, recourse had to be made to the personal practice or decisions of the Prophet in dealing with new situations, and so, by a necessary fiction, the vast amount of material which had been assimilated from the legislative and social practice of the conquered countries was justified by attributing it to the Prophet's practice. Later, when this method could no longer be maintained, it became necessary to admit *qiyās* or reasoning by analogy, and finally *ijmāʿ*, agreement between at first the Companions of the Prophet, later broadened to agreement of the faithful and in practice to agreement between the *ʿulamā*. *Ijmāʿ* in fact became the deciding authority. The whole system as revealed law (*sharīʿa*) is called *fiqh* (recognition) and these four are the 'roots' (*uṣūl*) of the *fiqh*. So there developed 'schools' of *fiqh* (called *madhāhib*, sing. *madhhab*, 'rite'). Four such schools became recognized as orthodox: that of Abū Ḥanīfa (A.D. 767), Mālik Ibn Anas (A.D. 795), Ash-Shāfi'ī (A.D. 820), and Aḥmad Ibn Hanbal (A.D. 855). The result of the foundation of these *madhāhib* was that the way to further development became closed, the system became rigid and no one was allowed to investigate the 'sources'. The Qur'ān and Ḥadīth came to 'have no more value than edifying literature' and the interpretative *fiqh*-books of a particular *madhhab* became the authoritative 'law-books' of an orthodox Muslim. Hence the *'ulamā*, the doctors of religion, could never be creative and orthodox Islam became a spent force.

So the *fiqh* came to be mainly an academic study, concerned with an ideal law, relating to an ideal state of society. It was divorced from practical life, the rulers had always had their own code of secular law, and the people their customs and popular beliefs, yet because of its divine character it always remained the foundation of Muslim education.

In the Sudan, as elsewhere, orthodox Islam is represented by: (1) the traditional educational system—the basis; (2) the courts administering the *sharī'a*; (3) the public mosques and their staff.

3. THE TRADITIONAL SYSTEM IN THE SUDAN

The nomad Arabs who conquered the Sudan had their own tribal codes and cared nothing for the *sharī'a*, whilst the Funj ruled arbitrarily over peoples who adhered to their own indigenous customs. But it was not long before some sort of orthodox influence began to affect the lives of the townsfolk and villagers. Wad Ḍaif Allāh begins his *Lives of the Saints*:

> Know that the Funj took control and conquered the land of the Nūba at the beginning of the 10th century in the year 910 (A.D. 1504).... In those lands there is no record of any schools for the Qur'ān nor religious learning. It is said that a man could divorce his wife and another marry her that very day without any period of probation[1] until Shaikh Maḥmūd al-'Araki[2] came from Egypt and taught the people about the probation period. He lived on the White Nile and built himself a castle known as the *Qaṣr Maḥmūd*. At the beginning of the second half of the 10th century the Sulṭān 'Umāra Abū Sakaikīn appointed the Shaikh 'Ajīb the Mānjilak (feudal governor), and

[1] *'idda*—the fixed period of continency (three menstruations) enjoined on the woman after separation from her husband either by divorce or death before she can legally contract another marriage. Islam, whilst accommodating itself to so much, has always insisted on certain reforms in the family life of pagans. Notice the account of the controversy of the Qāḍī Dushain with Muḥammad al-Hamīm (*Ṭabaqāt*, S. 150).

[2] Maḥmūd was a Sudanese born on the White Nile who went to Egypt to study the Mālikī Madhhab, and on his return (1510–20) founded fifteen *khalwas* on the White Nile.

early in his rule Shaikh Ibrāhīm al-Būlād came from Egypt to the Shā'iqiyya country and there he taught *Khalīl* and the *Risāla*[1] and the science of *fiqh* spread throughout the Jezīra. . . . Then came At-Tilimsānī the Maghrabī to Muḥammad Wad ʿĪsā ʿSuwār adh-Dhahab' and initiated him into the Ṣūfī Path and taught him *kalām* (dogmatic theology) and such Qur'ānic sciences as *tajwīd* (methods of Qur'ān recitation) and variant readings, and so knowledge spread in the Jezīra. . . . Then came Shaikh Muḥammad b. Qadam to Barbar district who introduced the Shāfʿī *madhhab* and his *madhhab* spread in the Jezīra. . . . Then came Shaikh Maḥmūd al-Miṣrī to Barbar where he taught *ʿilm at-tawḥīd* (doctrine of the unity), grammar, and the *Risāla*.

Islamic cultural development was therefore due to migrant *Kulturträger* who spread the traditional system of education throughout the Funj Confederation concomitantly with the mystical system and thus opened up a life-career for all and sundry who chose to follow the prescribed course. We find few traces of those bitter quarrels between the *ʿUlamā* and the Ṣūfīs which are a common feature of Muslim life elsewhere because the *ʿUlamā* and the *Ṣūfīs* in the Sudan were so often one and the same.[2] Such controversy only came to the Sudan with Azharite shaikhs during the Egyptian period[3] and is being intensified to-day. However ridiculous it may appear, one may say that these Ṣūfī doctors of law combined in their limited sphere the threefold way of Al-Ghazālī when he describes *fiqh* (jurisprudence) as the bread of life of all believers, *tawḥīd* (dogmatic theology) as the preventative medicine against heresy, and *taṣawwuf* (mysticism) the digester of the other two to the building up of a true religious life.

The System of Education. The aim of education is study of the *sharīʿa*—the only subject of true learning—and, since that consists of rules laid down in the past, the curriculum is fixed and the method is memorization.

The beginning, and for the majority the end, of education is recitation of the *Qur'ān*.[4] Ibn Khaldūn writes in his *Muqaddama*:

The practice of teaching the Qur'ān to children is one of the characteristics of Islam which believers have adopted and brought into practice in all their countries, because the result of memorizing it is to strengthen faith and (give

[1] Two text-books on *fiqh*.

[2] There are traces of such conflicts but they are very gentlemanly; cf. the controversy of Qāḍī Dushain with Sh. Idrīs over the question of smoking (*Ṭabaqāt*, S. 9–10) and with Muḥammad al-Hamīm over his marrying more than four women (*Ṭabaqāt*, S. 150, M. 142–3).

[3] Three *riwāqs* were founded at the Azhar: As Sinnāriyya (1850), Barābra, and Dārfūr.

[4] The Qur'ān was read according to Warsh in Donqola and Dārfūr and according to Abī ʿUmar in the rest of the Sudan. At the present day there is only one man in Donqola who recites according to Warsh, but a District Commissioner told me there are many in Dārfūr where many will not swear an oath upon any other reading.

a foundation for) the doctrines based on Qur'ānic verses and the text of certain traditions.[1]

Throughout the Sudan, in a *ḥōsh*, in the shade of a *rakūba*, or under a tree in the *sūq*, can be seen circles of boys around a feki reclining on his *ʿanqarīb*. All chant together in monotone, swaying back and forth in rhythm, droning the sections indefinitely until they are memorized. The feki dictates from memory and the sections are copied out on wooden slates with a pointed stick dipped in an ink solution of soot, gum, and water. For most Sudanese the Qur'ān is a closed book; they are not taught the meaning of the language because the chanting itself is a meritorious work. As Ibn Khaldūn says, the North Africans 'place more emphasis on the Qur'ān and its memorization by children with the variant readings and its mode of recitation, than on anything else'.[2]

In the past the feki of a *khalwa*, who combined many functions in himself, was a most respected member of the community. In general this is still so, though the educated look down on him because he is invariably so ignorant and incompetent. It would in fact, as Al-Jāḥiẓ says, be hard to find 'more of a sot than a teacher of *kuttāb*'.[3] Most fekis open a private *khalwa* because it is a most honourable occupation and an easy way of earning a living; other *khalwas* are connected with a mosque and supported by the mosque funds.

The same system is still the only form of education for the vast majority of Sudanese and some 1,500 *khalwas* are scattered about the Sudan teaching the recitation of the Qur'ān in the traditional manner. Even this education is somewhat restricted since so many children have to start feeding cattle at the age of four. The Education Department has tried to stimulate the fekis to reach a higher standard by instituting short training courses and subsidizing the *khalwas* of those who teach a little of the 'Three Rs'. But they now realize that there is no hope for rural education within such a framework and it still remains true that no one who leaves a *khalwa* is literate. Lord Cromer was quite right when he wrote that such schools are 'as nearly useless as any educational establishments could be'.[4]

The student of a *khalwa* is known as a *ḥuwār* (pl. *ḥairān*). Whenever he has completed a section (*qism*) the feki writes the first verse of the next on his slate and the boy takes it to his family, who then send the feki a present called *ḥaqq ash-sharāfa*. Every Wednesday each student takes some *dura*, cooks it and eats with the feki, and takes a

[1] *Muqaddama*, Cairo ed., p. 397.
[2] Op. cit., p. 398.
[3] Al-Jāḥiz, *Al-Bayān wa't-Tabyīn*, i. 139.
[4] *Modern Egypt* (1911 ed.), p. 879.

little to his home as *baraka*. Students act as the feki's servants, having duties of firewood collection, clearing the ground, and so on.

After about seven years' work the boy recites the Qur'ān three times before the feki. Then he is examined by another feki and if successful is pronounced a *ḥāfiẓ*. Unless he becomes a feki himself he soon forgets most of the Qur'ān.

The student lives normally at home and the feki belongs to the village, but in Dārfūr most Fūr boys leave their homes at the age of 7–9 and wander off with friends to a feki of whom they have heard. They are known as *muhājirīn* and cultivate for the feki as payment. Thus there grows up a village of *muhājirīn* varying in number from 20 to 100 boys and youths. These groups have often caused trouble in the villages and in 1927 they started a rising at Dār Tabella which was soon quelled. The boy reads until the age of 16 and then becomes a feki himself or returns home, or, if he fails, migrates east. Their day commences at four with the feki wielding a stick to get them up. They then chant in small groups around fires until sunrise. During the day they have other duties: they may work on the feki's cultivation or grind grain whilst others collect firewood and draw water. On Tuesdays the small boys only go out in groups to beg grain at more distant places and return on the Friday. During the rains they do little else than cultivate for the feki. The *muhājirīn* pay *faṭra* to the feki and if he happens to be the Imām of a village the villagers give him *zakā'* and *faṭra* at 'Īd al-Fiṭr. Learning the Qur'ān to them is almost a magical practice and its accomplishment brings a sense of power.[1]

In the east at about the age of 12 some boys continue their studies in *zāwiyas* or mosques. Such students are called in the Ṭabaqāt *fuqarā' l-'ilm* (also *ṭalaba*, sing. *ṭālib*) in contrast with the elementary *fuqarā' l-Qur'ān*. Here the curriculum consists of two branches of learning studied simultaneously: *Tawḥīd*—theology, according to the *madhhab* of Al-Ash'arī; and *Fiqh*, according to the *madhhab* of Ibn Mālik.

The *zāwiyas*, centring round the shaikh's home, combined the

[1] The following account from At-Tūnīsī (*Voyage au Darfour*, p. 293) shows that Dārfūr has advanced little since his visit (1803–13): 'L'instruction au Dârfour est fort peu avancée; la lecture du Coran y est très imparfaitement enseignée. Une des principales raisons en est que, dans les écoles, on n'apprend à lire le Coran que le soir, après la nuit close. Durant le jour, les enfants (les enfants mâles s'entend, car les filles n'apprennent jamais à lire) sont occupés à la garde des troupeaux; ce n'est que le soir, à leur retour des champs, qu'ils prennent leurs *planchettes* et vont à l'école. Chacun d'eux, à tour de rôle, doit y apporter du bois pour faire du feu; quand le feu est bien allumé, les enfants s'accroupissent alentour, et, à la lumière de la flamme, ils se mettent à lire, à écrire, à apprendre par cœur. Mais ces études ont de médiocres résultats, et ce que les Fôriens savent du Coran se réduit à bien peu de chose.'

functions of mosque, monastery, school, and college. Until the Egyptian period there were no other training establishments. Instruction is given in two ways. Usually the students sit around the feki whilst he recites the text and commentary, adding his own glosses. Sometimes the pupils go up individually to the feki and recite the portion of the text they have been memorizing; the feki will make some comments and set or dictate another portion. Books are rarely used and the students take down the section on slates.

The 'sources'—the Qur'ān and Ḥadīth—being without practical value, since dogma and legislation were fixed, have no place in their studies. The basis is *fiqh* and *tawḥīd*. But here again no critical study of the works of Ibn Mālik or other founders of *fiqh* is made. 'Abridgements' had been produced by obscure individuals and these the students learnt by heart. No doctor could be found who would dare to express a personal opinion on a law or doctrine or try to assess the value of the knowledge of these authors; they were limited to writing commentaries (*sharḥ*) or glosses (*hāshiya*) on these 'Abridgements'.[1]

In *fiqh* the two standard works used in the Sudan during the Funj period were the *Risāla* of Ibn Abī Zaid of Qairawān (d. A.D. 996) and the *Mukhtaṣar* (Summary) of Khalīl ibn Isḥāq (d. A.D. 1365). In theology they studied the *Muqaddama* of As-Sanūsī (d. A.D. 1490) and some memorized his three treatises on the Creed (*'aqā'id*). A few are stated to have read *kalām* (scholastic theology) which, however, from a notice on Muḥammad b. 'Adlān[2] seems to be merely As-Sanūsī's short catechism *Umm al-Barāhīn* ('Mother of Arguments').[3] Methods of reading the Qur'ān (*tajwīd*, the art of reciting it, and *qirā'āt*, variant-readings) were also subjects of study. A few odd individuals are mentioned who read *ḥadīth* and *tafsīr*. The majority, however, read and taught little more than *Khalīl* and the *Risāla* and the wide range of the school of the *Shā'iqī*, 'Abd ar-Raḥmān b. Asīd (d. 1715) is regarded as exceptional. The account of his school is worth quoting since it also gives us:

'A day in the life of a feki of Khalwa'.[4]

His pupil feki Muḥammad b. Ar-Raida al-'Awdī relates: As soon as he had finished morning prayers he read the last day's lesson on Khalīl and when he had finished it, the Qur'ān-students came to him and he corrected the tablets

[1] Al-Muḍawwī b. Muḥammad al-Misrī (d. 1684) of Shendī wrote four commentaries on As-Sanūsī's *Umm al-Barāhīn*, others on the *Wusṭā*, the *Ṣughrā* and a *hāshiya* (*Ṭabaqāt* M. 30–1, S. 32).

[2] Op. cit. M. 164, S. 172.

[3] A summary of the *Umm al-Barāhīn* is given in A. J. Wensinck, *The Muslim Creed*, pp. 275–6.

[4] *Ṭabaqāt*, M. 123–4, S. 130–1.

of the learners. Then he read the morning lesson on Khalīl. Then there come to him those who were reading Al-Kharāzī, Al-Jazarī, and Ash-Shātibī,[1] then those who were reading the *'aqā'id* and al-Akhḍarī and al-'Ashmāwī.[2] When he finished the muezzin came to him for the *ẓuhr* prayer and he performed the ablutions and prayed. When that was over he gave the midday lesson on Khalīl until the muezzin called the *'aṣr* prayer when he prayed. Then the students of *tajwīd* and *'aqā'id* and al-'Ashmāwī and al-Akhḍarī came to him and studied until the muezzin called the Maghrib Prayer. After praying he recited the text of Khalīl from memory and with a single verse he recited a commentary (*siyāq*) equal to a *maqra* of the Qur'ān. Then they brought him his *'anqarīb* on which he reclined whilst the Qur'ān-students recited,[3] two by two. Afterwards he performed the *'ishā* prayer and rested for a time whilst the *fuqarā* had supper, when he took his whip and sat to hear the Qur'ān-students recite the *sub'* of the day.[4] When they had finished he rose and entered his *khalwa* and one of the students brought a bundle of faggots, lit the fire, and started reading. The shaikh brought out his satchel in which were 16 *qubbāṣa*[5] and he faced the *qibla* whilst the student read to himself. When he had finished he took his whip and awoke the students for recitation and they washed their tablets and wrote (a new lesson). He had a thousand-bead rosary of tiny beads which he took and told whilst the students scribbled on their tablets. When they had written the lesson he occupied himself solely with correction until the muezzin called for the Morning Prayer, after which he tested the last lesson on Khalīl. On holidays he gave legal opinions (*fatwās*), judgements and wrote amulets. Such was his habit until he abandoned this world.[6]

The system of education outlined above: traditional, devoid of all joy and discovery, unadapted to rural needs, can never be made the basis of training of character and had it not been for the Ṣūfī influence the Sudanese mind would have been sapped of all initiative and vitality. Ibn Khaldūn realized this when he wrote that the constant reference to the past had 'sapped originality and independence out of the Muslim mind'.

4. THE MODERN ORGANIZATION OF THE 'ULAMĀ

Whilst a few of these fekis were *Shāfi'ī*, the majority were *Mālikī* and the Sudanese remain attached to this *Madhhab* to this day. The

[1] Died 1194. Wrote two poems in rhymed prose on the reading of the Qur'ān.

[2] These two were writers on *fiqh*. Al-Akhḍarī (tenth century A.H.), wrote a *Mukhtaṣar fi'l'ibādat 'alā madhhab Mālik b. Anas.*

[3] Coll. *'araḍa lōḥu*, to recite the set portion.

[4] *sub' ad-dirāsa* (seventh of the weekly section). They have been learning in small sections and now recite it in full, being flogged if they have been lazy.

[5] These may be 'pebbles' for use like a *sibḥa*; or for sortilege; or, after recitation over them, for sale for use on graves (cf. Burckhardt, *Nubia*, p. 269). There is a *v.l. qubbāḍa*.

[6] This is a long programme, but no one acquainted with a feki of *khalwa* will need to inquire when he goes to sleep.

Egyptian conquest introduced the *Ḥanafī Madhhab*, that of the Turkish Empire, as the official code of all the courts; and, with the exception of the brief exile of the *sharīʿa* codes during the Mahdiyya, the *Ḥanafī* has continued to be the official code, though so far as their private life and communal duties is concerned the Sudanese stick to the Mālikī code. We should remember that the *sharīʿa* only touches a section of life and the establishment of British rule did not mean that the *sharīʿa* ceased to be the law of the land. It never was the law of the land and was applicable, so far as its administration in the courts is concerned, only by the declaration of the sovereign power. The British, except that they abolished slavery, rule much the same sphere as that of any Muslim state, for most have adopted codes based on European models; only questions relating to family (marriage, divorce, minors, succession), religious usages, institutions, and pious endowments (*awqāf*) come under the *sharīʿa*.

Religious courts (*maḥākim sharīʿa*) exist in every province and district headquarters. The judges (sing. *qāḍī*, pl. *quḍāt*) are officials of the Legal Department of the Sudan Government. At their head are the Grand Qāḍī and the Muftī.[1] Their work is subject to a committee of supervision. The Legal Secretary decides all questions of discipline and administration and the decisions of the *qāḍīs* can be revised by the Higher Muhammedan Courts. The *qāḍīs* are chosen from Gordon College graduates and are trained at the Legal School attached to the College. Besides legal work their functions also include the administration of the mosques maintained by public funds. A board of *ʿulamā* exists to advise the Government with regard to the effect of legislation which might affect Muslim institutions and religious feeling.

The training of functionaries other than *qāḍīs* was in the houses of the *ʿulamā* until 1912 when Abū'l-Qāsim Aḥmad Hāshim succeeded Muḥammad al-Badawī as *Shaikh al-ʿUlamā*. Abū'l-Qāsim persuaded the Government to give land around the old mosque in Omdurmān as *waqf* for the building of a new mosque and a religious college attached to it to be called *al-maʿhad al-ʿilmī*. A subscription list was opened and £E16,000 collected and the Government allotted part of the market dues. It is administered by a Board of the *ʿUlamā*, acting under the authority of the Legal Department. Teaching in the *maʿhad* strictly followed that of the Azhar and the first examination took place in

[1] The *muftī* is a state adviser who can explain the law and his decision is called a *fatwā*. The *qāḍī* settles legal disputes. The Grand Qāḍī has always been an Egyptian until 1947 when, as part of the policy of Sudanization, a Sudanese was appointed.

1920. There are three stages in the training: (1) four years' elementary, leading to the *shahāda awwaliyya*—this training is not in the *ma'had*; (2) four years' intermediate, leading to the *shahāda ahliyya*, when he is qualified to be a *ma'dhūn* (notary of marriages), a *mu'adhdhin*, a *faqīh* teaching outside the *ma'had*, or a *qāḍī*'s clerk; and (3) four years' higher, leading to the *shahāda 'ālimiyya*, i.e. he becomes an *'ālim*. He is then qualified to be a Legal Assistant, or a teacher in the *Ma'had*, or *Imām* of a mosque.

The influence of this class is confined to the towns. The agriculturalists and pastoralists, as we have shown, are governed almost entirely by *'āda*. For instance, the most solemn oath a Sūdānī can take is usually on the tomb of his shaikh, although according to *fiqh* this is *makrūh* (reprehensible). The nomads are governed by it even in the spheres where the *sharī'a* rules more especially, such as problems of inheritance, guardianship, and marriage. The Baqqāra drove out a *sharī'a* judge who was sent to them. The custody of children after divorce is a right of the father, but it is an almost universal practice for the mother to get the girls. There is a clash going on at the present time between the marriage customs of the Zaghāwa and the *sharī'a*. The legal authorities of the Government in 1921 at the beginning of the process of decentralization (*The Powers of Nomad Shaikhs Ordinance*), recognized the ruling of *'āda*. This was extended in 1927 under an ordinance of a similar title with the significant omission of the word 'nomad'. Tribal laws therefore are valid for all local cases instead of the *sharī'a* law if both parties to a suit agree to trial by the Tribal Court.[1]

5. THE MOSQUES, THEIR STAFF AND CONGREGATIONS

The natural mosque to any Sudanese is not some ugly brick structure built to the designs of the P.W.D., such as one sees to-day in the principal towns, but an open space where a congregation can gather for *ṣalāt*. The mosque square in Omdurmān where the Mahdī and his Khalīfa gathered together their thousands is a typical Sudanese mosque. If you go to a village in the Central Sudan you find that a mosque is a thorn enclosure with a straw and grass *rākūba* at one side to shade the worshippers from the midday sun. In the north the mosque is a mud enclosure with either a *rākūba* or mud room for prayers during the heat of the day.[2]

[1] In urban centres if there is both a tribal and a *sharī'a* court in the same town, cases under the *sharī'a* must be tried in the *sharī'a* court.

[2] It is of interest to recall that the first mosque at Kūfa, built in A.D. 638, was an area enclosed by a ditch with a covered colonnade running the length of one side. Among the

Such an enclosure, although it may only be delineated by a few stones, is called a *masjid*, and before entering this area one must remove one's footwear. Such a *masjid* is usually connected with a particular dervish order and the *dhikr*, the main purpose of its existence, is performed there. It is then normally called a *zāwiya*. If there is a room within the enclosure for the performance of the Friday midday prayer, that room is called a *jāmi'*; if there is a Qur'ān school there it is also called a *khalwa*. Confusion is sometimes caused since these four terms may all be used in reference to the same enclosure. The *imām* of a *masjid* who leads the prayers may be the *khalīfa* of the order, or the feki of the *khalwa*, or any respectable Muslim present.

The large mosque in the town is always a *jāmi'*, which is the place where the *ẓuhr* prayer on Fridays ought to be performed. These buildings have been built by Greek builders with a good deal of government money. The normal Sudanese does not feel at home in them as he does in the religious club atmosphere of the *zāwiya-masjid*.

The personnel of such a *jāmi'* must consist of a minimum of four: an *imām* who leads the prayers; a *khatīb*, the preacher; a servant; and a *mu'adhdhin* to give the call to prayer. The larger mosques have many more. The functions of these officials need not be elaborated because they do not differ from those in other parts of the Islamic world.

It should be recalled that Islam in its efforts to preserve unity places its emphasis only on the externals of religion. Creed is less important than ritual observance, for it is ritual which divides and defines men in religion. No one can be a heretic who observes the external duties which Islam prescribes. *Īmān* (faith) and *iḥsān* (righteousness) are private matters between the individual and God. Lip-service is paid by all to the *sharī'a* rules, but observance naturally varies even within the same family. Compulsion is necessary to get general observance such as in the days of the Mahdiyya. Few perform all five ritual *ṣalāts* daily and those who do have some incentive; either they belong to the teaching class, or are merchants who find a reputation for piety good for business, or are old men with plenty of time on their hands. The *muzāri'īn* and people working in towns find two *ṣalāt* all that they can manage. The effendiyya are hindered by the wearing of trousers and the nomads know no more than the ritual gestures. Spiritual emotion is for most men absent from *ṣalāt*, though there are Islamic values in the discipline and regimentation of a religious

Ya'qūbāb in the Jezīra the *rākūba* is very high with many pillars which A. J. Arkell has suggested may be a survival of the motif upon which the Egyptian temple was built.

exercise. The very orthodox are more stirred by the ornate chanting of the Qur'ān at feast or fast and the masses moved to ecstasy in the *dhikr*.

The fast (*ṣawm*) of Ramaḍān is much more strictly observed than ritual *ṣalāt* by the *muzāriʿīn*, though not by the nomads. Here they have been influenced by the dervish orders and not the *sharīʿa* because the orders all stress the need for abstinence, whereas they have a substitute for *ṣalāt* in the *awrād*. It has been suggested that there is a belief that the observance of the Ramaḍān fast is an atonement for sins committed during the year. I have found little evidence of a belief in that form, though the belief is very universal that the observance brings special rewards in the hereafter. The effects of Ramaḍān are universal. It is a month of inertia. Everyone is sleepy and sulky-tempered, for, owing to the disarrangement of feeding at night, the digestive system is upset, even with the non-fasting children.

No account is taken of the obligatory *zakāt*, the 2½ per cent. income-tax for the relief of the poor, but most people who can give voluntary *ṣadaqāt*. The *zakāt* of the breaking of the fast (*zakāt al-fiṭr*), though only *sunna* according to the Mālikīs, is scrupulously observed at any rate in the towns.

The pilgrimage (*ḥajj*) to the Holy Places is a great ambition, but in spite of nearness to the Ḥijāz not very many go.[1] He who does returns under heroic conditions to be feasted and honoured, for his *ḥajj* brings to his family the *baraka* of the Holy Places. Henceforth he is called *al-Ḥājj* and his achievement is commemorated on his house which has its façade whitewashed and designs illustrative of his journey painted on it. The Sudan always possesses a large floating pilgrim population of West Africans who spend a considerable time in it working for the means to proceed farther. The pilgrimage arrangements are under the supervision of the Government. Most sail from Sawākin where they are medically examined. The pilgrimage is important because the returned pilgrims are strongholds of orthodoxy.

In respect of *sharīʿa* prohibitions, that against the use of intoxicants has always been disregarded. *Merīsa* forms an important item of ordinary diet and many *merīsa*-houses are licensed.

The chief festivals have received official recognition as public holidays. These are *al-ʿĪd aṣ-Ṣaghīr* (the lesser feast) or *ʿĪd al-Fiṭr* (the festival of the break-fast), treated as the greatest festival, during the three days after Ramaḍān and *al-ʿĪd al-Kabīr*, 10th to 12th Dhū'l-Ḥijja (also called *ʿĪd al-Qurbān* or *ʿĪd al-Aḍḥā*, during which an

[1] Of the 8,404 pilgrims who embarked from Sawākin during the 1946 *ḥajj* season only 500 were from the Anglo-Egyptian Sudan, all the rest were 'westerners'.

unblemished sheep of a fixed age is killed by each family in memory of the sacrifice of Abraham. The Festival Prayer (*ṣalāt al-ʿĪd*) is common to both these. It is *sunna* and always celebrated in the open air in the desert or open country. It consists of two *rakʿas* followed by a two-part *khuṭba*. During these festivals new clothes are worn and visits are paid to friends for congratulation and present-giving and to the cemeteries and saints' tombs. The *Mawlid an-Nabī* (the birthday of the Prophet) will be described in the following chapter.

5

Beliefs and Practices of Popular Islam

A. SAINT-WORSHIP

1. *Saints in Islam: Muslim Idea of a Holy Man*

> Ho, verily upon the friends (*awliyā'*) of Allah there is no fear neither do they grieve. (Qur'ān, x. 63.)

EVERY Muslim believes that beside the visible order of believers there exists an invisible order of saints who, under the direction of Allāh, manage the affairs of the world for Him. So bound up are the saints with the religious life of Islam in the Sudan that to think of Allāh without His intermediaries is impossible.

Men of piety attracted attention through their alleged powers from the beginning of Islam, but no regular theory about them nor special cult developed until the rise of the dervish orders in the twelfth century A.D. All authority then came to be invested in the shaikh of the order who claimed to have powers of intercession with God and to perform miracles. Naturallv when dead his followers continued to venerate him still as a 'friend' of God and their protector.

The word *walī* in its religious sense may have to be translated as 'saint', but we must avoid reading our own conceptions into the word. The idea of 'nearness' (to God)[1] which lies behind it needs to be brought out because it is essential in the development of the Muslim theory of saintship. In the Qur'ān *walī* does not have a strict meaning,[2] but in the course of time it came to be applied to those who were felt to have a personal relationship with God. The word then lays stress not on saintliness but on personal relationship with God. The *awliyā'* are those who live in the presence of God.

As a result of the development of this usage of the term *walī*, the theory developed that God has granted to some of them special powers which even make the subsistence and governance of the world depend upon them.

[1] *Walī*, plur. *awliyā'*, is derived from *walā*, to be near.

[2] *Walī* in the Qur'ān is applied to God as 'Patron' or 'Guardian' (ii. 258, iii. 61, xlv. 18, &c.); it is used for 'guardian' in a general sense (ii. 282); and as 'Friend' or 'Ally' of God (x. 63). The popular sense of the word became common during the ninth century A.D.

ʿAlī al-Hujwīrī states that God has chosen the saints to manifest His actions:

God, then, has caused the prophetic evidence (*burhān-i-nabawī*) to remain down to the present day, and has made the Saints the means whereby it is manifested, in order that the signs of the Truth and the proof of Muḥammad's veracity may continue to be clearly seen. *He has made the Saints the governors of the universe*; they have become entirely devoted to His business, and have ceased to follow their sensual affections. Through the blessing of their advent the rain falls from heaven, and through the purity of their lives the plants spring up from the earth, and through their spiritual influence the Muslims gain victories over the unbelievers.[1]

This government of the world has a nightly meeting of the saints, both dead and living, as its directive organization. Their head is the *Quṭb* (Axis) who is a saint living on earth in different incarnations. He is God's official administrator in the world and constitutes the most vital link in the chain of union between the Creator (*al-Ḥaqq*) and the creatures (*al-khalq*).

Many of the Ṣūfīs have asserted heretically that by virtue of having attained unity with God the saints are higher than the prophets in rank. In actual fact to the masses they are. A prophet is certainly of less value to the community than a saint, for in the saint is embodied that longing for salvation which is inherent in all men. He is regarded as an embodiment of saving power quite apart from his personal piety or impiety. This is because the Muslim idea of a holy man has nothing to do with his personal merit, or attainment of holiness through pain and suffering, prayer and meditation; it is rather a mechanical conception and does not involve the personal will. The saints are people 'honoured' by God with His special favour, and the way in which this honour is manifested is through their possession of *baraka*, whereby miracles (*karāmāt*) are performed on their behalf. A miracle (*karāma*) is an honour.[2] The purity of a saint's life or doctrine is of secondary importance; if he can work miracles, that is enough, he is a saint and therefore one to be feared and one whose protection is to be sought.[3]

[1] *Kashf al-Maḥjūb*, trans. R. A. Nicholson, p. 213.

[2] D. B. Macdonald has pointed out that the *karāmāt* (thaumaturgic gifts) of the saints are closely akin to the χαρίσματα of 1 Cor. xii. 9, worked by divine grace. *Muʿjizāt* has become synonymous with *āya* (sign), i.e. miracles in the conventional sense, which are recognized by orthodox Islam only in the prophets and are Acts of God performed through a prophet to prove his mission (*daʿwa*).

[3] The same attitude is adopted to the tombs of Christian saints in Muslim countries, many of whom, of course, are in the Muslim calendar. In the Sudan, which does not have indigenous Christian saints, the only example is that of the festival of Mār Jirjis (the Prophet al-Khiḍr of popular Islam) at the church dedicated to him in Ḥalfāya. As a result of the cure

A saint without miracles is no saint at all; but when it is remembered that converting a sinner,[1] clairvoyance, telepathy, and *firāsa* (the art of divination from the physiognomy or actions of a person) are *karamāt*, and that these are the commonest of phenomena among ecstatics, it will be seen that it is not difficult to attain to *walī*-ship. It is absurd to look for ethical signs of saintship, for if the holy one's consciousness is absorbed into God, his body can hardly be held accountable for its actions. This does not mean that the ascetic virtues are not admired, but that they have nothing to do with the holiness.

Baraka, literally 'benediction', means holiness in the Muslim sense of something given by God. The whole conception has its roots in pre-Islamic beliefs in a wonder-working force, re-set in a new form in Islam, and therefore with new tendencies, through it being regarded as a '*blessing*' from God. *Baraka* is possessed in its highest degree by the saints and is bestowed arbitrarily by God regardless of merit; although the conception is not absent that exceptional piety and asceticism, can, as it were, force God's hand and make Him bestow it. It is universally believed in the Sudan that the *baraka* of a saint can also be transmitted to his posterity. This accounts for the fact that men whose conduct is so vile as to offer the worst possible example to others, are yet venerated because they are regarded as having inherited this supernatural power from a *walī* ancestor. Thus we get in the Sudan whole feki villages which live to a large extent on the credulity of the masses. *Baraka* can also be claimed by certain acts such as the recitation of the *Fātiḥa*, which is caught by the symbolic act of raising the hands during the recitation and then transferred by drawing the palms down over the face.[2]

The Christian must beware of judging the saints of Islam by his own standards and strive to understand Muslim requirements in a saint. The saints were the product of a religious environment which needed them and they have been a real means of providing a living religion to the masses to whom orthodox Islam was an empty show. Compare the attitude of the worshippers at a mosque, with its dignified formal ritual, with that of those at the shrine of a saint, where the people,

of a madman his feast (16 Nov.) has come to be associated with his miracle-working presence and on that date hundreds of Muslims as well as Christians visit the church, perform sacrifices, and make vows.

[1] Cf. *Ṭabaqāt* of Wad Ḍaif Allāh, biographies of ʿAwūdo b. ʿUmar and Salmān aṭ-Ṭawwālī.

[2] *Baraka*, as we shall see later, can be possessed by natural objects as well as humans. Harmless idiots are also thought to possess *baraka*, since God has taken their personality to Himself; but maniacs are thought to be possessed by *jinn* or devils, whereby the participle *majnūn*, possessed.

men, women, and children alike, freely express their devotion to one who was the guardian of their ancestors and is their protector to-day, one who is 'near to God' now as then, who hears their pathetic supplications and intercedes with the remote One.

2. *Peculiarities of Saint-worship in the Sudan*

Belief in holy-men, both living (*shuyūkh* or *fuqarā*) and dead (*awliyā'* or *ṣāliḥīn*) and their cult, all came ready-made to the Sudan, where it found a fertile field for its reception; for the Sudanese entered into the cult with an enthusiasm which formal observances could never evoke. To-day, in spite of the spread of modern education, there has been almost no diminution in saint-worship. Some of the effendiyya, it is true, such as Gordon College graduates and also the ultra-orthodox, may scoff at it, but to the masses belief in the saints and the efficacy of their *baraka*, with all that this involves of powers of intercession and miracle, is the essence of their religious life. Even the effendi has no control over the *ḥarīm* and would on no account refuse to allow his son to be ornamented with the charms of some pious feki, nor would he throw away his own *ḥijāb*.

The saints of the Sudan, in spite of the comparatively recent islamization of the country, are innumerable and most of them are indigenous. Their names spring immediately to the people's lips at times of illness, distress, and danger. Pilgrimages are constantly made to their shrines both to show reverence and to receive a share of the blessing (*li't-tabarruk*). The saints are all connected with the religious orders and many of the most important will be mentioned in the following chapter. The lives of those who flourished under the Funj régime for the three centuries from A.D. 1500 to 1800 are to be found in the *Ṭabaqāt* of Wad Ḍaif Allāh (d. 1809).[1] This book not only gives 260 biographies of a motley throng of ascetics, mystics, and thaumaturges, revealing their diverse personalities and mode of life, their visions and miracles, but also gives an illuminating insight into the religious life of the Sudanese masses of to-day; for these biographies are a mirror in which are reflected the ideals and yearnings, the humour

[1] The *Ṭabaqāt* has been studied by H. A. MacMichael (*Hist.* ii. 217–306) and S. Hillelson (*S.N.R.* vi. 191–230) both of whom give copious extracts. S. Hillelson also edits and translates two biographies in his *Sudan Arabic Texts* (pp. 172–203). There are two editions from different manuscripts, Mandīl (1930) and Ibrāhīm Ṣidaiq (1930). In the references which follow Mandīl's will be indicated by M. and Ṣidaiq's by S. The Arabic of the book is fascinating because of its colloquial style and freedom from the turgidity of the schoolmen. It differs considerably from other lives of the saints, like that of Sha'rānī, in that they are composed mainly of 'sayings', whereas Wad Ḍaif Allāh's book is mainly biographical.

and pathos, the common sense and folly, of the people who worship them. Caricatures as they are of the inner life of the Sudanese, they are also idealizations of it.

These men vary considerably in type and direction; some lived lives of religious intoxication; others quiet lives of sober sobriety; some were ascetics, living in retreat, subjecting themselves to great austerities; others savoured to the full the pomps and vanities of the world. Mysticism so completely pervaded the Sudan that most of the representatives of the *sharī'a* were also representatives of this deeper aspect of religious life. Most of these holy men therefore claim to have studied both formal law and Ṣūfism under accredited teachers whose names are invariably mentioned by Wad Ḍaif Allāh. A typical example is that of Khōjalī b. 'Abd ar-Raḥmān (d. 1742):

> He was born on the Island of Tūtī and entered the *khalwa* of the *faqīra* 'Aisha bint walad Qaddāl. He studied *kalām* (dogmatic theology) and *taṣawwuf* (mysticism) under *faki* Arbāb and mastered Khalīl under Az-Zain walad Saghairūn, being one of those who united the study of Ṣūfism and *Fiqh*.[1]

Some, however, did not regard the dryness of orthodox study as compatible with progress in the Ṣūfi Path. Others were quite illiterate. One saint it is related read the Qur'ān as far as the Sūrat az-Zilzila and then gave it up. It is related of 'Abd ar-Rāziq Abū Qurūn (d. A.H. 1070, A.D. 1659) that

> when a disciple of Sh. Bāsbār, named 'Alī wad Mōj, saw the people flocking to 'Abd ar-Rāziq, seeking his intercession with God and his *baraka*, he said, 'how can these people follow an illiterate man! Bāsbār deserves this popularity more than he'. 'Abd ar-Rāziq read his thoughts and said, 'may God make you see what I see'. He touched him and Wad Mōj saw the *Ka'ba* before his very eyes.[2]

We read of one 'Abd al-Mājid b. Ḥamad al-Aghbash (d. 1710) that he was

> one of those who practised what he preached, following closely the laws of the Qur'ān and the *sunna* and taking no notice of censure when following the way of God. He was one of the masters of esoteric sciences so that he could tell men the secrets of their consciences, yet, when his two disciples, Sa'd and Ḥammād, the sons of the faki Samīḥ, asked his advice about studying Khalīl at al-Qoz, he said to them 'go and get married and have children to succeed

[1] *Ṭabaqāt*, M. 71, S. 74.

[2] Op. cit. M. 135, S. 142. 'Abd al-Qādir al-Jīlānī makes use of the tradition that God has created 70,000 veils of light and shade between the believer and the Ka'ba, here symbolizing 'that Presence unseen by the eye which indwells the Divine world' (Al-Ghazālī, *Iḥyā*, i. 242).

you, for your lives will be shortened in studying Khalīl'. The event happened as he foretold. They completed eight readings of Khalīl and then God brought their lives to an end.[1]

The Sudan has its own peculiar theories of saintship. Idrīs b. al-Arbāb said:

there are three categories of saints, higher, middle and lower. The lower is that the saint can fly in the air, walk on the surface of the water, and has powers of clairvoyance. The middle is that God gives him creative powers (*ad-darajat al-kawniyya*), which means that he says to a thing 'Be!' and it is (*kun wa kān*). This is the category to which my 'son' Daf' Allāh belongs. The highest degree is the *Quṭbāniyya*.[2]

Their theories about the *Quṭb* are not at all clear. 'Shaikh Ḥasan wad Ḥasūna was asked about the rank of Mūsā ibn Ya'qūb. He said, "he holds the rank of *fard* among the Ṣūfīs. This is other than the *Quṭb*, the four *awtād*, the seven *nujabā'* and the forty *abdāl*. Their number (i.e. the *afrād*) is equivalent to that of those who took part in the Battle of Badr (that is 300) and they hold in relation to the *Quṭb* the status of privates (to the general)." '[3] Here he is clearly referring to the *Quṭb* as the 'Axis of the universe'. But normally when applied to a saint it means that he has reached this third degree of saintship. This same man Mūsā b. Ya'qūb is called by Daf' Allāh 'the divine Axis and eternal Helper (of the epoch)'.[4] Again, it may mean no more than a 'graduate', for we read of Daf' Allāh wad Idrīs that 'many benefited from his teaching and forty of his disciples attained the degree of *quṭbāniyya* in *'ilm*, *ṣalāḥ*, and *dīn*, not the *quṭbāniyya* known to the Ṣūfīs'.[5] In an *ijāza* (certificate) given by 'Abd ar-Raḥmān ibn Jābir to Ibrāhīm ibn Umm Rāb'a we read, 'I appoint him a *quṭb* in rank.'[6]

How does a Sudanese become a saint? If we examine the lives of these *awliyā'* we find that many members of the family of a *walī* tend to become saints. The tendency seems to be dormant in them, but can become manifest through election or special exercises. The *khalīfa* of a great saint, who is usually of his family, automatically inherits his *baraka* along with the office. Some seem to have attained saintship by

[1] Op. cit. M. 121–2, S. 129.

[2] Op. cit. M. 79–80, S. 86. Cf. also the account of 'Awwūda b. 'Umar (op. cit. M. 118). The saint mentioned above is Daf' Allāh b. Muḥammad Abū Idrīs.

[3] Op. cit., biog. of Mūsā b. Ya'qūb, M. 145, S. 152–3.

[4] Al-Quṭb ar-rabbānī wa'l-ghawth aṣ-ṣamadānī.

[5] Cf. the modern usage of *quṭb* applied to one who is pre-eminent in his profession, e.g. *huwa quṭbun min aqṭābi' s-siyāsa*—he is unequalled in diplomacy.

[6] Op. cit. M. 32, S. 33. See below p. 203, n. 2.

genuine asceticism. Most marked the professional religious life out as a career in a land where few other careers were open, by simulating ecstasy and practising magic. There are not wanting in the accounts of the *Ṭabaqāt* references to many women saints though the author does not give them special notices in his Lives.[1]

There are a number of accounts in the *Ṭabaqāt* of the occasion when illumination first came to a man that he was one of the chosen. It will be seen that there is no question of personal merit nor of attainment by procession from one stage (*maqām*) to another culminating in the *fanā'* (absorption into Deity) of the Ṣūfī philosophers. *Fanā'* was attained without any preparation. They would have agreed with the saying, 'one "attraction" (*jadhba*) from God is equal to all the work of mankind and *jinn*'.

Visions are the pretext alleged by these saints, and visions still play an important part to-day in Sūdānī religious life. In many of the accounts the vision is that of flying through the various heavens and having audience with the Prophet, for vision of the Prophet is regarded as authentic since Satan cannot assume his form.[2] This kind of vision has some connexion with the *mi'rāj* legend. The Mahdī was later to follow the same method. There can be no doubt about the reality of the occurrence of these visions and hallucinations, for a dervish to-day who lives in a continual hypnoidal state has similar visions. Here is an example from the nineteenth century. It is related of Aḥmad al-Hudā, a follower of Muḥammad b. al-Mukhtār (d. 1882) who introduced the Tijāniyya into the Sudan, that

he reached an extreme state of *jadhb* (rapture) and wandered about in many lands. *Ḥāl*[3] used to overpower him and he reached *fanā'*. He used to go into a trance and remain in it, prostrate on the ground, neither eating nor drinking and not recovering consciousness for forty days until he associated with our shaikh who completed his training. When the Sayyid (Muḥammad b. al-Mukhtār) used to speak about the divine verities to the chief *'ulamā* the speech used to go higher and higher until it passed far beyond their comprehension, so that he used to say, 'Now you don't understand what I say, but this inanimate object sitting here understands', and points to Aḥmad al-Hudā who was possessed by a *ḥāl*, so that one looking at him would suppose him to be inanimate.[4]

[1] Cf. Abū Dilaiq's nomination of his daughter 'Ā'isha to succeed him as *khalīfa* (op. cit. M. 16, S. 18).

[2] In the *Ṣaḥīḥ* of Bukhārī (iv. 135) on the authority of Anas it is reported that the Prophet said, 'He who sees me in a dream, actually sees me, for Satan cannot impersonate me.'

[3] *Ḥāl* is the state of ecstasy as a divine gift.

[4] *Ar-Risālat as-sādisa*, p. 20.

The account of how illumination first came to Sharaf ad-Dīn, shows how the call came to one who did not consciously seek to follow the religious life. It was told to Wad Ḍaif Allāh by his father as follows:

The story of his initiation was told to me by faki Ḥijāzī, the grandson of Shaikh Idrīs. He said that the faki ʿAbd ar-Rāziq wad ʿIwaiḍa said: 'I went into seclusion for purposes of worship and suffered greatly from a pain in my side. It troubled me so much that I left the *khalwa* (cell). Shaikh Sharaf ad-Dīn was staying in Al-Ḥijair, so I went to visit him. I found him reclining in a *rākūba*, facing the *qibla*, and with people surrounding him. I sat down behind the people saying to myself: I'll see him when he finishes. But he called me without having looked in my direction, and said, "Is it that fellow ʿAbd ar-Rāziq?" I said "Yes". He said, "Does a pain in your side make you leave your retreat?" He said to a man sitting in front of him, "O Maḥfal, the reason for my taking the *ṭarīqa* from Shaikh ʿAbd Allāh al-Ḥalanqī was that I was engaged to my cousin and left for the south together with my uncle's son whom I wanted to hire out for recitations so that I might gain sufficient to enable me to marry her. When we arrived at Abu Ḥarāz we found that the trading-caravan had left before us for Wad Madani, so we said 'Let us visit Shaikh ʿAbd Allāh and then we'll overtake the caravan.' We found him reclining in the shade of the mosque and facing it." A *faqīr* was massaging him. He called out to me without having seen me, "Is it that fellow Sharaf ad-Dīn wad Burri?" "Yes," I replied. He said, "Three days ago a saint came to me and said, 'A boy will come to you on his way south. Detain him, initiate him into the Way, and be his *murshid*.' " Then they brought us food and we ate. The brethren said to me, "You are very fortunate." I said to them, "But I want nothing better than my cousin." Then the Shaikh said, "Rise and wash your clothes and your body." I did so and returned and found him with a gourd of milk. He then gave me a handful of the milk and a thousand-bead rosary and said, "Go into retreat for eight days and recite *Al-Ḥayy al-Qayyūm* 50,000 times after each prayer." Whilst I was in retreat a man came to me carrying an iron rod with which he struck me, but neither did I turn to him nor stop my reciting. On the eighth day a *faqīr* came to me and said, "The Shaikh calls you." I found that he had performed his ablutions for the Noon Prayer. He started[1] the prayer and I followed. Thereupon I saw the world from the ground to the Throne of God and the thoughts of all men were revealed to me. I became greatly distressed and when one of the disciples blamed me for it, I told him all that had happened to me. When I told him he said, "We have been seeking this and have not seen it." From the moment that I told him all that I was seeing vanished. Then the Shaikh asked me saying, "What have you seen?" and when I told him "I saw this and that, but when I told the disciples

[1] *Aḥrama li-ṣ-ṣalāti*, i.e. to say 'God is greatest', the *takbīratu' l-iḥrāmi*, with which words one 'enters into prayer', and from which moment any action outside the prayer is *ḥarām* (unlawful).

of it, it vanished" he said, "In my opinion you are like a naughty *jinni*.[1] You aren't worthy to be trusted with the secrets of God." I wept bitterly. Then he ordered me to wash my clothes, take a bath and go into retreat a second time. This I did and by the grace of God what I saw the second time has not left me to this day. That was how I started.'[2]

The following about al-Musallamī'ṣ-Ṣaghīr might be regarded as a Sudanese parallel to the conversion of al-Ghazālī:

He started in this wise. After he had completed the reading of Khalīl and the *Risāla*, he travelled to see Shaikh Daf' Allāh (al 'Arakī b. Abū Idrīs). He entered the *khalwa* where the children were being taught. He said to the teacher, 'I have come from the desert.' So he started him off with his A.B.C.s and the children helped him with his slate and laughed at him. Then the Shaikh came and found him so engaged. He said 'Come here, O *faqīr*'. Aren't you a learned man?' He said, 'No.' The Shaikh said, 'I see on you the mark of learning, unless you tell us the truth you won't benefit from us.' He replied, 'My knowledge has profited me nothing. I have come seeking your spiritual help.' Then the Shaikh initiated him into the Path, slaughtered for him a goat and ordered him to eat it. He went into retreat for seven days and when he came out he could see the universe from the Throne to the earth.[3]

There are not wanting among these men saints who went as far as Al-Ḥallāj, identifying themselves with God by virtue of having attained *fanā*'. 'The Shaikh Balal ash-Shaib b. aṭ-Ṭālib said: "the name of my 'father' Daf'Allāh is the Greatest Name of God." When he used to write an amulet he wrote nothing else but "Daf' Allāh, Daf' Allāh, . . ." throughout.'[4]

Many of these saints, like Ṣūfīs elsewhere, claim that they are not subject to the *sharī'a* rulings which govern the lives of ordinary folk. Such men when they actually contravene the *sharī'a* are called

[1] *Atārīk jinniyyan maṭmūsan*. The above translation is the Sudanese usage. Lane gives *maṭmūs*, one who keeps nothing in mind.

[2] Op. cit. M. 91–2, S. 98–9. Hillelson (*S.N.R.* vi. 213–17) translates accounts of the coming of the initial illumination to Ḥasan wad Ḥasūna and Ṣāliḥ b. Bān an-Naqā.

[3] Op. cit. M. 22, S. 24.

[4] Op. cit. M. 80, S. 86, biog. of Daf' Allāh b. Muḥammad Abū Idrīs. The ecstatic theophanic utterances of one in the state of *fanā*' are called *shaṭḥāt* (cf. As Sarrāj, *Kitāb al-Luma' fi' l-Taṣawwuf*, edit. R. A. Nicholson, pp. 375–409). *Shaṭḥāt* in the Sudan is applied to any kind of extravagant sayings or poems uttered during the ecstasy of the *dhikr*-exercises. The *Ṭabaqāt* quotes some uninteresting examples. In the *Tijāniyya Majalla* (vi. 22) we read of Shaikh Muḥammad al-Khair that he lived in state of perpetual *fanā*' in the society of his Shaikh, Muḥammad b. al-Mukhtār, the introducer of the Tijāniyya to the Sudan during the Turko–Egyptian period and uttered such weak *shaṭḥāt* as 'my father is Al-Yazīd and the Ṣūfīs are all drunkards'.

malāmatiyya (blameworthy, antinomians).[1] We read of Muḥammad al-Hamīm that

> he belonged to the *malāmatiyya* who are a class of Ṣūfīs who do blameworthy things in contravention of the *sharīʿa* in order to incur the people's disapproval. Some seek to destroy their critics, whilst others seek such disapproval for the good of their souls and from fear of the dangers of popularity.[2]

We are told that Muḥammad al-Hamīm stole someone else's concubine, married two daughters of one father, and had seven wives at the same time, all contraventions of the *sharīʿa.* At the celebrations of his marriage to Ḥalīma, daughter of the *makk* of Atbara, one of ninety women he married, the slave girls sang 'the shaikh worships God and curses Iblīs, but is a slave to the coaxing words of Ḥalīma', and he answered, 'It is even so.'[3]

God's favour (*karāma*) is shown to these men in two ways. All saints are believed to possess esoteric knowledge (*ʿulūm al-walī*) and to associate freely with the Prophet, Al-Khiḍr, the Quṭb, and other eminent saints (*rijāl al-ghaib*), whereby they speak intuitively about hidden things; and also that they possess the power of performing miracles or rather that God performs miracles on their behalf. These are often called *khawāriq al-ʿādāt*—what breaks the natural order of things.

The ability to perform miracles depends on the strength of the saint's *baraka.* A Sūdānī's faith always tends to be placed in persons. To-day they say of healing by *ʿazīma* (incantation), 'the *baraka* is in the palms and not in the letters',[4] though with some methods (e.g. inhaling burnt texts), they think of the *baraka* as being in the *ḥurūf.* The double process is usually necessary—the interaction of the *baraka* of the feki and that of the symbol.

The *karamāt* of the saints are infinite in their variety. The most notable saint of the Jezīra, Ḥasan wad Ḥasūna (d. A.D. 1664), whose grandfather came from Spain, had the widest range. Some of the *karamāt* may be explained psychologically, but most are deformed or exaggerated accounts of some simple happening, or of those states common to

[1] A Ṣūfī was thought to be free of *sharīʿa* restrictions owing to his special relationship to God; being one with God he naturally obeyed God's laws. In time some found this a useful pretext to live an immoral life under a cloak of sanctity. ʿAlī al-Hujwirī writes, 'he who abandons the law and commits an irreligious act, and says that he is following the rule of "blame", is guilty of manifest wrong and wickedness and self-indulgence' (*Kashf al Maḥjūb*, edit. R. A. Nicholson, p. 65).

[2] *Ṭabaqāt*, M. 142, S. 149. See also account of Ismāʿīl b. Sh. Makki'd-Daqalāshī (M. 27, S. 29).

[3] Op cit. S. 150, M. 142.

[4] Al-baraka fi'l kufūf mush fi'l-ḥurūf.

ecstatics, or, more generally, the inventions of their followers. It may be interesting to give some examples from the treasury of the *Ṭabaqāt* since they are continually on the people's lips and help us to understand them. They may be arranged under the following grouping:

(1) *Healing*, usually by *'azīma*,[1] though here is an example of healing by psychological methods, when *'azīma* failed, by Khōjalī b. 'Abd ar-Raḥmān, who died in 1742, and whose *qubba* is at Ḥalfāya. He is reckoned as one of the greatest saints:

Fāṭima bint 'Ubaid was seriously ill and at the point of death. The Feki an-Nūr went to Khōjalī and said: 'My Lord, Shaikh Ḥasan used to bring the dead to life, now I want you to ask God to revive her and I have vowed for you her male slave Qasm Allāh.' So he made an incantation in the water of the *rakwa*,[2] and gave it to Feki an-Nūr for her. They spooned the water into her mouth, but she rejected it, because she was at death's door. Very late at night she addressed an-Nūr in a very faint voice, saying, 'I am well, for I have seen Shaikh Khōjalī standing by this chest and he prodded me with his stick and said, "arise."' Thereupon Feki an-Nūr rose up immediately and rode to Tūtī Island. He found the Feki Aḥmad, the son of the Shaikh, going to the mosque and cried, 'Good news, Bitt 'Ubaid is well!' Aḥmad said, 'the Shaikh has been shut in the *khalwa* up to this very moment. He said (to me), 'I am exhausted, I and the Angel of Death have contended together for the spirit of Bitt 'Ubaid and he left her to me.'[3]

(2) *Mukāshafāt* (unveilings, divination) knowledge of hidden things: thoughts, the future, clairvoyance, telepathic gifts, &c. This is a vast field. Here is an example of the commonest type, the foretelling of the future:

The Shaikh Bān an-Naqā was once seriously ill. Some of the brethren visited him and said to him, 'You are ill and haven't a male child, all your children are females.' He said, 'My wife Bitt Ṣāliḥ is pregnant and will bring forth a male child and I will not die until he becomes as tall as a sword.' It happened as he said, for his son Shaikh Ṣāliḥ relates, 'I didn't attain maturity until seven years after my father's death.'[4]

It is related of Al-Musallamī that:

He went out with his disciples and put up with a hermit. The man was very sorry for himself saying (in his heart) 'he who has neither society nor wealth will always mourn his lost years'. Al-Musallamī penetrated his thoughts and said, 'Society is valueless and money will not last for ever. He who doesn't engage himself in remembering God will die grieving. We are sufficient unto ourselves.'[5]

[1] On healing by *'azīma* see p. 167.

[2] Leather ablution bottle. Here he makes incantation in the water itself, not by washing words off a *lōḥ*.

[3] Op. cit. M. 75, S. 78–9.

[4] Op. cit. M. 36, S. 38.

[5] Op. cit. M. 23–4, S. 25.

(3) *Metamorphosis* of themselves, or others, or things. We read of ʿAlī al-Labadī that:

ʿAbd al-Ḥafīẓ al-Khaṭīb Abū'l-Khaṭīb ʿAmmār asked for the hand of his sister who was called Labadiyya and his mother said to ʿAli, 'O Entranced, ʿAbd al-Ḥafīẓ, the son of butter and honey, wants to marry your sister.' He said to her 'Bring a capacious *zīr*, call the water-carrier and fill it with water.' She did as he ordered. Then he said, 'Bring another and fill it with water also', and she did it. But when he said 'bring a third and fill it', she and her women began to laugh and said, 'Fill us just these two'. But he said, 'Bring a third, the bounty of God is unbounded.' She refused, thinking that he was talking in a trance. Then he dipped his cudgel into the two *zīrs*, one after the other and stirred them saying, 'In the name of God the Compassionate, the Merciful, alif, bā, tā, thā, jīm, ḥā, khā.' Thereupon that water was transformed into yellow clotted butter and the second into honey. His mother said, 'Let us bring you the third.' He said 'The opportunity has gone.' Then they married ʿAbd al-Ḥafīẓ to Labadiyya.[1]

To-day they still say of any powerful feki, 'he is a feki who can curdle water'.[2]

(4) *Power over the elements*: levitation, walking on water; control over animals and inanimate objects.

Hajā ibn ʿAbd al-Laṭīf b. ash-Shaikh Ḥamad wad Zarrūq was born at Shanbāt. A wonderful *karāma* was manifested on his behalf[3] which was witnessed by Shaikh Khōjalī. He relates, 'the Shaikh Hajā married a woman of Tūtī Island called Zainab bitt Balla. He died one afternoon (*ʿaṣr*) and it was impossible for the people to take the bier to the East owing to the shortness of time and the river was in flood and overflowing the bank. While the people were wondering what to do, the sun changed from west to east. Thereupon they carried the corpse to the East and buried him with his fathers (on the mainland).' Someone said to Shaikh Khōjalī, 'Did you see this with your own eyes or did you hear about it?' He said, 'I saw it plainly, I and the other children were playing tip-cat (*ḍaqal*); and the people who were sitting in front of the mosque in the afternoon shade had to change over to the forenoon shade behind the mosque. The women ceased wailing and started luluings of joy.'[4]

Here is a flying story related of Muḥammad Qaili by Mūsā Wad Rayya:

I left Ḥalfāya for Egypt and with me was a *faqīr* called Wad Feki travelling for the pilgrimage. We were entertained at the *khalwas* of Muḥammad Qaili whilst waiting for the caravan. We used to pray the five daily prayers with him and one day we were awaiting him to lead us in the Morning Prayer when we saw him flying between heaven and earth. He alighted at the door

[1] Op. cit. M. 112, S. 119.
[2] Hū faki yarawwib álma (colloq.).
[3] Ẓaharat lahu karāma ʿajība.
[4] Op. cit. M. 169, S. 178.

of his *khalwa* and made a few hops as he alighted like a hawk. Then he entered his *khalwa* and didn't pray with us. As for Wad Feki as soon as he saw him flying immediately he left the *khalwa* a bewildered wanderer and no one has heard since whether he is living or dead. The Shaikh came out of the *khalwa* in a distressed state and counselled me to keep my mouth shut about what I'd seen.[1]

(5) *Restoring the dead to life*: It is related of the versatile Ḥasan wad Ḥasūna:

Wad Abbakr was drowned in the river at al-Khushshāb and remained three days under water. They asked Ḥasan to perform the prayers over his disciple. He said, 'I cannot be the same Ḥasan in the eyes of my Lord otherwise my disciple could not have been drowned for three days and I not know it.' When he saw the corpse he said 'Rise', and he rose and his spirit pervaded his body.[2] After that he married and had a son called Bakr. . . . It is related that Shaikh Ḥasan always went bareheaded. Shaikh Idrīs related, 'Shaikh Ḥasan said that if he put anything on his head and said to a dead person "rise", he will rise. A man came to him carrying two dead birds. The Shaikh took them, put the sleeve of his *qamīṣ* over his head and they flew away.'[3]

This *baraka* was not only used to do good but could be used destructively to punish evil-doers. The saint is then called *ʿaṭṭāb li-ẓ-ẓalama* (destroyer of tyrants):

Badowī wad Mirnāt seized by force the house of a disciple of ʿAbd al-Qādir ibn Idrīs called Abraq Abū Shaʿbān. The Shaikh sent a messenger to ask him (Badowī) about it. He took a handful of earth and said, 'give him this'. When the Shaikh heard about it he cursed him (*daʿā ʿalaihu*) saying, 'May this (i.e. earth) enter your mouth and come out of your anus.' Immediately it entered his mouth and came out of his anus and he died. Then the Shaikh went down to the river on his tawny horse to take a bath. They screened him with a *firka* (woman's wrap) whilst bathing. The brother of Badowī came and yelled from the east bank, 'You fellow there having a bath, what's that wailing from Shaikh Badowī's?' He didn't reply. Then the man shouted to him a second time and the Shaikh said, 'If God will, may you follow him,' and he died at that very moment, so they were both buried at the same time.[4]

They often seem to have used it too for their own purposes on someone who annoyed them. Those who disbelieve and scoff at their pretensions are made to suffer for it. The Sūdānīs are very susceptible to suggestion and the curse of such a man had great power. Their

[1] Op. cit. M. 158, S. 166–7.

[2] *Tamālat rūḥuhu*. According to Islamic thought *rūḥ* is a material or semi-physical substance; cf. *Kashf al-Maḥjūb* (196, 262) where it is called a fine, created substance (*ʿain*) or body (*jism*) placed in the sensible body like sap in green wood.

[3] Op. cit. M. 49, S. 51–2.

[4] Op. cit. M. 137, S. 145.

belief in fatalism kept them from questioning acts which we should consider immoral. We read in the biography of Sharaf ad-Dīn of such a cursing related as miracle:

He was honoured with many miracles. One of them is that he was afflicted with syphilis and the people of Nasrī said, 'the Shaikh has contracted syphilis.' So he prayed against them (*daʿā ʿalaihim*) with the words, 'O God, if (it is true that) I have not visited the place of syphilis, then smite them with it, by the power (*baraka*) of Shaikh ʿAlī wad Burrī.' Thereupon everything in Nasrī was smitten, human beings, animals, children, and even trees, were covered with ulcers.[1]

The process of canonization is continuous and new saints are always being added to the calendar. Omdurman, which is a new city,[2] though to-day the nerve-centre of Sudanese religious life, now has three *qubbas*, numerous other tombs, and at least a hundred *bayānāt*. One of the *qubbas* is that of Qarīb Allāh (d. 1930), a khalīfa of the Sammāniyya Order, whose following call his branch (*farʿ*) of the Order, the Qarībiyya. The other two are Dafʿ Allāh 'al-Gharqān' (d. 1917) of the Qādiriyya, a pupil of Muḥammad Badr, and Wad al Badawī (d. 1911) who is not a *walī*, but was *shaikh al-ʿulamā* in the early days of the present régime. In the Jezīra, the Yaʿqūbābī khalīfa, Shaikh Hājju ʿAbd al-Qādir al-Māsiʿ (d. 1930) became a recognized *walī* in his own lifetime.[3]

The Muslim idea of a holy man opens up a vast field for imposture and many who pose as such live immoral lives. There are always some such as Qarīb Allāh who have genuine claim to be honoured on account of lives of real piety and asceticism. Then there is the large group of fakis who have a reputation for the possession of *baraka* and magical powers. This group includes the heads of the dervish orders who in the Sudan have fekiship thrust upon them, and members of the many feki-families whose profession it is. They vary in the different areas. In the Jezīra with its tradition they are often genuine in the Islamic sense; in Kordofān generally charlatans, living on the people by their wits. Further, there are dervishes and idiots who may well be classed together. There was an idiot wandering about Omdurman,

[1] Op. cit. M. 92, S. 99. See also account of ʿAlī wad ʿIshaib, M. 107–8, S. 114–15.

[2] Omdurman existed before the Mahdiyya as an insignificant village and is first mentioned in the *Ṭabaqāt* as the residence of Ḥamad b. Muḥammad (1646–1730) whose tomb is south of Omdurman where it is called Wad Umm Maryūm. Omdurman grew up out of the camp which the Mahdī pitched there for the siege of Khartoum.

[3] Hājju lived in a hollow tebeldi tree during the Mahdiyya, having entered through a cleft which later closed up. Years afterwards the cleft opened again and he had acquired such fame that the Yaʿqūbāb asked him to become their shaikh.

who died recently, whom all the women called *walī* Dā'ūd. Lane's words hold good for the Sudan too when he wrote 'most of the reputed saints of Egypt are either lunatics, or idiots or imposters'.[1]

It might be well to say something about the characteristic type of living holy man. One who is alive will rarely be called a *walī*. That term is reserved until, after his death, he proves his right to the title by the continued exercise of power from his tomb. The general term is the vague one of *faki*[2] 'which is applied indiscriminately to the scholar and the mystic and, at the lowest point of the scale, to the ignorant hedge-priest and to the dubious dealer in charms and amulets'.[3] Le Comte d'Escayrac de Lauture's remarks still hold good for a great part of the Sudan:

> We find in the villages only a clergy of a secondary order; a clergy low and poor, unknown elsewhere, holding their powers only by the general confidence, living on alms and privations. . . . Men of this category are called fekis. Many have accomplished the pilgrimage to Mecca, all can read (more or less fluently). All read the Qur'ān and some know it by heart. Each village at all important has its feki, it is he who teaches reading and writing to the children, presides at marriages and burials, fills the functions of judge or *qāḍī* in all minor disputes. He adds to these functions that of exorcist; he evokes at the bedside of the sick the demon who agitates them, writes on bits of paper the *sūrat al-Falaq*, a talisman which protects him who carries it from the obsessions of the enemy of men, and even, according to some, the injuries and illnesses to which they might be subjected. He draws from the sale of these talismans some small profits which enable him to live. This industry is quite innocent, the talismans do no one any harm and always produce a favourable effect upon the imagination. Besides the feki does not seek to deceive others, he believes as fervently as they in the efficacy of these hamaïl (charms). Nor does he limit himself always to exorcising the sick or administering to them bits of paper or the water in which a pious invocation has been washed, he often adds to this illusory medication the employment of vegetable essences of whose efficacy he has learnt through long experience or the traditions of his predecessors.[4]

Whilst most of this still holds good, it will be wise if one is told that So-and-so is a feki, to inquire what kind of feki. The word can have

[1] *Modern Egyptians* (Everyman), p. 234.

[2] Originally *faqīh*, jurisconsult. In the Sudan the word has been corrupted to *faki* with no precise meaning, though it seems to have reverted somewhat to the old sense of a wise person. The plural *fukahā*, is not used, *fuqarā*, the plur. of *faqīr*, being used instead, e.g. *waddar kullu mālu fi'l fuqarā*—he wasted his substance on *fakis*. *Faqīr* usually means a dervish, though it is sometimes applied to a *faki*. In other Arabic dialects the corruption *faki* signifies a *kuttāb*-teacher, which is only one of its usages in the Sudan.

[3] S. Hillelson, *J.R.A.S.*, 1937, p. 664.

[4] De Lauture, *Le Désert et le Soudan*, 1853, pp. 446–8.

many meanings: (1) If your cook produces a new *sufraji* and says he is a feki, all he probably means is that he is a 'pious' man (*rājil taqī*). Here again one must guard against reading a wrong meaning into the term pious, for he means no more than that he is strict in observing his religious practices, not that he is honest or trustworthy. (2) He may be a *healer*. As such he is primarily a religious man whose function it is to supply preventive charms and to heal by means of prayer, charms, and incantations, or, in the case of serious illness, by more elaborate methods of exorcism. This kind of fekiship is usually hereditary, and his power has much to do with that and his reinforcement of it by cures and, if necessary, some supernatural manifestation. Although to-day the people are making increasing use of hospitals in the case of illness, they will still visit the feki to make doubly sure, because of the place the 'unseen' holds in their lives. They believe too that they can detect a thief, locate the stolen articles, and cure the effect of the evil eye. (3) Holders of certain offices, such as the head of a dervish order. Here it is a question of unusual power, since he inherits the *baraka* of a dead saint ancestor. The founder of the Ismāʿīliyya was always known in his lifetime as the feki Ismāʿīl.[1] In this group women will sometimes be found such as ʿAlawiyya and Maryam al-Mirghanī. Again the guardian of a *qubba* has this title. He is usually a descendant of the dead saint. (4) Finally, it is applied to the schoolmaster of a *khalwa* or Qur'ān-school. In the village community he is still a very important figure. With the minimum of knowledge he tries to teach reading and writing but mainly the memorization of the Qur'ān. He also acts as imām in the communal prayers.

In the past the functions of (2) and (4) were inseparable and to-day they overlap considerably. Most fekis of *khalwas* are healers; but the exercise of such functions by those who are in any way brought under the general educational scheme of the government is not encouraged. Although the gradual spread of modern education is modifying their influence among limited sections of the population, the fekis are still a power in the land.

3. *Shrines and Practices connected with them*

The people may not always be sure of the efficacy of the *baraka* of living fekis, but they have a blind faith in that of their dead saint, normally spoken of as 'our shaikh' and always as though he were living. He is in fact supposed to be slumbering and manifests himself to people in dreams or trances. His powers to bless or blight cover

[1] See de Lauture, *Le Désert et le Soudan*, 1853, p. 448.

almost every category of human need.[1] His power is testified by the miracles performed on behalf not only of one's dead ancestors, but also of one's living family. It is impossible to manage one's affairs properly without his help, whether it is the curing of a sick child, the winning of a wife, or the blessing of children.

The tombs of these holy men are to be found chiefly along the Main Nile north of Khartoum and the Blue Nile from Khartoum to Sennār, they are less frequent on the White Nile and there are others scattered in most settled districts. In Kordofān the various local fekis are buried under a tree with only a couple of stones and a few fluttering flags to mark the site.

There are various kinds of shrines, for any place that is in some way connected with a saint may partake to some degree of his *baraka*.

1. There is the *qubba*, the domed tomb of a noted saint. It may be a square *jālūṣ* building with an egg-shaped dome,[2] or a high *tukl* of the same conical shape. This is erected over his grave which is often the place where he died. His *baraka* must naturally be strongest at the place where he lived and died and still spends a great deal of his time. Not every *qubba*, however, marks the burial place. Sometimes it may be no more than a memorial shrine, or it may be the place where the placenta of the saint was buried.[3] There is one such at Jadīd where

[1] In view of this universal veneration for the saints it is surprising to discover this proverb 'I supposed the *qubba* held a saint' (*ana qāyil fi'l qubba shaikh*) as the equivalent of 'all that glitters is not gold'.

[2] This type of Sudanese *qubba* also appears among the nomads of the High Algerian Plateau and 'follows the local style of building in clay of the nomad country with the egg-shaped dome and the usual tapering lower structures' (*Enc. Is.*, Suppl. vol., 128). Burckhardt (*Nubia*, 274) gives a sketch of a cone-shaped tomb and remarks that he only saw two such during his journeys. The *qubba* of Shaikh Idrīs al-Majdhūb at Kuēka is of the stepped *maṣṭaba* form almost as old in Egypt as the First Dynasty. The normal *qubba* is on this form:

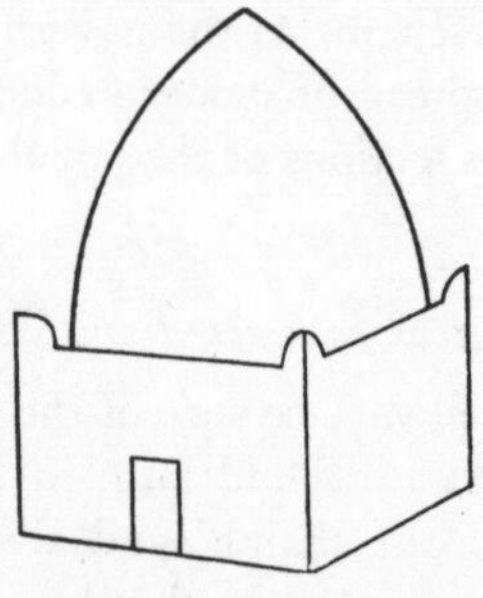

[3] Seligman believed that in ancient Egypt the placenta was regarded as the double, physical and spiritual, of the infant it had nourished (*Hamitic Problem*, p. 658). Among sections of the conglomerate of Omdurman a similar belief prevails.

Bakrī wad Idrīs was born, others are that of Bakrī b. 'Abd Allāh b. Ḥasōba at Sōba Bakrī who is buried at Umm Laban on the White Nile; also at Bāra that of Al-Ḥasan, son of the founder of the Mirghaniyya, who is buried at Kasala. *Qubbas* are usually in charge of a feki who is a descendant of the dead saint; sometimes the khalīfa appoints the guardian. He is maintained by the community and the gifts of pilgrims.

2. Secondly, there are simpler mud buildings with a flat roof or a *tukl* in the form of an ordinary *quṭṭiyya* (often called *ḍarīḥ*); others with no roof at all, just a plain *turba* marked at head and foot and with four mud walls around it. Especially numerous are shrines called *bayān* (manifestation) which mark the places where a saint has been seen in a dream. Omdurman, not having many saints' tombs, is full of them. There is one outside my house and I have been told that some devotee dreamt that he met a *walī* called Shaikh Mas'ūd at that spot. The *walī* told him that his *baraka* would adhere there to help people and to receive honour. The man then built a mud wall and women visit it and leave their *karāma* in the form of small coins, coffee, &c., which are then taken by the poor or children. At Wad Medanī there is an unusual *bayān* to Ḥasan the son of Muḥammad 'Uthmān al-Mirghanī which is built of brick with a roof of reeds. Inside is a *turba*, though there is no body there, covered with a purple pall, at one end of which is a hole containing earth to be taken to the sick to bestow his *baraka*. *Bayāns* to Sīdī Ḥasan, as he is known, are very numerous: I have seen three at least in Omdurman. Some *banayāt* are visited for special services. There is one in Khartoum of Shaikh Maḥmūd Abū Shaiba, who is buried at Nōfalāb, which is visited by bridegrooms on their wedding night, as also are the tombs of Khōjalī and Ḥamad at Ḥalfāya.

3. There are shrines marked by neither building nor *turba*, except perhaps a ring of stones or a cairn sometimes with a stick and a flag. Such enclosures are often *bayānāt*, or they may mark the spot where a saint went into retreat or performed a miracle.

4. There are further various holy places and objects which are associated with saints and partake of his *baraka*; or, in districts till recently pagan, they may be objects, such as trees, springs, wells, rocks, once associated with pagan worship, now personified or identified with saints.

The *qubba* is always a sanctuary (*ḥaram*), and sometimes the fenced area around it. It therefore acts as an asylum for people fleeing from vengeance or justice. There is a general feeling too that wild animals should not be killed near a tomb; for it is possible that such an animal may have some connexion with the saint, many of whom granted their protection to certain animals. Among the Bishārīn and ʿAbābda is the curious belief that animals sacrificed at a tomb turn into gazelles or ibex which enjoy the protection of the *walī*, who punishes any attempt to shoot them.[1]

The saint, too, protects objects deposited at his tomb for safe-keeping. Ploughs will be left by cultivators whose *dura*-patches are scattered over a wide area. MacMichael mentions having seen such articles as a hair-tent, bowls, grindstones, left by Arabs at the tomb of Ḥasan wad Ḥasūna until their return at the end of the season.[2] Merchants going to Egypt still leave surplus goods at the grave of Abū Ḥamad as when Caillaud passed in 1821. Hair, nail clippings, and teeth are often left to prevent others getting them for purposes of witchcraft. Dust or stones taken from their graves also protect. They are usually attached to the cross-beam of an unused *sāqiya* (water-wheel) to prevent its being stolen. The most solemn oath that can be taken for most people is that at their saint's tomb, whereas they do not mind swearing falsely on the Qur'ān.

The manner of worship at tombs is very simple in character. It is quite free, with no fixed forms of devotion, though since most are connected with a *ṭarīqa*, there are set methods of saying the Fātiḥa, special Qur'ānic passages and *murāqabāt* (meditations). Visiting a tomb is called a *ziyāra*. If regular visits are not paid to them the saints tend to appear in dreams to complain and utter threats. The visitor at his first sight of the shrine 'draws' the blessing of the saint by first saying the Fātiḥa holding out and looking at the palms of his hands, then raises his hands and draws them down his face (*at-tabarruk*).

Two types of visits are paid to the tomb: one for the benefit of the saint and the other for the worshipper. The first is the paying of honour to the saint merely by the visit and the repetition of the Fātiḥa, but usually offerings (*zuwāra*) are brought—food, candles, incense, &c. Gifts are usually made at the various stages of life, such as the shaving of a child's head, circumcision, marriage, to secure their protection. Failure to do so might cause harm to fall on the child. The people firmly believe that the saint enjoys the immaterial 'substance' of the food, &c., offered him. Orthodoxy says that, since the distribution of food is a pious work, the 'merit' of this, which normally would be received by the alms-giver, is transferred to the saint. The materials must be consumed, either burnt in his honour (candles, oil, incense) or eaten by a living person, preferably the feki in charge, the poor, or

[1] G. W. Murray, *Sons of Ishmael*, p. 154.

[2] *Hist.* ii. 287.

children. The important thing is the *intention* to transfer the 'substance' or the 'merit' to the saint.

For the second, the worshipper sits or stands facing the shrine and tells the saint of his desires or troubles and, in order to move his compassion more effectively, makes a conditional vow (*nadhr*) that if the saint is gracious, he will return and hold a Qur'ān-reading, or make a sacrifice (*dhabīḥa*), or whitewash his tomb, or give money to the poor. The night of 27th Ramaḍān (*Lailat al-Qadr*) is believed to be especially propitious for making requests. When a vow is made, sometimes they go alone, sometimes with a few friends, or, if it is a very special desire, in procession. Failure to carry out the vow after the granting of the request would be visited with the direst of consequences, such as the illness or death of a son who has been granted. Stories of such catastrophes are common. Amongst most groups visits are paid to the shaikh's tomb during marriages, circumcisions, and other festivals. Sick animals are also taken to a tomb and driven around it seven times.

Contact with a shrine is believed to be beneficial, therefore in order to keep the saint in mind of the request something which has been in contact with the person is usually left. Normally this is a piece of rag attached to the door or to sticks planted in the walls for that purpose.

A saint is believed to retain his living characteristics after death. Therefore if he was noted for a particular miracle during his life he continues to exercise that power. Sometimes a particular cure becomes his speciality only after his death. Thus the *qubba* of Al-Khōjalī at Ḥalfāya is good for children cutting teeth, that of 'Abd al-Ma'rūf at Berber for evidence; most people will be very chary of swearing falsely at his tomb. Mud from the tomb of Aḥmad wad aṭ-Ṭaraifī near Wad Medani is good for curing dog bites, hence the saint is called Aḥmad Dābī as-Sa'ar (the viper, i.e. enemy, of rabies). If you have been robbed, a nail driven into the ground before the *bayān* of Shaikh Zinzīr in Khartoum will result in the Shaikh visiting you during sleep and showing you or telling of the thief.

The *qubba* of Shaikh Aḥmad Ṭaraifī of Ṭalhatain and the eighteen 'Arakī *qubbas* at Abū Ḥarāz, especially that of Sharīf Yūsuf Abū Shara, are famous for fertility. The women must spend seven Thursday nights inside or outside the *qubba* within its area. They are usually accompanied by their husbands and other relatives and the night is spent in drinking and singing. After the seventh night the khalīfa gives them a paper inscribed with Qur'ānic verses. If they conceive successfully, they bring the child to the khalīfa when it is four months old. He shaves it and the mother gives him a *waqiyya*

(1·32 oz.) of gold for a boy and half the amount for a girl. These visits are very popular and lorry-loads of women will arrive from Wad Medani and surrounding villages on Thursday nights.

The saints who were fools during their lifetime are still regarded as such. The Bishārīn have one in Wādī O Sirairāb and 'to obtain his favour it is sufficient to take a sheep there, make the usual little pile of stones to cover the blood, notify the saint that the sheep has been slain in his honour, *and take the animal away again*'.[1]

Some saints have acted as oracles from their tombs. In the account of Medanī an-Nāṭiq b. ʿAbd ar-Raḥmān, we read:

> The reason for his being called the Oracle (an-Nāṭiq) is that when he died the people disputed as to who should succeed him. Some suggested the Khalīfa Mālik because he was exceedingly learned; others the *feki* Shaikh al-Aʿsar (the left-handed) owing to his piety and asceticism. The dispute waxed long when one of the 'westerner' *fekis* sat down before the tomb and said to the Shaikh Madanī 'the people are disputing about your successor'. He then replied from his tomb, 'the Khalīfa is Shaikh'. This man (i.e. Shaikh) was his full-brother. The feki went and informed the people of what Madanī had said. An 'easterner' would not believe it, saying, 'you are a liar'. So the people went to his tomb and the entrance straitened upon the denier so that he feared destruction. They then gave the appointment to the feki Shaikh.[2]

The *Mūlid* or *Ḥōliyya* of a saint is the great village festival. Each year at the anniversary of the saint's birth or death—the great day of his reception into heaven—the inhabitants will be seen arriving at the tomb carrying their offerings. If it is a famous saint they will come from the whole area. It is at the same time a homage to the saint and an expression of the need for an ideal beyond the tomb. On arrival they carry out the traditional rites: tour of the *qubba*, chantings of *mūlids*, and usually a *dhikr*. It is a time of general rejoicing and the meeting of friends, as well as of religious observances, for religion and social life are inseparably bound up together. Pedlars are always present and at some *mūlids* a *sūq* is set up.

The *Mūlid an-Nabī*, the anniversary of the Prophet's birth, is to-day the most important of all such festivals since it is celebrated

[1] G. W. Murray, *Sons of Ishmael*, p. 152.

[2] *Ṭabaqāt*, M. 159, S. 167; also repeated in biography of Shaikh al-Aʿsar, M. 90, S. 97. Cf. also a similar story of Bān an-Naqā, M. 36, S. 38; and the following from Doughty's *Arabia Deserta* (ii. 160): 'Amân told me of a yearly miracle in the cave of Bedr Honeyn, where lie buried the "Martyrs" that fell in the Néby's first battle with the (unbelieving) citizens of Mecca. "On a certain day, when the people go thither on pilgrimage, they hear as it were a blissful murmur within of the martyrs' voices. And they only may enter in who have preserved their lives pure from grievous crimes: but the polluted, and wrongdoers . . . be not able to pass; for the passage straitens before them, and in the midst they stick fast".'

universally over the whole of the Sudan even in the smallest villages, and with great brilliancy in Omdurman and other towns. Although it is not one of the official festivals ordained by law and came to the Sudan as late as the Egyptian period, it has in fact received general recognition because of popular sentiment.[1] During the Mahdiyya it was celebrated by a great parade in the presence of the Khalīfa lasting four hours. The present Government have given it official recognition.

Though the 12th of Rabī' al-Awwal is accepted as the birthday of the Prophet and the chief feast-day (the actual celebration is the eve of the feast), the commemoration occupies the whole of the preceding week. On 1st Rabī' I all the principal towns have a procession (*zaffa*) which starts from the government headquarters in the town, proceeds along all the principal streets, and ends up in the *mūlid* square. It is headed by a band followed by the *ma'mūr* and other officers with mounted police, then come the *ṭarīqa* groups on foot with flags and drums, the general public on horses, donkeys, or on foot, and is completed with a string of carts carrying lustily yelling children.

At Omdurman sections of the large square, which was once the *jāmi'* of the Mahdī, are allotted to some twenty or more different *ṭarīqa* groups[2] who erect large and small tents (*siwāns*) according to their means. In the matter of show there is a yearly competition between the Mirghaniyya and the Mahdiyya group. The Government and the 'Umda of the town also have tents. Torchlight processions to the square are a feature of the celebration. Outside the *jāmi'* are the usual stalls and amusements inseparable from any festival. Private *mūlids* are held in houses and these culminate in a feast.

Throughout this week recitations of *mawālid* are held.[3] These are panegyrics in poetry or rhymed prose based on the legendary life of the Prophet, just those stories which are most untrue receiving particular attention, and concluding with a *dhikr* in the case of the dervish orders. The Mahdist Sect chant all kinds of extravagant poems (*anāshīd*) in

[1] It is a late development in Islam. Maqrīzī (ii. 292 f.) describes celebrations in A.D. 1122 during the Fāṭimid period, but these did not become a matter of popular observance until the time of the Seljūqs, when, as part of the religious reaction of the period, they became associated with popular Ṣūfism.

[2] It may be of interest to record the groups in 1939: Khatmiyya (1), Aḥmadiyya (2), Bayūmiyya (1), Rifā'iyya (1), Sammāniyya (4), Ismā'īliyya (1), Qādiriyya (9), 'Azmiyya (1), Khalwatiyya (1).

[3] The *mawālid* I have found in the Sudan are: Al-Barzanjī (Qādiriyya and Sammāniyya); Ad-Daib'i (?), Al-'Azab (Yemanīs in the Sudan); Yūsuf al-Hindī (Sammāniyya); Muḥammad ibn al-Mukhtār ash-Shanqītī (Tijāniyya); Muḥammad 'Uthmān (Mirghaniyya); Ismā'īl al-Walī (Ismā'īliyya). A description of such a recitation is given on pp. 215–17. The *Burda* of al-Būṣīri, a panegyric of the Prophet, is recited at home and mosque gatherings.

honour not only of the Prophet, but of the Mahdi and especially of his son, the present leader. The recitation of *mawālid* is not confined to this week but is now a feature of the regular gatherings of many dervish orders.[1]

B. ESCHATOLOGICAL ELEMENTS

1. *Belief in a Mahdī*

The messianic elements in Muslim thought have played a great role in the history of the Sudan and a few general remarks are necessary if we are to understand the specifically Sudanese manifestation. The myth of the Second Coming of an historical figure has, since the days of Judaism and Christianity, been adopted by other peoples and groups who have been in a disappointed or frustrated state. In Muslim lands the concept was derived in the first place through converts to Islam, and quickly established itself in popular belief. As the years went by Muslims became dissatisfied with the worldliness of their rulers, some turned to asceticism as an escape, whilst the masses clung to the idea of a future deliverer who would restore Islam to its pristine purity before the End.

Eschatological tradition ascribed to the Prophet began to circulate early. These declared that the Last Day would be heralded by a period of confusion and oppression brought to an end by the appearance of one called the Mahdī (the God-guided one). The chiliastic kingdom of the Mahdī would then be destroyed by the Dajjāl (Anti-Christ),[2] but the Prophet ʿĪsā would return, kill the Dajjāl, and fill the earth with justice by ruling according to the Law of Islam. This doctrine about the Mahdī constitutes the main line of divergence between Sunnī and Shīʿa, but we are not concerned here with Shīʿa doctrine because it did not affect the Sudan.

Orthodox Sunnī belief attempted as usual to incorporate the belief of the masses, but many did not go so far as to introduce a new element, that of the Mahdī. Strict orthodoxy, it is true, states that there will be a final restorer of the faith in the Last Days, but that he will be the Prophet ʿĪsā (al-Masīḥ al-Muhtadī—the rightly-guided Messiah). This belief is based on *Sūra* xliii. 61, 'and He (Jesus) shall be a sign of the Last Hour'.[3] Farther than this the Ḥanafites did not care to go, though the other Madhhabs have admitted a Mahdī belief in a modified form. Neither of the two great collectors of Traditions, Muslim

[1] See Chap. VI, p. 216. [2] From Aramaic—*meshīḥā daggālā*.

[3] This is the accepted Muslim interpretation, though Prof. Margoliouth once suggested to me that probably the passage should be translated, 'Verily there is knowledge of the Hour.'

and Bukhārī, nor the great systematic theologians, mention the Mahdī. Al-Baiḍāwī gives what he regards as accepted as follows:[1]

Jesus will descend on a hill in the Holy Land called Afīq. In His hand He will hold a lance with which He will slay the Dajjāl. He will then enter Jerusalem at the time of the morning *ṣalāt*. The Imām will make way for Him, but He will refuse and perform prayer behind him, following the rites of the Law of Muḥammad. Thereupon He will kill the swine, break the Cross, destroy the chapels and churches and kill the Christians, except those who believe in Him.

But the masses came to have a passionate belief in the future saviour called Al-Mahdī. Ibn Khaldūn states this popular belief in his Muqaddama:

It is a universal belief amongst the Muslim masses throughout the ages that at the End of Time a man of the family of the Prophet must manifest himself to confirm the faith and proclaim justice. The Muslims will follow him and he will establish his rule over the Islamic Kingdoms. He will be called the Mahdī. The appearance of the Dajjāl after him and what succeeds him are among the signs of the Hour which are based on sound tradition. 'Īsā will either descend after the Mahdī and kill the Dajjāl, or He will descend with him and assist at his killing. He will follow the Mahdī as Imām in worship.[2]

Around this belief were built up all kinds of signs which would presage the coming of the Mahdī and prove his mission. One is that he should bear the same name as his ancestor, the Prophet, Muḥammad ibn 'Abd Allāh, following an alleged tradition, 'his name will be as my name and his father's name as my father's name'. He will resemble the Prophet in disposition (*khulq*), but not in appearance (*khalq*).

The messianic doctrine of Islam is at once both political and religious and an exceedingly important element to be taken into account in the constitution of the Muslims of Africa. It sunk very deeply into the popular mind in its moderate (non-Shī'a) form and whenever the people have been oppressed by their rulers, Mahdīs have tended to arise in response to their longing for a deliverer. Since Islam does not distinguish between Church and State, the result has been that any religious reformer must inevitably use political means, preach the *jihād*, not only against polytheists but against other Muslims, and, if successful, form a state. In Africa, where the Arab-Negroid and Arab-Hamite peoples form very susceptible material to mass suggestion, with their innate anthropolatry saving the would-be-Mahdī the laborious work of gaining adherents, Mahdīs have been especially

[1] Comm. on Sūra xliii. 61. Cf. Bukhārī, *Anbiyā'*, § 49.

[2] Cairo ed., p. 218.

frequent and have almost always been reformers and deliverers, and whenever successful have inevitably founded states. One such was the Shīʿite propagandist Muḥammad ʿUbaid Allāh, the founder of the Fāṭimid dynasty, who manifested himself in A.D. 908 at Jebal Māssa, in north Morocco, and expelled the Aghlab dynasty from Tunisia, and whose dynasty overran Egypt and Syria in A.D. 969–70. Others were the 'Almohade' Muḥammad b. ʿAbd Allāh Ibn Tūmart, who, at the beginning of the twelfth century, introduced the heterodox Ismāʿīliyya doctrine into the Maghrib and proclaimed himself the Shīʿa Mahdī; and Muḥammad al-Mahdī, the second Sanūsī, who made use of his name to reinforce his claim.

In the Anglo-Egyptian Sudan the sole recorded instance of a Sūdānī proclaiming himself a Mahdī before Muḥammad Aḥmad is in the biography of Ḥamad an-Naḥlān (*d.* 1704), commonly known as Wad at-Turābī, who, during a pilgrimage to Mecca, claimed to be the Mahdī.[1] He was treated with scant courtesy there, but sent a messenger to the Sudan to announce his mission who was killed by King Bādī. There is no description of any characteristic Mahdī elements in his actions on his return. He was a *Malāmatī* and his claim to be the Mahdī was regarded as one of his excesses.

2. *Mahdism in the Sudan*

We have given but a brief historical sketch of the Mahdiyya,[2] because this period of history will already be familiar to all who are interested in the Sudan. Now we need to treat this drama from the religious-social point of view, to try to estimate its religious influence, to treat of innovations of doctrine and practice, and to see how this theocratic state was organized.

Muḥammad Aḥmad the Donqolāwī was neither an impostor nor utterly unscrupulous, otherwise this Sudan epic would be an effect without a cause. Muḥammad Aḥmad had been recreated through a profound spiritual crisis, and the Mahdiyya was the attempt to re-create in his own milieu the mutation which he had achieved in himself. The actual success of the movement it is true was not so much through its own strength, as through the weakness of its opponents. The people joined and died for the movement because they were in despair. But it must be remembered that a long period of tyranny had not been able to unite the Sudanese groupings. It was religion which provided the stimulus though economic conditions determined the response. The

[1] *Ṭabaqāt*, M. 59, S. 61–2; Hillelson, *Sudan Arabic Texts*, p. 181.

[2] See Chap. III, sect. 6.

result is that, because Muḥammad Aḥmad has lived, because he stirred the Sudan to belief in a divine order, the Sudan can never be the same again. New factors have been brought into play in the psychology of the Sudanese which every administrator must take into account, and which have little to do with the messianic expectations which were there before and still colour their lives.

The secret of Muḥammad Aḥmad's achievement was the strength of his personality and his power of influencing the susceptible Sudanese by suggestion. He was the 'leader', thrown up by the times, of a peculiar type of Sudanese nationalism. Behind all was his very real and unwavering belief in his divine call—a belief which exercised a compelling influence on others. His absolute certainty that he was the Mahdī of Allāh gave him an authority against which there was no appeal. As a simple Ṣūfī protesting against the worldliness and oppression around him he could accomplish nothing, but once convinced that he was the Mahdī, the divinely appointed leader proclaiming the millennium, the masses obeyed his call and swept triumphantly through the land.

To begin with, when convinced of his call, in order to provide the superstitious background, he selected from the mass of vague undigested Mahdist tradition those elements which applied to himself, such as his name and ancestry, the mole on his right cheek (the 'seal of prophecy'), and doctored others such as the site of Jabal Māssa.[1] He refers to many of these 'signs' in his letters and proclamations to support his claim.

He had followed the path of the traditional Sudanese Ṣūfī by being initiated into the Sammāniyya and Idrīsiyya orders and one of his early needs was to combat the ready taunt that he was but another *majdhūb* carried away in ecstasy and therefore not worthy of credence. In his manifesto to the people of Khartoum he writes:

> All that I have told you of my succession to the Mahdiyya was told to me by the Lord of Being (the Prophet) when I was awake and in good health, free from all transgressions of the Law, not in a state of sleep or ecstasy (*jadhb*), nor of drunkenness, nor madness, but enjoying a sound mind, keeping to the *sunna* of the Prophet, adhering to what he ordered and avoiding what he forbade.[2]

In spite of his defence his Ṣūfī background is evident in his letters,

[1] He performed a *hijra* to Jabal Qadīr in the Nūba Mountains which he renamed Jabal Māssa, in accordance with the belief that the Mahdī will come from the hill of the name where the people will swear allegiance to him (cf. Al-Qurṭabī (1272), *Tadhkira*). The Jabal Māssa of the Mahdist tradition is in the Maghrib.

[2] Shuqair, *Tārīkh as-Sūdān*, iii. 123.

'the Prophet said to me, "you are created from the light of the inmost depths of my heart"'.[1] In his reliance upon visions, too, he followed the traditional type of Sudanese holy men and in all his letters he brings forward visions of the Prophet and saints as the main proof of his mission:

As God had preordained to confer upon His humble slave the highest succession (*khilāfa*) from God and His Prophet, the Prophet told me that I am the awaited Mahdī and appointed me to succeed him by repeatedly making me sit in his chair in the presence of the four Khalīfas, the Quṭbs and al-Khiḍir. God helped me with His favourite angels, with the saints both living and dead from Adam to this day and likewise with the believing *jinn*. In time of war the Prophet appears in person with them before my army; likewise the Khalīfas, the Quṭbs and al-Khiḍir. He gave me the Sword of Victory, and I was told that no one, not even the *Thaqalān* (mankind and jinnkind), can defeat me when it is with me. The Prophet said to me, 'God has made for you a Sign of Mahdiship', and it is the mole on my right cheek. He made for me another sign as well—a banner of light will appear and will be with me in time of war and ʿAzrā'īl will carry it. God will strengthen my friends with it and fear will descend into the hearts of my enemies.[2]

Mahdist State Organization. The Mahdiyya was a new world state—the rule of God on earth. It was revolutionary in character. Only one allegiance was possible. It was the tie of faith alone which could prevail over tribal bonds and feuds so that concerted action could be taken. So they were given a universal name of *darāwīsh* which arose because of the patched *jubba* (called *maraqqaʿa*, another sign of equality) worn by his followers. This name was later changed to the more honourable one of *anṣār*—they were to consider themselves the equivalent of the Prophet's *anṣār*. The decree ran:

All the faithful have already been cautioned not to call themselves *darāwīsh*, but *ansār*, that is to say, those whose hearts are entirely consecrated to God and whose souls have become enlightened by a desire to possess the joys of the world to come, quitting the pleasures of this life and having full faith in the power of the Almighty who has created Paradise for those who are truly faithful to Him. The joys of Paradise are such as eye hath not seen, nor ear heard, nor hath entered into the heart of man to conceive. A man who is in hope of gaining such a reward should certainly cease to be called a *darwīsh*, that is to say a poor man. But, on the contrary, he should be called an intelligent, far-seeing man, a defender of God's cause, a follower of God's will, an abstainer from all things which would displease Him.[3]

This change also symbolizes the change of direction. The Mahdī did

[1] Shuqair, op. cit. iii. 122. [2] Ibid. iii. 122.

[3] R. F. Wingate, *Mahdism and the Egyptian Sudan* (1891), pp. 47–8.

not want it to be thought that his movement was in any sense a new *ṭarīqa*. He was the initiator of a new world order.

Devotion to the Mahdī naturally dissolved all tribal and religious allegiances. The dervish orders were abolished because loyalty to the shaikh conflicted with loyalty to him. The four *madhhabs* also could have no further significance and one universal ritual was adopted.

Those who denied the claims of the Mahdī were not even Muslims: 'the Prophet informed me saying "he who doubts your Mahdiship is a disbeliever in God and His Apostle"'.[1]

He exacted a *bai'a* (oath of allegiance) from his followers. In the case of an important adherent it was given with the hand in that of Mahdī, grasping his thumb, and repeating the formula sentence by sentence after him as at the initiation into a *ṭarīqa*. The normal method was repetition of the formula by a whole group of adherents without the handclasp. The formula after the *basmala* ran:

> We swear allegiance to God, His Prophet and to you, by God's unity, that we will not associate anything with Him, nor steal, nor commit adultery, nor accuse anyone falsely, nor disobey you in rightful things. We swear that we will renounce this world, being content with what God has decreed, desiring God's mercies in this world and the next, and that we will not flee from the *jihād*.[2]

The people who were most susceptible to his call were especially the *muzāri'īn*, the most oppressed, who were longing for a deliverer. Then followed detribalized blacks, Danāqla, and certain Arab tribes, especially the Baqqāra, who are fanatical and susceptible to feki-suggestion and to whom the attractions were fighting and love of booty. The Baqqāra, being rich cattle-owners, were at first very apathetic. They attacked Hicks's rearguard, but did not join in the march to Khartoum. When they did come over fully they formed the backbone of the military strength of the Mahdiyya. Most other nomad tribes violently opposed a system which abolished their inherent tribal constitution. The *muzāri'īn* of the Jezīra, not having been severely oppressed and with their loyalties to their religious shaikhs, did not respond to the emissaries he sent when he was in Kordofān, but joined later like the rest of the Sudan from expediency.

The Beja remained uninterested, for they had been little affected by Egyptian rule, until the arrival of 'Osmān Diqna after the fall of El-Obeyd. When 'Osmān Diqna was sent to them by the Mahdī he was joined by the followers of the Majādhīb *ṭarīqa* and the worst elements of the tribes, but the majority always remained lukewarm, joining him

[1] Shuqair, op. cit. iii. 123. [2] Ibid., 139.

only when a general summons was issued, after which they again dispersed. Even this was only accomplished by heavily bribing the chiefs.

Whatever their motives for joining Mahdiyya, it had at first an extraordinarily unifying effect; tribal loyalties were abolished, Baqqāra and black slaves fought under one banner and the slave could rise to the highest positions in the state. There was equality between rich and poor, though it was an enforced communism, maintained by plunder. But after the Mahdī's death control passed from the hands of the riverain tribes to the wild Baqqāra followers of the Khalīfa ʿAbd Allāh, whose rule exhibited military autocracy at its worst.

Winston Churchill well described the changing character of Mahdist fanaticism when he wrote:

> All the warlike operations of Mohammedan peoples are characterised by fanaticism, but with this general reservation it may be said—that the Arabs who destroyed Yusef, who assaulted El Obeyd, who annihilated Hicks fought in the glory of religious zeal; that the Arabs who opposed Graham, Earle and Stewart fought in defence of the soil; and that the Arabs who were conquered by Kitchener fought in the pride of an army. Fanatics charged at Shekan; patriots at Abu Klea; warriors at Omdurman.[1]

The organization of the Mahdist state, like that of the Prophet and for the same reasons, was military in character. The Mahdī chose four Khalīfas: ʿAbd Allāh the Taʿaishī who succeeded him, ʿAlī Wad Ḥilū, the Shaikh Muḥammad as-Sanūsī of Kufra, and Muḥammad Sharīf, his cousin. The Sanūsī declined his invitation.[2] The policy of the Khalīfa was to divide and thus weaken the tribes. Each subsection would be given its own independent *amīr*. The Jezīra, for instance, was under a Donqolāwī, Shaikh Muḥammad ʿUthmān Abū Jirja. Each flag (*ar-rāya*) was given its quota to furnish for the army. During winter and summer a large part of the population had to be present in Omdurman but in the 'rains' they returned to their cultivation and tax collection was made before their return to Omdurman.

An important institution was the *bait-al-māl*, the Treasury, or really the State Storehouse. There was a law that all spoil of war should be brought to the *bait-al-māl*, which financed the *jihād*. The *anṣār* were to be a kind of military caste; but this proved unworkable in practice, the *anṣār* were allowed to return to their cultivation periodically and a standing army was built up by the Khalīfa. When

[1] *The River War*, p. 36.

[2] The Mahdī's second letter to the Sanūsī is reproduced in Shuqair, op. cit. iii. 170–1. Wingate (op. cit., p. 36) says that the Mahdī then appointed Ādam Wad al-ʿIwaisir the third Khalīfa. I have not been able to confirm this.

the period of conquests was over the *bait-al-māl* was kept stocked by taxation and confiscations.

Taxation was based on the recognized *zakāt* in various forms.[1] The innovation was that this was not a tax, but a free-will offering for the poor and was made a direct government tax. Over each area (*jism*), following the custom of the Prophet, an *'āmil* (agent) was appointed to be responsible for tax collection and see that religious regulations were followed. The *jism* was again divided into sub-districts called *shūnas* (lit. granaries). Agents collected through local shaikhs of tribes or areas who were known as *muttaḥidīn* (contractors or tax-farmers). The system in practice involved every form of oppression and together with army recruitment led to deep resentment of the new order.

Doctrine and Practice of the Mahdist State. The teaching and precepts of the Mahdī were those of a visualized primitive Islam which was communicated to him by direct revelation. His rigorous ordering of life shows analogies with the Wahhābī rule, although there is no evidence of any direct Wahhābī influence and certainly the bases of Muḥammad Aḥmad and 'Abd al-Wahhāb were very different. It was a revolt against the new order of foreigners, begotten out of bitter suffering, to establish an ideal order.

The central point of his teaching upon which the organization was based was eschatological—the rule of God on earth through His representative, the Mahdī. The call to arms was the dominant note and the subjection of the Sudan was to have been followed by that of Egypt, Syria, 'Irāq, and Arabia. In a vision in 1883 the Prophet told him: 'that as I prayed in the mosque of El-Obeyd I should also pray in the mosque of Khartoum, then in the mosque of Berber, then in the mosque of Mekka, then in the mosque of Jerusalem, then Al-'Irāq, and then Al-Kūfa'.

Loyalty to himself as sole representative of God involved innovations in the practice of Islam. The 'Pillars of Faith' (*Arkān*) were changed:[2] (1) The *shahāda* had an addition—'I bear witness that there is no god but Allāh, and that Muḥammad is the Prophet of Allāh, and that *Muḥammad Aḥmad ibn 'Abd Allāh is the Mahdī of Allāh and the representative of His Prophet*'.[3] Doubt of his Mahdiship was an act of

[1] The four recognized forms of taxation seem to have been: (i) *zakāt*, one-tenth of crops and animals born, collected in kind; (ii) *fuṭrā*, originally an offering, but fixed by Khalīfa at a poll-tax of P.T. 1 per head; (iii) *hawāmil*, stray animals and slaves; (iv) *at-tabarru'* (lit. free gift) which was some form of super-tax to make up a bad year.

[2] Cf. Shuqair, op. cit. iii. 365.

[3] The additional words are '. . . wa anna Muḥammadan Aḥmada'bna 'Abdi'llāhi huwa mahdīyyu'llāhi wa khalīfatu rasūlihi'.

apostasy punishable by death. (2) The *jihād*, which was essential for the establishment of God's rule, took the place of the *ḥajj* which being unnecessary was forbidden.[1] Sunnī practice has never admitted the *jihād* as a pillar (*rukn*) of faith. (3) *Ṣalāt* in congregation. This practical method of social drill was given great emphasis as the symbol of unity. (4) Obedience to God's commandments as taught by the Mahdī, which he claimed to be based on the *sunna* of the Prophet communicated by direct revelation. He was preparing his own *sunna* in a work called the *majlis*, which was uncompleted at his death. (5) Recitation of the Qur'ān and the *Rātib* of the Mahdī. These came to be the only two books allowed in the Mahdiyya. Religious instruction disappeared, all learning was discouraged and all books of *sunna* and *tafsīr* were burnt. The burning of books is a common phenomenon in new dispensations. The *rātib* is a compilation of prayers, texts, and exhortations from the Qur'ān and *ḥadīth* in which no mention of himself and his pretensions occurs, which had to be recited twice daily after the *ṣubḥ* and *ʿaṣr* prayers and took about three-quarters of an hour.

The Mahdī set to work strenuously to reform the morals and revolutionize the customs of the Sudanese. He preached renunciation of all earthly vanities. He forbade intoxicants, tobacco, amulets, magic, music, processions, marriage and circumcision feasts,[2] mourning (*bikā*), and visiting saints' tombs—all of which are the very essence of Sudanese social life and all remained underground and returned in full after the Mahdiyya. The life of his followers was to be the life of men living in the Last Days: 'I destroy this world and I construct the world to come.'[3] As an example of his proclamations to asceticism, we may quote the following:

> Always pray whether you are walking or riding or with your friends. Abstain from all amusements, for through prayers alone can this world be kept in peace. Abstain also from the pleasures of music, do not beat the big and small drums .... Put aside everything that has the slightest resemblance to the manners and customs of Turks and infidels ... All their dresses, therefore, as well as drums, bugles, and other articles, must be put aside; adhere only to the customs of the *ṣaḥāba* (Companions of the Prophet). This is now the time to come to God and make a covenant with Him.[4]

Great stress was laid on the *jihād*. It was true, the Mahdī said, that

[1] By an ordinance of the Khalīfa, visiting the Mahdī's tomb was allowed as a substitute, though it was not to be regarded as a pilgrimage but a pious visit.

[2] The wedding ceremony was regulated and the bride price (*mahr*) reduced to £E.2 for a virgin and £E.1 for others. Those who asked for more were punished.

[3] Slatin, *Fire and Sword* (1895), p. 230.

[4] Wingate, op. cit., p. 59.

'God could destroy the infidel without war, but for the honour of His people He wished to carry out His design through them. It is said that the Turks can be reformed by sermons and preaching, but they can never be reformed except by the sword.' With the *jihād* was linked *liqā' bi'llāh*, the Beatific Vision, which gave such great confidence to his followers. In a vision the Prophet said to the Mahdī, 'these warriors who have gone forth for the religion of God shall be welcomed by God in the world to come. They shall be allowed into the paradise wherein are lofty palaces, chaste wives, and the greatest happiness and prosperity.'[1]

After the death of the Mahdī there was a natural decline in those who believed in him and his programme; but the Khalīfa worked strenuously to keep the faith of his followers alive. He reinforced his rule and flogged religious enthusiasm by broadcasting the visions he received from his old master. He enforced strictly the purely religious side of the Mahdī's revelations and was able to maintain the fierce fanaticism of many sections of his followers right up to the Battle of Omdurman.

3. *Persistence of Belief in a Mahdī and Mahdism*

Legends began to develop about the Mahdī long before his death. The Mahdī encouraged the Qāḍī Ismā'īl b. 'Abd al-Qādir, son of the founder of the Ismā'iliyya and one of his most devoted followers, to chronicle the events of his reign, and after the Mahdī's death the Khalīfa ordered its continuance.[2] The Mahdī, too, had his own poets, such as Muḥammad at-Tiwaim and Abū Sharī'a,[3] who eulogized him and the Khalīfa. These laid the foundations for the development of a Mahdist cult.

The death of the Mahdī before his mission was accomplished in no way discredited him in the eyes of his followers. The Khalīfa was careful to justify his actions and stimulate the zeal of his followers by alleged visions of the Mahdī, so that Mahdist fanaticism, more especially amongst his immediate following, continued though with diminishing force right up to the Battle of Omdurman. His tyranny

[1] Wingate, op. cit., p. 48.

[2] It was entitled: *Kitāb al-Mustahdī ilā sīrat al-Imām al-Mahdī.* Cf. Shuqair, op. cit. iii. 559–60; Slatin, op. cit., p. 515. It covered the years A.H. 1298–1306 (A.D. 1880–8). Ismā'īl fell into disgrace and all copies of this work were ordered to be burnt. Shuqair says that he was able to find a copy, but if it still exists it has never been published.

[3] A volume of Abū Sharī'a's poems has been published (Khartoum, 1931), but it only contains his poems in praise of the Prophet. He is stated to have burnt the others at the reoccupation. I have heard of collections, for they were certainly preserved by the reciters.

alienated the allegiance of the Mahdī's most devoted followers and, after his overthrow, the majority of the people accepted the new order passively, completely rejected the Mahdism which they had joined from religious enthusiasm or expediency or by force, and returned to their old tribal and religious allegiances. The nomad tribes were reconstituted, the riverain and Jezīra cultivators renewed their loyalty to their religious tribal shaikhs, the heads of orders such as the Mirghaniyya won back their followers, and the pagan tribes relapsed into paganism.

On the other hand, the Baqqāra were dissatisfied and longed for a return of the old times of blood and plunder, whilst certain groups of Arabs and cultivators—the old *anṣār* and especially the West Africans—maintained their allegiance to Mahdism. These die-hards, believing that Muḥammad Aḥmad was the true Mahdī,[1] believed that the other Mahdist prophecies were being or would be fulfilled. Lord Kitchener was given the role of the Dajjāl and some believed that the Mahdī's son 'Abd ar-Raḥmān was the *nabī* 'Īsā. The majority, however, still awaited his coming. Spurious prophecies began to circulate, such as that attributed to Farāḥ wad Taktōk: 'At the end of time the English will come to you, whose soldiers are called police: they will measure the earth even to the blades of the sedge-grass. There will be no deliverance except through the coming of 'Īsā.'[2]

Since the coming of the *nabī* 'Īsā was awaited with expectancy, 'Īsās (and in some cases Mahdīs) did appear with persistent regularity,[3] more especially during the early days of the reoccupation. The twenty or so risings which these fekis initiated have, however, never been widespread and have in most cases been localized to one district or the particular following of the feki. They have always appeared amongst ignorant and superstitious groups and in many parts of the Sudan, but especially in the Central Sudan and the west. A number of them have

[1] Kitchener, alive to the dangers of the development of a Mahdist cult, destroyed the body and the tomb of the Mahdī. I have come across the belief that the Mahdī's body still lies beneath the ruins, but it cannot be general because, whilst women will often be found praying at the gates of the enclosure, their number is surprisingly few compared with the crowds who visit other saints' tombs. This may be due to the fact that they have a living symbol of him to visit in the person of his son. [Since this was written the Government have allowed Sayyid 'Abd ar-Raḥmān to rebuild his father's tomb as an exact replica of the old one. The tomb was reopened on 15 June 1947 and since then there has been a great increase in the number of pilgrims.]

[2] Quoted from Hillelson, *Sudan Arabic Texts*, p. 159. Farāḥ lived in the seventeenth century.

[3] 'Īsās arose even in the Khalīfa's time after the death of the Mahdī, cf. account in Slatin, *Fire and Sword*, pp. 423–4, and Shuqair, op. cit. iii. 470–3, of the 'appearance' of a Takrūrī, Ādam Muḥammad al-Barqāwī, as the *nabī* 'Īsā in Gallabāt.

been Fellātas for there used to be a belief in the Blue Nile colonies that they would be led back to Nigeria by a Mahdī. They have been quickly suppressed by the authorities ever on the watch for such 'manifestations'.

The most serious was the Katfiyya Rising of 1908, when an old Mahdist, 'Abd al-Qādīr, a feki of Kāmlīn, preached a *jihād* and murdered a British official. This disturbance had most important consequences because it served to show the Government how closely linked were economic and social conditions with outbreaks of fanaticism; and was a contributory cause to the development of the Jezīra.

The Nyāla rising in southern Dārfūr in 1921 in which two British officials were killed had both economic and religious motives. There had been discontent in *dārs* Maṣālāṭ and Fellāta over the institution of a system of taxation, but when a feki arose proclaiming a *jihād* the people all developed religious motives. The rising as it developed was primarily anti-Christian and his followers felt they were driving out Ad-Dajjāl, that is the Christian Government. This feki was a Maṣālīṭī, 'Abd Allāh as-Siḥainī, and called himself, not the *nabī* 'Īsā, but 'the Khalīfa of God on His earth'. After he was captured he gave the following account of his call:

> one night . . . six angels came to me, named Zaibūn, Kalla, Mesrī, Zubardī, Ghōyā'īl, and 'Azrā'īl. They told me that this was the year 1340 and that I had been appointed to collect the people and lead a *jihād* against the *Turuk* to exterminate. After this I and my people would govern the land for 10 years. Then another leader would be appointed to continue the war. In 1370 the sun would rise in the west and set in the east. In 1380 would come the end of the world and the *nabī* 'Isā would appear.[1]

The last such outbreak was in Dārfūr in 1927 when a mixed Dāju-Fūr, who called himself 'the Pilgrim Feki' (*al-feki al-muhājir*), headed a purely local rising which was quickly quelled by a police sergeant.[2]

The passage of time has witnessed two developments in Sudanese Mahdism—the formation of a Mahdist propagandist cult and its running underground, and the organization of the bulk of Mahdist adherents into an orthodox religious society which is usually referred to as the neo-Mahdiyya.

As a cult Mahdism is a millenniarist sect. It regards Muḥammad

[1] Statement preserved in the 'Nyala Rising' File in Fāsher. There is a note on the Rising in H. A. MacMichael, *The Anglo-Egyptian Sudan*, pp. 136–7.

[2] A list of such risings is given in H. A. MacMichael's *Anglo-Egyptian Sudan*, pp. 98–9, 176–9.

Aḥmad as the true Mahdī and his son ʿAbd ar-Raḥmān as the *nabī* ʿĪsā after whom it is sometimes called Raḥmāniyya. He has not, however, 'manifested' himself and his followers await the Day of the Manifestation when he will drive out the British and usher in the millennium. This is believed more especially by colonies of 'westerners'[1] settled on Abā Island, his agricultural colony, along the White Nile, in the Jezīra and Kordofān, by the Baqqāra of western Kordofān and Dārfūr,[2] the Berti, Zaghāwa, Maṣālīṭ, and many other negroid tribes of Dārfūr. In Dārfūr, which was pagan in all but name before Mahdist agents arrived, the cult has canalized Islamic thought and feeling into this heretical current, so that the belief that ʿAbd ar Raḥmān is the *nabī* ʿĪsā whose 'time' is near is almost universal. The belief in sweeping through Dārfūr, which is connected more with the west than the east, has spread into French Sudan and Nigeria, especially Bornū and Wadā'i. There is a strong centre at Dumbulwa in Bornū and in Baqirmi where westerners are often influenced whilst on their way to Mecca.

Its rapid spread westwards is due to organized propaganda through agents among peoples filled with that widespread expectancy of a Messiah who will drive out the Christians which we have mentioned as a characteristic of West African Islam. By many of these followers a visit to ʿAbd ar-Raḥmān on Abā Island is regarded as a substitute for the Pilgrimage itself.[3] He is known as Aṣ-Ṣiddīq, the Truthful. Many perform two additional *rakʿas* in his honour and say *raḍī Allāh ʿanhu* whenever his name is mentioned. The following is the type of *madīḥ* they sing of him:

We pray God who answers prayers; the Lord has aided him in his rule.
The Prophet in whom the age puts its hope; follow him, O men of Islām.
The Mahdī in his day killed the unbelievers.
The Truthful One has saddled his horse; mounted on thoroughbreds he upholds the faith.

[1] This term includes negroid tribes of Dārfūr as well as Fellāta. Many of his most fanatical followers are Fellāta, especially those of Abā Island and cattle-owning nomad Fellāta. But of the two greatest emirs in the Sudan, Mai Wurno is Tijānī and Mai Aḥmad, ex-emir of Missau, Qādrī, with their followers. There was a spurious letter circulating in 1923 that Alfa Hāshim, Khalīfa of the Tijāniyya, had recognized the Mahdī as genuine, but Alfa Hāshim was at pains to refute the letter and visited his followers in the Sudan.

[2] The Taʿaisha are the only exception among the Baqqāra.

[3] This pilgrimage reached such proportions in 1923–5 that ʿAbd ar-Raḥmān was encouraged to go on the *ḥajj* to Mecca himself and agreed to discourage the pilgrimage to Abā. The volume of western visitors has slackened owing mainly to the efforts of the Government at interception and many tribal leaders oppose it because allegiance to Mahdism weakens their authority. It still goes on because the movement eastwards has economic as well as religious motives.

O Prophet bearing the mark of truth; he whose ancestor bore a birthmark on his shoulder.
Many a one who disobeyed him is fed on fire in the next world.
Disobey not the Truthful One; he beareth the very burden of the Mahdī.
I call upon you to turn to the pilgrimage (*to Abā*) with pure intention.
ʿAbd ar-Raḥmān, the Truthful, in a vision has called upon his horsemen.
Blessed is he who lives in his time, who believes his message, and obeys his commands.
He has ordered his affairs as in a *dīwān*; with the Mahdī's *wird* he leads us.
Our leader and our refuge; behold the gates of mercy open before us.
This is his time; behold the Mahdī and the Prophet before him.
He is the seal of all prophets; fully sealed with divine secrets.
The Prophet of mercy, the Lord of plenty; love for him has brought life to the Island.
He who is not with thee is blind of perception; he who loves thee thou wilt save in the next world.
O Lord, accept this verse containing greetings on him; and distinguish the poet with a mark.
The Truthful One has ordered his affairs; through thee I hope to attain salvation.
ʿAbd ar-Raḥmān, the Truthful; may the Lord exalt his state.'

Refrain (repeated after each line).
The Truthful One, the son of our Imām, has illumined the universe from childhood; be purified through him in his congregation.

There were evident dangers in this development of Mahdism and its rapid spread since 1917 beyond the original followers of the Mahdī to the Negroids of Western Sudan and Wadā'i, for these ignorant adherents are more readily inflamed to fanaticism by agents than in lands where orthodox institutions have been long established; but the Government were well aware of the dangers and prohibited Mahdist agents from Kordofān and Dārfūr.

Then there is the development of neo- or modern Mahdism in the Eastern Sudan. In the east a form of the cult exists, but it does not have the same milleniarist form or danger. Mahdiship became hereditary, not in the eldest son ʿAlī, but in ʿAbd ar-Raḥmān, a posthumous son by a Dārfūrian woman. His most devoted followers in the east are the surviving eastern *anṣār* and their less sophisticated children. To them the English are still *Turuk* and *Naṣāra*. 'We regard him as part of his father,' they have told me, 'his *baraka* descended into the Sayyid.' He is therefore to them the Mahdī not in himself, but as the bearer of the *baraka* of his father. He is not regarded as *nabī* ʿĪsā by his eastern followers. This is because they are somewhat more educated and sophisticated by contact with outside currents and are not attracted by the extreme manifestations of Mahdism. The majority of Eastern Sudanese are not his followers, but belong to a dervish order. In Dārfūr, on the other hand, there was no such pre-existent influence and the orders do not flourish there except amongst the 'foreigners' (i.e. easterners) of Al-Fās͟her itself.

Again, as a further development of the neo-Mahdism of the east there were many Sudanese, especially among the effendiyya, who revered the Mahdī as a great religious reformer and national leader, and ascribed the misgovernment of the Mahdiyya to the K͟halīfa. These felt an allegiance of a different kind to Sir ʿAbd ar-Raḥmān al-Mahdī Pās͟hā and came to look upon him as a national leader. ʿAbd ar-Raḥmān's own aspirations are secular rather than religious and he favours this development to increase his influence. He uses the general prestige which he inherits as son of the Mahdī and is ready to foster other forms of belief in himself since a mass of fanatical followers are a useful political weapon. He says, however, that he is 'the founder of a new movement, following the good order of the Government and the rules of justice and peace in general', and with no political aspirations. But he has a large following of the effendiyya whose motives are certainly political.

It was as a result of this development that Mahdism came to have the status of a religious and political society in Islam. It claims that it is not a new sect, and that it is quite orthodox; although that is impossible because it rejects the four *mad͟hhabs* for that of the Mahdī.[1] No claims are made openly for the Mahdī as such, nor for his son, nor is it opposed to the present Government; nor is it a *ṭarīqa* for it has no *d͟hikr* or esoteric teaching. Its followers recite the *rātib* of the Mahdī after certain prayers and they chant eulogies of him and his son at their gatherings. Many believe in Mahdism as a reformist movement and they observe such Mahdist prohibitions, like that against smoking, as do not cut across any deeply-rooted Sūdānī custom.[2] Attempts have been made to revive other of the Mahdī's regulations, such as in the £E.2 dowry campaign (called *al-Kōra*), but with little success outside the colonies. The annual 'day of weddings' (27 Rajab), instituted by the Mahdī in 1882, has for many years been kept up by his son.

[1] Opponents call the Mahdists *Al-K͟hāmsiyya*, i.e. members of the fifth *mad͟hhab* and by implication non-Muslims.

[2] The Mahdī wrote in one of his proclamations, 'Remember also that the crime of those who smoke tobacco is greater than that of drinking wine. He who drinks wine is punishable by eighty blows of the Kourbash, but the smoker of tobacco by one hundred blows' (Wingate, *Mahdism*, p. 62).

Fanaticism is a product of universal religions such as Islam and the psychology of the Western and certain Eastern Sudanese makes an outbreak of certain forms of it an ever present possibility, less perhaps in connexion with this new Mahdist group than through the appearance of the new Mahdī, for the mood of expectancy is already prepared. But there is little real danger whilst the Government maintains its vigilance and the present comparative prosperity continues, for disaffection arising out of poverty is the only thing that could cause such a rising to spread. They would be unwise to slacken this vigilance for this dormant but smouldering flame of Mahdism would be ready material for use in a political revolution in the Nile valley.

C. ANIMISTIC INFLUENCES IN SUDANESE ISLAM

1. *Islam and Animism*

Say, 'I seek for refuge in the Lord of the Daybreak,
from the evil in what he has created;[1]
from the evil of the moon when it is eclipsed;
from the mischief of women blowing on knots;
from the evil of the envious when he envies.' (Qur'ān cxiii.)

Assimilation of primitive religious elements was inherent in Islam from the beginning. The Prophet, being born into an environment deeply saturated with animism, had to reckon with and incorporate many such elements. He preserved, for instance, the primitive religious force associated with the fetish Black Stone at Mecca and harnessed it in the service of his own system. He was compelled to reckon with magic and witchcraft because he himself believed that 'the devil did teach sorcery to men' (Qur'ān ii. 96). He had revelations prohibiting the old sorcery *(siḥr)* and fortune-telling *(kihāna)*, but traditions exist in which he sanctions the use of spells: 'There is nothing wrong in using spells so long as you do not associate anything with God.'[2] These traditions, whether or not they derive from the Prophet, show the need felt by Muslims to justify the prevalence of magic among them and to find a religious sanction for it.

[1] Lit. 'From the evil of the night when it cometh on.' The above is ʿA'isha's interpretation (cf. E. H. Palmer (World's Classics), p. 537).

[2] *Mishkāt* xxi, c. 1; (see Hughes's *Dict.*, p. 72). *Bukhārī* (iv, c. 76) deals with sanctioned and prohibited magic. Exorcism, he shows from tradition, can be used to cure illnesses provided that the Qur'ān is used, the two *sūras* 113 and 114 (*al-muʿawwidhatān*) being valuable as incantations (§ 32). Magic (*ar-ruqya*) is useful against the evil eye and against poison (§ 37). Divination (*al-Kihāna*) is forbidden, and the true things the diviners (*al-Kuhhān*) sometimes say are stolen from the *jinn* (§ 46). Sorcery (*ṭibb*, *siḥr*) is forbidden (§ 49). Cf. Muslim, ii. 180–3.

From the beginning then an inner nexus was established between animism and Islam which enabled it to be so easily assimilated by the peoples of Africa and Asia and attracted kindred elements of their systems. By its inherent syncretism it can assimilate them, even though they may seem at utter variance with its doctrine.

These beliefs in wonder-working powers, in *jinn* and spirits innumerable, must not be regarded as mere excrescences, for although they may not be in harmony with Islamic Law, they are inherent in the Islamic system. The very remoteness of the Islamic conception of God necessitated the retention in its system of a world of intermediate spirit-beings which provided the monotheistic Muslim with an inner connexion with polytheism. Just as the early Christian Church assimilated into its system many pagan customs and seasonal festivals, so Islam absorbed all the irradicable beliefs and customs of its new adherents. Muslims could hardly continue to contemplate the persistence of forbidden things which they had no power to root out, so they were incorporated and made permissible by providing them with explanatory Muslim legends, formulae, and orthodox interpretations. Snouck Hurgronje writes:

> A custom or idea does not necessarily stand condemned according to the Moslem standard, even though in *our* minds there can be no shadow of doubt of its pagan origin. If, for example, Mohammedan teaching is able to regard some popular custom as permissible enchantment against the devil or against jéns hostile to mankind, or as an invocation of the mediation of a prophet or saint with God, then it matters not that the existence of these malignant spirits is actually only known from pagan sources, nor does any one pause to enquire whether the saint in question is but a heathen god in a new dress, or an imaginary being whose name but serves to legitimize the existing worship of some object of popular reverence.[1]

An Islamic colouring then may be given to assimilated animistic beliefs and practices simply by introducing the name of God, which is regarded as ensuring the efficacy of the incantations and practices. The belief in a wonder-working power (*mana*) becomes the *baraka* which God gives to certain humans, and which can be transmitted through relics, stones, trees, by association. So the belief in the materialization of spiritual values is carried on. Thus in practice the conception of the unity of God tends to be lost in the bewildering field of God's gift of *baraka*, since this is dispensed through persons and objects which may come to be regarded as the power itself

[1] Snouck Hurgronje, *The Achenese*, trans. A. W. S. O'Sullivan (1[illegible]

The effect of the coming of Islam amongst pagans, as H. A. MacMichael says, was to

> wrench the ancient custom from its original setting and *re-set* it in a modified form among the unobjectionable, if not quite orthodox, observances of the local True Believers; and the latter would never fail to represent their prayers as directed to the One God, however much their fears might really centre upon the hidden demon known to their forefathers.[1]

In the face of this syncretism one of the ironies of Islam is the maxim: 'Islam cancels all that was before it.' The rhythm of life for the African Muslim remains much the same as before. This is the main reason why Islam is so successful in Africa and retains such an intense hold over its adherents. Doughty realized this when he wrote, 'The pre-Islamic idolatrous religion of the Kaaba was the cause that the soon ripe Mawmetry rotted not soon again'.[2]

Islam, when it came to the Sudan, had passed through centuries of growth and was saturated with all kinds of animistic and magical elements, therefore certain elements of the new religion were assimilated by its peoples without dislocation. The idea of a supreme God did not overthrow their previous beliefs, but was correlated to them.[3] A tree or stone associated with previous heathen beliefs became associated with a saint and imbued with his *baraka*. The cult of spirits, whether propitiatory or exorcistory, though associated with Islamic formulae, remains much the same as it was before the coming of Islam. All their old customs still persist: family life, for instance, is governed very definitely by Islamic Law, yet every single practice connected with it is indigenous, even the marriage contract needs to have a propitious date and hour found for it by the Muslim feki who has replaced the pagan *kujūr*.

Over against all these tolerated practices there is the universal practice of 'black' magic (*siḥr*) and all kinds of other underground regional pagan practices such as the worship of the Sōba stone in Dār Funj and the cults of Dār Fūr.

Although with the progress of education many of these things are losing their terror, there can be few, if any, Sudanese who believe that sorcery and spirit influence on men are not things to be afraid of and guarded against.

[1] *Hist.* i. 73–4.

[2] *Arabia Deserta*, i. 101.

[3] Animistic peoples possess a remnant conception of a high God who plays no part in the affairs of men and is neither feared nor loved with which Islam has a point of contact. Whilst assimilating the animist's spirit-world, it develops this faded belief in a high God to one of an omnipotent Deity.

The Sudanese Muslim lives in an atmosphere of the supernatural, in which the fear of evil things emanating from man and spirit is prevalent. But one must not think that the Sūdānī is perpetually haunted by this unseen world. When life is running smoothly, he is just like a care-free child. Yet the unseen is never far away. Crises especially are a recurring element in his life. Such things as birth, circumcision, marriage, and death are crises for they mean entry into a new and untried experience in life. Also illness, disease, and calamities are crises. It is to these things that the old pre-Islamic superstitions still cling, for the function of religion with the pagan is to give him confidence, not only in the normal conduct of daily life, but above all in life's crises. The rites which are connected with crises have been called by Van Gannep[1] *rites de passage*, by which confidence is restored. Crises are then the states when special protection must be given, and it is here that Islam helps the pagan as he loses confidence in his own safeguards, and, above all, one who has lost tribal ties. Having lost the spirit, the sanction of his customs, they are re-orientated in Islam. This explains the attraction of Islam to him. Islam cannot free him from his fears, but by joining this great community he insures himself against unseen dangers by the close association of Islam with the primitive functions of his life and to a lesser degree by the use of its standardized rituals. Yet he can bring with him all his old *mores* which are re-set in Islam. Thus he inhales burnt Qur'ānic texts as an antidote to evil influences opposed to Qur'ānic teaching. His old customs are not disrupted, but reintegrated; they can still serve a vital function; but now between him and the unknown stands more than his old custom.

2. *Non-Islamic Superstitions and Pagan Practices*

For from within, out of the heart of men proceed evil thoughts . . . the evil eye. (Mk. vii. 21–2.)

The result of all this mutual interaction is that present-day Islam in the Sudan is bound up with a substratum of animistic beliefs and practices which vary between race admixture, tribe, and district. It is impossible to treat of these adequately until a more detailed study of regional Islam has been made. But though the superstitions of the people vary so much in detail they are often identical in kind and the following sketch may serve to give some conception of the general tendencies.

Many of these beliefs and customs appear to be common to all

[1] Cf. *Les Rites de passage* (1909), esp. ch. iv.

Muslim peoples. But that is because (apart from the general world uniformity of superstitions) Islam was always obliged to do some labelling, modification, and alteration in its incorporation of them. For instance, the Qur'ānic name of *jinn* has spread to incorporate the various spirits of the indigenous peoples, but the *jinn* of Kordofān are by no means identical with the *jinn* of Donqola, let alone the *jinn* of other Islamic countries.

Causes of diseases and misfortunes and methods of prevention and cure

In order to understand the Sudanese it is necessary from the beginning to distinguish clearly between our ideas of cause and effect based on scientific facts, and their ideas of cause and effect based on supernatural visitations of external malign powers or mistakes in conduct or custom which affect physical and mental health. For instance, it is believed that abortion is caused either by the pregnant woman hearing the cry of an owl (i.e. the spirit incarnated in it), or by the jealousy of her *qarīna*, if she possesses one, or the malice of the *umm aṣ-ṣubyān*.

Because of this need for protection and exorcism we have the practice of magic, and in the Sudan as elsewhere the sanction of 'white' magic led to the retention of feki practitioners who flourish on the credulity and superstition of the masses. Instead of going to the hospitals and dispensaries for treatment the majority will still visit the fekis. These men also carry on a flourishing trade in preventive medicine in the form of charms to ward off the evil eye and ensure protection against evil spirits.

The practice of sanctioned magic is sometimes called *da'wa* (invocation). *Da'wa* or, as they say, *ṭalab min Allāh* (supplication), covers all practices which Islam sanctions, but applies more especially to the systems of incantation.[1] The commonest forms of white magic are: (1) *'azīma*, the mumbling of Qur'ānic incantations and *awrād* with spitting after each verse to transfer the *baraka*. If the feki is unable to visit the patient his expectoration is mixed with water and taken to the patient. Fever in a child with convulsions, for instance, is treated by marking a black cross on its forehead and reciting a special incantation transferred by spitting three times over him. (2) *bakhra* (incensing), which involves folding a paper into (say) twelve squares,

[1] Such systems of *da'wa* can be used to work evil on a person. In this case from *da'ā 'alā*, to pray against, to curse, not *da'ā ilā' llāh li fulān*, to pray for someone; prayer thus becoming a spell. Persons who are unfortunate in life are called *mad'ī*, they are supposed to have been 'cursed'. For such 'prayers against' see above pp. 138–9.

and separating them, then writing on each piece words, phrases, and symbols (such as the Khātim Sulaimān or five-pointed star). The patient is instructed to burn two in the morning and two in the evening with frankincense or ambergris and allow the smoke to circulate around his whole body. (3) *miḥāya* (erasure). Here the feki writes texts and symbols on a wooden slate or skin and washes it off with water which he bottles and gives or sends to the patient. Sometimes writings will be made on (medicinal) roots which are then boiled and the patient drinks the water, or burnt and the patient fumigated by the smoke.

Black magic is called *siḥr* and the word *sāḥir* (sorcerer) is used for (1) a feki practising black magic, (2) anyone believed to possess the evil eye, and (3) were-animals. There are also female soothsayers or sibyls. The *sāḥir* will sell his services to one who wishes to injure an enemy. Sudden death or paralysis is often attributed to a *sāḥir*.

The operation of injury is called *'amal*. It is produced through performing magic with something, such as a hair, a nail-paring, a garment in which he has perspired, anything in fact which has come from the body of the one to be injured containing some soul-substance; or it is performed by the use of an image on paper or on the skins of animals and birds, especially the chameleon, or a mud image, and their destruction. The simplest method is to get the feki to write an injurious spell on a 'paper'. Then an efficacious bone or shell is wrapped inside the paper and it is buried in the sand or soil or thrown into the river with an incantation stating how the person is to be injured or destroyed. This often takes the form of a prayer that the person may suffer a similar fate to that of the paper or piece of wood, either be destroyed by white ants, burning, or drowning, and so on. If the spell is found the enchantment is broken. There is a Funj story of al-Ḥijāzī b. Abū Zaid putting a spell on King 'Adlān II by taking some soft clay, moulding it to the form of the King, and then baking it until it cracked. Sometimes birds or lizards are taken, their wings or feet sewed so that they cannot move, and left to die on the housetop or other place belonging to the one to be injured where they will escape notice. If the animal is released the patient recovers.

Siḥr is a form of induced auto-suggestion connected with the association of ideas by similarity and its efficacy is due to this as well as to the use of charms and the assistance of *jinn*. The victim is in some way brought to realize that he has incurred a curse and the effect is such that he becomes ill and wastes away, unless he can have his confidence restored by a counter method.

Preventive methods are chiefly by the use of amulets. Every Sūdānī will be found wearing at least one against the evil eye, another against evil spirits, and probably some kind of love-charm. The men wear theirs in leather drums or pouches above the bend of the elbow. The effendiyya in European dress wear them on the left flank next to the skin suspended by a cord round the neck. The women wear whole bunches of all shapes and sizes hanging down below their waists and sometimes in their hair. They are also hung round the necks of domestic animals.

The charm called *ḥijāb* consists of a square of paper written by the feki, containing Qur'ānic verses,[1] and cabalistic signs arranged within squares called 'the seals'. The *ḥiriz* are much more varied. They may consist of printed *awrād*, beads, bones of animals and fish, dried chameleon heads, the skin of a *waral* or iguana lizard, pounded Egyptian antiquities, cowry shells, or the hair, nail-cuttings, bits of cloth of a *walī* or earth from his tomb, and the species called *'urūq as siḥr* (magical roots) which may consist of the pounded heart of a tree or pieces of special woods such as the *fakiqāna*. The *ḥijāb* and *ḥiriz* are usually found together. A Kordofān charm for a long journey consists of the tusks of a wart-hog with *ḥijābāt* in pouches on either side. The efficacy of these *ḥijābāt*, however, is believed to lie in the *baraka* of the feki who supplies them and the price is consonant with his reputation. Again they have value only for the particular person for whom they are prescribed. Charms are worn if preventive or curative, but destroyed or put in a special place if they are used for witchcraft. The efficacious method is chosen by the feki according to the 'nature' (*ṭabī'a*) of the one to be bewitched.

The usages of the *ḥijāb* may be: to prevent an illness or disease; to protect against evil spirits, the evil eye, or someone's jealousy or anger; *jalab*, that is, to attain success in commerce, matrimony, or in obtaining a situation; to change the heart of a coveted man or woman or to retain someone's love; to obtain children.

The *tamīma* are strings of beads with tassels tied to a child's hair to avert the evil eye. Itinerant *faqīrs* also wear them. These are to be seen in the *sūq* singing songs in honour of the Prophet and then dancing, making the beads rattle and stand upright. Women will press forward to touch them to receive *baraka*.

The preventive *'uqda* are seven 'knots' tied and blown upon by the feki with incantations over each which are obtained especially for

[1] The most common are the Throne Verse (ii. 256), Sūras 1, 113, 114. These are supplemented with the ninety-nine names of God, names of angels, and *jinn*.

pregnant women and for the prevention and cure of fevers in children. Sometimes string or thread is passed through the skin and then knotted. A Sīdī Ḥasan of Tōkar was noted for the efficacy of his knots.

Other forms of *'uqda* are Black Magic. Shuqair writes of the Qarab, a sub-tribe of the Atbara Bishārīn, 'if they want to "bind" a person to a place they make incantations against him. Then he cannot leave the spot until they undo the knot. If they put food before him and "bind" him he is unable to stretch out his hand for the food.'[1] A form of *'uqda* which I have heard is common and effective is to bind a man to make him sexually impotent. The knots which may be of any material must be concealed in some way, either thrown into a well or river, or burnt or buried. The cure is obtained by the feki writing a *ḥijāb* which is worn on the right side. Then certain letters are written on a vessel which is filled with honey or olive oil, the writing is erased with water and drunk by the afflicted one.

The Evil Eye (*'ain ḥārra*) is greatly feared and the Sudanese would agree with Hamza that 'a person possessing the power of the evil eye . . . exudes venom as deadly as the viper's breed', and one who gets the reputation of a *sāḥir* often leads a very unpleasant existence, being hounded from pillar to post. He is greatly feared since a glance from his eye may wither a vital organ and cause the victim to die in torments. Slatin Pāshā describes the Khalīfa 'Abd Allāh's dread of the 'eye'. A one-eyed Syrian who unintentionally cast his blind eye in his direction was instructed never to come near him again. He remarked to Slatin, 'nothing can resist the human eye. Illness and misfortune are generally caused by the evil eye.'[2] Children are thought to be particularly susceptible to 'the evil of the envious when he envies' and are always protected with *ḥijābs*. In its simplest form anyone who envies may cast the evil eye. For that reason one should not comment on the health or handsomeness of a child, except by using such expressions as *mā shā' allāh*. If a child complains of a sudden pain, they immediately say, 'he was struck by the eye'. The cure involves first discovering the *sāḥir*. This is done by dropping a piece of alum with salt, acacia pods, and cumin in an incense burner and censing the victim. Then water is sprinkled on it and it coagulates into a mass. From the shape this takes they claim to tell the inflictor. There are many methods of removing the cause. They may wash the eye of the *sāḥir* whilst he sleeps if he is one who is believed to have acquired it innocently. In

[1] Op. cit. i. 237. An example of an *'uqda* carried by a rebel against the Government to 'bind the senses of the rulers' is given in *S.N.R.* i. 53–5.

[2] *Fire and Sword* (1895), p. 519.

other malevolent cases the 'scapegoat' method of evil transference is used. A little earth may be taken from the *sāḥir*'s track and if possible a hair or something else partaking of his substance. They are then burned with alum, herbs, and incense and the child is censed with it. Afterwards the mass which has now absorbed the evil must be destroyed. They may go into the street or desert and throw it behind their backs or into the river taking care not to see where it goes.

One man in the Jezīra had power to cure spells which cause the afflicted one difficulty in breathing and eventual death, said to be due to a piece of the stomach having been taken and his throat stopped with it. His treatment was to draw a formula of the usual geometrical pattern on a slip of paper, roll it up, put it up the nostril of the patient, and light it. The bewitched cries out in the voice of the afflictor 'let me out', and the explosion which results, by driving out the spirit, completes the cure.

Again, there is the realm of the Evil Spirits as the cause of suffering, misfortune, and death—the *jinn*-family with its many sub-divisions of *ʿafārīt*, *s̲h̲ayāṭīn*, *riyāḥ*, *zairān*, and so on. The cultivators especially are afraid of them. The attitude of the nomads, whether Arab or Beja, is that of the Maʿāza shaikh, Salīm Faraj, quoted by G. W. Murray as saying: 'The *jinn* abound in our mountains, but nobody but a *fellāḥ* would fear them. Now, wolves are really dangerous!'[1]

The beliefs connected with the *jinn*, like other animistic beliefs, can be divided into three strata: those from old Arab paganism; those accepted by Islam from many sources, including Western Sudanese,[2] in the course of its development during the centuries (both these have lost all regional peculiarities through syncretism and are part of the Islamic legacy to the Sudan); and, finally, those taken over from the beliefs of the indigenous people of the Sudan. Insufficient material, however, has been collected to allow of analysis.

The spirits may be external influences or they may enter into a person, that is, take possession of him. It is thought that someone who has done wrong lays himself open to such possession or they may enter at times of crisis (*mus̲h̲āhira*). The *jinn* are the world of supernatural powers between angels and men. As elsewhere they are thought to be crafty and mischievous demons, formed of fire and vapour and dwell in cemeteries and uninhabited places. As such they are personifications of the terrors of the desert. They are invisible but may take the form of snakes, lizards, or other loathsome things. Some are Muslims,

[1] *Sons of Ishmael*, p. 156.

[2] Cf. Westermarck, *Ritual and Belief in Morocco*, i. 379.

others unbelievers. All are under the rather nominal sway of the prophet Sulaimān. They are capable of doing good or evil and must be propitiated to avert their evil influence or exorcised when affected by them. After an illness the name of the child is often changed in order to deceive the spirits. Many fekis claim to have *khuddām* (subject-*jinn*). Occasionally the *jinn* marry humans. The Fellāta and the Hadendiwa, in popular legend, owe their origin to the union of *jinn* with Abyssinian girls. One of my friends had a white unblemished lamb born in his *ḥōsh* and an old woman who had never been married on seeing it was persistent in her wish to buy it. He asked for the reason and she replied reluctantly that she was married to a *jinn* and the feki had told her that such a lamb was necessary as a sacrifice to prevent its turning upon her.

Whilst the *jinn* are really feared there are certain superstitions connected with them which are regarded as mere *khurāfāt* (legends). For example, the 'dust-devil' is popularly regarded as a *jinn* riding a horse. Shooting-stars are thrown at *jinn* by angels. A well is never dug nor a house built without a *karāma* to propitiate the *jinn* 'lord of the place' (*ṣāḥib al-maḥal*) who may have been disturbed.

Whilst the *jinn* are a species and in general lack individuality, there are *jinn* having individual names and special characteristics. The great curse of women is the spirit called *umm aṣ-ṣubyān* (mother of children, a euphemism for enemy of children) or *ghazāla*. She is pictured as a skinny and loathsome old woman of immense powers of destruction, to counteract or propitiate whom only certain powerful fekis can write effective *ḥijābs*. She is the curse of pregnant mothers and is the cause of miscarriage, sterility, and infantile paralysis. Anyone afflicted with epilepsy (*ghazāl*) is regarded as being possessed by her and therefore the Sudanese are very averse to touching anyone in a fit for fear of possession.

There is the *Qarīn* or *Qarīna* (companion). In Omdurman it is a spirit which possesses. The Egyptian conception of it as a double born with every individual is not known.[1] Only certain people are possessed and such people cannot marry or the *qarīna* will harm them. It does not seem to be at all identical with the *bint iblīs* (*silūt* with the Bishārīn) which has relations with the unmarried during sleep and can cause them to waste away physically. It is not the cause of mental deficiency or imbecility as in Egypt. That is due to *shaiṭāns* substi-

[1] For the Egyptian conception see Zwemer, *Studies in Popular Islam*, ch. v. The Sudanese usage as spirit-husband or spirit-wife seems to be similar to its usage in the Qur'ān: 'Whoever has Satan for his mate (*qarīn*), an evil mate has he' (iv. 43).

tuting one of their own imbecile children for a human child. Therefore when reviled an imbecile is called a 'changeling' (*mubaddal*). To guard against such substitution children must never be left alone for the first forty days after birth (*ayyām al-arbaʿīn*), during which the mother is confined to the house. *Jinn* which are in possession are usually classified as either *hādī*, quiet and controlled, or *ḥāsid* (lit. envious), which excite and cause mania. *Junūn* (madness, i.e. *jinn*-possession) is strictly only to be used of lunatics. This is treated by special feki-families only who have inherited the particular *baraka*. The method of treatment is by imprisonment in a dark room, fasting on a little *kisra* and water, followed by severe beating with sticks on which Qur'ānic verses have been written, incantations with the usual spitting at the patient to convey the *baraka*, and recitation of the Qur'ān. This treatment often results in the death of the patient. Another method involves swinging by the shoulders and feet, slowly over a hot fire with incantations. People mildly possessed are called *mishōṭin*. In all treatments of the different kinds of possession it should be noticed that the *daʿwa* may be practised either with the object of pacifying the spirits or actual exorcism.

The *Umm aṣ-Ṣubyān* and these possessive spirits are really dreaded; but there are also many other spirits which are used as bogies to frighten children. The *ghūl* is pictured as a *jinn* with seven heads and a large comb. It sleeps for a year and is active for a year when it lures men away to lonely places to destroy them. The female is known as *Suʿluwwa*.[1] Other species are the *shakalōta*, which is a one-eyed, one-legged, one-handed, noseless thing with long finger-nails with which it attacks the faces of the people it meets. The *Dūdū* and *Umm Buʿullū* seem to be the equivalent of the Egyptian *Buʿbuʿ*. Nightmare is said to be caused by *Abū-Kabbās*, a shaiṭān who puts his hand over one's mouth in order to stifle one. He does not succeed because of a hole in his palm through which one can breathe with difficulty.

There is a living belief in the reincarnation of people who have died, missed Paradise, and returned to live a normal human life in some other district or country. Their ghosts (called *baʿātī*) usually visit their relatives immediately after death and tales are often told of encounters years later with people who knew them in their previous existence.[2]

[1] *Ghūl* is a feminine noun from a root meaning 'to destroy', but it is regarded as a male demon in the Sudan. All I can connect the form *suʿluwwa* with is the Arabian pre-Islamic demon (*siʿlāt*). See Masʿūdī, *Murūj*, iii. 318.

[2] This belief may have been derived from Fūr slaves, for H. A. MacMichael writes (*Hist.* i. 103): 'Popular belief throughout Dārfūr still attributes to all the Fūr a power of metamorphosis, and the word *nabātī* there is a common expression of abuse implying that the

The riverain people believe that the Nile is inhabited by some kind of mermen and mermaids called *awlād al-ḥūr* and *banāt al-ḥūr*. The albinos who are sometimes born of black parents are supposed to be changelings of theirs and such a child is called a *ḥūrī*. They also believe in other inhabitants of the Nile called 'Angels of the River' (*malā'ikat al-baḥr*).[1]

The skull and horns of cattle, crocodile skin, black kettle, bottles, and plates which are to be seen over the gates of *ḥōshes* are sometimes represented to be a kind of fetish to guard against the entrance of evil spirits, or they are said to be there to attract the evil eye so that it will not harm anyone in the *ḥōsh*. The animals' skulls which will be seen erected on poles in the midst of growing crops are also to attract the 'eye'.

The *zār* is a form of propitiation of the genius *zār* or *ar-rīḥ al-aḥmar* (the red spirit) by means of music and dancing. It is certainly not indigenous to the riverain Northern Sudan for it is not practised in the villages, nor do the Jezīra, Funj, and Blue Nile districts practise it. It seems to have been introduced into Egypt during the nineteenth century by black slaves from pagan Sudan or more probably Abyssinia.[2] From Egypt it entered the Northern Sudan where it is now practised mainly in Sawākin, Barbar, and Omdurman. Its prevalence in Sawākin rather suggests that it was introduced from the Ḥijāz which may have got it from Abyssinia.

The women of Omdurman are brought up in an atmosphere of *zār*-fear and when they become hysterical or get any kind of wasting illness they regard it as *zār*-possession. This nearly always shows itself by the patient being thrown to the ground in convulsions which may last for hours, and during which the patients are sometimes very wild and raging. They are left afterwards with fixed, straining, wide-open eyes. The theory behind *zār*-possession is simple; once let another spirit get possession of one's body then one is to all intents and purposes another person.

person to whom it is addressed is in his second existence, that he had died, that is, and instead of dwelling in Paradise, has come back to lead a second existence upon earth.'

[1] Cf. Crowfoot's article on them, *S.N.R.* ii. 183 ff.

[2] The word *zār* is an Amharic loan-word thought to have been derived from the ancient Agau religion of the pagan Kushites whose Sky-god was called *jār* which word degenerated in its usage by the Abyssinians (christianized Agao) to denote an evil spirit (see Paul Kahle, *Zar-Beschwörungen in Ägypten*, Der Islam, iii. 1–41, Plowden's account in his *Travels in Abyssinia*, pp. 259–60, and E. Cerulli, *Etiopia Occidentale* (1933), ii. 34–7). The Sudanese quite naturally derived it from *zāra*, to visit. Women possessed always refer to it as the *jamā'a* (company). It should be noted that Lane in his *Modern Egyptians* (1st ed. 1836) never mentions the *zār*, so presumably it had not been imported then. It has also spread to the Ḥijāz (cf. Snouck Hurgronje, *Mekka*, ii. 124 ff.).

Some Sudanese say that everyone possesses a *zār*, that normally it is hidden, but certain conditions, such as a mental shock, can make it active. But mostly it is regarded as a spirit which possesses and the one possessed is called a *mazyūr*. There are many types of *zairān*, a Ḥabashī (Abyssinian), an Egyptian Pāshā, a Fellāta, a Coptic priest, a group of nuns, and certain *darāwīsh* (such as ʿAbd al-Qādir al Jīlānī and Aḥmad al-Badawī). But the spirits called up seem to be more malevolent than these names would justify. However, the woman afflicted by a *zār* often wears a ring with the name of, say, ʿAbd al-Qādir engraved on it and she will throw bread into the corners of the house for him as she would for any other *jinn*.

The ceremony of propitiation is also called a *zār*. The essence of it is appeasement of the *zār* by means of the ecstatic dance, gifts, and sacrifices. The whole thing is pagan and is too far removed from Islam for there to have been any attempt made to islamize it.[1] The practitioner or *zār*-priestess is usually a woman, though not necessarily a negress, who is called a *shaikha* or a *kūdiya*. If someone is mentally or physically ill, and *zār*-possession is thought to be the cause, the *kūdiya* is brought to the house for the ceremony called 'opening the box'. This box contains incense, during the burning of which the *kūdiya* decides whether the person needs a *zār*-party or not. She can tell of course whether the patient will be susceptible to this influence or is likely to get worse or die from the treatment. If so they avoid performing the *zār* by suggesting treatment by a feki. This is because their reputation (unlike that of a feki) suffers if the patient becomes insane or dies. There have been many cases of suicide and insanity in Omdurman as a result of *zārs*. The practice is supposed to be forbidden, but little attempt is made to put a stop to it, although a *zār* cannot be concealed on account of the infernal noise of the drumming which keeps the whole neighbourhood in a state of tension.

The *kūdiya*'s first task is to find out what *zār* or *rīḥ* she has to deal with and the correct tune with which to exorcise it or them, for sometimes the patient is possessed by more than one. One tune after another is tried accompanied by its appropriate drumming and dancing

[1] I have already shown that the incorporation of primitive conceptions in Islam is dependent upon their compatibility with the claims of Allāh as supreme ruler. The basic formulae of the *ḥijāb*, for instance, should be the Word of Allāh and it is wrong to associate pre-Islamic demons with Him on the paper as is so often done; it is wrong to use it to work evil (*ʿamal*) on another, that is, to violate the sanctity of the Qur'ānic word; similarly the *zār*, as representing a pre-Islamic demon, cannot be elevated like a *walī* to be a 'friend' of Allah. Orthodox magic, unhappily, is ineffective to control the *zairān* and the primitive rites have had to be retained.

until the patient (sometimes the *kūdiya*) becomes ecstatic and goes into a spirit trance. This proves that the right *zār* has been found and the chanting of that tune and the drumming continues interminably. The identifying of the *zār* causes him to lose much of his power. Each tune requires the putting on of special clothes, which may be that of men, women, boys, girls, or hermaphrodites according to the sex of the *zār*. The *zār* always has certain desires and it is the *kūdiya*'s task to find these out before it can be pacified. These they express sometimes in Arabic, sometimes in a *zār*-language, to the *kūdiya* through their victims, though sometimes the *kūdiya* may be a medium. These desires tend to take the form of clothes, jewellery, and other coveted things.

The meetings for exorcising the *zār* usually continue for seven nights. During the sixth night the greatest feast is prepared. The *kūdiya* and others possessed who have been treated previously by the same *kūdiya*[1] remain the whole night, and the next morning they sacrifice a ram. First a procession is formed when the ram is driven seven times round the room, sometimes with the woman seated on it, to the singing of the special incantations. It is then killed and the patient and others are smeared with its blood; then she, the *kūdiya*, and other possessed women, drink some blood and eat of the flesh.[2]

Two classes are subject to the *zār* superstition: the patient who has tried fekis and doctors and has not been cured, women of unstable mental temperament, or women who wish to obtain gold ornaments from their husbands as an insurance policy against the day of their divorce. There is a strong but ineffective opposition to the *zār* by the men, not on the ground of its being a pagan ceremony, but as a trick of women and an expensive last resort of incurables. The *kūdiya* takes

[1] It should be remembered that the *zār* is only appeased, not exorcised. The women say that certain fekis in the past had power to exorcise *zārs*, but that the art was lost during the Mahdiyya.

[2] Muslimized Negroes in Omdurman perform a somewhat similar ceremony on Thursday nights. The officiant is called *shaikh aṭ-ṭumbura*. The *ṭumbura* is a large drum which is used with a *rabāba* (psaltery). The shaikh has a skin full of cloven hooves and a long stick and decorates himself with ostrich feathers. He ties the hooves round his waist and leaning on his stick shakes his hind-quarters to make the hooves rattle. Others who suffer from the *jamā'at aṭ-ṭumbura*, as they are called, are also invited. The spirits are driven out by the monotonous beating of drums, chanting, incense, playing on the *rabāba*, and clapping which have a hypnotic effect on the patient, who goes into a trance. This ceremony lasts for one night only. The Omdurmānīs say that it is this ceremony which entered the Northern Sudan and Egypt, was suppressed during the Mahdiyya, and returned afterwards from Egypt with new excrescences, especially in the way of expense. Cf. also account of ceremony of Bangala on Upper Congo (J. H. Weeks, *J.A.I.* xl. 425).

a pound a day for seven days. It would be impossible for most people to produce this sum were it not for the fact that the drums attract the *zār*-possessed of the neighbourhood who all share in the expense.

The belief in were-animals is prevalent throughout the Sudan. Certain *sāḥirs* (in this case called *saḥḥārīn*) are credited with the ability to transform themselves at night into crocodiles and hippopotami in riverain districts, or hyenas in Dār Funj and among the Maṣālīṭ, or lions in Dārfūr. These metamorphosed human-beasts roam about seeking to destroy and are reputed to hold cannibal feasts. In Dārfūr whole Fūr villages are supposed to turn out at night on such hunting expeditions.[1] That this belief is no mere legend is shown by the experience of a former General Manager of the Sudan Railways who told me that he had once to raise a boat which had sunk at the mouth of the Atbara. He had great difficulties in obtaining labour from a nearby village and eventually found out that a man of the village was credited with the power of transforming himself into a crocodile, and the villagers were afraid to enter the water. During the reconquest Kitchener issued an order that crocodiles should not be shot in the Baṭn al-Ḥajar because of the belief of the inhabitants in metamorphosis. In Dārfūr the 'lion-men', known as *ahl al-ʿawāʾid*, levy dues upon the villagers.

Throughout the Sudan there is the reverence of certain holy trees, wells, and stones universal in Islam. To-day of course they have mostly been given an Islamic colouring. Similarly one often sees at markets performances of sand-divination (*ḍarb ar-raml*), shell divination (*ḍarb al-wadʿa*), and bibliomancy (*fatḥ al-kitāb*); all following the well-established Islamic forms based on literary sources. The practice of *istikhāra* (divination by dreams) is universal. The book of Ibn Sīrīn is normally used in the interpretation of dreams and that of Ad-Dairabī is common among the *fuqarāʾ*. *Ḍarb al-mandal*, which is the method of arriving at the knowledge of hidden things through the mediumship of spirits, is practised by Fellāta throughout the Sudan. The method follows the usual form which has often been described.[2] Using a boy as a medium the magician traces the *Khātim* of Solomon on the sand, writes the word Allāh in the centre, and the boy gazes until he is in a trance. He then calls upon 'the king of the devils' who answers questions through the boy. Sometimes a glass of water or a mirror or a drop of ink will be used.

Actual pagan practices are to be found amongst the purely nominal

[1] Cf. At-Tūnisī's account, *Voyage au Darfur*, p. 358.

[2] Cf. Lane, *Modern Egyptians*, i. 348 ff.

Muslim Negroids of Dār Funj, Dār Nūba, and Dārfūr. The Ghodiāt, between Jebel Kordofān and Lake Rahad, are regarded by their neighbours as possessing magical powers. Women soothsayers, rain-makers, and sacred stones and trees are to be found among the Fūrs, Zaghāwa, and Mīdōb. E. Lampen writes of the Mīdōb:

> Their recent and still lingering religion seems to have focussed on three points, sacrifice and worship before sacred stones and trees, a great harvest festival, and resort to wise women as oracles. There is one magnificent tree near Malha with a small enclosure round it which I have always believed to be a sacred tree, but I could obtain no definite information of it or of any other. Sacred stones are more common. I have spoken of that in Malha crater. Another I have seen in a gorge of the Wadi Goldonut. It was covered with smaller stones which passers-by placed on it for good luck. There are several such.... The sacred women or *todis*, who used to divine by throwing shells on the ground, still exist and no doubt are still consulted. All Meidobis are very shy of speaking of their old faith, and are ashamed of their backwardness in the practice of Mohammedanism. But there is no doubt that the great majority of the tribe are still animists at heart.[1]

Concerning the Dājo of W. Kordofān, S. Hillelson writes:

> Though strongly permeated by Arab influence, and nominally and perfunctorily professing Islam, the Dago maintain rites of a purely pagan nature with which the *togonyē* (or *kujūr*) are particularly associated. In charge of the *togonyē* there are shrines dedicated to the High God of the Dago, Kalge, whom they identify with Allah.[2]

There is the cult of the Sōba Stone among the Hamaj of Jebel Gūli. They claim a queen-ancestress called Sōba and the stone was her throne. It is still the 'throne of the kingdom' (*kursī mamlaka*) and plays its part in the ceremonies when the *mānjil* assumes office by the ceremonial washing of his feet upon it. This and other Sōba stones play their part in other rites, such as the dance in honour of the first time a newly delivered mother leaves her house, and offerings are placed on the stone at the first cutting of the grain. Sōba is also invoked to cure illness.

The Beja, most of whom are very imperfectly Islamized, retain many pagan practices. G. W. Murray writes: 'The Bishārīn have still a few sacred rocks and cliffs, to which ceremonial visits are performed and sheep sacrificed. Such a place is Kanjar Aweib, "the runaway stone", in Wādī Kajūj, a tributary of Wādī Irib'.[3]

[1] *S.N.R.* xi. 60–1. [2] Ibid. viii. 63–4. [3] G. W. Murray, op. cit., p. 157.

3. *Pagan Influences on Social and Family Life*

A. *Traces of the Matrilinear System*

It has already been shown that the Nubians and Beja, and probably most other tribes of the Sudan were originally a matrilineal people, as were the Arabs until the time of the Prophet. Maqrīzī wrote of the Beja, 'Their relationships follow the female line; they pass the inheritance to the daughter's son or sister's son to the exclusion of the "son of the loins".'[1] It was this system which the immigrant Arabs took advantage of to obtain chieftaincies. This is also shown by the fact that the traditions of many tribes, such as the Hadendiwa and Baṭn al-Manāṣīr, go back to a female ancestress.[2]

To-day under the *sharīʿa* this system does not exist in law and descent is patrilineal, but it survives in the customs of the people. Matrilocal conditions exist in that the husband goes to live with his wife in the *ḥōsh* of her family and he remains there under the rule of the bride's mother until the first child is born and often longer. Even when custom has slackened the woman returns to her own people to be delivered. The Sudanese woman is surprisingly independent of her husband, who in certain spheres of life has no control whatever over the domestic side of the house, even after she has removed to his house. The women always resist successfully any desire of the husband even to move to another part of Omdurman, though they know that this often means that he acquires another local wife. The association of the children also is largely with the mother's family, especially where the husband has more than one wife. In practice, though not in law, the family of the wife, especially the mother's brother, exercises authority over the children. The Baqqāra divorced woman returns to her uncle and not her parents. The avoidance by a man of his mother-in-law and by a woman of her father-in-law (*istiḥyā'*) is almost universal with Arab, Beja, Nubian, and Negroid alike.[3] Thus out of respect, a man will avoid meeting his mother-in-law and will never speak to her or eat in her presence. A man may speak to his father-in-law, but will avoid eating out of the same dish. Among the Hadendiwa a man goes to the woman's village to be married and stays there from one to three years; almost the whole of the marriage hut is

[1] *Khiṭaṭ*, i. 194.

[2] Many *ḥijābāt* refer to a man's mother (*fulān ibn fulāna*). I have been told, however, that this was due to the necessity of referring to the right person, otherwise the *ḥijāb* might be ineffective and blight instead of blessing. There can be no question as to a person's mother.

[3] Cf. MacMichael, op. cit. i. 106.

provided by the bride's relatives; he also travels with the herds of his father-in-law, and their relationship is that of father and son.

The matrilinear system actually exists among the nominal Muslim Mīdōb of north-eastern Dārfūr in both inheritance and succession, a *mek* being succeeded by his sister's son. 'The bone', they say, 'is from the mother, the flesh from the father.'[1]

B. *Family Festivals and Customs*

Family and social life, we have said, whilst governed by Islamic law, is more vitally connected with indigenous graduation rites (*rites de passage*). These rites are to insure protection to the individual during the dangerous period of transition from one stage of life to another. The name *mushāhara*[2] is that given to the 'unknown peril' resulting in illness or disaster connected with these crises. This is thought to be connected with the moon and the calamity to have been caused by some defect in these protective rites (*sibr*),[3] such as the materials of the *jirtiq* not being complete or not visiting the river. To counteract the *mushāhara* the *jirtiq* ornaments[4] are worn at marriage, circumcision, from the seventh month of pregnancy to the end of the forty days, and, in the past, at the investiture of a king.

Customs connected with birth. Amongst the riverain peoples, that is, the Danāqla and so-called Arab tribes such as the Ja'aliyyīn and Rubāṭāb, when a woman is in the seventh month of her pregnancy a 'knot' is sought from a feki and tied around her waist, the *jirtiq* ornaments assumed, her child is promised gifts, and her peculiar fancies satisfied. A Maria Theresa dollar must be placed under the pillow of the woman. All this is to guard the mother and child. Three days after the birth of the child a ram is killed and distributed uncooked to the poor. This is called *hurrāra*. On the seventh day is the naming (*simāya*) which involves a large party and probably a *dhikr*. The *sharī'a* recommends the cutting of the birth hair of the head on that day and the sacrifice of a sheep (called the *'aqīqa*), but in Omdurman, though they always sacrifice a sheep at the *simāya*, it is rarely combined

[1] Cf. MacMichael, op. cit. i. 59 ff. He also mentions traces of the system amongst the inhabitants of Al-Ḥarāza in Kordofān (*Tribes*, p. 91) and amongst the Kabābīsh eight generations ago (op. cit., p. 185).

[2] Der. from *shahr* (month), i.e. a moon. 'The sun shall not smite thee by day, nor the moon by night' (Ps. cxxi. 6). The verb is not used, *itkabas* being used for 'to be smitten by the "peril" ', *kabsa* being an alternative for *mushāhara*.

[3] It is important to distinguish between *sibr* and *'āda*. *Sibr* refers to these customary *ceremonial* practices. *'āda* or *sawālif* (Arabic but used by Beja) is 'custom' in the wider sense of the customary mode of action to be adopted in any given situation.

[4] See 'wedding customs', pp. 182–3.

with the idea of *ʿaqīqa*. The 'ignorant one's first hair' (*ʿaqīqat al-jāhil*) is shaved after seven months, leaving tufts. In towns the practice of leaving tufts is dying out, there is no *ʿaqīqa* sacrifice and so no celebration. On the fortieth day (*arbaʿīn al-wilāda*) the woman goes after sunset with a company of women friends and relations for a purification ceremony to the Nile. She first throws some *belīla* into the river, then washes her hands, face, and feet, and the face of the child.[1] The child's faeces, which have been collected during the forty days, are also emptied out and she asks that all the evil which may cling to her or her child may be washed away. After she has finished, the rest of the company bathe and eat the rest of the *belīla*. During the forty days they mark a cross in *kuḥl* on the forehead of the child as a safeguard against the evil eye. The Beja keep a fire burning continually during this period.

Circumcision, called *ṭahūr* in the Sudan, is of course an indigenous rite practised before the Arabs came to the Sudan. It is islamized by being regarded as admission into the Islamic community, but there is clearly, in the accessory rites attached to it, relationship with an initiation ceremony. The boy is dressed like a girl, wears the *jirtiq* and gold ornaments to deceive *jinn* (though a man's sword to guard against *jinn*), he rides surrounded by men to keep him from falling, charcoal, frankincense, mimosa pods, and salt are burnt, there is recitation of *dhikrs* and *awrād*, and the slaughtering of a victim. Sometimes a visit is paid to a tomb, and during the preceding fourteen days he can demand gifts from relatives and friends. All these are to avoid the graduation dangers, the *mushāhara*, the evil eye, and the evil spirits. The ceremony is sometimes called *al-ʿirs* (wedding) and there is a proverb: 'The Arab is a king on the day of his wedding and the day of his circumcision'. Among the Beja the boys live together with the operator in a special hut erected for them. This shows its connexion with a primitive initiation ceremony.

Boys are circumcised at varying ages according to tribal usage or family finances, the majority perhaps about the ages of 8 to 10. Some of the Beja perform it immediately after birth and hold the festival some years later.

The circumcision of women is not a rite of this kind and is not covered with mystery, though there are ceremonies and the *jirtiq* is worn. It takes the form of the severe rite of infibulation (*ṭahāra firʿawniyya*), a characteristically Hamitic rite which has been adopted

[1] The rule of the Coptic and Abyssinian Church is that male children should be baptized on the fortieth day after birth.

by the immigrant Arabs.[1] The Baqqāra, who used to practise the *sunna* form, resisted it longest. In the time of At-Tūnīsī and Browne it was not universal in Dārfūr but coming in,[2] the eastern Misairiyya being the first to adopt it. Now it is almost universal among the Baqqāra. Northerners do not trouble to justify the practice. It is *'āda* (custom). But tribes such as the Baqqāra who have adopted it recently justify the practice by saying that it is supposed to be a protection against untimely pregnancy (for the Baqqāra women have great freedom); and that it is regarded as rendering the victim more attractive to men. It is unorthodox and half-hearted efforts are sometimes made to get it condemned and to substitute the milder legal form (*ṭahāra sh̲ar'iyya*) in its place. These efforts have failed owing to the indifference of the men and the determined opposition of the *ḥabōbāt*.[3]

Wedding Customs. The *jirtiq* type of wedding[4] is common over most of the Northern Sudan—amongst the riverain tribes (Maḥas, Danāqla, Ja'aliyyīn, and Sh̲ā'iqiyya), in Northern and Central Kordofān, the Blue and White Niles, and the Benī 'Āmir. It has been adopted by most of the camel-nomads, but not the Sh̲ukriyya, the Baqqāra, the Bedawie-speaking Beja, nor the Nubian Kenūz and Sukkōt in Egyptian Nubia.

The *jirtiq* ceremony is only one of the many elaborate ceremonies connected with marriage. The nomad tribes tend to be simpler than

[1] Mentioned by Herodotus (ii. 104) and Strabo (xiv. 4, 9). Ibn Salīm mentions the practice among the Beja.

[2] Cf. MacMichael, op. cit. i. 107.

[3] The orthodox attitude is condemnation of the extreme form as a mutilation, but the schools vary in their ruling on the milder legal form. This is obligatory (*wājib*) with Sh̲āfi'ī, but desirable (*mustaḥabb*) according to Mālik and most others. The following is a translation of a *fatwā* by the Mufti of the Sudan about female circumcision: 'Dr. as Sayyid 'Abd al Hādī has written a full statement, which appeared in *An-Nīl* of 25–7–39, on the evils of female circumcision in the Sudan, explaining its social and pathological harmfulness, and its injurious effects on women throughout life. He blamed, quite rightly, the educated class and persons of position for tolerating the continuance of this barbarous practice of female circumcision which has no origin and which has never been known in the Moslem world, or any other country. In this statement, which needs no addition, he suggested to me that I should make clear the *Sh̲arī'a* ruling on this question. My answer is that female circumcision is only desirable, i.e. not compulsory, and that it consists in cutting off part of the clitoris. More than that is forbidden in view of the Umm 'Aṭiyya report; "Circumcise but do not go too far, for thus it is better for appearance and gives more pleasure to the husband". This is the female circumcision that is desirable in Islam. Other forms such as that known among us as the pharaonic, are mutilations and mutilations are categorically forbidden' (*An-Nīl*, 31. 7. 39). Legislation has recently been introduced, but naturally with no effect upon so deeply-rooted a custom. The Sudanese should be allowed to find their own way towards its gradual and peaceful extinction.

[4] See articles by J. W. Crowfoot, 'Wedding Customs of the Northern Sudan', *S.N.R.* v. 1 ff. and S. Zenkovsky, 'Marriage Customs in Omdurman', *S.N.R.* xxvi. 241–55. For the customs of the camel-nomads, cf. *The Sudan from Within*, pp. 120–4.

villagers and town dwellers. The *jirtiq*, which is worn at all periods of danger, is, however, central and is only worn at the *first* marriage, of either the boy or girl. The *jirtiq* proper is a red silken cord on which is threaded a green or blue bead, the vertebra of a fish and a tassel, hanging from a bracelet. This is assumed at a special ceremony, and with a man 'to put on the *jirtiq*' also includes all the other protective female ornaments which he wears.

The emphasis in the marriage is on the correct performance of the protective rites. There are other rites to promote fertility, but there is no climax of consummation, probably owing to the practice of female circumcision, in contrast to its centrality in other Islamic countries. Consummation has no fixed time, it is often delayed by the *ḥabōba*'s demands for money and frequently involves an artificial preparation by a midwife.

Among the Beja the *sunkāb* takes the place of the *jirtiq* since it is only used at the *first* marriage.

> This is made of the young leaves from the heart of the dōm palm tied with black, white, and brown wool, somewhat after the fashion of a fly-whisk. To it are attached miniature tethering ropes for camels and boys' sandals. This is prepared by the women and placed over the entrance of the house where it remains for two years, or more, until it has completely disintegrated.[1]

To-day many Beja brides and bridegrooms wear a tassel on the wrist for the first marriage only, but this is an innovation.

Death and Mourning Customs. These are much the same as those in other Muslim countries and, though full of their own rites, the important tenets of orthodox Islam are complied with.

On the death of a person the women trill the *sakalī*.[2] The body is washed immediately,[3] and the women howl, put ashes on their heads, and beat the *manāḥa*.[4] At the death of notables and young married women their clothes are heaped on an *'anqarīb* and the women dance around it. Then they wear them (or the slaves if a tribal shaikh) and afterwards they are given to the poor. Just before the body is taken for burial (which is within a few hours of death) there is the second (the legal) washing, the body is shrouded, perfumed, and covered with the costliest coverlet possessed. The women do not accompany the *'anqarīb* to the grave, where the orthodox 'funeral office' (*ṣalāt al jināza*) is performed.

[1] W. T. Clark, 'Manners, Customs and Beliefs of the Northern Beja', *S.N.R.* xxi. 11.

[2] This is very similar to the *zagharīṭ* employed only on happy occasions.

[3] Called *khurūj ar-rūḥ*—departure of the spirit.

[4] The *manāḥa* (lit. wailing) is used only for funerals. It is made by putting a gourd upside-down in a large basin of water and beating it with old slippers.

The period following the burial is called *ayyām al-furāsh* (also *ayyām al-bikā*) because the near relatives of the deceased spend from three to seven days and nights (among nomads sometimes forty days) squatting on mats (*furāsh*) in order to receive visits of condolence from friends and neighbours, only leaving the room or tent if very necessary. It is considered a mortal insult not to visit. Women visitors are expected to embrace the chief mourners and wail. Men simply pronounce the *Fātiḥa* and wait quietly until they are given permission to go. It is the duty of neighbours and friends to do the work of the house and provide food. On the last day of *furāsh* they make *ṣadaqa*, that is they slaughter and cook one sheep or more according to their means for the poor. This, they say, is to 'remove the earth from the mouth of the buried one'. The same day the whole of the Qur'ān is read, sections being gabbled through by different people simultaneously. On the fortieth day *karāma* is made for the poor only and women are then allowed to visit the grave. An upright stone or palm frond is placed at the head and foot of the grave, which is usually surrounded by a circle of stones.

The Beja take little notice of death ceremonies and have no *furāsh*, though friends will come some days after a death to offer their condolences. The period of mourning with the women lasts a year, during which they cannot use *ḥinna* or perfume or plait their hair. Nomad Arabs sacrifice a sheep every day, but this is due to the necessity of having to feed visiting mourners.

The women visit the graves on Friday evenings, and on the last Friday in Ramaḍān offerings (*raḥmatāt*) are made for the dead. These are collected from the houses and eaten by children. It is called the 'supper of the dead' (*'ashā' al-mayyitīn*).

C. *Other Indigenous Social Customs*

We have shown in the previous chapter[1] the ineffectiveness of the *sharī'a* over the field of tribal customs (*'āda* or *sālif*) upon which shaikhs and tribal courts base their decisions. Among the Beja for instance the penalty for adultery is the payment of a fine of £8 to the husband. Proof only is required of 'entry into the house' (*dukhl al bait*), which is the term used for adultery.

Such customs do not vary greatly amongst the various Arab groupings, and those upon which the shaikhs' decisions are based were in the main brought in by the Arabs. Some naturally approximate to the *sharī'a* rulings because the Prophet's legislation of expediency often

[1] See iv. 4, p. 122.

consisted of the sanctioning or only slight changes in the customary observances of pagan Arabia.

Those of the Beja differ more considerably, though being nomads there is a family resemblance between theirs and the Arabs. The decisions of the tribal courts, however, are coming more and more closely to those of the Arabs. Their inheritance custom is very different and it is unlikely that the *sharī'a* will modify this because it is based upon the Beja belief in the inalienability of territory.

Other social ceremonies include the calendar usages kept up by the women in the north, milk-ritual among the Beja, the initiation of the harvest season by the chiefs in Dār Funj and Dārfūr, and other harvest and rain-making rituals in central and western Sudan.

The Beja, along with certain other Hamitic tribes, such as the Galla, retain a dairy-ritual. Milk possesses a certain virtue which is not only lost if any of the ritual is omitted, but may cause harm to the person partaking of it. The chief rules are that: men only must milk; no man may drink of the milk he has drawn until someone else has drunk of it; milk must only be drawn into gourds or basketry vessels; it must never be boiled and may only be cooked in certain ways; it may not be sold. A shaikh is also splashed with milk at his installation. This milk ritual seems to be the making of something sacred or taboo permissible for human consumption.

A. C. Beaton has given a description of Fūr rain cults.[1] The office of rain-maker is hereditary and involves a prayer for rain addressed to the ancestral spirits who are associated with the sacred snakes, spears, and trees at a shrine. It is suggested from the phallic symbolism of the ritual and the part played by children in the rites that it is a survival of an old fertility cult. Here the ritual is the expression of the spirit of the tribe, and until the ritual becomes dissociated such a tribe can hardly be called Muslim.

An example of the way in which such pagan ceremonies become islamized is shown in the following descriptions of rain ceremonials by A. C. Beaton. Referring to the Estate of Ja, he says that the people attend the pagan rain ceremonial at the Estate of Komoro but 'have a minor ceremonial of their own whereby the feki climbs a tree and reads out the appropriate chapters of the Qur'ān letting the leaves of his book fall one by one as he reads. The leaves are picked up by a few of the villagers stationed at the bottom of the tree, while the rest are

[1] *S.N.R.* xxii. 186 f. The accounts of the two rain-making ceremonies which follow are taken from notes by A. C. Beaton in a Dārfūr Province file. For accounts of other Fūr pagan customs see MacMichael, *Hist.* i. 100–8.

seated some way off telling their beads.' Again in the Estate of Kaalu, 'the Imām is in charge of a rain ritual. After counting the beads and reading the Qur'ān for many days, the people collect a large heap of stones, and while the Imām is reading the prayers for rain, they all remove the stones, one by one, until the heap has disappeared. A ram is bought by general contribution, sacrificed and eaten.'

There is no need to do more than indicate that with the black tribes which are Muslim in name in the area 12°–10°, that is, the various Nūba–Funj communities and the tribes of Dārfūr, their whole life is governed by pagan customs, a study of which belongs properly to that of pagan communities.[1]

[1] They are treated as such by Seligman in his *Pagan Tribes of the Nilotic Sudan.*

6

The Religious Orders

I. THE DEVELOPMENT OF ṢŪFISM IN ISLAM

IN this chapter we shall try to show the place that Ṣūfism, in the form transmitted through the dervish orders, holds in the life of Islam in the Sudan. Ṣūfism has been studied in great detail and this section is merely an introductory sketch for readers not already acquainted with its history.

Islam contained from its earliest days the perception of absolute dependence upon God and submission to His will, so that for many devout souls the conquest of self by the ascetic life offered an alternative *jihād* to the conquest of the world. Original Islam had no deep connexion with mysticism, in spite of the attempts that have been made to read it into the meagre hints in the Qur'ān,[1] but the expansion of Islam into Egypt, Syria, 'Irāq, and Persia brought large Christian populations into the Islamic fold. These naturally brought with them their religious attitude to life, expressed it in Muslim forms and strongly influenced the ascetics of Islam from within. We are told that one of the Prophet's companions, Tamīm ad-Dārī, who had formerly been a Christian, passed the whole night in religious exercises, repeating a single verse (xl. 20) from the Qur'ān.[2] On the other hand, the policy of Islam with the *dhimmīs* left them complete freedom of worship, so that the Muslims could hardly fail to be familiar with Christian practice.

Ṣūfism arose out of this asceticism of the first century of the Hijra. Wandering ascetics were first called Ṣūfīs because of their practice, like that of the Christian ascetics, of wearing a woollen habit (*ṣūf* = wool) and so the word came to mean first ascetic and then mystic.[3] The normal word for mysticism being *taṣawwuf*—putting on wool.

[1] Such hints are, 'everything is perishing except His face' (xxviii. 88); 'everyone on earth is passing away (*fānī*), but the face of thy Lord, full of glory and honour, will endure for ever' (lv. 26–7). These phrases play a vital part in later Ṣūfism but had little to do with the awakening of the mystical element in Islam.

[2] Sha'rānī, *Lawāqiḥ al-Anwār*, Cairo, n.d., p. 21.

[3] According to Al-Qushairī, *Risāla* (Cairo, A.H. 1319, pp. 7–8), the word came into general use during the period of transition from asceticism to mysticism towards the end of the second century A.H. Al-Jāḥiẓ (d. A.D. 869) was one of the first Arabic writers to use the term when he speaks of 'the Ṣūfīs among the pietists' (*aṣ-Ṣūfiyya min an-nussāk*). Wool went out of fashion in the eleventh century A.D. in favour of the patched coat.

Ibn Khaldūn shows that Ṣūfism during the first century was ascetic and quietistic. He writes:

> The 'Way' of these people (the Ṣūfīs) has been current from the early days of Islam. It was adopted by the Companions and the Successors and those who followed them as the Way of Truth and Guidance. It meant originally, being zealous in worship, devoting oneself to God, shunning the pomps and vanities of the world, abstaining from the attractions of pleasure, wealth and position, and involving seclusion from men in a retreat for devotional purposes. Such was the normal thing among the Companions and early believers; but when love of the world became rampant, from the second century onwards, and people adhered to worldly things, those who were drawn to piety were distinguished by the name of Ṣūfīs.[1]

During the second century there was the development from asceticism (*zuhd*) to quietism (*riḍā*). The social, political, and intellectual conditions of the age favoured its growth. The rigid and barren dogmatism together with the sterile sectarianism of the schoolmen could not fill the hearts of people yearning after a harmony that is not of this world, so many of whom were converted from eastern Christianity. The devastating wars and tyrannical rulers of the Umayyad period, followed by the brilliant worldliness of the ʿAbbāsid period, with its sceptical and rationalistic currents, resulted in a turning away on the part of many of the devout from material things to an ascetic and quietistic life. These people were characterized by an overwhelming consciousness of the majesty of God and submission to His will, together with intense religious exaltation leading them to the perception of eternal truths. No organized community life developed at this stage, nor was there any attempt at theory until the transitional period at the end of the century when new tendencies begin to make their appearance. Maʿrūf al-Karkhī (d. A.D. 815), Rābiʿa al-ʿAdawīyya (A.D. 717–801), and Ḥārith b. Asad al-Muḥāsibī (A.D. 781–857) foreshadow the new development of ecstatic mysticism which characterizes the next stage. They sought, through the Way of Purgation, to bring their every thought and deed into harmony with the divine Will, and as that led to freedom from worldly attachments it gave birth to a doctrine of illumination and divine love. Maʿrūf al-Karkhī is the author of the first recorded definition of Ṣūfism: 'the apprehension of the verities and the renunciation of that which is in the hands of God's creatures' —a definition which contrasts in its simplicity with later definitions.

Another great ascetic-mystic of this interim period was Dhū'l-Nūn al-Maṣrī (A.D. 796–857) whose father was a Nubian slave.[2] It was

[1] *Muqaddama* (Cairo), p. 467.

[2] Al Qushairi, *Risāla*, p. 8.

he who gave a theosophical trend to the mystical doctrines of Ṣūfism and his teaching on the mystic gnosis (*ma'rifa*) constitutes a new development.

During the third century Ṣūfism entered upon this new phase. The quietistic spirit which had so far characterized it became overwhelmed by speculative and pantheistic tendencies. The *zāhid* (ascetic) developed into the *'ārif* (gnostic). These tendencies, arising through diverse forces working together, were derived from Neoplatonic speculation transmitted mainly through Syriac-speaking Christians, Nestorians, and Jacobites or Monophysites, for mysticism had reached a very considerable development in the Eastern Churches.[1] At first it came through personal contacts and later through written sources when translations from the Greek of books like the *Theology of Aristotle*[2] (tr. A.D. 840) were made by Christians such as Ḥunain ibn Isḥāq and his son. Ibn Masarrah of Cordoba (A.D. 883–931) was the precursor of this Illuministic (*Ishrāqi*) School.

Undoubtedly the Ṣūfīs arrived independently at the conclusion that Allāh was the only real Being, but the development and systematization of their experiences was strongly influenced by external influences through contact with oriental syncretism.

So the central doctrine of Islam, *tawḥīd*,[3] became pantheistic. The transcendent God became revealed in all created things. To the Ṣūfī not only is there no god but Allāh, but there is nothing but Allāh and the mystic finds his true self by losing his individual consciousness in ecstatic self-abandonment in the divine Oneness.

The next stage in the development of Ṣūfism is that in which it gains official recognition. Because of the speculative element Ṣūfīs had come to be regarded with suspicion and even as heretics, but through

[1] Jewish Neoplatonic influence is also undeniable, but not that of Manichaeanism as has often been stated. It is true the Ṣūfīs must have been in contact with it, but Manichaeanism does not seem to have had much influence over them. The term *zindīq*, though derived from the Syriac *zaddīqē*, was applied to the disciples of Mānī, with the meaning of 'heretic', by the Persians of the Sassanian period and was always used by the Muslims in a bad sense to mean 'atheist', 'Manichaean'. Ṣūfīs could not possibly have been influenced by 'atheists'. As to the terms supposed to have been borrowed from Manichaeanism (the 'hearers', the 'elect', the 'righteous'), they are really borrowed from the categories of the 'elect' (*οἱ ἐκλεκτοί*) among the Nestorian Christians. Ṣūfism has, therefore, been greatly influenced by Persian Christianity. It has also been influenced by the West Syrians or Jacobites, of whom the semi-pantheist Bar-Sudaili was one. This is especially true of the purely Arabian section of the Ṣūfīs—a section though which was not very important numerically.

[2] The so-called *Theology of Aristotle* is a translation into Arabic of Porphyry's commentary on the *Enneads* of Plotinus, iv, v, and vi.

[3] *Tawḥīd* is the acknowledgement of divine unity and the denial of all causes other than the One.

the extraordinary influence of one man, it was purged of these tendencies and gained a firm and assured position in the Islamic religious system by the *ijmāʿ* or 'catholic consent' of the faithful. This man was Al-Ghazālī (d. A.D. 1111)[1] who, driven to accept the Ṣūfī position through his own personal experience, by incorporating it into orthodox belief and giving an assured place to the religious Muslim, unsatisfied by formalism, who followed its path, gave new meaning to Islam itself.

Al-Ghazālī it is true can hardly be regarded as a typical Ṣūfī. He remained fully orthodox in his view of the nature of God and in his reverence for the *Sharīʿa.* He ruled out of Islam all pantheistic mysticism such as *hulūl* (incarnation or the union of the divine spirit with man)[2] and annihilation of individual personality, with the result that this type of speculative thought became unorthodox.

The effect of Al-Ghazāli's work was to bring about a truce rather than a true reconciliation between the *ʿulamā* and the Ṣūfīs and did not deter Ṣūfism, especially in Persia, from reaching the most extreme forms of pantheistic excess, which had already brought individuals, such as al-Ḥallāj, under the condemnation of orthodoxy. Thus there is a further development, of which Ibn al-ʿArabī (A.D. 1165–1240) is the central figure, which brought about a clear rupture between Ṣūfism proper and that mystical quietism which devout souls needed to give them a living religion in a formalist system. Thus, says D. B. Macdonald, 'the devout life within the Muslim Church led to a more complete pantheism than ever did the Christian Trinity'.[3]

With Ibn al-ʿArabī Ṣūfism becomes a hidden science which must only be divulged to a circle of initiates, or, as Massignon calls them, 'supernatural opium dens'. Sheltering behind this esoteric knowledge, the Ṣūfīs affected conformity to the Qur'ān, but interpreted everything allegorically.[4] They were universalists holding that God was active in all religions and, since all things are manifestations of Him, He may be worshipped in a star or an idol. Their speculations led orthodox Islam to keep careful watch on the doctrines of the mystical orders which now began to consolidate themselves as vehicles for the transmission of these esoteric doctrines.

So Ṣūfism, whether in its contemplative, emotional, or theophanistic form, showed the inadequacy of the religious doctrine of Islam, bound

[1] The way had been prepared by Abū'l-Qāsim al-Qushairī, who, in his *risāla* (A.D. 1045), attempted a reconciliation between Ṣūfī doctrine and Muslim law.

[2] He uses *hulūl* of the descent of God to Man in His Qur'ānic Word. A more theosophic type of mysticism is found in his later books which anticipates Ibn al-ʿArabī's pantheistic system.

[3] *The Religious Attitude and Life in Islam*, p. 39.

[4] Cf. *Tafsīr* of Ibn al-ʿArabī.

as it was in the bonds of formalism and statism. Ṣūfism was the upsurging in Islam of that spirit which insisted on the necessity for an inner life lived with God. It was the soil upon which Islam flourished and without which it would wither and decay.

2. THE RISE OF THE RELIGIOUS ORDERS

We have sketched the origin and development of Ṣūfism, but this forms only one aspect of its study. Pure theophanistic Ṣūfism has only a philosophic influence. But Ṣūfism in practice, which is emotional mysticism, is neither a philosophical system nor a sect, but a way of life—the way of purification. We need now to consider this practical aspect, the way in which the teaching was spread throughout the Islamic world through the growth of the religious orders, which have been the real agent for the spread of this transformed Islam. In this development we get a real difference of direction. Another aspect—the creation of a new power, that of the saints—we have already treated in the previous chapter.

The early Ṣūfīs usually wandered about alone, but the mystical experience can never be completely solitary, it is also exogenous. Though Ṣūfism in practice consists of feeling rather than knowledge, there is a natural succession which involves example and training. Further, conscious as they were of the dangers inherent in Ṣūfism through the development of heterodox theophanistic mysticism, they felt the need for guidance and training. So, gradually, aspirants to the mystical *ṭarīqa* ('path') came to put themselves under the guidance of older men. A *ṭarīqa* at first meant no more than the graded method of contemplative mysticism followed by one who had had a mystical call. Circles of disciples would gather round some venerated shaikh, such as al-Junayd (d. A.D. 909) and Sarī Saqatī (d. A.D. 866), and a community would be formed. Although the community was always mobile and its members wandered about the country supported by alms, a retreat or rest-house (*khalwa*, *khānqāh*, or *ribāṭ*) would often be founded as a centre. We hear of such a retreat at Damascus as early as A.H. 150 (A.D. 767) and in Khorāsān about A.H. 200 (A.D. 815).[1] These developed into monasteries and became very numerous in the Middle East during the eleventh century A.D. The development of fortified monasteries (*ribāṭ*), which played such an important part in the later Ṣūfism of the Maghrib, goes back to the foundation of the *ribāṭ* of Monastīr in A.D. 796.

[1] D. B. Macdonald, *Muslim Theology, Jurisprudence and Constitutional Theory*, p. 177.

These schools, however, represented only the teaching of the shaikh, having a very fine but limited philosophic influence. Therefore, for centuries these groups broke up on the death of the shaikh. They were not the definite orders we now know, but simply groups of disciples gathered around a loved and honoured teacher which disintegrated after his death—the bond of allegiance being a personal one. Al-Ghazālī, for instance, gathered a school around him which did not survive his death. It was not until the early thirteenth century that we find one of these schools, the Qādiriyya, some fifty years after the death of ʿAbd al-Qādir in 1166, developing into a definite self-perpetuating order, designed to carry on, not only the teaching, but also the name and rule of the eponym.

Certain eminent pupils would ascribe themselves[1] to their leader and bestow the *ṭarīqa* on others as from the dead shaikh. The shaikh ceased to train his disciples directly and a special cult then developed around his person. This is one aspect of the change. The other is a change in the constitution of the body of adherents. The dedicated darwīsh-disciples devoted themselves to asceticism and the duties of the order, but membership was now extended to include lay-adherents who 'took the *ṭarīqa*' from the shaikh or his *khalīfas* but were allowed to carry on the normal duties of life. The *ṭarīqa* by this width of membership thus became a kind of religious-philanthropic body.

Such a body came to be called a *ṭarīqa* (plur. *ṭuruq*) which word then meant the particular system of spiritual training attributed to the founder of an order. Each *ṭarīqa* is supposed to have been handed down through a continuous chain (*silsila*) and adherents can produce an *isnād*, or spiritual succession, from the Prophet through ʿAlī or Abū Bakr to the existing shaikh of the order. So the shaikh is regarded as being the spiritual heir of the original founder deriving his authority from his immediate predecessor. These orders were not intended to replace the formal Muslim religious organization, which the Ṣūfīs regarded as a necessary concession (*rukhṣa*) to human weakness; nor were they sects, for they were regarded as being orthodox and their differences were in organization, method of training, and ritual, not in doctrine; but they were centres for the higher development of the spiritual life under the guidance of one endowed with special gifts. They did, however, constitute a mystic church within Islam and introduced a hierarchical system foreign to primitive Islam. The distinctive traits of the dervish were voluntary poverty, the solitary conventical life passed in prayer and mortification, often missionary

[1] *intasaba*, *intamā*, or *tasammā*.

zeal, but not continence or chastity. Along with this went the parallel development of the cult of the saints as the religion of the masses, whilst pure Ṣūfism appealed to the educated. No real dividing line, however, could be drawn between the two. Ṣūfism provided a philosophy of life which was adapted to the needs of the masses by the orders. They taught that God has given every soul the potentiality of union with Him, but since this cannot normally be developed except under the guidance of one already illuminated, the aspirant (*murīd*) must attach himself to such a one as his *murshid* or *shaikh*. A Tijāniyya book, *As-Sirr al-Abhar*, begins: 'Praise be to God who has given to everything a means and made the mediating shaikh the means of union with God'.

It was not then until the thirteenth century A.D. that corporations established themselves with the definite purpose of carrying on the name and rule of life of the master; but once started they developed a vigorous life and multiplied with great rapidity.[1] Although at the present day all the orders claim to have been founded by celebrated early Ṣūfīs such as Ibrāhīm Ibn Adham (d. A.H. 161) and Abū Yazīd al-Bistāmī (d. A.H. 261), these spiritual *nisbas* were made up later. The earliest definite orders which still exist are the Qādiriyya, attributed to ʿAbd al-Qādir al-Jīlānī (A.D. 1077–1166); the Rifāʿiyya which started at Baṣra under Aḥmad ar-Rifāʿī (d. A.D. 1182); the Suhrawardiyya attributed to Ḍiyā' ad-Dīn Najīb Suhrawardī (d. A.D. 1167), but founded by his nephew Shihāb ad-Dīn (d. A.D. 1234/5); the Badawiyya of Aḥmad al-Badawī (d. A.D. 1276), whose shrine at Ṭanṭā is one of the most popular in Egypt; the Naqshabandiyya of Turkestan, founded by Muḥammad Bahā'ad-Dīn an-Naqshabandī (d. A.D. 1389); the Shādhiliyya, attributed to Abu'l Ḥasan ʿAlī ash-Shādhilī (d. A.D. 1258); and the Mawlāwiyya, the 'whirling dervishes', founded by the famous Persian poet, Jalāl ad-Dīn ar-Rūmī (d. A.D. 1273). From Asia they spread to Africa, their tendencies changing considerably in the process to fit in with the needs of Berber and African Islam.

A great growth of unspecialized Ṣūfī centres also characterized this period. Maqrīzī[2] gives a long list of *zāwiyas*, *ribāṭs*, and *khānqāhs* in Egypt in the times of Ṣalāḥ ad-Dīn, the overthrower of the Fāṭimid Empire, and his successors, which was the period of their greatest

[1] The definitive formation of the orders is an example of the way in which established (i.e. Sunnī) Islam assimilates other elements and thus avoids schism, for one result of the failure of the Shīʿite social movements such as that of the Buwayhids in Persia in A.D. 1055, and the Fāṭimids in Egypt in A.D. 1171, was the development of the Ṣūfī orders and the absorption of many Shīʿite theories into them.

[2] *Khiṭaṭ* (ed. A.H. 1324), iv. 273–306.

influence. The first *khānqāh* in Egypt was the Dār Sa'īd as-Su'adā[1] which was constituted a *waqf* in A.D. 1173/4. It was intended to act as a hostel for the residence of foreign Ṣūfīs, but soon lost this character and developed into the chief centre of Egyptian Ṣūfism. Its head had the title of *shaikh ash-shuyūkh*, which title was soon extended to all heads of *khānqāhs*. Ibn Baṭūṭa describes many of the *khānqāhs* and their rules at the time of his visit to Egypt in A.D. 1326.[2] He says that the *fuqahā'* in them were chiefly Persians. The *khānqāhs* were not yet specialized to particular orders, and remained independent until the Shaikh al-Bakrī was appointed in A.D. 1550 as head of all the orders.

A definitely new order can never now arise. Often the sons or the *khalīfas* of a *walī* will quarrel about the succession and make themselves independent, so that the parent order will become weak and decentralized. Sometimes a saint of outstanding gifts will arise within a *ṭarīqa* and found a daughter order with the consent and blessing of his old shaikh. He then traces his succession back to the original founder of the parent *ṭarīqa*. As Abū'l-Faḍl puts it, 'any chosen soul who, in the mortification of the deceitful spirit, and in the worship of God, introduced some new motive of conduct, and whose spiritual sons in succession continued to keep alight the lamp of doctrine, was acknowledged the founder of a new line'.[3] His branch is then an independent organization in spiritual communion with the parent order.

The doctrines of the orders are not so important. The main thing is the bond between the *shaikh* (or *murshid*) and the *murīd* (aspirant or novice); nothing else really matters, for the shaikh, if he wishes, can order the *murīd* to cease to believe in God.

Their organizations are very similar, differing mainly in secondary details such as grades, litanies, and ritual, though sometimes in direction and effort. At the summit of the visible hierarchy is the *shaikh* whose dignity is usually hereditary. Immediately under him is his *khalīfa* or *nā'ib*, one in charge of each area. Then there is sometimes a *naqīb* or guardian of the liturgy (*dhikr*). Under the regional *khalīfa* are the sectional leaders (*muqaddam*, North Africa; *murshid*, Irān; *'ām*, Egypt; or simply *shaikh*), who enrol and initiate new members, engage in the work of propaganda and management, and to whom the dervishes[4] and lay brethren are subordinate. The dervishes or begging

[1] Op. cit. iv. 273–5.

[2] *Riḥlat* (Cairo, 1939), i. 37–8. Cf. also many other references to the *Khānqāhs* of the Ṣūfīs at Damascus (i. 84), *zāwiyas* at Kāzarūn (i. 168), Kawrastān (i. 218), Ẓafār al-Ḥamūḍ (i. 204), specialized to particular shaikhs.

[3] *Abū'l Faḍl 'Allāmī*, *Ā'īn-i-Akbarī*, tr. H. S. Jarret, iii. 357.

[4] *darwīsh*, pl. *darāwīsh*, has been thought to be derived from Persian 'seeking doors',

friars in the Sudan are often called *fuqarā* (sing. both *faqīr* and *faqīh*) and *talāmidha* (sing. *tilmīdh*, disciple); but these form only a small section of the membership of the orders. The various terms and the functions of the officials vary between the different *ṭarīqas*. All classes of the populace can be enrolled as lay brethren or affiliated members. These carry on their normal occupations and mode of life, but are all subject to the guidance of the *shaikh* and *khalīfa*, receive their instructions from them, and take part in the collective repetition of remembrances of God (*dhikr*). Some orders admit women as members, but to-day these are only affiliated members. Certain classes, trades, districts, or tribes affect particular orders, and there has been a tendency in the Sudan to form tribal groups.

3. INTRODUCTION OF THE ORDERS INTO THE SUDAN

The Islam of the Sudan during the Funj period was influenced not from Egypt, but the Ḥijāz, and this gave it a different tendency which endures to this day. The holy places being easily accessible, the pilgrimage played an important part in the process by bringing Sudanese into touch with the centre of Islam. Some Meccan scholars and holy men were induced to migrate to the Funj kingdom and many Sudanese studied in Mecca and Medina. These men introduced the nominal Muslims of the Sudan to a type of Islam they could readily appreciate and assimilate, and brought a measure of culture to a barbarous people.

The main result of this connexion with the holy places was the bringing of a living religion to the Sudanese in the form of that double aspect of one process—saint-worship and the religious orders. These orders were not organized in the sense that we now know them. Individual holy men came to the Sudan, established Muslim cells, and became objects of reverence. They initiated their followers into the Ṣūfī path they themselves followed; but since Ṣūfism at this time was at a very low ebb, for mysticism in Islam is not only its highest but also its most degraded form, it was materialized in the form of the cult of mysterious powers, now islamized in the form of *baraka*, therefore personal allegiance and abject reverence for the shaikh was the thing that mattered.

Though a superstitious throng, bringing a degenerate type of mysticism, yet they brought the fervour, devotion, and vitality begotten of long contact and discipleship with spiritual leaders in ʿIrāq and the Ḥijāz.

i.e. mendicant, but probably connected with Avestan *drigu* (poor), M.Pers. *drgwš*, Pazand *daryōš*.

The wealth of biographies in the *Ṭabaqāt* help us to understand how their teaching and influence was impressed on the land. They found a fertile soil among the sedentaries in the Sudan and easily won the hearts of the intellectually backward masses with their devotional fervour and miracle-mongering, whilst many of their successors, now all Sudanese, became influential guides of the Funj kings and princes, not only in spiritual but political affairs as well. At the same time the common people sought their intercession, not only with God but with their rulers as well, for they were a means by which the opinion of the masses could be expressed. During their life they enjoyed royal favour and the adoration of the people; and after their death they became intercessors with God and their tombs places of pilgrimage.

There were two main stages of the introduction of the *ṭarīqas*. The earliest tradition which has come down to us says that the Shādhiliyya was brought to the Sudan before the fall of the kingdom of ʿAlwa by a son-in-law of Al-Jazūlī called Sharīf Ḥamad Abū Dunāna who settled in Berber district in A.H. 849 (A.D. 1445) and whose descendants continued to exercise the khalīfaship to this day.

One, Tāj ad-Dīn al-Bahārī, is said to have been the first to introduce the Qādiriyya (*c.* A.D. 1550) from the seat of the order, Baghdād, and to have lived at Wādī Shaʿīr in the Jezīra for seven years. He appointed a number of khalīfas, amongst them Muḥammad al-Amīn ibn ʿAbd as-Ṣādiq, founder of the Ṣādiqāb branch of Sūki; Bān an-Naqā aḍ-Ḍarīr, founder of the Yaʿqūbāb;[1] Sh. ʿAjīb ʿAbd Allāh Jamāʿa of the ʿAbdallāb, the viceroy of Qerrī; and ʿAbd Allāh Dafaʿ Allāh al-ʿArakī, founder of the ʿArakiyyīn (who later changed over to the Sammāniyya *c.* 1800). These men were the temporal and spiritual heads of families and their descendants continue in the double function in the Jezīra to this day. The members are thus born into the *ṭarīqa* and do not receive any special initiation. The first shaikh of the group is regarded as their patron saint whose *baraka* has descended to his successors.

But a Maḥasī, Idrīs ibn Arbāb (A.D. 1507–1651), is also stated to be the first khalīfa of the Qādiriyya in the Sudan. The confusion probably arises from the fact that neither then nor to-day is the work of the order centralized. This Idrīs is one of the most famous of all the saints of the Sudan and his *qubba* at ʿAylāfūn is an important place of pilgrimage.

During the reign of Bādī ibn Rubāṭ (1651–89) there also came

[1] They take their name from his eldest son Yaʿqūb.

'at-Tilimsanī, the Maghrabī, to Shaikh Muḥammad b. 'Īsā "Suwār adh-Dhahab" and initiated him in the Ṣūfī Path'.[1]

The Shādhiliyya acquired further influence during the Funj régime through one Khōjalī ibn 'Abd ar-Raḥmān (d. 1743), a Maḥasī born on Tūtī. He was at first a Qādirī, but also joined the Shādhiliyya when in Mecca. In the *Ṭabaqāt* we read of Khōjalī, 'as regards the origin of his *ṭarīqa*, the foundation of it was Qādiriyya, but in his methods of *awrād* (litanies) he was a Shādhilī, and indeed his "Shaikh" was a pupil of Shaikh Muḥammad an-Nāṣirī the Shādhilī'.[2]

In the north, the Majdhūbiyya Ṭarīqa (a derivative of the Shādhiliyya) was started in the early eighteenth century by Ḥamad ibn al-Majdhūb (1693–1776), who joined the Shādhiliyya in Mecca. His family became a considerable force in Dāmar district.

These orders, with the exception of the Majdhūbiyya, had no cohesion and, as we see from the accounts in the *Ṭabaqāt*, were only thought of as religious schools. Islamic religious organization in the Sudan at this time was 'cellular', the *zāwiya* of the feki being a kind of monastic cell in a pagan environment nursing the new Islamic culture. The 'path' was taught independently by the fekis who concentrated their work in a *zāwiya* where they had their family, slaves, servants, and disciples, and in which the traveller or pilgrim could find rest and hospitality. The sanctity of the founder of the *zāwiya* extended sometimes very far and pilgrims thronged to receive his *baraka*. This attachment to the holy men led to a grouping of adherents by villages[3] or districts under a khalīfa whose office became hereditary, though it did not necessarily descend to the eldest son. Sometimes the temporal authority went to one son and the spiritual to another. Usually succession was settled by the head of the order before his death and failure to do so often led to disputes among the descendants and a split in the order. The biography of 'Alī an-Nīl gives the account of such a testamentary deposition:

When he was about to die he was asked who would be khalīfa after him. He said, 'the herdsman', meaning Al-Junaid although he was illiterate and had done nothing but herding cattle. Sharaf ad-Dīn (another son) was present too and he knew the Qur'ān by heart and was learned, as were 'Alī's brothers Muḥammad Aṣ-Ṣāfi and Muṣṭafā, the sons of Muḥammad al-Hamīm. The people said, 'Shaikh 'Alī is the most learned of us and knows God best, and had he not seen goodness and piety in this man he would not have appointed him.' Then he made him khalīfa over them and said, 'A saint can guide

[1] *Ṭabaqāt*, M. 4, S. 5.

[2] Op. cit. M. 74, S. 77.

[3] The piety of Idrīs b. al-Arbāb attracted Maḥas from Donqola to his house at 'Ailāfūn which is now one of the largest villages in the Blue Nile Province.

whether alive or dead.' They brought Al-Junaid to him and he pressed him on his chest and belly and said, 'This one will sit on my *sijjāda* and will hold my rosary. All that I have had he shall have.'[1]

The shaikhs were mainly powerful in the Jezīra under the Funj. They were highly regarded and subsidized by the Funj kings and would intercede with them and could rebuke them with impunity. We read of Ṣāliḥ ibn Bān an-Naqā (1681–1773), who, we are told, 'was the third of the khalīfas who lit the fire of Shaikh ʿAbd al-Qādir in the land of the Funj', that 'the court gave him a share in the river-lands and rain-lands', which, however, 'he divided among the people as though it had been a banquet'. Of powers of intercession with kings (*ash-shifāʿa ʿinda'l-mulūk*) we read of Ḥamad b. al-Majdhūb (d. 1776) that 'God made him exceedingly popular with both great and small. He used to intercede frequently with kings and sultans, especially the Jaʿal, and normally his intercession was not rejected for he who rejected it would be quickly blighted.'[2]

Some of these shaikhs were invested with the Funj symbols of authority. We read of Dafʿ Allāh b. ash-Shaikh Muḥammad Abū Idrīs:

> Shaikh Muḥammad wad Dā'ūd al-Agharr came to him from the village of Wad ʿAjīb and brought him the *kukāra*,[3] flags, *jubba* and *kufiyya* of Ḥabīb Allāh al-ʿAjamī[4] and the *jubba* of ʿAbd Allāh al-ʿArakī 'Umm Kiraisha' (the Pot-bellied) in which are inscribed 'the Names'. He said, 'these things were left in my hands by your forefathers who said to me, "if Dafʿ Allāh grows up give them to him". So take your legacy.'[5]

The second stage was the result of events outside the Sudan. The stagnant period through which the Islamic world had been passing was now changing and new life was stirring at the beginning of the nineteenth century. This was due mainly to the reaction caused by the rapid expansion of European countries into Muslim lands. In the Ḥijāz Wahhābism was becoming powerful and through its puritanism and 'back to primitive Islam' movement was intensifying religious differences within Islam and intolerance of external interference. It attacked the popular saint-worship and superstitions and led to an accentuation of the differences between the religious orders. New orders sprang up full of renewed missionary zeal, whilst the old orders, many of which existed only in name as mystical schools, lost their

[1] Op. cit. M. 134, S. 142; cf. also the story of Medanī an-Nāṭiq b. ʿAbd ar-Raḥmān speaking from tomb, quoted above p. 146.

[2] Op. cit. M. 70, S. 73.

[3] Plur. of *kakar*. See above, p. 87.

[4] Ḥabīb Allāh was the son of Tāj ad-Dīn al-Bahārī.

[5] *Ṭabaqāt*, M. 80, S. 87.

apathy and tolerance in a counter-reformation. The resurrected Qādiriyya was turned into a vital and effective missionary force throughout Africa, although it never gained any definite cohesion.

In A.D. 1800 the Sammāniyya *ṭarīqa* was introduced into the Sudan by a certain Jamū'ī, Aḥmad aṭ-Ṭayyib al-Bashīr, who had been studying at Al-Medīna under Muḥammad ibn 'Abd al-Karīm as-Sammānī. In a short time he gained a great following among the Jamū'iyya, Kawāḥla, and the Ḥalāwiyīn in the Jezīra.

But the man who influenced the Sudan more than anyone else, though he never entered the country, was the Sayyid Aḥmad ibn Idrīs, known as Al-Fāsī (d. 1837). Whilst a genuine mystic he was also a religious reformer,[1] influenced by the Wahhābī reformation, and the result was that the activities of his followers were of a missionary character amongst both Muslims and pagans. Though he founded an order, the Idrīsiyya, which is still active in the Sudan, he influenced it mainly through being the teacher of other men who founded or introduced orders. The most important of these were:

(1) Muḥammad al-Majdhūb aṣ-Ṣughayyir (1796–1832), the great-grandson of the founder of the Majdhūbiyya. He studied under Aḥmad ibn Idrīs whilst in exile in Mecca and on his return to the Sudan revivified his *ṭarīqa* and extended it in the east among the Beja.

(2) Shaikh Ibrāhīm ar-Rashīdī (d. 1874), a Shā'iqī, who was of the family of the founder of the Algerian Rashīdiyya, carried on the propagandist tradition of his master Aḥmad ibn Idrīs and established the Idrīsiyya order in the Sudan amongst other places.

(3) Muḥammad 'Uthmān al-Mirghanī (1793–1853), who made extensive missionary journeys in the Sudan and established his *ṭarīqa*, the Mirghaniyya or Khatmiyya in the north and east, where it spread rapidly through the propaganda of the founder's numerous family.

The most famous of Aḥmad b. Idrīs's pupils, Muḥammad ibn 'Alī as-Sanūsī (d. 1859), scarcely influenced the Eastern Sudan.

[1] On Aḥmad and his *ṭarīqa* see pp. 228–30. His biographer writes: 'His concern was not confined to teaching *awrād* and *adhkār*, to urging people to shut themselves up in retreat and isolate themselves from mankind. Such practices might be of advantage for the personal development of the individual disciple, but were not suitable for the higher purpose at which he was aiming, that is, the unity of the word of the Muslims and their unification in the bond of Islam. He was shocked when he saw how disagreed they were in their opinions, how broken up was their unity and disordered their mutual affairs. God had sent him as a reformer (*mujaddid*) to this Ḥanifite religion following the tradition narrated by Abū Dā'ūd in his *Sunan* and the Imām Aḥmad in his *Musnad*, that "God will send to this nation at the opening of every epoch one who will reform her religion". He was a reformer of this religion and propagated this spirit of reform in the hearts of his companions' (*Kanz as-sa'ādati wa'l-irshād*, pp. 16–17).

Another order introduced into Berber shortly before the Mahdiyya was the Tijāniyya. It was brought from Egypt by Muḥammad b. al-Mukhtār (d. 1882), known as 'Wad al-ʿĀliya'. Later West Africans such as the Hausa, ʿUmar Ganbo, spread the order in Dārfūr and Kordofān.

Chatelier mentions the Syro–Egyptian order of the Saʿdiyya[1] (a branch of the Rifāʿiyya), the Raḥmāniyya (a branch of the Darqawiyya), the Badawiyya of Aḥmad al-Badawī of Ṭanṭa, and the Burhāmiyya or Disūkiyya of Ibrāhīm ad-Disūkī as having been introduced during this period. The founder of the Raḥmāniyya, Muḥammad b. Muḥammad b. Masʿūd ibn ʿAbd ar-Raḥmān (d. 1878), built a *zāwiya* at Mecca in 1857 and afterwards preached all along the south-west coast of the Red Sea from Sawākin to Maṣawwaʿ, where his khalīfa, Aḥmad al-Hajūnī al-Ghafrūnī, made himself independent (Ghafrūniyya). Some of these Egyptian orders have disappeared from the Sudan, or have only small urban groups of Egyptian adherents.

The only order other than the Majdhūbiyya truly native to the Sudan is the Ismāʿīliyya which was founded by Ismāʿīl ibn ʿAbd Allāh (1793–1863) in El-Obeyd by permission of his shaikh Muḥammad ʿUthman al-Mirghanī. It has spread mainly in Kordofān.

The whole spirit of these new orders was different. Initiation was purely an act of blind submission to the shaikh. The great aim was to increase the power of the orders by augmenting their numbers and centralizing the organization. The culmination of the reactionary spirit in the Sudan was the Mahdiyya outburst.

These orders, especially the Egyptian, were encouraged by Muḥammad ʿAlī after the Turko-Egyptian conquest and their legal existence recognized.[2] In Egypt they had all been placed under a *shaikh aṭ-ṭuruq*, having the title of Shaikh al-Bakrī, so that they would be under central control. This shaikh's authority extended to the Sudan which did not have its own *shaikh aṭ-ṭuruq* as in other parts of the Turkish Empire; but he had little influence over the established

[1] Chatelier writes of the Saʿdiyya: 'L'histoire de la propagande des confréries égyptiennes au Soudan paraît avoir été fertile en épisodes. Les chefs des différents ordres se firent, en effet, une concurrence active. L'un d'eux, celui des Saadiya, pour mieux établir la supériorité de sa règle, ne craignit pas de reculer de plusieurs centaines d'années, dans un "tract" destiné aux néophytes soudanais, la date de la naissance du Cheikh el Triqā, du fondateur de l'ordre. Ce procédé paraît avoir été couronné de succès, car les Saadiya comptaient, au moment de l'insurrection mahdiste, parmi les plus importantes confréries du pays' (*L'Islam au XIXe siècle*, pp. 90–1). The Mahdist insurrection must have wiped out the order in the Sudan because I have never heard of any members.

[2] ʿAli Mubārak (*Khiṭaṭ Jadīda*, iii. 129) gives a long list of the orders which were active in Egypt in 1888.

groups where all emphasis was placed on personal allegiance to the shaikh of the order. In Egypt, on the contrary, he acted not only as an intermediary between the authorities and the orders with regard to such things as the *awqāf* (religious endowments), participation in national and public ceremonies and use of the mosques, but gradually came to lay claim to a general authority.[1]

This recognition of the shaikhs by the new government led to their becoming wealthy and respected members of the community and the natural leaders of the people under a foreign rule. When therefore the Mahdī raised his standard in Abā Island they were all, with the exception of the Majādhīb, hostile to his claims which they knew assailed their authority.

In districts where the *ṭarīqas* were strong the people were not immediately prepared to accept a type of belief which abolished their deep-seated belief in saints and substituted that of God and His Mahdī alone. But as soon as he confirmed his Mahdī-ship by his military successes they readily transferred their allegiance to him. The first effect of Mahdist control was that all *ṭarīqas* were abolished since the leaders denied his claims. The shaikhs then either joined the Mahdī, or opposed him, or fled the country. The Mahdī himself, at first a shaikh of the Sammāniyya, refuted all who thought that he was founding a *ṭarīqa* by his change of the name of his followers. His coming initiated a new dispensation, the 'bridegroom' was with them, and his *anṣār* were equal to the saints. He wrote in a letter to the Shaikh al Islām, 'the Prophet . . . announced to me that my followers are as his followers and that the commonest of them in the sight of God is like unto ʿAbd al-Qādir al-Jīlānī'.[2]

After the reoccupation the shaikhs of the orders returned to the Sudan with official recognition and quickly reclaimed the allegiance of the people who were attached to them by personal loyalties, except in certain parts of the White and Blue Nile provinces, where many clung to a superstitious belief in the Mahdī's son.

Though some orders like the Sanūsiyya and certain branches of the Tijāniyya are anti-European, the more powerful Sudan orders have until recently been favourable to the present government. Competition between the orders and internal quarrels occupy them a great deal. The Mirghanī leaders opposed the Mahdī and aided the British considerably during the reconquest, and to-day the hostility between the

[1] The present Sayyid al-Bakrī, who succeeded his father in 1940, is a Cambridge graduate and western in outlook. His father belonged to the old school.

[2] Wingate, *Mahdism*, p. 48.

Mirghaniyya and the Mahdist sect is intense, but the reasons are purely political and in no sense religious. The attitude of the orders depends wholly upon that of the shaikh and naturally those of assured position do not encourage fanaticism. This attitude, although inspired by their own interests, and not by any sympathy for the British, has been very valuable for the development of a stable rule in the Sudan.

Though the *ṭarīqas* have a very strong hold upon the people they are more likely to decrease than increase in importance in the future, for the new conceptions of Islam are either indifferent or hostile to them. In other countries which have been longer under western influence they have declined considerably. The orthodox *ʿulamā* are no less hostile than the modernists. Still, it would not be wise to under-estimate their strength for it is they, and not official Islam, that are the organized expression of Sudanese religious life.

4. METHOD OF ORGANIZATION

There are considerable differences between the organization of the various orders, for the terminology, powers, and authority of the functionaries vary considerably, but a few general lines may be indicated.

At the head of each order is the *shaikh* who is the spiritual heir of the founder, to whom the revelation has been passed on and to whom it is personal and inherent. He is called *shaikh as-sijjāda* because he inherits the prayer-carpet (often a sheep-skin) of the founder as the symbol of his authority. He lives usually at the place where the founder's tomb is situated. Thus the head of the world-wide Qādiriyya lives at Baghdād as keeper of ʿAbd al-Qādir's tomb. To-day the Qādiriyya is split up into numerous branches and in practice only nominal allegiance is paid to him. The shaikh to any Qādirī of the Sudan is his local head (technically a *khalīfa* or deputy) who claims absolute allegiance, and not some remote person in Baghdād. So it is with the other external orders, though they are not all so decentralized as the Qādiriyya. Of the orders which are Sudanese rather than anything else, the head of the Ismāʿīliyya resides at El-Obeyd where his grandfather, Ismāʿīl b. ʿAbdallāh, is buried; Al-Bashīr Aḥmad Jalāl ad-Dīn of the Majdhūbiyya at Dāmar, where is the tomb of Ḥamad b. Muḥammad al-Majdhūb. One of the Mirghanīs always lives at Khatmiyya, a township of Kasala which was founded by Al-Ḥasan, the son of Muḥammad ʿUthmān, as his see, and has gained great prestige from the miracle-working powers of Al-Ḥasan's tomb and because it is essentially a Sudanese order.

The shaikh need not be of the family of the founder since the succession is spiritual, but in practice the hereditary principle is invariable. He usually nominates his successor amongst his sons, though not necessarily choosing the eldest. In the Mirghaniyya, each regional head is recognized as a *shaikh as-sijjāda*, for the *baraka* resides in each of them. The hereditary principle is bad as regards spiritual direction, and leads often to incompetence in organization, for they are surrounded by sycophantic toadies who are out for what they can get. It does, however, serve to hold an order together. In the Sudan the prestige of some of the shaikhs is such that they have become a kind of royalty. The people have an unquestioning veneration for them which is based upon the great claims they make for themselves as inheritors of the *baraka* (holiness) of the founder. This *baraka*, which has descended upon them from the prophet, as we have already seen, is a far greater thing than a blessing. It includes all the miraculous and intercessory power of a *walī*. The member obtains a share in the *baraka* through the initiation (*akhad al-wird*)[1] of the shaikh or his khalīfa, who in return demands absolute allegiance.

Under the shaikh are a number of khalīfas appointed directly by him to take charge of regional areas to whom he gives a certificate (*ijāza*).[2] In some orders they are invested with certain of his powers and can confer the *wird* through delegation by the shaikh. The

[1] 'To take the *wird* of shaikh So-and-so' is to take his *ṭarīqa*, that is, his 'rule', for *wird* (pl. *awrād*) is the term used for special daily or seasonal collects which the new *murīd* (novice) promises to repeat. The ordinary way of referring to initiation is *akhada'ṭ-ṭarīqa*, 'he took the ṭarīqa', and 'to initiate' is *salaka'ṭ-ṭarīqa*. *Talqīn*, also 'to teach the *awrād*', i.e. to initiate, is only used in books.

[2] Two kinds of *ijāza* are given, the one to a *darwīsh* permitting him to practise in the name of his master, and the other to a *khalīfa* or *muqaddam* giving him authority to confer the *wird*, i.e. admit others into the *ṭarīqa*. An *ijāza* usually runs on this form: 'This is to certify that Muḥammad Aḥmad the son of (full genealogy) who took the *ṭarīqa* from the *khalīfa* Muṣṭafā (then follows the chain (*silsila*) of khalīfas back to the founder) has found his adept (Ṭāhā ibn . . . with genealogy) to be a worthy follower of the order. He is therefore given authority to act according to the rules of the Order, since all its secrets have been revealed to him.' The khalīfa affixes his seal to the document and it is usually worn in a tubular case on the flank. Sir Richard Burton (*Pilgrimage*, App. III) gives a full translation of the *ijāza* of a *murshid*; and the *Ṭabaqāt* (S. 33, M. 31–2) reproduces part of an *ijāza* given by Ibn Jābir in 1574 to one of his disciples, as follows: 'Praise be to God the Lord of the universe and peace be upon the Apostles. Verily the brother of faqīh Ibrāhīm, the pious, learned and humble one, the son of Umm Rāb'a, I believe to be worthy of mastership and leadership. I therefore appoint him a *quṭb* in rank, an interpreter to his age and time, a tutor to the aspirants, an example to those who guide, a refuge for the poor and destitute, a revivifier of the sun of knowledge after its setting. I authorize him to pass on and teach to the people all that he has truly received and heard from me. I also authorize him to propagate and broadcast the knowledge we have referred to. Let any one to whom such knowledge is communicated be exceeding careful lest he should be spiritually destroyed.'

<u>kh</u>alīfas of the Qādiriyya in the Sudan, by virtue of the hereditary principle, have the authority inherent in them whether or not they receive it from the actual shaikh. On the other hand, the <u>kh</u>alīfas of the Mir<u>gh</u>aniyya cannot confer the *awrād*. They are simply ordinary lay members who have charge of the ordering of a small group or a <u>kh</u>alwa, and over each ten or so is a <u>kh</u>alīfat al-<u>kh</u>ulafā.

An important official of the large centralized orders is the organizing head, the *wakīl* of the *shaikh as-sijjāda*, who administers the property of the order and organizes large functions. He sends out 'collecting parties' which collect dues from the followers. These parties have often caused trouble because of the number of parasites who attach themselves to get free entertainment.

The members of an order are of two groups. The first, a minority who are supposed to be wholly devoted to the religious life and to be following the 'Path' under the direction of the shaikh. These are the professional *darāwī<u>sh</u>* or *ḥairān.* (disciples): 'In his hand the rosary of women; In his eyes the symptoms of the drunken.'[1] Some are men who have taken the *ṭarīqa* from the shaikh, learn his *awrād*, practise his cures, live in his *zāwiya*, accompany him when travelling, and help to enliven the *dhikr*.

Other *darāwī<u>sh</u>* own no allegiance to a particular order or a living shaikh; their shaikh is a dead saint who revealed himself to them in a vision and whose shrine they frequent. Such a one never calls himself a *darwī<u>sh</u>*, but the *tilmī<u>dh</u>* (disciple) of shaikh So-and-so, or he will say 'my father is Shaikh Fulān'. They are therefore simply called by the people *wad ash-shaikh* (son of the shaikh). A *tilmī<u>dh</u>* of Shaikh <u>Kh</u>ōjalī told me that he had a vision of the shaikh outside his *qubba* in which the Shaikh offered him some *kisra*. His acceptance and eating of it made him his disciple. He had not been initiated by the present-day <u>kh</u>alīfa of Shaikh <u>Kh</u>ōjalī. Such men haunt the neighbourhood of their saint's tomb and carry around sand from his grave to drop into the hand of the faithful, who are then expected to reward them. *Darwī<u>sh</u>* is also applied in a general way to any half-witted or simple-minded person. Once when I spoke to a mentally-deficient child his mother explained him by saying, 'he's become a darwī<u>sh</u>' (*iddarwash*). None of these self-constituted dervishes know anything of Ṣūfism and they are usually half-witted. They are beyond any recognized standard and their disregard of the laws of conventional Muslim morality and mental deficiency is ascribed to their being so absorbed in God that their bodies cannot be held responsible for their actions.

---

[1] Al-Ḥarīrī, *Maqāma* of Damascus.

There are comparatively few dervishes in the Sudan, for the fekis are the conventional Sudanese religious men, and, whilst the illiterate have some regard for them, they are often objects of derision to those with a smattering of education. Some orders, such as the Mirghaniyya, do not have any professional dervishes at all.

The majority group are the masses of the people who, whilst retaining their ordinary occupations and mode of life, are devoted to their shaikh and acknowledge his leadership. They satisfy their religious needs in the *dhikr*. These ordinary members may be known variously as *awlād aṭ-ṭarīqa*, *khuddām* (Jezīra), *ḥairān*, in a specialized sense *aṣḥāb* and *anṣār*; but it is uncommon for them to talk of themselves as we should speak of members of a society. In contrast with other countries where it is only certain groups or strata of the population who belong to a *ṭarīqa*, all Muslims in the Sudan have attachment to some one or other. This is probably the result of the standard level of life in the Sudan and the weakness of orthodox religion. But particular districts or tribes affect particular *ṭarīqas*. Their importance in the Sudan is due to this vast membership and they rival each other in extending their influence. None of them are taught the Ṣūfi Path. Members learn the *wird* or *ḥizb* of their order as a condition of their admittance and are supposed to recite it at stated periods of the day and take part in the congregational *dhikr* ritual.

Each order possesses a number of *taqīyyas*. These are not the great organizations associated with this word in other countries, but simply a place for the accommodation of dervishes and travellers. They all possess *zāwiyas*, which is the term used for any small privately-owned mosque, in which the *dhikrs* are performed. The main one is known as *umm zāwiya* where the shaikh of the order presides. These act as a kind of brotherhood centre or religious club for ordinary members; their attitude to them being much more intimate and personal than to the ordinary mosques which they enter, if at all, only for the Friday noonday prayer. The *khalwa* should also be mentioned; used in reference to a dervish it is equivalent to being 'in retreat', but any place where one can be alone can be called a *khalwa*.

Initiation

Their methods of initiation vary only in the details. Initiation is usually called 'taking the *ṭarīqa*'. Sometimes it is called *'ahd* (contract or covenant), and for most is rarely more than a simple *bai'a* (vow of allegiance to the shaikh), a promise to be a good Muslim and to perform certain prescribed daily prayers (*awrād*). The pivot of the ceremony is the vow of allegiance to the shaikh, given sacramentally whilst the hands are clasped (*muṣāfaḥa*) under the sleeve of the shaikh. This initiation is necessary for all who hold office, but in practice the attachment of lay members is often very weak. Rarely do they 'take the *ṭarīqa*'. When quite young the father takes his child along to a *dhikr* and he grows into it. He does not regard himself as being the spiritual child of the founder in quite the same sense as those who have been formally received, nor is he obliged to contribute to the finances, but he does feel that he belongs to that order and has a right to ask for the intercession of its saints and receive their *baraka*.[1]

The initiation of a *darwīsh* may be more complicated. The aspirant (*murīd*) to the religious life must present himself to his shaikh who proceeds to examine the state of his soul. His main purpose is to test whether the *murīd* is sufficiently simple-minded to be supple in his hands. Then he gives him preliminary vital instructions: 'Be with your shaikh like the corpse in the hands of the washer: he turns it over as he wishes and it is obedient.'[2] At his initiation he vows to hand himself over body and soul to the shaikh at the sacramental *muṣāfaḥa*. He is sprinkled with water or milk, vested with a habit (*kharqa*, or *daliq*, patched cloak) and handed the book of *awrād* which he promises to recite as given permission by the shaikh. He is then attached to a *zāwiya* to lead a life according to rule, to pray, fast, keep silence, and so on. That is the beginning and end of his training.

Undoubtedly the main reason why the man in the street joins an order is because it is part of his religious inheritance, and what keeps him there is the social life of the brotherhood and the colour and satisfaction brought into his life by this emotional self-hypnotic method of worship in community. The brotherhoods minister to a definite need amongst a people devoid of intellectual culture and the main criticism of the method of worship is that, whilst it is a satisfaction, it is not re-creative and does not lead to a change in life.

A minority with a modicum of western education affect to despise the orders, though it is with great difficulty that they can avoid attending a *ḥaḍra* held in their *ḥōsh*.

5. DOCTRINES

Our aim is to understand living Islam, therefore we shall not attempt to deal with Ṣūfī doctrines except in so far as they underlie

[1] I have been told that many do not 'take the *ṭarīqa*' because they are afraid of the curse they invoke upon themselves if they fail to carry out the rules.

[2] From the Mirghaniyya compilation, *Minḥat-al aṣḥāb*, p. 75. This simile was first used by al-Ghazālī and has been adopted by all the orders.

Sudanese Islam of to-day. Ṣūfī doctrine is behind the orders, otherwise their existence would be an effect without a cause, and they are the means by which aspects of the Ṣūfī philosophy of life has been applied to the needs of the man in the street.

The doctrine of many orders is difficult to extract because it is not always systematically formulated. The *ḥuqūq aṭ-ṭarīq* deal with the rules for the relationship between shaikh and follower, follower with follower, *zāwiya*-conduct and rules for reciting *dhikr* and *awrād*. The doctrine has therefore often to be extracted from these rules and the *awrād* and *qaṣā'id* (pious songs).[1]

First, all the orders claim to be orthodox. Since Ṣūfism is always regarded with suspicion by the orthodox doctors of religion (*'ulamā*), the first object of the founder of an order is to prove his orthodoxy, otherwise it would be regarded as schismatic. This, however, is very simple and can be produced artificially. It is sufficient in order to avoid the reproach of innovation (*bid'a*)—the equivalent of heresy—simply to have followed the course of some well-known orthodox Ṣūfī. He can then prop all his teaching on the authority of his master and those who transmitted it to him from the Prophet himself. This is that chain of doctrine and authority called the *silsila*.

Further, they claim the Law (*sharī'a*) as the starting-point of the Ṣūfī Path, a basis for further progress in the directed life. This is expressed in the following quotation from a Mirghaniyya manual which can be paralleled in all orthodox orders:

> Hold firmly, my brother, to the *sharī'a*, because you cannot approach the 'Path' except through the *sharī'a*, nor can you approach the 'Truth' (*Ḥaqīqa*)[2] except through the *ṭarīqa*. . . . *Sharī'a* is the root, *ṭarīqa* is the branch and *ḥaqīqa* is the fruit. You cannot expect to find fruit except through the existence of root and branch, and the branch could not exist except through the root. He who sticks to *sharī'a* and does not follow a Path is corrupt. He who follows a Path and does not stick to the *sharī'a* is a heretic (*zindīq*).[3]

Now Ṣūfism, as we have seen, had during its history accumulated a philosophy totally foreign to Islam. Its doctrine of God, Muḥammad and the saints, and man's relation to them, cannot be reconciled with orthodox Islam. A professed Ṣūfī was God's *'āshiq* (lover) and therefore his relationship to God was unusual. He could do and say things which would be blasphemous if done by others. Since all the founders of the orders were professed Ṣūfīs, their writings are necessarily full of

[1] Many of their ideas are treated in Chap. V, A. 2.

[2] *Ḥaqīqa* is defined as direct vision of the Divine (*mushāhadāt ar-rubūbiyya*).

[3] *Minḥat al-aṣḥāb*, by Aḥmad b. 'Abd ar-Raḥmān ar-Ruṭbī, p. 96.

the 'path' they laid out for others to follow. The founder's particular bent settled its tendency and emphasis which might range from the extremes of ascetic quietism to pantheism.

A perusal of those writings which give the principles of the practice of the founder, the teaching to be given to his followers and especially the *awrād* and songs, although some excellent orthodox teaching is included, would, however, give reason for their condemnation by orthodoxy. Yet it is difficult, as R. A. Nicholson has pointed out,[1] to be convicted of heresy in Islam where everyone is judged by his actions, merely on the ground of speculative teaching, provided that in practice the teachers and adherents continue to act like normal Muslims by worship in congregation. Only if they brought in innovations in religious law could they be accused of heresy.[2]

It is impossible in this place to treat fully of the teaching of the different orders and we shall give the merest sketch of a few general tendencies. The orders all assert that they possess an esoteric system which had been inherited through the *ahl as-silsila*, but everywhere in the Sudan there is a complete ignorance of the meaning of even the simplest technical Ṣūfī terms. In order to make their orders acceptable to the masses the shaikhs, suppressing abstract doctrines, have insisted on the Ṣūfī forms of devotion, ascetic discipline, and material obligations, and the spiritual experiences and miracles of the saints. Sometimes, it is true, one hears glib talk of the 'Stages' (*maqāmāt*), of being '*ā<u>sh</u>iq li'llāh* (lover of God) and *fanā'* (passing away from self), yet the shaikhs themselves are quite incapable of understanding true Ṣūfism. I want to emphasize this because of the exaggerated statements which have been made concerning the teaching of the orders to-day as though it were that of the great Ṣūfis of the past. At the same time one cannot completely ignore the teachings because many of the speculative ideas of Ṣūfism are to be found in a perverted sense influencing popular religious life and thought.[3] These are related to the special needs of the Muslim masses.

[1] *Studies in Islamic Mysticism*, p. 57.

[2] Whenever the influence of leaders of orders began to overshadow that of the '*ulamā* in Mecca means were always found for bringing a charge of heresy against them. Sayyid 'Alī b. Ya'qūb b. al-Mur<u>sh</u>idī of the <u>Sh</u>ā<u>dh</u>iliyya was executed as a heretic in 1886, others like Shaikh Aḥmad b. Idrīs were forced into exile, whilst Ibrāhīm ar-Ra<u>sh</u>īd had to vindicate himself from two charges of heresy (*c.* A.D. 1856).

[3] Cheap, badly printed copies of Ṣūfī classics, such as the *Dīwān* of Ibn al-Fāriḍ, are to be bought in the market and are used at the chantings which take place on special occasions such as the Ḥōliyya of a saint. Nobody understands them, for most are illiterate, but they do have the effect through words and rhythm of lulling one into a dream world. They are used therefore in a magical sense—the very obscurity of the words tending to this. Other less

We have already shown that mysticism, working within the purely unitarian system of Islam, led necessarily in two directions, both closely related—to pantheism and a saint-cult. The God of Islam being incredibly Transcendant and Unknowable cannot be an object of human devotion, therefore in speculative mysticism a Logos doctrine developed which, without impairing the Divine Unity, provided a philosophical basis for that practical devotion to prophet and saint which had already sprung up out of the people's need. Ibn al-ʿArabī, through his doctrine of the Unity of Being (*waḥdat al-wujūd*), taught that 'all things pre-exist as ideas in the knowledge of God, whence they emanate and whither they ultimately return'.[1] Out of this he produced a doctrine of the pre-existence of Muḥammad. This is the doctrine of the *nūr al-muḥammadiyya*—the Light of Muḥammadness[2]—a primary entity in the image of God which is the first thing God created. The world is a manifestation of that Light; it became incarnate in Adam and all the prophets and saints, each of whom is the Perfect Man (*al-insān al-kāmil*) in varying degrees, until it was perfectly manifested in Muḥammad, the Perfect Man *par excellence*. R. A. Nicholson writes:

> This of course is an Islamic Logos doctrine. It brings Mohammed in some respects very near to the Christ of the Fourth Gospel and the Pauline Epistles. But if the resemblance is great, so is the difference. The Fatherhood of God, the Incarnation, and the Atonement suggest an infinitely rich and sympathetic personality, whereas the Mohammedan Logos tends to identify itself with the active principle of revelation in the Divine essence.[3]

difficult, often doggerel, poems, are used before the *dhikr* to attune the group to a kind of harmony of aspiration.

[1] R. A. Nicholson in *The Legacy of Islam*, p. 224. Note the Trinitarian basis of the Divine nature in Ibn al-ʿArabī (*Tarjumān al-Ashwāq*, ed. Nicholson, xii. 4: 'My Beloved is three although He is One, even as the (three) Persons (of the Trinity) are made one Person in essence.'

[2] The doctrine of the pre-existence of Muḥammad, which is also called *al-ḥaqīqat al-muḥammadiyya*, i.e. Muḥammad in his absolute reality, is attested by early Sunnī tradition (Ibn Saʿad, i. 1. 95; Ibn Hanbal, iv. 66. 127). It appears in Al-Qumait (d. 743) with its descent into the family of ʿAlī; and Al-Ḥallāj, with whom it is Jesus who is the Perfect Man:

> Praise be to Him who manifested His humanity, the secret of His glorious divinity,
> And then visibly appeared to His creation in the form of One who eats and drinks,
> So that His creation could perceive Him in the flicker of an eyelid.

The first line refers to Adam and the rest to Jesus. The source of the doctrine is to be found in the Philonic and Neoplatonic theory of the Logos. Cf. with ἀνὴρ τέλειος of Pauline theology. It may have been influenced by the Avestic fable of a similar Light handed down through Yima Khshaeta. Its development has also been influenced by Christianity.

[3] *Studies in Islamic Mysticism*, p. 87. It should be noted that the Muslim conception of the Logos is akin to that of Arius who taught that God, absolutely One and inaccessible, created the Logos to be His intermediary in creation. It was not the *eternal* Word of God,

Since the work of the founder of an order was to apply the philosophy of Ṣūfism to the needs of the man in the street, so, through teaching and the popular devotional manuals of the Orders, these theosophical doctrines have been absorbed into the popular religion of the people, though in a perverted way. Such ideas are more apparent in eastern Islam, where they have led to schism. They came to the Sudan with the introduction of *mawālid*. In the *mūlid* of Muḥammad 'Uthmān al-Mirghanī we read:

When God wished to project these higher and lower worlds He took a fistful of His Light and it was Muḥammad b. 'Adnān. He (the Prophet) said to Jābir, 'The first thing God created was the Light of your Prophet as an answer to His problem and I was a prophet when Adam was yet water and clay.' The Prophet said to Gabriel, 'How old are you, O Gabriel?' He said, 'I do not know, except that a planet appears in the Fourth Heaven once every 70,000 years (these are the concealed signs) and I have seen it 72,000 times exactly.' The Prophet said, in order to make known his rank and the secret of his light, 'By the glory of my Lord, I am that planet which you have seen, O Gabriel, in the sky of the Benefactor, and other things which pens cannot put to paper and even the two writers of good and evil cannot preserve.'[1]

It will be seen that this conception has more than an academic interest because the adherents hear it at every *dhikr*-gathering. It means that the place of the *nūr al-muḥammadiyya* in popular cosmogony, among people to whom the arid unitarianism of the scholastics is unintelligible, is much like that of the Logos in Christianity. The pre-existence of Muḥammad is described in words obviously borrowed from the Johannine statements about the Logos. Tradition ascribes to Muḥammad such sayings as the one quoted by Muḥammad 'Uthmān, 'The first thing which God created was the Light of the Prophet;' and also, 'I am the Light of God and all things are from my Light'. It need hardly be said that the Prophet would have been the first to condemn such heretical beliefs, but his religion is such that Muslims have been driven to the belief that the only way they could obtain grace was through his intercession; so the doctrine of Muḥammad and of his pre-existence claims an intense hold over uneducated masses. It is mainly through the songs, which are an essential part of every gathering, that this idealized conception of Muḥammad is spread, and it is held together with complete attachment to the doctrine

who was 'with God and was God'. For this reason it is unwise to make any comparison between the two conceptions. In Islam the Logos doctrine is nothing but an aberration, not a fundamental element of the faith.

[1] *Mūlid al-Mirghanī*, chap. ii. The conception is found in all the *mawālid* used in the Sudan.

of the One God. This Muḥammad-centrism of later Islamic mysticism condemned Muslims to a spiritual ignorance fatal to the development of spiritual life because it shifted the emphasis from the real to the unreal.

The conception comes still nearer to the people in the *Quṭb*. The Sūdānī feels the need for personal knowledge of the Word of God. Muḥammad, the Logos, in every epoch takes on the form of a living saint, the *Quṭb*, who manifests himself to true mystics. Muḥammad ʿUthmān, for instance, was the *Quṭb* of his age and therefore the manifestation of the *nūr al-muḥammadiyya.*[1] It lies behind all such instructions as the following: 'In the first stage the disciple is expected to love and look to the Shaikh as his all in all. He acts, talks, and prays like the shaikh, and constantly meditates upon him. Having been, by this process, spiritually transformed into the shaikh, the student (*murīd*) is spiritually introduced to the Prophet.'[2] That is why Ṣūfism in practice centres round the idealized personality of the shaikh.

The development of such a theory in Islam and its spread in popular religion clearly reflects the Muslim need for a true Incarnation. The difference between Christ and *al-insān al-kāmil* is the difference between Truth which can draw men's hearts to Him and give the power to act in a re-creation and a substitutive abstraction which fails entirely in its effect on life.

Apart from this, there is that vague kind of pantheism lying behind the exercises of the *dhikr* as practised in the Sudan; and one who becomes *majdhūb* is regarded as having lost his consciousness temporarily in the Divine Oneness. Antinomism also expresses itself in the *malāmatīs*. Orthodoxy, by continual pressure on all kinds of heterodox mysticism, is continually striving to thrust it back to narrow limits, for the people absorbed such elements in perfect good faith from their shaikhs and there is no conscious departure from orthodoxy. What is really unorthodox is their relationship to their shaikhs.

It must be understood that the intellectual value of the Ṣūfism of

[1] His descendants also make these extravagant claims (cf. the song by Jaʿfar on pp. 215–16, in which he also says 'I am the first who existed') in which they identify themselves not only with the *Quṭb* of the Ṣūfī hierarchy but the Logos *Quṭb*. It is therefore not surprising that these leaders demand and obtain from their followers a reverence almost akin to worship. Jīlī writes of these reincarnations in *al-insān al-kāmil* (R. A. Nicholson, op. cit., p. 105): 'The Perfect Man is the *Quṭb* (axis) on which the spheres of existence revolve from first to last, and since things came into being he is one (*wāḥid*) for ever and ever. He hath various guises and appears in diverse bodily tabernacles (*kanāʾis*): in respect of some of these his name is given to him, while in respect of others it is not given to him. His own original name is Mohammed. . . . In every age he bears a name suitable to his guise (*libās*) in that age.'

[2] *Moslem World*, viii. 252–3.

the orders is to-day of the slightest and its ideals are not by our standards high. The axis of the orders is not the teaching, which is but vaguely assimilated, but the shaikh who possesses *baraka* inherent in him.

6. RITUAL AND PRACTICE

The Dhikr.

The liturgic element in Ṣūfī practice began to develop in the second century A.H. and centres around the technical term *dhikr* (remembrance).[1] In the Qur'ān the word is used in the sense of worshipping God, but it has come to mean a particular method of worshipping God in order to attain spiritual ecstasy (*wajd*) by the constant repetition of His name either mentally (*dhikr khafī*) or aloud (*dhikr jalī*). Orthodox Islam has its own liturgic prayer (*ṣalāt*) which the Ṣūfī performs if he wishes to be regarded as of the community of Islam; but he believes that *ṣalāt* is a concession to men's weakness and that the *dhikr* is the very centre of true religious practice. It is based on the Qur'ānic injunction, 'remember God with frequent remembrance' (xxxiii. 41). Each order has its particular method of recitation and the devotional manuals which are so common give the various methods of practising the *dhikr*. The vocal method has always been regarded by true Ṣūfīs as vulgar and more fitted for lay members. There are two main groups of the silent *dhikr*: that of the heart called the *dhikr* of adoration, which can be practised by anyone with the time and inclination, and the very advanced stage of the *dhikr* of the whole personality. In both the mystical idea is predominant and they are undoubtedly a valuable aid to spiritual meditation. But the *dhikr* degenerated along with the orders and the Sūdānī is content to leave contemplative methods to more mystically minded races. The vocal method satisfies his emotional need and provides further a strong bond of common worship with others.[2] He takes part in the *dhikr* at an early age and boys from ten upwards are to be seen at the *ḥalqa* (circle) imitating the movements of their elders. Quietist methods are, however, practised in the Sudan (Tijāniyya and Idrīsiyya) and satisfy certain sections of the population.

At the regular services in the *khalwas* the ritual consists first of the recitation of the 'office' of the order composed by the founder. This

[1] Connected with Syr. *dukrāna*, used by Syriac Christians in the same technical sense.

[2] It is true that the simple *dhikr* of the *awqāt* ('hours') to be repeated after the five regular prayers is observed. But this is as mechanical as the prayers and few except the aged repeat them more than twice a day. In the Qādiriyya it consists of the repetition of *subḥān Allāh*, *al-ḥamdu li'llāh* and *Allāhu akbar*—each repeated thirty-three times with the aid of a rosary (*subḥa*).

may consist of *awrād* and *aḥzāb*, or a *rātib*,[1] or of a *mūlid* (an allegorical life of the Prophet), whence *mūlid* often means a *dhikr* evening's entertainment. Once a year with the Mirghaniyya on the night of Muḥammad's night-journey (the night before 27th Rajab), a *quṣṣat al mi'rāj* is chanted. Whatever the 'office' may consist of, it is all interspersed with the singing of spiritual songs in praise of God or in honour of the Prophet or the saints of the order.

This is usually a preparation for the *dhikr* proper which consists of the repetition of the formula 'lā ilāha illā'llāh', the word 'Allāh', and certain attributes such as 'Al-Ḥayy', the Living. There is a strong belief in the magical power of words and each order has its own peculiar methods of intonation for the prayers and especially the *dhikr*. In the Sudan the older orders have developed distinctively African elements in the chanting of songs and the *dhikr* which eastern Ṣūfīs regard as utterly barbaric.

Gradually with the repetition and corresponding rhythmical movements a strong emotional exaltation is produced which finds an outlet in more and more violent movements until it results in an orgy of ecstatic excitement. Very frequently the *dhākirs* fall out in a trance and when in this state they are referred to as *majdhūb*.[2] The abnormality of such a state the simple Sudanese take to be a real contact with the divine or with the founder shaikh. It is in this state of *jadhb* that the *dhākir* does strange things, such as the Egyptian practices mentioned by Lane,[3] but these performances are foreign to the Sudanese.

The performance is accompanied by the chanting of songs, the poetry of which is doggerel, the subject usually the Prophet or the founder and the music of a monotonous but thrilling and poignant

[1] The word *ḥizb* (pl. *aḥzāb*) is also used with the same significance as *wird* (pl. *awrād*) for the special prayers or Qur'ānic passages to be recited at different times of the day or on particular days. There is a much used collection in the Sudan called *Majmū' al-awrād wa-l aḥzāb wal-ad'iya*, which contains the *aḥzāb* of many famous leaders such as Ash-Shādhilī, An-Nawawī, Ar-Rifā'ī, Ad-Dasūqī, and Al-Baiyūmī. The *Dalā'il al-Khayrāt* (The Proofs of the Excellencies) of Al-Jazūlī (A.D. 1464), a propagator of the Shādhiliyya in Morocco, which is a collection of prayers for the Prophet, a description of his tomb, names, and virtues, is very well known, though more especially used by the old orders and Shādhiliyya derivatives. *Waẓīfa* is used by the Tijāniyya and *rātib* by the Ismā'īliyya for 'office'.

[2] *Majdhūb*, lit. 'attracted' (by love of God), an ecstatic in a state of unconsciousness absorbed in the Divine Oneness. The term is also used of a dervish who lives in a trance-like state, and talks strangely, unintelligibly or childishly; whence it comes to mean weak-minded.

[3] *Modern Egyptians* (Everyman's ed., pp. 248 ff.). Such performances do take place in the Sudan, but not by Sudanese. Rifā'īs who have been in the army and have settled in the Sudan used to do them openly in Khartoum. The *ḥairān* of Aḥmad al-Badawī of Ṭanṭa come to Omdurman and exhibit their tricks for the entertainment of the Sudanese who look upon it as a show.

nature. In the Sudan the *dhikr* misses all call to true spiritual heroism, but once heard one ceases to wonder at its place in the religious life of the Sudanese, for it brings into it vividness and colour. It shows that the heart of these people, whose mind is too static to be influenced, can be profoundly moved through their emotions.

It must be clearly understood that the *dhikr* for the vast majority has nothing to do with true mysticism. It is merely a method of psycho-physical enthusiasm tending, by concentrated repetition, rhythm, singing, and drumming, to develop a religious neurosis under different forms; hysterical phenomena, interpreted by Africans as the working of a new power which has entered the person's body, becoming the equivalent of sanctification. In some orders it is these effects they are trying to produce and the whole purpose of the performance. Some leaders, realizing the dangers, keep a tight hold over too great extravagances. Over-indulgence in *dhikrs* is bad for ordinary members of society, they come to live in a permanent hypnoidal state and relapse into a state of inactivity.

The silent *dhikr* is a real form of prayer, but the communal *dhikr* in general is an orgiastic type of mysticism in which the spiritual is swallowed up in the psychical and corporeal effects. That is why it does not re-create and has no effect on the moral life, for true worship is essentially bound up with conduct. Sometimes it leads to actual moral degradation, for it is not uncommon for a visit to a prostitute to follow the *dhikr*.

There is no better commentary on the Ṣūfism of the Sudan than this criticism by Abū Naṣr as-Sarrāj:

> Some suppose that Ṣūfism is song and dancing, accepting invitations and seeking company, wasting time over meals and listening to poetry, artificial ecstasy and dancing, knowledge of composing tunes for good voices and sorrowful melodies and the art of making love-poetry which resembles that of true Ṣūfīs. This is a mistake, because the music and ecstasy of every heart that is polluted with worldliness and every soul that is accustomed to vanity and heedlessness will have a hidden motive and therefore his action is a pretence. He who thinks that, by his pretence and trickery and desires, he can become of the true Ṣūfīs at the times of music and motion and ecstasy and so on, has made a mistake.[1]

Since it is impossible to describe the practices of the orders in detail, we will content ourselves with describing a *lailiyya* of the Mirghaniyya Order.

[1] As-Sarrāj, *Kitāb al-Luma' fi'l-Taṣawwuf*, edit. Nicholson, p. 419.

Lailiyya of the Mirghaniyya Order

The regular Monday and Friday service[1] is called a *lailiyya* or a *ḥaḍra*,[2] and can be held in a mosque or *zāwiya*, but is usually held in the *ḥōshes* of these buildings or that of the shaikh, khalīfa, or one of the members, or even in the street. Apart from the regular *ḥaḍras*, a member may ask for one to be performed in his *ḥōsh* on any occasion connected with thanksgiving, such as the naming of a child (*simāya*), circumcision, recovery from illness, sudden fortune, or return from pilgrimage; in Sawākin, but not elsewhere, at weddings. They also take place during the *ḥōliyya* or anniversary of the death of a *walī*.

The service is always under the charge of a *khalīfa* who directs it and keeps order. He calls those regular members who support the service *jamā'at al-lailiyya* (these bring such things as sugar, tea, coffee, and oil), but any member may join in. Still, if he comes regularly he is expected to contribute something towards expenses. If it is a regular *ḥaḍra* no food is provided, but if performed in a private *ḥōsh* the man thus honoured entertains all the company and usually gives the *khalīfa* a present of money.[3]

The *lailiyya* if in a private *ḥōsh* begins with a procession (*zaffa*) starting from the khalīfa's house where the company have assembled. All should be ritually clean and have performed the evening prayers. Flags are only carried on big occasions. The Mirghaniyya colour is green. During the procession the *munshids* (singers) chant the following *shaṭḥ* by Ja'far al-Mirghanī which they call the *safīna* (ship):

By the power of my design did I quaff the cup of knowledge;
By the welcome of every gift was I called.
My Beloved refreshed me with a draught of knowledge;
I am the Sayyid famous for my knowledge of the unseen.
You see, my friend, my judgement is above all creatures,
I am a pillar of the universe—a gift from my Lord.

---

[1] That is, our Sunday and Thursday night, because the Muslim day is from sunset to sunset.

[2] *Ḥaḍra* means 'presence'. It is the equivalent of 'meeting for worship', and is taken to refer to the presence of God. The Mirghaniyya, however, say that it is the Prophet who is present, since naturally God is present in every place. This belief is based on the account of a dream in which the founder of the order saw the Prophet. Here is his description of the occurrence taken from the beginning of his *mūlid*: 'He (i.e. the Prophet) ordered me to write a *mūlid* rhyming in *ḥā* and *mīm*, which I did, and he gave me the good news that he will be present when it is read. So I have written this that people may be honoured by his coming when it is read.'

[3] The food consists of *fatta* made of *kisra*, soup, rice, and meat, and *liqimāt* which is made of a dough of flour, allowed to ferment, separated into lumps (*luqma*), fried in oil, and covered with powdered sugar. In the Red Sea district *qahwat lōz* (tea with milk and crushed almonds) is provided instead of the usual mint tea.

I am of the descent of pure-ones—God is my witness;
I am the treasure of lights in the midst of creation.
I am the glory of the people of the age, know, O my friend!
I am a lantern light on the throne of Judgement Day.
I am the chosen of the chosen, above the heavens;
I am the door, my authority is over east and west.
I am the flash of light above creation. . . .[1]

Between each verse of this effusion the whole company chant this chorus:

For God's sake,[2] O Mirghanī; for God's sake, O Mirghanī—the Meccan, the Medīnan.

On arrival at the *ḥōsh* the performers squat in a circle with a lamp, an incense burner, and all their footwear in the centre. At one side are the four *munshids*. First of all the khalīfa exclaims, '*Al-Fātiḥa*', and all recite it in concert. Then they chant the *tahlīl* (*lā ilāha illā'llāh*) a hundred times and the *munshids* sing the *madḥa* called *al-munbahya* in which the help of God is besought.

The second stage is the chanting of the *Mūlid an-Nabī* written by the founder of the order, Muḥammad ʿUthmān al-Mirghanī. It is divided into fourteen chapters called *alwāḥ* (sing. *lōḥ*, tablet). It opens with a chapter on the uniqueness of Islam, followed by an account of the founder's dream in which he saw the Prophet, of how God created that luminous substance, the 'Light of the Prophet', first of all before Adam, of his physical birth with an account of his ancestry, the story of the angels taking out his heart and its cleansing, the *miʿrāj* story, the prophetic call, and a description of his physical appearance and character.

The *khalīfa* chants the first chapter and afterwards he indicates those of the company whom he wishes to continue. Many of them although illiterate know some section by heart. The *khalīfa* also reads the chapter on the Prophet's birth and when he gets to the words 'he was born . . .' all rise and chant a *madḥa*. When this *lōḥ* is finished the hymn of welcome to the Prophet (*taḥiyyatu qudūmihi*) is chanted still standing; all the rest is done sitting. After the chapter on the *miʿrāj* a special *qaṣīda* is sung of which the first hemistitch of the verse is by Ibn al-ʿArabī and the second by Muḥammad Sirr al-Khatm (d. 1915). The *mūlid* lasts about two hours.

There now follows an interlude of chanting by the *munshids* of one or more *qaṣīdas* in honour of the Prophet (*qaṣā'id al-madīḥ*), during

[1] *Quṣṣat al-Miʿrāj*, pp. 135–7.

[2] *Shai'un li'llāh*—a suppliant's cry.

the singing of which the company is refreshed with the Sūdānī tonic, mint tea.

The final stage is the *dhikr*. Here the real attempt to produce effects begins, the other has all been preparatory. It commences very slowly, the *dhākirīn* all standing in a circle, with the formula *lā ilāha illā'llāh*, chanted 100 times, accompanied by a rhythmical bowing of the head and body first to the right then to the left, the hands hanging loosely. The recitation and movements naturally control the breathing —an important thing if emotional effects are to be produced. Then the measure is quickened, more stress being laid on the last syllable and the movements change to forward and backward jerking. With each change the voice is made more raucous until, at the final stage of jumping up and down, the words have degenerated to an almost unrecognizable 'Allāh' pronounced in a kind of pectoral barking voice or like a rough saw. The first syllable is exhaled, the second inhaled, then the process is reversed to inhalation—exhalation. Such a section of one formula is sometimes called a *ḍarb*. Other *ḍurūb* are simply '*Allāh*' or '*Huwa*' or '*Ḥayy Qayyūm*'. Each taking of a new word or formula constitutes a new time for the *dhikr*. All this may be modified freely by the *khalīfa*. A *qaṣīda* is usually sung between each *ḍarb*, but the singing is going on during the whole of the *dhikr*, the *munshids* walking round and round the circle to excite the performers, sometimes crying out '*madad*, *madad*, *yā Mirghanī*' when the *dhikr* is going well.[1] In this order they are usually kept well in hand by the *khulafā* who are always ready to restrain any extravagances.

The *dhikr* is closed by the *ḥizb* called the Prayer of the Khatmiyya Ṭarīqa, the prayer for mankind (*du'ā li'l-insān*), and the *Fātiḥa*. After that they all relax and the names of persons who need prayer are mentioned when they say the *Fātiḥa*. Finally the food is brought in.

7. QĀDIRIYYA

The Qādiriyya was the first definite order to develop in order to perpetuate the rules and teachings of a shaikh, and its subsequent development shows signs of this in the weakness of its organization, the incoherences in its doctrine, and varieties of its practice.

The founder was 'Abd al-Qādir al-Jīlānī (d. A.D. 1166) who had a school (*madrasa*) and a *ribāṭ* (an institution similar to the later *zāwiya*) at Baghdād. 'Abd al-Qādir did not himself plan a self-

[1] *Madad* means '(supernatural) help' and may be uttered either out of joy or to encourage the performers.

continuative order, but his teaching and his ecstatic practice constituted the foundation for a body of rules, doctrine, and practice which was spread by his numerous progeny and followers who continued to ascribe themselves to him and to initiate followers in his name. His methods became very popular and even in his lifetime his followers had spread his system to Syria, Egypt, and the Yemen; and afterwards it spread throughout the whole Islamic world, so that he has been ever since the most universally popular saint in Islam. Each khalīfa taught as he wished and the organization, *dhikr*, and *awrād* vary in every country. Rinn writes:

By reason of its dispersion over the whole extent of the Muslim world, by reason also of its general character of tolerance and charity, the Qādiriyya Order does not have that homogeneity of rules which is to be found in other congregations, which seem to form small exclusive churches outside which there is no salvation. The Qādiriyya Order on the contrary is open to all.[1]

The doctrine taught has varied from the extremes of worship of ʿAbd al-Qādir as semi-divine to the attitude of reverence for a great saint. The numerous branch orders have only nominal connexion with the Shaikh in Baghdād and some of them have come to be organized on new and rigid lines.

It is claimed that the 'fire of ʿAbd al-Qādir' was first lit in the Sudan by Tāj ad-Dīn al-Bahārī in the second half of the tenth century A.H., 'by leave of the Prophet of God and Shaikh ʿAbd al-Qādir al-Jīlānī'. The suggestion that he should visit the Sudan actually came from Dā'ūd b. ʿAbd al-Jalīl Muḥammad (*c.* 1550), a wealthy slave-trader of Arbajī, who met him whilst on pilgrimage 'at the beginning of the reign of Shaikh ʿAjīb' (d. *c.* 1604) and became his patron, and with whom he lived at Wādī Shaʿīr. He only remained in the Sudan seven years, but during that time, like all Muslim missionaries he married into the people, initiated many into the 'Way', and left behind khalīfas in different areas qualified to admit others.[2]

A story which is very popular in the Jezīra tells of how he tested the first group who came to be initiated. The *Ṭabaqāt* gives it as follows:

People came to him to be initiated into the Ṣūfī Path. He hid some rams in a store room (*qaṭīʿ*)[3] and said to the people, 'I am going to initiate and guide you and slaughter you, then you will die in the faith.' Thereupon the people

[1] *Marabouts et Khouan*, p. 186.

[2] *The biography of Tāj ad-Dīn* is given in *Ṭabaqāt*, M. 42–3, S. 44–5.

[3] *Qaṭīʿ* is used in the Jezīra for the store-room which leads off the one living-room of the hut.

dispersed except Shaikh Muḥammad (al-Hamīm) wad ʿAbd aṣ-Ṣādiq who was then a youth wearing a silk shirt. He removed it, performed his ablutions and prayed two *rakʿas*. The Shaikh took him inside the store-room, initiated him and slaughtered one of the rams and the blood flowed from the store-room. The people thought that he had slaughtered him. Then came Shaikh Bān an-Naqā who was very old. He said, 'I am a bull who has served his days.[1] I prefer to join my Lord.' So he performed the ablutions, prayed two *rakʿas*, and went in. He initiated him and slaughtered another ram and the blood flowed towards the people. He said to them 'Come! Don't be envious, annoyed or stingy.' They refused and after that the two came out safe and sound.[2]

We have already said that many of these khalīfas became temporal-spiritual heads of families in whom the succession continues till to-day. Thus Muḥammad al-Hamīm founded the Ṣādiqāb of Sūqī district between Wad Medani and Qedāref. The second, Bān an-Naqā 'aḍ-Ḍarīr', retired from the royal service to serve Tāj ad-Dīn as his disciple, who, before his return to the Ḥijāz invested him with the Funj symbols of authority, the *taqīya* (head-dress) and the *kakar* (wooden stool), which are still with the Khalīfa of the Yaʿqūbāb to-day. Amongst others whom he initiated were Shaikh ʿAjīb al-Kabīr al-Mānjalūk, the great leader of the ʿAbdullābī.[3] It is said that he travelled to Taqalī (southern Kordofān) where:

he initiated ʿAbd Allāh al-Hammāl, grandfather of Shaikh Ḥamad wad at-Turābī, together with other people. When he wanted to leave for the Ḥijāz he said to his neighbours, 'I came from Baghdād on account of this lad. I have nominated him my successor. Deal with him as you have dealt with me.' Then he taught him the names and attributes of God, how to enter into retreat and perform spiritual exercises. . . . He departed leaving all directing themselves to God.[4]

The apparent confusion to be noticed in the *Ṭabaqāt*, whereby we read for example that both ʿAlī an-Nīl and Ṣāliḥ ibn Bān an-Naqā were each the third 'to light the fire of Shaikh ʿAbd al-Qādir',[5] is due to each belonging to a different order of succession from Tāj ad-Dīn; Ṣāliḥ, for instance being the third khalīfa from Shaikh Idrīs.

[1] Proverb: *ana tōran kammal kirāhu.*

[2] *Ṭabaqāt.* biog. of Bān an-Naqā, M. 33, S. 35. This is the Yaʿqūbāb version of the story (cf. Reid, *Tribes of Blue Nile Province*, pp. 65–6, 77–8), in which only two men are mentioned, but that ʿArakiyyīn and others mention four who professed themselves willing, the courage of one of whom failed after seeing the other three disappear. His name varies according to the group to which the relator belongs.

[3] ʿAbd Allāh b. Dafaʿ Allāh al-ʿArakī, the founder of the Arakiyyīn, is stated to have been one of those who failed Tāj ad-Dīn's test, but when he saw the miracles manifested by Tāj ad-Dīn's followers he repaired to Mecca only to find him dead. He was then initiated by Tāj ad-Dīn's successor Ḥabīb Allāh (op. cit. M. 105–6, S. 112–13).

[4] Op. cit. M. 42–3, S. 44–5.

[5] Op. cit. M. 133 and 97, S. 141 and 104.

The most famous of all the holy men of this period was the Maḥasī Shaikh, Idrīs ibn Arbāb,[1] who, we are told on the authority of Shaikh Khōjalī, was the first to light the fire of ʿAbd al-Qadīr. 'Then appeared the saintship of Shaikh Idrīs without the mediumship of a *shaikh* and it is said that he took it directly from the Prophet. Others say that a man from Algeria (al-Maghrib) called ʿAbd al-Kāfī initiated him into saintship (*khaṭwa*).'[2] Hs is supposed to have studied under Shaikh al-Bandarī at Ḥalfāya. One who has not been properly initiated is normally regarded in dervish circles with suspicion, but the personal influence of Shaikh Idrīs was very great.

His son Ḥamad succeeded him as khalīfa, though we also read of other successions from him; for instance, 'Shaikh Khōjalī once said, "Shaikh Badawī (wad Abū Dalaiq, d. 1706) succeeded Shaikh Idrīs in keeping ablaze the fire of Shaikh ʿAbd al-Qādir" '.[3] He was followed by Ṣāliḥ b. Bān an-Naqā (1681–1753) 'who related that the divine revelation[4] came to him giving him leave to keep ablaze the fire after the death of Shaikh Badawī' in A.D. 1706. The narrative goes on to say how his son, Az-Zain, carried on the 'fire', to be followed in turn by his son.

Some of these hereditary khalīfa groups later changed over to other *ṭarīqas*. Thus the khalīfas of Shaikh Idrīs became Mirghaniyya; the Yaʿqūbāb, the ʿArakiyyīn, and Awlād Turābī changed to the Sammāniyya.

The Qādiriyya, sometimes called Jailāniyya, in its character as *ṭarīqat al-qōm* (the 'Way' of the Holy Ones), numbers more nominal adherents than any other in the Sudan. It is strongest in the Jezīra where these tribes with a hereditary Khalifate live, though groups which are not tribal are to be found all over the Sudan. The Badrāb, centred at Umm Dubbān, whose founder Muḥammad Badr (1810–84) was initiated by Shaikh ʿAwaḍ al-Gid of Efaina, are Qādiriyya, and since they maintain a famous school where many boys who seek religious posts get their early training, many fekis and religious shaikhs claim to be Qādiriyya. The Musallamiyya are strongly Qādirī because they claim that their ancestor al-Musallam was the son of the sister of ʿAbd al-Qādir al-Jīlānī. The Qādiriyya was active in Dārfūr when At-Tūnīsī lived there (1803–13), for he writes of the *dhikr*-method

[1] The Sennār Chronicle, which is unreliable, says he lived 147 hijriyya years from A.H. 913 (A.D. 1507) to A.H. 1060 (A.D. 1650). His biography in the *Ṭabaqāt* is incomplete but the date A.H. 981 (A.D. 1573) is mentioned.

[2] Op. cit. M. 4, S. 5.

[3] Op. cit. M. 37, S. 39.

[4] *Al-madad al-ilāhī*, lit. supernatural help or sustenance.

and rivalry between the followers of Ḍaif Allāh and Shaikh Ya'qūb.[1]

The camel nomads, Ammar'ar and many Beja sections, claim 'Abd al-Qādir as their patron saint, though they know little or nothing of the cult. Those in the north ask for his protection before setting out on a journey or at a crisis of life at a *bayān* dedicated to him near the rock of Abū Sīr at Wādī Ḥalfa.

The order is regarded as orthodox and because of its localized or tribal character the rivalries which characterize it are tribalistic and not connected with the gaining of adherents. An ordinary Qādirī is concerned essentially with the cult of his family saint.

We should infer from accounts in the *Ṭabaqāt*[2] that the investiture of a *khalīfa* in the Jezīra involved the shaving of his head by the initiator, the singing of *anāshīd*, seating on the *kakar* of the founder, handing over of the *kukāra* of former khalīfas, turbanning with the green *'imma*, investing with the *jubba* and the sheepskin *sijjāda* of the founder, and the allotment of pupil-servants.

Some Jezīra shaikhs were invested with other Funj symbols of authority, including in addition to the *kakar*, iron spears and shaibas or sceptres. These may originally have been connected with temporal authority because investiture with a *kakar* involved a grant of land. The Ya'qūbāb of to-day, who have become Sammāniyya,[3] and most other groups keep these symbols in their ceremonial and they are brought out at festivals.

An example of the simple *bai'a* (oath or *'ahd al-yad*) used to-day for admitting ordinary members is the reciting three times each of 'I ask forgiveness of God the Great', 'there is no god but Allah', and the *ṣalāt 'alā'n-nabī*. Then, with his hand in that of the shaikh, he recites after him 'I swear allegiance to you in the faith and truth and law. I have become a *murīd* to Shaikh 'Abd al-Qādir al-Jailī after myself—may God illuminate his tomb and hallow his Secret and his Fātiha.' The two then recite the Fātiḥa together, the newly admitted member kisses the shaikh's hand and the ceremony is concluded.

The *lailiyya* in charge of the sectional leader (*muqaddam*) consists of the occasional recitation of the *mawlid* of al-Barzanjī, the *dhikr*[4]

[1] At-Tūnīsī, *Voyage au Darfour*, pp. 245–9.

[2] *Ṭabaqāt*, M. 79–80, S. 86–7. See also account of Muḥammad b. Dā'ūd al-Agharr (op. cit. S. 151).

[3] The change was simply due to their choosing one Hājju (d. 1930) an ascetic who lived in a tebeldi tree, who was a Sammānī, as shaikh of the tribe after the Mahdiyya. See above, p. 139, n. 3.

[4] They still often use the word *kirair* for *dhikr* as in the *Ṭabaqāt* (M. 132, S. 139), 'I stood in the *dhikr*-circle (*ḥalqat kirair*) of the Awlād Burri . . . and the feki 'Abd al-Ḥalīm, was singing in the ring'.

with drums (*nōba*) and the chanting of *madīḥ*, before and during the *dhikr*. In procession they sing only *lā ilāha illā'llāh*. On Friday they perform the *dhikr* in the mosque after the midday prayer.[1] Their performances are more distinctively African than any other order.[2]

8. SHĀDHILIYYA

This order might almost be described as a school of Ṣūfī doctrine rather than an organized order and is found in the Sudan as elsewhere mainly in derivatives, such as the Majdhūbiyya.

The founder, Abū'l-Ḥasan ʿAlī b. ʿAbd Allāh ash-Shādhilī, was born in A.D. 1196 at ash-Shādhila near Jabal Zafrān in Tunisia. He studied in Fās where he came under the influence of the Ishrāqī (Illuministic) School of Ṣūfism. Persecuted for his teaching and popularity he took refuge in Egypt where he achieved great renown not only among the populace but even with the ʿ*ulamā*. He used to go on *ḥajj* every year and he died somewhere in the Atbai Desert whilst returning from one of these in A.D. 1258.[3]

Abū'l-Ḥasan was an itinerating master of the Way (*shaikh sā'iḥ*) and did not initiate his pupils into any special rule or ritual. His teaching was carried on by his disciples and one Abū'l-ʿAbbās al-Mursī (d. 1287), who resided in Alexandria, was regarded as his successor.[4] But the order never consolidated itself, probably because the founder left no son to succeed him. His pupils collected his scanty literary remains (chiefly *awrād*) and carried on his teaching in scattered *zāwiyas* having little or no connexion with each other, and no hierarchical system grew up. Sometimes prominent shaikhs of such congregations would receive the required special permission of the Prophet to found new orders; such were the Shaikhiyya, Ṭayyibiyya, Jazūliyya, and Darqawiyya.

[1] A Qādirī is supposed to say the 'minor office' (*al-wird aṣ-ṣaghīr*) after each of the five *ṣalāt*. It consists of each of the following said 100 times with the aid of the *sibḥa*: at-tasbīḥ, al-ḥamdu, al-ḥawqala, al-basmala, al-istighfār, at-tawba, aṣ-ṣalāt, and at-tahlīl. The *wird al-kabīr* consists of the *tahlīl* repeated 70,000 times.

[2] I met an Indian Army Officer in Wad Medanī who told me that being a *qādirī*, he was invited to attend a *dhikr* and was so shocked by the performance that he denounced them for using the name of ʿAbd al-Qādir al-Jīlānī.

[3] The Hadendiwa claim him as a saint of theirs and say that his tomb is at Halus. The Ilaiqāt claim a tomb at ʿĪd al-Khashab between Halāyib and Dirr as his, and there was another at Ḥamaithrā built by a Mamlūk Sulṭān (cf. Ibn Baṭūṭa, 1939 ed., i. 42, and Burckhardt, *Nubia*, p. 463).

[4] An account of the life and sayings of Abū'l-Ḥasan and Abū'l-ʿAbbās is given in the *Laṭā'if al Minan* of Tāj ad-Dīn ʿAṭā'-Allāh al-Iskandari composed A.D. 1284 (on the margin of Ash-Shaʿrānī's *Laṭā'if al-Minan*).

The propagator of the order in Morocco was Abū 'Abd Allāh Muḥammad b. Sulaimān al-Jazūlī (d. between 1465 and 1470), the author of the famous *Dalā'il al-Khairāt*.[1] One of his daughters is said to have married a Sharīf Ḥamad Abū Dunāna who travelled to the Sudan with his son, As Sayyid ibn al-Ḥasan al-Baitī, settled at Saqādī Gharb (now called Mahmiyya) in the year A.H. 849 (A.D. 1445), and initiated the Shādhiliyya teaching in the Sudan. He is buried at Abū Dalaiq. The khalīfa to-day is Sharīf Muḥammad Aḥmad b. 'Abd ar-Raḥmān al-Baitī who resides in Omdurmān where he has a mosque and *khalwas* for students and *darāwīsh*.

The Shādhiliyya liturgies also came to the Sudan through fekis who were taught whilst on pilgrimage. We read of the Tūtī Island saint, Khōjalī b. 'Abd ar-Raḥmān (d. 1743),[2] that, although he was a Qādirī in origin, he taught the Shādhilī ritual:

He went on pilgrimage to the venerable House of God and took the *ṭarīqa* from Shaikh Aḥmad at-Tumbuktāwī, the Fellātī, the divine Quṭb, who was settled in Al-Medīna. As for the origin of his *ṭarīqa*, the foundation was Qādirī and the *awrād* Shādhilī, in fact his Shaikh was a pupil of Muḥammad an-Nāṣiri ash-Shādhilī.[3]

In his worldliness he was typical of many a modern religious leader:

He modelled himself on the Shādhilī Sayyids in word and deed. He used to wear magnificent clothes, such as the green Baṣrāwī robe with a red ṭarbūsh on his head turbanned with rich muslin and shoes on his feet. He censed himself with India wood and perfumed himself, putting Abyssinian civet on his beard and clothes. These he did in imitation of the Shaikh Abū'l Ḥasan ash-Shādhilī, and as a manifestation of God's grace to him, and in order to praise Him for that. Someone mentioned to him that the Qādiriyya only wore patched *jubbas* he replied, 'my clothes announce to the world "we can do without you"; their clothes say "we are in need of you" '.[4]

Khōjalī had a very great reputation and numerous disciples. He was succeeded by his son Aḥmad who was khalīfa for sixty years, but the Sammāniyya won away his adherents in the Jezira, the Majdhūbiyya those around Dāmar, and the Mirghaniyya all the others north of Khartoum.[5] The Shādhiliyya has considerably influenced the

[1] See above, p. 213, n. 1.

[2] See above, pp. 130, 136. His life is given in the *Ṭabaqāt* (M. 71–7, S. 74–83), extracts from which are translated by MacMichael, *Hist.* ii. 250–2.

[3] Op. cit. M. 71, S. 74.

[4] Op. cit. M. 73, S. 76.

[5] There still exists a khalīfa of al-Khōjalī at Ḥalfāya but he considers himself Qādiri. In Sennār district is a group calling itself Shādhiliyya; the feki Sulaiman Muḥammad Shādhli (d. 1924) being the last khālīfa who had any training. The village of Shādhli near Sennār mentioned by Bruce (*Travels*, vi. 384) is now ruined. Many of the Ḥaḍramawt and Jidda people on the Sudan Red Sea coast are Shādhiliyya.

doctrine of many of the Sudan orders and the recitation of the *ḥizb al-baḥr* is almost universal.

For the *dhikr* the Baitiyya group sit either in a circle or in two rows facing each other and commence by reciting the *tahlīl* (*lā ilāha illā'llāh*) in a loud voice continuing for about two hours, no count being made. Then the shaikh makes a sign and they continue reciting in silence for half an hour. Next the word Allāh is repeated for half an hour aloud, followed by *huwa*, *ḥaqq*, *ḥayy*, *qayyūm* and *qahhār*, the five taking another half an hour. After that the *dhikr* is closed by the recitation of one or more long prayers from the collection *al-mafākhir al-'aliyya*.[1] The *mūlid* of Al-Barzanjī is recited at festivals only.

The initiation is very simple. The *murīd* sitting in front of the shaikh repeats after him the following *'ahd*:

O God, I have repented before Thee and accepted my teacher so-and-so as my shaikh in this world and the next, as guide and leader to Thy presence and as director in Thy Path. I will disobey him neither in word nor deed, by gesture nor in silence. Confirm me, O God, in obedience to him and his *ṭariqa* in this world and the next, and in the *ṭariqa* of the shaikh of shaikhs and imām of imāms, the *quṭb* of the people, my Lord Abū'l-Ḥasan ash-Shādhilī, may God be pleased with him!

After the *'ahd* all recite the *Fātiḥa* and the *tahlīl*. The shaikh holds regular classes (*majlis at-tarbiya*) in which the instruction given is mainly on duties towards God and man, and at these progressively the *murīd* is given permission to recite various *awrād* and *aḥzāb*.

9. MAJDHŪBIYYA

This *ṭarīqa* started as a localized order through attachment to a Ja'alī, Ḥamad ibn Muḥammad al-Majdhūb al-Kabīr (1693–1776), early in the eighteenth century in Dāmar district. The family was Qādiriyya, but we read in the *Ṭabaqāt* that Ḥamad became Shādhilī:

He memorized the Qur'ān under the feki Ḥamad b. 'Abd al-Mājid and learned khalīl and the *Risāla* under the feki Madanī b. Muḥammad and 'Alī al-Fazāri, and *'ilm al-kalām* under al-Ḥājj Sa'd. He performed the pilgrimage to the venerated House of God and was initiated in the Path by Sh. ad-Dirrāwī, pupil of Sīdī Aḥmad b. an-Nāṣir ash-Shādhilī. He devoted himself to teaching all branches of learning, legal decisions and religious rules, to initiating in the Path of the saints. His asceticism, meditations, performance of the *Dalā'il al-Khairāt*, concern for the welfare of Muslims, was wonderful. God made him exceedingly popular with great and small. He used to intercede much with Kings and Sultans, especially the Ja'aliyyīn. Usually his intercession was not refused and he who rejected it would be blighted quickly.[2]

[1] Aḥmad b. M. b. 'Ibād, *Al-mafākhir al-'aliyya fī'l-ma'āthir ash-Shādhiliyya* (Cairo, A.H. 1327).

[2] Op. cit. M. 70–1, S. 73.

Ḥamad acquired a great reputation and concentrated the rule of the district into his own hands. Dāmar became the main centre of education for the riverain tribes, Jaʿaliyyīn, Shā'iqiyya, Ḥasaniyya, &c., and the Dāmar shaikhs, being universally respected, became important mediators in quarrels between the tribes. Burckhardt's account of the 'little hierarchical state' of the fekis of Dāmar is worth quoting to show something of the reputation of Dāmar for learning and the respect and the power enjoyed by religious men of this type in the Sudan. Writing of Dāmar in 1814 under the rule of Ḥamad's grandson, Muḥammad al-Majdhūb aṣ-Ṣughayyir (1796–1832), he says:

It is inhabited by the Arab tribe of Medja-ydin, who trace their origin from Arabia; the greater part of them are Fokara, or religious men. They have no Shikh, but a high pontiff, called El Faky el Kebir (the great Faky), who is their real chief, and decides all matters in dispute. The family of Medjdoule, in whom this office is established, has the reputation of producing necromancers, or persons endowed with supernatural powers, from whom nothing remains hidden, and whose spells nothing can withstand. Innumerable stories are related of their magic powers, of which the following is a specimen: Abdullah, the father of the present Faky, caused a lamb to bleat in the stomach of the thief who had stolen, and afterwards eaten it. The Faky is resorted to in all cases where property is stolen, and as everybody entertains the greatest terror of his supposed omniscience, it is generally an easy task with him to perform wonders. If I am not mistaken, the office of the great Faky is hereditary; of course it is essential that the successor should be a shrewd man, and well instructed in the Mussulman law, these being absolutely necessary to enable him to act his part. The great Shikh, however, is not the only person in the place who possesses magical powers; there are many Fakys of less note, who enjoy a similar credit, in proportion always to their sanctity and learning, and thus the whole town of Damer has acquired great reputation. Here are several schools, to which young men repair from Darfour, Sennaar, Kordofan, and other parts of Soudan, in order to acquire a proficiency in the law, sufficient to enable them to make a figure as great Fakys in their own countries.[1]

The rule of Muḥammad al-Majdhūb aṣ-Ṣughayyir marks a new stage in the history of this order. The Majādhīb resisted Ismāʿīl Pāshā's invasion, but were crushed. Later, when as a result of his murder by *Makk* Nimr at Shendī all the Jaʿaliyyīn were subjected to severe reprisals, Dāmar was destroyed and Muḥammad al-Majdhūb fled to Sawākin and from there to Mecca where he was initiated into the Shādhiliyya by Sh. Muḥammad Ẓāhir al-Madani and came under the revivalist influence of Aḥmad ibn Idrīs. He returned to Sawākin in 1830 with his own *awrād* and acquired a following in that district.

[1] *Travels in Nubia*, p. 266.

Amongst others, 'Alī Diqna, uncle of 'Osmān Diqna, became one of his khalīfas. In 1832, when all the Ja'aliyyīn were given the amnesty, he returned to Dāmar and died the following year.

The Majādhīb, who believed that the Mahdī would come from the west, warmly supported the Mahdī. The original khalīfa at Sawākin, Shaikh aṭ-Ṭāhir al-Majdhūb, made an impressive act of submission to 'Osmān Diqna, one of his own followers, when the latter arrived there as envoy of the Mahdī, which brought over all the Majādhīb to Mahdism. He remained always a firm and fanatical supporter of the Mahdī and many of his family were killed in 'Osmān's battles.[1]

This order is an example of a family *ṭarīqa*. They call themselves collectively the Majādhīb; other followers who settled around Dāmar often being absorbed into the tribe. Their numbers to-day are stationary at about four thousand. They are still a force in Dāmar and district where half of them (Ja'aliyyīn) live. The Egyptian conquest scattered many and to-day they have adherents amongst Beja tribes on the Red Sea coast (Shara'āb and Tirik sub-sections of the Hadendiwa), at Sawākin, where they have a mosque, at Kasala, Qadārif, and amongst the Bishārīn of the River Atbara. Many of the Rashā'ida, a Red Sea tribe which came over from Arabia in 1846, have joined the Majādhīb for they were Shādhiliyya in Arabia.

All the adherents have a strong belief in the localization of the *baraka* of the family at Dāmar where all their *walīs* (with the exception of Madanī at Kasala and Aḥmad at Qadārif) are buried and where they possess two mosques. The present Khalīfa is Shaikh Bashīr Aḥmad Jalāl ad-Dīn.

10. SAMMĀNIYYA

The Sammāniyya is a branch order of the Khalwatiyya.[2] It was introduced into the Sudan by a Jamū'ī, Shaikh Aḥmad aṭ-Ṭayyib ibn

[1] Cf. H. C. Jackson, *Osman Digna*, p. 27.

[2] The parent order is very weak in the Sudan. There was a group at the Omdurman *Mūlid* in 1939, and the people of Masid (Blue Nile) call themselves Khalwatiyya. There were two main stages in its development. 'Umar al-Khalwatī (d. 1397/8) is regarded as its founder, though he was a teaching shaikh of the old type. The order spread rapidly in Turkey, Ḥijāz, and India for a time, and then decayed. The second stage was its revival and expansion in Africa. This began when Muṣṭafā ibn Kamāl ad-Dīn al-Bakrī (d. 1121/1709) sent to the Western Sudan four missionaries to propagate Islam amongst pagans. Three of these disputed the succession after al-Bakrī's death and formed three new groups, the Ḥafnawiyya by Muḥammad b. Salīm al-Hafnīsī; the Sharkāwiyya by 'Abd Allāh ash-Sharkāwī; and the Sammāniyya by Muḥammad b. 'Abd al-Karīm as-Sammānī (1718–75). The present Shaikh of the Sammāniyya, As-Sayyid Muḥammad al-Ḥasan as-Sammānī, who lives at Al-Medīna, paid three visits to the Sudan and stayed for some time collecting dues.

al-Bashīr, khalīfa of the *khalwa* at Umm Meraḥi (twenty-five miles north of Omdurman) who was initiated and appointed a khalīfa whilst at Al-Madīna on pilgrimage either by As-Sammānī or his successor. He returned to the Sudan about the year 1800, and his *ṭarīqa*, influenced by the new reactionary movement in Islam, spread with vigour.

He left his home for the Jezīra to attempt to cure the paralysed *wazīr* Muḥammad Abū Likailak. He did not succeed, but was granted lands there, founded a *khalwa* called Umm Maraḥi Sa'īd and his *ṭarīqa* spread rapidly among the Jamū'iyya, Kawāḥla, and Ḥalawīn. He achieved a great success when he appointed as his khalīfa the Shaikh at-Tōm of the Bān an-Naqā Qādirī family, so that all the Ya'qūbāb became Sammāniyya. His encroachment upon the followers of Yūsif Abū Shara, khalīfa of the 'Arakiyyīn, led Yūsif to visit him, with the result that the Shaikh aṭ-Ṭayyib sought permission from the King to return to his home at Umm Meraḥi where he died in 1823.[1]

Shaikh aṭ-Ṭayyib's grandson, Muḥammad Sharīf ibn Nūr ad-Dā'im, had a famous pupil in Muḥammad Aḥmad the Donqolāwī. The events leading to the latter's expulsion from his order are well known. Muḥammad Aḥmad then attached himself to Shaikh Qurashī az-Zain of Masallamiyya, a khalīfa of Nūr ad-Dā'im. Shaikh Qurashī did not live long and Muḥammad Aḥmad acquired great merit by building his tomb.

The Sammāniyya is most strongly represented along both banks of the White Nile in its numerous family branches. The main line, the family of Shaikh aṭ-Ṭayyib, is now represented by Shaikh Jaili 'Abd al-Muḥammad Nūr ad-Dā'im of Lake Tabat, that of Shaikh al-Qurashī by Shaikh aṭ-Ṭayyib at Ṭayyiba. Those of Tabat consider themselves superior to Mahdists because their ancestor initiated the Mahdī. Those of Ṭayyiba, whilst holding to their order, believe in the sanctity of Muḥammad Aḥmad al-Mahdī. The Sammāniyya is the basic *ṭarīqa* of the Ḥamar tribe of Kordofān and of the Fadniyya East, sub-tribe of the Ja'aliyyīn. The Sulaim Baqqāra belong to it, though Mahdism has strongly influenced them. One of the great present-day religious leaders of the Sudan, the Sharīf Yūsuf al-Hindī (d. 1943), was the head of a branch which is beginning to be called the Hindiyya or Sharīfiyya. His followers, who are mainly Kawāḥla, had a superstitious reverence for him and related *karāmāt* of him. One related to me that Yūsif was sent to the *sāyir* (prison) by the Khalīfa, but all the chains that were fastened on him fell off miraculously

[1] The present tomb at this village, which is now called Shaikh aṭ-Ṭayyib, was built in 1906.

and the Khalīfa, impressed by this evidence of supernatural power, released him. Four Sammānī groups are represented at the Omdurman *Mūlid*, the most important being the Qarībiyya, who are descended from an Omdurman ascetic Qarīb Allāh Ṣāliḥ who died in 1930. This group, still under the genuinely good influence of its late head, in contrast to most orders require a period of discipleship from the *murīd* who must perform *ṣalāt* and *awrād* with the shaikh and receive instruction.[1]

The *shaikh as-sijjāda* appoints subsidiary leaders from those who are living with him. At the ceremony of investiture a *dhikr* is performed, then the shaikh invests the *murshid* with an *'imma* and reads the certificate of appointment (*ijāza*). Afterwards he presents him with a *rakwa* (leather ablution jug), *sibḥa* (rosary), *'aṣāya* (stick), *farwa* (prayer-skin), and a Qur'ān. A shaikh so appointed has power to admit *murīds*.

II. IDRĪSIYYA (AḤMADIYYA)[2] AND RASHĪDIYYA

The founder, Aḥmad ibn Idrīs al-Fāsī, played an important part in the reactionary movement in Islam at the beginning of the nineteenth century. A reformer, as well as a mystic, he aimed at the unity of Islam and was in sympathy with the Wahhābīs. As we have shown he initiated a new phase in the religious life of the whole of Central and Eastern Sudan through the missionary activities of his pupils.

[1] I append a genealogical tree giving the more significant names since it is not given in MacMichael's *History*:

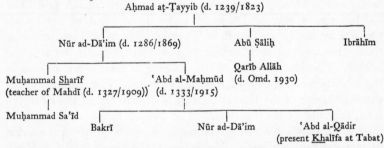

- Aḥmad aṭ-Ṭayyib (d. 1239/1823)
  - Nūr ad-Dā'im (d. 1286/1869)
    - Muḥammad Sharīf (teacher of Mahdī (d. 1327/1909))
      - Muḥammad Sa'īd
    - 'Abd al-Maḥmūd (d. 1333/1915)
      - Bakrī
      - Nūr ad-Dā'im
      - 'Abd al-Qādir (present Khalīfa at Tabat)
  - Abū Ṣāliḥ
    - Qarīb Allāh (d. Omd. 1930)
  - Ibrāhīm

'Abd al-Maḥmūd was a follower of the Mahdī but hated by the Khalīfa whom he was rash enough to tell he did not know how to pray. He was imprisoned and eventually sentenced with others to receive 1,000 lashes but he was preserved by a miracle, not even his skin being broken and his untorn pants are still preserved by his followers at Tabat. He wrote three histories of the Mahdī, the Khalīfa, and Famous Pupils of Aḥmad aṭ-Ṭayyib which are now held by his Khalīfa 'Abd al-Qādir at Tabat.

[2] This order must not be confused with the Aḥmadiyya of Aḥmad al-Badawī of Ṭanṭa which is called the Bedāwiyya in the Sudan where its followers are mainly Egyptians, except in Omdurman where it attracts town-bred natives of slave origin.

He was born at Maisūr in Morocco in 1173/1760 and was trained at Fās where he was admitted to the Shādhiliyya *ṭarīqa* by ʿAbd al-Wahhāb at-Tāzī. After performing the Pilgrimage, he taught in Cairo from 1214/1799 until he went to Mecca in 1234/1818. In the Ḥijāz he continued to seek after shaikhs until he was told to turn exclusively to the Qur'ān. There he found his own path and received guidance to propagate it. The Prophet said to him, 'I have given thee, O Aḥmad, the keys of heaven and earth, and these are the Special Supplication, the Prayer of Glory and the Act of Forgiveness.' After he came out as an independent shaikh he became the outstanding religious figure of his age and grouped around him a great number of pupils. His fame excited the envy of the *ʿulamā'* of that city and a charge of heresy was brought against him. He was forced to fly for safety to Ṣabyā in ʿAsīr in 1243/1827. The Wahhābīs, who were then contending with the Egyptians in Yemen, left him in peace, for many of his reformist tenets agreed with theirs, and he died there in 1253/1837.[1]

The subsequent history of his order is one of dissension and discord. After his death his two most famous pupils, Muḥammad ibn ʿAlī as-Sanūsī and Muḥammad ʿUthmān al-Mirghanī, contended for his spiritual heritage and caused a schism in the order. Both established *zāwiyas* in Mecca. The bedouins ranged themselves under As-Sanūsī, the most outstanding personality of the two, whilst the ʿUlamā' and Shurafā' supported Muḥammad ʿUthmān. Although these two took very widely diverging paths, both in their writings acknowledged their indebtedness to their master and Aḥmad Ibn Idrīs is widely revered by their followers.

Muḥammad ʿUthmān had travelled widely in the Sudan nominally on behalf of his master, but the attachment of the Sudanese was naturally to the shaikh they knew and, after Aḥmad's death, Muḥammad ʿUthmān sent his son to organize his followers.

Aḥmad's son Muḥammad recognized Ibrāhīm ar-Rashīd, another of Aḥmad's pupils, as his father's successor, and all the followers in Ṣabyā paid allegiance to him. ʿAbd al-Mutaʿāl, another son of Aḥmad, attached himself at first to the Sanūsī and spent some time with him at Jaghbūb. Then he went to Donqola to attempt to reconstruct his father's order there, and had considerable successes, winning many of

[1] A short account of his life and teaching is given by the present head Shams ad-Dīn b. Muḥammad ʿAbd al-Mutaʿāl in a copy of Aḥmad ibn Idrīs's *wird al-ʿaẓīm* called *Kanz as-saʿādati wa'r-rashād* (Khartoum, 1939) and also in the collection of his *aḥzāb wa awrād wa rasā'il* (Cairo, 1940).

Q

the followers of the son of the Sayyid Aḥmad al-Ḥasan al-Mirghanī. His tomb at Donqola'l-Urḍī iṣ a famous shrine and his *ḥōliyya* (21st Rajab), celebrated there and in Omdurman, where some member of the family is usually present, is a great event and has been attended by heads of the Mirghaniyya and Rashidiyya. The present head is his grandson Shams ad-Dīn b. Muḥammad ʿAbd al-Mutaʿāl.

The head of the Arabian branch, Muḥammad ibn ʿAlī b. Muḥammad b. Aḥmad Idrīs (1876–1923), founder of the Idrīsī dynasty of ʿAsīr, also had considerable influence in Donqola where he had married and established himself, until he went in 1905 to ʿAsīr, where his family had been long settled,[1] to succeed to the Imāmate and begin his long and indecisive struggle with the Turks for the independence of ʿAsīr. He was the first Arab ruler to join the Allies in the 1914–18 war. He died in 1923 and the dissensions which broke out between members of his family finally resulted in civil war. In 1930 ʿAsīr was absorbed by Ibn Saʿūd by a treaty which gave it the status of a dependency. In Donqola, where he is regarded with great affection, Muḥammad ibn ʿAlī is known as Muḥammad al-Yamanī.

Claims have always been made by the family of Aḥmad ibn Idrīs to leadership of the followers of the Mirghaniyya and the Sanūsiyya on the grounds that the founders were pupils of their ancestor, and stress is laid on Aḥmad's teaching as a reformer and unifier of Muslims. But these claims are not treated seriously. To-day the Mirghaniyya is said to be extending its influence in Donqola at the expense of the Aḥmadiyya.

The Aḥmadiyya is a somewhat puritan order like the Wahhābiyya and objects to tomb-worship. To-day many signs of deterioration are setting in. Their *dhikrs*, however, remain sober. They use Aḥmad ibn Idrīs's *wird al-ʿaẓīm*. The instructions concerning its recitation state that 'the *dhākirs* sitting in a circle should have the intention (*nīyya*) of being near to God, recalling to their minds the presence of the Prophet in the form of the prophetic qualities (*shamāʾil*) and conducting themselves soberly by reason of that presence, with attentiveness of the heart and senses, pronouncing clearly and giving every radical its full enunciation'.

Rashīdiyya

This *ṭarīqa* does not claim to be a new order, but that it is the true Idrīsiyya in direct and genuine succession from Aḥmad b. Idrīs. It

[1] The population of ʿAsīr and the surrounding villages is largely of Sudanese blood, both freed and unemancipated slaves and *muwalladīn*.

is regarded by others as a branch (*far'*) of the Idrīsiyya. It is certainly not a separate order because Ibrāhīm ar-Rashīd did not receive the usual revelation and permission by prophetic vision to start one, but he carried on the *wird* of his master, using his *awrād* and giving the *ṭarīqa* in his name.

Ibrāhīm ar-Rashīd ad-Diwaiḥī[1] claimed to belong to the family of Sīdī Aḥmad ar-Rashīdī (d. 1524), the founder of the Rashīdiyya in Algeria. He joined Aḥmad ibn Idrīs at Ṣabyā and Aḥmad died in his arms. Aḥmad's son Muḥammad refused the succession himself and proclaimed that his father had appointed Ibrāhīm his successor, so that all the followers in Ṣabyā followed Ibrāhīm. Ibrāhīm is stated by his enemies to have reverted to the Shādhiliyya. He went to Egypt in order to avoid becoming involved in the Sanūsī-Mirghaniyya rivalry and to try to extend his own influence. He succeeded in establishing *zāwiyas* at Luxor and among the Shā'iqiyya in Donqola (Merowe), where he stayed for some time, then he returned disappointed to Mecca. Here he took up the claim to be the legitimate head of the Aḥmadiyya and acquired a rapid notoriety because he was attacked by both the Mirghaniyya and the Meccan shaikhs attached to Aḥmad ibn Idrīs. He had to face two charges for heresy (*c.* A.H. 1273) before the court of the '*ulamā'* but emerged from the trials triumphantly and with an enhanced reputation. Indian pilgrims in particular flocked to his *zāwiya* and an Indian Begum sent him a present of 1,000 gold rupees to enable him to build a great *zāwiya*. He died at Mecca in 1874.

He was succeeded by his nephew, Muḥammad Ṣāliḥ, who died at Mecca in 1919, and the present *khalīfa* is his son Ar-Rashīd. Subordinate leaders are also called khalīfas. The importance of using Mecca as the centre of influence is shown by the fact that the order has spread to India, Eritrea, Somaliland, Syria, Ḥijāz, and the Sudan.

The Rashīdiyya in the Sudan, where its followers are often called the Rashā'ida,[2] is active among the Shā'iqiyya at Merowe and Salama (Shendi where the *khalīfa* is Sa'īd ibn al-Amīn), on the White Nile around Kawa where there is a *zāwiya* (Sīd Aḥmad b. 'Abd Allāh ad-Dufārī), and Omdurman which has a mosque and *zāwiya* (Sharīf Muḥammad at-Taqalāwī).

12. MIRGHANIYYA OR KHATMIYYA

One of the most famous of the pupils of Sayyid Aḥmad ibn Idrīs in the Ḥijāz was Muḥammad 'Uthmān al-Mirghanī (1793–1853).

[1] The Diwaiḥ is a section of the Shā'iqiyya of Donqola.

[2] Not to be confused with the Arab tribe of that name.

His family, who were <u>Sh</u>erīfian in origin, had been settled in Turkestan and later India, but had returned to Mecca. His grandfather, 'Abd Allāh al-Mir<u>gh</u>anī al-Maj<u>dh</u>ūb (d. 1792/3), was a noted Ṣūfī whose *karāmāt* are mentioned by Al-Jabartī (d. 1821) in his *'Ajā'ib al-Āthār*.

Muḥammad 'U<u>th</u>mān is stated to have been very precocious in his youth and quickly mastered the religious sciences.[1] But Ṣūfism was his real field, and he followed one Path after another until he branched off on his own with the Seal of all Ṭarīqas. He was initiated first into the Naq<u>sh</u>abandiyya by Shaikh Aḥmad Muḥammad Banna; then into the Qādiriyya by Sayyid al-Qadūmī, the *muqaddam* at Mecca; the Indian Naq<u>sh</u>abandiyya by Sīd 'Abd ar-Raḥmān, Muftī of Zubaid; and into the Junaidiyya, the Mir<u>gh</u>aniyya of his grandfather, and the <u>Sh</u>ādhiliyya by Aḥmad ibn Idrīs.

Aḥmad ibn Idrīs was pre-eminently his shaikh and sent him to the Eastern Sudan as a propaganda agent. Muḥammad 'U<u>th</u>mān sailed first to Sawākin, but finding the land route dangerous owing to internal troubles, he went up the Red Sea to Kosair, then ascended the Nile to Aswān. In Egypt his mission had no success, but once he got amongst the Nubians his passage from Aswān to Donqola was a triumphal procession and the Nubians, impressed by the splendour of his equipage, flocked to offer him allegiance. From Donqola he crossed the desert to Kordofān where he stayed for a time, proselytizing without much success among the pagan Nuba, and winning the Muslims over to Aḥmad ibn Idrīs. Thence he proceeded to Sennār and the Funj Chronicle records:

In 1232 (A.D. 1817) the most learned and pious Sherīf, the noble Sayyid Muḥammad 'U<u>th</u>mān al Mir<u>gh</u>anī al Mekki, visited Sennār and met its rulers and called upon all men to follow his *ṭarīqa*; but only a few people did so, and the rulers paid no heed to him but wished to test him by examination; so they brought forward the *feki* Ibrāhīm wad Baqādī, one of the most brilliant of the *'ulamā'*, to examine him. And the *feki* Ibrāhīm arrived at Sennār with a racking headache, and the pain increased until he died—and this before he had ever met the Sherīf. So the Sherīf left Sennār; and at that time his age was twenty-five years.[2]

In spite of this special *karāma* and the exaggerated accounts of his success, it is to be inferred that he was not outstandingly successful in the Sudan. He had, however, laid foundations for the future and like all Muslim missionaries created a permanent bond with the Sudan by marrying a Donqolāwiyya whilst in Kordofān, and her surviving son

---

[1] Apart from his numerous Ṣūfī writings he left behind him commentaries on the Qur'ān, the Mālikiyya Ma<u>dhh</u>ab, and a grammar.　　　[2] MacMichael, *Hist.* ii. 383-4.

Al-Ḥasan was the 'Seal' by which he bound these African adherents to him when later he set himself up as an independent master of the Way.

On his return to the Ḥijāz he continued to serve Aḥmad ibn Idrīs, following him into exile in Ṣabyā, until Aḥmad's death in 1837.

Muḥammad 'Uthmān and Muḥammad ibn 'Alī as-Sanūsī now contended together for the leadership of the order and the result was a schism, each setting himself up as an independent shaikh. Owing to his Sharīfian origin Muḥammad 'Uthmān was able to win the support of the Sharīfs of Mecca against the Sanūsī. He established a central *zāwiya* at Dair Khaizarān, with branches at Medīna, Jidda, and Aṭ-Ṭā'if. Then, having completely modified the rule of Aḥmad b. Idrīs and developed his theory of the peculiar hereditary sanctity of his family, he sent out his sons to proselytize in other regions. The eldest Muḥammad Sirr al-Khatim went to the Yaman and the Ḥaḍramawt. Al-Ḥasan, who was being educated in Mecca, went to Sawākin where he won over the Beja tribes of the Banī 'Āmir, the Ḥalānqa and Ḥabāb who had been previously influenced by his father. Thence he travelled to Sennār, Kordofān, and north to Donqola trying to establish *zāwiyas*. In the central regions he had little success, but in northern Kordofān, Donqola, and Nubia, especially amongst the Danāqla and Shā'iqiyya, his success was outstanding.

Muḥammad 'Uthmān's success drew upon him the enmity of the 'Ulamā' of Mecca and he retired to Aṭ-Ṭā'if where he died in 1853, leaving his order firmly established in western and southern Arabia and the Northern Sudan. After his death his eldest son, Muḥammad Sirr al-Khatim, was recognized as *shaikh aṭ-ṭarīqa*, but his death shortly afterwards opened the era of internal rivalry which is the main feature of the history of the order. The unity of the order was broken and Muḥammad 'Uthmān's descendants became the heads of regional clans. We are concerned only with the order in the Sudan where Al-Ḥasan remained the great regional leader. He settled at Kasala where he founded the township of Khatmiyya which has remained the centre of the order. He died there in 1869 and to-day is more revered by the Mirghaniyya followers in the Sudan than the founder himself. He has numerous *bayāns* throughout the country and the most binding oath is one taken on his tomb. He was succeeded by his son Muḥammad 'Uthmān Tāj as-Sirr. On the Mahdiyya outbreak the family, with everything to lose, supported the Egyptian Government and headed the Bani 'Āmir and Shukriyya against the dervishes. Eventually Muḥammad 'Uthmān was forced to fly to Cairo where he died in 1886.

After the reoccupation his two sons Aḥmad and ʿAlī returned to Kasala and succeeded in completely re-establishing the order. The Government rebuilt their mosque at Kasala which had been destroyed by the dervishes and subsequently ʿAlī was created a K.C.M.G. and K.C.V.O. and Aḥmad (d. 1928) a C.B.E., in recognition of their support and loyalty to the Government.

None of the Mirghanīs is recognized as the paramount head and the order is organized in regional spheres of influence: the Kasala, Qadārif, and Qallabāt areas and the Shukriyya and Hadendiwa are under Muḥammad, the son of the above-mentioned Aḥmad; Kordofān, Khartūm, Barbar, Donqola, and Ḥalfa under ʿAlī; the Red Sea Hills under the *Sharīfa* Maryam al-Mirghanī; and Eritrea under *Sharīfa* ʿAlawiyya[1] and Jaʿfar b. al-Bakrī. All these, and it should be noted that they include two women, are equal in status in theory, since all possess the peculiar *baraka* of the family. Politically As-Sayyid Sir ʿAlī al-Mirghanī is the most important.

The order is very strict in insisting on the extreme sanctity of the family and therefore refuses to allow its adherents to affiliate themselves to any other order or even to take part in their ritual.[2] It is opposed more especially to the Idrīsiyya and the Majdhūbiyya, and is in bitter political rivalry with the Mahdiyya.

Some of the doctrines and practices have already been treated.[3] Muḥammad ʿUthmān we have said was initiated into many Paths and his numerous writings show the influence of eastern Ṣūfism. He belonged to the class of ecstatic mystics and the doctrinal and reformist influence on him of Aḥmad ibn Idrīs was negligible. When he became *shaikh aṭ-ṭarīqa* he formulated his own rule and adopted the formula NAQSHJAM.[4] as the symbol of the spiritual 'chains' concentrated into himself. Whence his order is called *Khātim aṭ-Ṭuruq*, 'the Seal of the Paths', and its popular name is the Khatmiyya. The direct descendants of the founder have the title of *Sirr al-Khātim*, 'the Secret

[1] ʿAlawiyya al-Mirghanī has since died (Oct. 1940).

[2] The following statement by D. B. Macdonald (*Aspects of Islam*, p. 155) should be corrected. He writes: 'one man, a Syrian Christian and the editor of one of the most important newspapers in Cairo, told me that there was a certain fraternity, the Mirghanite, the predominant one in the Sudan, which was quite prepared to accept Christians; that they would put no bar in their way; and that there was nothing in their ritual to prevent a Christian from using it.' The Mirghaniyya would never accept a Christian and no Christian could use their ritual without denying his faith.

[3] Above, §§ 5 and 6. Cf. *Ar-Rasāʾil al-Mirghaniyya* (1939), which is a collection of treatises on doctrine and practice, by the founder and others.

[4] The initial letters of the Orders into which he had been initiated, i.e. Naqshabandiyya, Qādiriyya, Shādhiliyya, Junaidiyya, and Mirghaniyya; cf. *Minḥat al-Aṣḥāb*, pp. 77–8.

of the Seal', that is, they are by their very nature trustees of that mysterious power entrusted to the family. So they are regarded as semi-divine by their followers, who place themselves and all that they possess in their hands.

13. ISMĀ'ĪLIYYA

The founder was Ismā'īl al-Walī (1793–1863) ibn 'Abd Allāh al-Kordofānī of a family originally domiciled in Donqola.[1] His father went to Kordofān trading and there Ismā'īl was born. He memorized the Qur'ān when quite young and began teaching in a *khalwa*. When Muḥammad 'Uthmān al-Mirghanī came to Kordofān he became one of his followers and later, after his return from Pilgrimage (1842), was allowed by his shaikh to form his own branch which became known as the Ismā'īliyya. He became very famous for his charity and learning and composed some forty-five books.[2]

Ismā'īl al-Walī was succeeded by his eldest son Muḥammad al-Mekkī (d. 1906), who was one of the Mahdī's first and foremost adherents in Kordofān and was trusted by the Khalīfa.

Ismā'īl's second son, Aḥmad Al-Azharī, Shaikh al-Islām in Western Sudan, who studied at Al-Azhar for twelve years, on the other hand, is famous for his opposition to the Mahdī and wrote a *risāla* refuting his claims.[3] When returning to Cairo in 1881 Ra'ūf Pāshā, the Governor-General, asked him to accompany an expedition against the Mahdī as an ambassador of conciliation. The party was almost annihilated and Al-Azharī was killed.

After the death of Muḥammad al-Mekkī in 1906, disputes arose between his grandson, Muḥammad Mirghanī Ismā'īl al-Mekkī, who was the head of the family by descent, and Muḥammad Mirghanī's uncles as to the headship and there were occasional affrays between the adherents of the various parties. To-day the influence of Muḥammad Mirghanī is negligible. He resides at Omdurman and visits Al-Ubayyiḍ perhaps twice a year.

Although derived from the Mirghaniyya it is a distinct order, owing to the influence of Ismā'īl al-Walī and his composition of rules and *awrād*. Its influence is confined mainly to Kordofān. The *Nāẓir* and almost the whole of the Badairiyya tribe and the El-Obeyd natives

[1] He claimed to belong to the Dahmashiyya section of the Bedairiyya and was therefore of the Ja'aliyyīn, but was of partly Takrūrī origin (MacMichael, *Tribes*, p. 70).

[2] Seven at least have been printed: these are (1) *Dīwān ash-Shaṭrāt*, (2) *Al-Burāq*, (3) *Al-Khaira*, (4) *Al-Mawlid*, (5) *Mushāriq al-Anwār* which treats of the seven heavens and seven earths, (6) *Al-'Uhūd*, which gives the rules and method of the order, and (7) *awrād*.

[3] Quoted in Shuqair, op. cit. iii. 383–91.

of slave extraction are adherents. The various <u>kh</u>alīfaships have tended to be kept in the same family.

The *mūlid* written by the founder is read, not before the <u>dh</u>ikr, but once a week after the *ṣalāt al-jum'a*. At the twice-weekly *ḥaḍra* the founder's *rātib*[1] is read first, *qaṣā'id* are sung and they <u>dh</u>ikr for about two hours; *qaṣā'id* and *madā'iḥ* being sung continuously and during the pauses. Unlike the Mir<u>gh</u>aniyya the drum (*nōba*) is used at the <u>dh</u>ikr.

14. TIJĀNIYYA

The Tijāniyya is one of the most active of the African orders and has been one of the chief agents for the spreading of Islam in West Africa. Its founder, Aḥmad b. Muḥammad b. al-Mu<u>kh</u>tār at-Tijānī[2] (b. 1737 at 'Ain Māḍī), travelled widely and was affiliated to many orders. But it was not until 1781 that:

... the Prophet permitted him to initiate others, at a period when he was avoiding meeting with people, owing to his caring only for his own (spiritual) welfare and not daring to call himself a shaikh until he was permitted by him, awake and not in a dream, to train people generally and totally. He showed him the *wird* he was to teach in 1196 (1781). . . . When he permitted him to found the *ṭarīqa* and he received divine inspiration, through the medium of the Prophet . . . he said to him, 'you owe no favour (*minna*) to any of the shaikhs of the Path, for I am your mediator and your provider in very truth. Leave all that you have taken in anything concerning the Path.'[3]

At-Tijānī, therefore, developed his own rule on strict lines. He adopted the <u>Kh</u>alwatiyya chain for his mystical succession, though his teaching, philosophical rather than ecstatic mysticism, seems to owe most to the <u>Sh</u>ādhiliyya. Obligations, as are necessary in a missionary order, were simple. There were no prolonged penances and retreats and the ritual was simple. He emphasized above all the need for an intercessor between God and man; that intercessor being himself and his successors. His followers were strictly forbidden from invocations to any *walīs* other than those of his order.

At-Tijānī travelled about the West establishing *zāwiyas* and nominating *muqaddams* and the order spread with great rapidity. He settled at Fās and died there in 1815. In his will he nominated the *muqaddam* of the *zāwiya* at Temasin, Al-Ḥājj 'Alī b. 'Īsā (d. 1844), as

---

[1] This is given in the book of rules called *Al-'Uhūd al-Wāfiya*, p. 13.

[2] An account of his life is given in *Jawāhir al-Ma'ānī wa Bulūgh al-amānī fī faiḍ a<u>sh</u>-<u>sh</u>ai<u>kh</u> at-Tijānī*, known as the *Kunnā<u>sh</u>*, compiled by 'Alī Harāzim under Aḥmad's direction. This book and the *Rimāh* on the margin by 'Umar b. Sa'īd al-Fūtī contain the main body of Tijānī doctrine.   [3] *Jawāhir al-Ma'ānī* (ed. 1929), p. 43.

his successor and directed that the succession should be alternately in his own family and that of Al-Ḥājj ʿAlī.

No great split in the order occurred until 1875 when the groups at ʿAin Māḍī and Temasim separated owing to a dispute about the succession. These two places have to-day little more than local authority and groups have made themselves independent all over Africa where it is now the most widespread *ṭarīqa*. At the present time, As-Sayyid Muḥammad al-Ḥāfiẓ, who lives in Egypt, is regional shaikh of Egypt, the Anglo-Egyptian Sudan, and the Near East.

The *ṭarīqa* was introduced into the Anglo-Egyptian Sudan by Sīdī Muḥammad b. al-Mukhtār b. ʿAbd ar-Raḥmān ash-Shanqītī, popularly known as Wad al-ʿĀliya.[1] He was born at Tashīt in Algeria, studied under many leaders, though he 'attributed himself' mainly to Muḥammad as-Saqqāf, a pupil of the founder in Egypt, and received the *ijāza* of *muqaddam* from Ṣāliḥ b. Aḥmad Balqāsim in Al-Medīna in 1847. He travelled considerably, trading in the Sudan and Egypt, and acted as ambassador between the Sulṭān of Dārfūr and the Sublime Porte. He is stated to have given the *ṭarīqa* to Saʿīd Pāshā, Khedive of Egypt.

He was a rich trader, but it is related that he sometimes escaped from luxury, put on the patched *jubba*, and acted as a water-carrier. 'Once in Dārfūr he passed some graves and saw the state of their inhabitants. Nearby he saw a group playing musical instruments and dancing and was overcome by a profound *ḥāl*. He distributed all his wealth and freed all his slaves and most of his women, and fell on the ground lying prostrate for seventy days.'[2] He lived for a time in Sawākin, then went to Barbar with Zain al-ʿAbdīn al-Maghrabī. On the latter's death, owing to some dispute with his family, he went to settle amongst the Jaʿaliyyīn on an island near Qōz where he died in 1882. He married more than thirty wives, his concubines are stated to be numberless, and he buried more than sixty children.

He initiated many into the *ṭarīqa* throughout the Sudan, including Ḥusain, Ṣulṭān of Dārfūr and Shaikh Muḥammad al-Badawī, who became Shaikh al-Islām in the early days of the present government and whose tomb at Omdurman is famous.

He died in 1882 having previously ordered his grave and shroud and the cause of his death was an 'overplus of love' (*shiddat al-maḥabba*). He left a *Dīwān* in Arabic (published), and another in

[1] He was a *sharīf* on both sides, but his mother was especially noted as a learned woman. An account of his life and a long list of his pupils in the Sudan is given in *ar-risālat as-sādisa* issued by the Jamāʿat al-waḥdat al-islāmiyyat at-tijāniyya, Cairo, 1355 (1936), pp. 17–23.

[2] *Ar-risālat as-sādisa*, p. 18.

Sudanese colloquial, a *Mūlid Insān al-Kāmil* (published), and a *Kitāb al-Wāridāt*.

There is evidence to show that the Tijāniyya were persecuted under the Egyptian occupation from the life of an Egyptian ʿAbd al-Munʿim b. Aḥmad b. Salāma who spent his life in the Sudan and died at Umm Saʿdūn near Bāra in 1935, at a very advanced age. On coming to Khartoum we read 'he concealed his *ṭarīqa* at first and pretended to serve those interested in propagating other *ṭarīqas*. Some of the Tijānīs were persecuted and killed, but God willed to preserve him.'[1]

The Anglo-Egyptian Sudan was also influenced by Tijāniyya from Western Sudan and the main body of its followers are West Africans. One of these was a Hausa, ʿUmar Janbo, a disciple of Muḥammad as Ṣaghīr b. ʿAlī of Temasin. He lived for a time at Al-Fāshir under ʿAlī Dīnār, who was nominally a Tijānī, but who, when he came to consider himself a saint, was suspicious of all other religious influences. ʿUmar Janbo was accused of using witchcraft to cause illness to the Sultan and had to flee. Afterwards he lived in El-Obeyd and Omdurman and died at Mecca in 1918. The celebrated Nūba Khalīfa, Shaikh Dardairī Muḥammad, Khalīfa of Jebel Harāza, was initiated by a Western feki.

In 1906 Sultan Mai Wirnū, son of the ex-Sultan of Sokoto, settled at Shaikh Talḥa, near Sennār Dam, and to-day his Fellāta settlement, some 10,000 strong, recognize him as Khalīfa and a saint. Alfa Hāshim, a Fellāta *muqaddam* of the Tijāniyya,[2] visited the Sudan in 1925 and gave the *Ṭarīqa* to large numbers of West Africans. About fifteen years ago a Maghribī *ʿālim* named Shaikh ad-Dirdābī (d. A.H. 1355) came to the Sudan and gave the *ṭarīqa* to various people, amongst whom was Shaikh Marzūq, who has set up a red-brick prayer-house at Wad Nubāwī, North Omdurman.

Most *muqaddams* are allowed to initiate others. At the initiation the *murīd* asks for the *ṭarīqa* and is told that he is required to know its principles and rules and to perform certain *awrād* as he is given permission. He agrees and the *muqaddam* recites his chain of authority, gives him the *ṭarīqa* by the *muṣāfaḥa*, hands him the book of rules (*al-fatḥ ar-rabbānī*), and orders him to recite certain *awrād* regularly. Later he will be given more *awrād*.

The *dhikr* in congregation is performed only once a week on Friday afternoons before the *mughrib* prayer. At the *dhikr* the worshippers

[1] *Ar-risālat as-sādisa*, p. 34.

[2] Alfa (i.e. ḥāfiẓ) Hāshim fled as a political refugee from Nigeria to Al-Medīna in 1903. He died in 1934 and has now been succeeded by his son Ibrāhīm.

sit in a circle, recite the *ta'wīẓ* to clear the air of devils and *jinn*, and commence the *dhikr* with *lā ilāha illā'llāh* a specified number of times. This is performed in a low voice, and pronounced clearly. There is no singing of *madīḥ*.

The Tijāniyya has quite a vogue amongst the educated in Omdurman, owing perhaps to its philosophical mysticism and liberalism, and many unexpected people such as secondary school teachers have adopted it.

15. MINOR ORDERS

(*a*) *Sanūsiyya*

Muḥammad b. 'Alī as-Sanūsī (1791–1859) on leaving Mecca centred his *ṭarīqa* in Cyrenaica and never visited the Eastern Sudan nor sent any missionaries there. His successors also have taken little interest in such propaganda except in Dārfūr, whose links have always been much more with Central than Eastern Sudan. Muḥammad al-Mahdī (1844–1902), the son and successor of the founder, it will be remembered, was asked by the Sudanese Mahdī to act as his Khalīfa number three, which invitation, since he was himself the Mahdī, he scorned.[1]

The same Muḥammad al-Mahdī or his successor wrote three times to Sulṭān 'Alī Dīnār requesting the establishment of Sanūsī *zāwiyas* in Dārfūr. 'Alī, fearful of Sanūsī power, desiring neither Sanūsī activities nor to alienate the Brotherhood, contrived to put him off for a time, though he did eventually allow a *khalīfa* to come and open a *zāwiya* in Al-Fāshir itself. In 1911 there was an influx of Kenin (Ṭawārek) refugees from the French into Dārfūr who were Sanūsī, but these were not well received. They are still settled south of Al-Fāshir with a Khalīfa, Abū Bakr al-Ghadamsī. At the beginning of the 1914–18 war 'Alī Dīnār got into touch with the Sanūsī and when he resolved on revolt he permitted a Sanūsī establishment north of Jebel Mīdōb.

To-day these various immigrant groups from the West, with the few Tibbū negroid groups (Qura'ān and Bedāyāt) that are to be found in the Sudan, are the only Sanūsiyya and the influence of the order is negligible.

(*b*) *'Azmiyya*

This was founded in the Sudan by an Egyptian Shaikh, Muḥammad Māḍī Abū'l-'Azā'im (1870–1936), who was a teacher at Gordon

[1] Al-Mahdī was originally his proper name to which he contrived to give the popular application.

College from 1905 to 1915 when he was deported to Egypt for his tendentious political principles. In Egypt he established his seat at Maṭariyya in Minya Province. His son Aḥmad has now succeeded him.

Muḥammad Māḍī, originally a Shādhilī, had been strongly influenced by Wahhābī reformist principles. He aimed at the destruction of the influence of the great hereditary religious shaikhs, urging that sanctity had nothing to do with heredity. He condemned the veneration of shaikhs, worship at tombs, and mourning at funerals.

The *ṭarīqa* membership reached its zenith in the Sudan, where his followers are called ʿAwāzma, in the nineteen-twenties, but has now declined since saint-worship is the essence of Sudanese religious life. Although he tried to be a reformer, Muḥammad Māḍī only succeeded in fact in forming another *ṭarīqa.* In 1915 his representative at Sawākin was condemned as a heretic by the khalīfas of the other orders. He wrote two books called 'The First Principles of following the Prophet' and 'The ʿAzmiyya *Ṭarīqa* and Heavenly Inspirations'.

The hierarchy consists: (1) the shaikh, (2) his regional *wakīls*, the one in the Sudan lives at Atbara, and (3) the *khalīfas.* All these can admit new members. Ordinary members are called *fuqarā'*, and there are two higher grades *najīb* and *naqīb* who have special functions at the *dhikr*.

With the worshippers sitting in a circle, the *dhikr* commences with the *taʿwīdh* (the formula: 'I take refuge with God from Satan'), then they recite *awrād* such as *allāhu akbar*, pronouncing clearly. These are interspersed with *madīḥ*, the first line of which is repeated in chorus between each line of the poem. It concludes with prayer on the Prophet, individual prayers, and finally Fātiḥat al-Qur'ān.

(*c*) *Jamāʿat Abū Jarīd*[1]

ʿAbd Allāh b. Dafʿ Allāh al-ʿArakī who went on Pilgrimage twenty-four times, introduced certain sharīfs from the Ḥijāz into the Sudan. One of these was a Shādhilī called Maḥmūd al-Ghaib who married a Jezīra woman and had a son called Abokr. This Abokr was the founder of a sect (early seventeenth century) which came to be regarded as heretical and was known as *Az-Zabālʿa*[2] (the deceived) and *Al-Millat al-Khāmisa* (the Fifth State).[3] Abokr was associated with two others, Abū Jarīd and Kirēn, who, according to one tradition,

[1] S. Hillelson has given an account of this sect in *S.N.R.* i. 176 f.

[2] Sing. *Zabla'*, deceived people, cf. Dozy, *Dict.* i. *Zablah.*

[3] The fifth *madhhab*, i.e. non-Muslim.

were his brothers. The sect came to be popularly associated with the name of Abū Jarīd owing to his being the missionary leader.

It is not known how they came to be regarded as heretical and so distinctly marked off from other associations. It could not be on account of their beliefs, such as the claim to possess esoteric teaching, nor because of the ecstatic outbursts (*shaṭḥāt* or *ḥayūt*) of its leaders, even if Abū Jarīd did associate himself with the Prophet or Allāh. Rather it must have arisen through practices which caused them to be shunned or to dissociate themselves from other Muslims. The accusation, which they deny, that they claim Abū Jarīd as a prophet would easily arise through their exclusiveness. They themselves rank Abū Jarīd below Abokr who is the repository of their esoteric knowledge. It is quite probable that immoral practices used to take place at the *dhikr* in the past, which, if condemned, caused the order to take the form of a secret society.

The organization of the sect, which is not very important numerically, is that of an exclusive tribal *ṭarīqa*, though different tribal groups are associated, the main group being Kināna. The followers only marry within the group and avoid association with others. There are three khalīfas, the descendants of Abokr (al-Imām al-Busatī of Ḥillat al-Jiwaizāt in Sinja district), Abū Jarīd (Aḥmad an-Nūr, Sinja district), and of Kirēn (near Karkōj).

Under the khalīfas are *muqaddams* and ordinary members are called *fuqarā'*. At their *dhikrs* they are said to use the ordinary Shādhilī formulas and when *majdhub* break out into theopathic utterances in a language called *ḥayūt* said to have been taught to Abokr by angels.

(*d*) *Egyptian Orders*

Egyptian orders came in first with the Ja'farā[1] and received special recognition during the Egyptian occupation. They exist to-day in towns only amongst Egyptians, *muwalladīn*, and some blacks of slave origin who had no *ṭarīqa*. The following orders are active: Ibrāhīmiyya (Dasūqiyya), Rifā'iyya, Aḥmadiyya (Badawiyya) which has a large following in Omdurman, Bayūmiyya, and Naqshabandiyya.

[1] The Ja'farā originally came from Banban and Ramadi, north of Aswān, in the time of the Funj and settled eventually at Dueim from where they expelled the Shilluk. There are now settlements at Barbar, Dāmer, Omdurman, El-Obeyd, Dueim, and Roseires. They retain *fellāḥīn* characteristics in that they are good cultivators and traders.

7
Islam and Pagan Sudan

I. ISLAM IN CONTACT WITH PAGAN SUDAN

THE Anglo-Egyptian Sudan, like the French Sudan, is an actual battle-ground between Islam and Animism. Islam has gained in some regions, regressed in others. We have shown in Chapter III that the influence of the Arabic-speaking northerners upon the Negroids of the Southern Sudan has been disastrous and that although Islam had apparently all the odds in its favour the pagan tribes south of lat. 10° clung to their own beliefs upon which their tribal life was based. Those between lat. 10° and lat. 12° which had had earlier and more continuous contact with Islam were more influenced; though there are many tribes in Dārfūr, the Nūba Mountains, and Dār Funj who, though literally surrounded by Muslims, have remained pagan to this day. Others in these areas have adopted Islam in variable proportions without animism having been dethroned from their consciousness.

(*a*) *Tribes east of the Nile*

There is a natural border on the White Nile between Islam and pagan tribes at Banjang (eighteen miles south of Renk). At this point the populated area narrows down to a bottle-neck stretching eight miles inland on either side of the river. Blacks are continually moving through it. This is therefore a strategic point.

In this area the only contact of Arab with pagan tribes is that of the Baqqāra[1] with Dinka and Shilluk and of the Rufāʿa[2] with the Mabān.

Muslims in the Government have had an eye to strategic values for they have suggested turning over the whole area (eighteen miles north to ten miles south of Renk) to Islamic influence. At the moment they are trying to organize an Arabic school at Renk. It should be noted that the northern extremity of Dinka country is at a point eighteen miles north of Renk, and that this move would open up the

[1] The Salīm tribe on the left bank from Jabalain to Kāka and on the right bank from Jabalain to near Renk. MacMichael (*Hist.* i. 276 ff.) writes: 'they mix largely with the Dinka, and not being cultivators themselves rely upon them and the Shilluk for their grain supply'.

[2] Rufāʿa al-Huoi, on the left bank between Geshaish and Ad-Disa.

Dinka country to more persistent Islamic penetration. Arabic has begun to be used as a lingua franca in this area.

There are also villages of Malakiyya in this district. These are descendants of garrisons stationed there during the Mahdiyya. They are mixed groups of de-tribalized Negroids, who speak Arabic and are Muslims.[1]

To the east, south of the Jezīra between the White and Blue Niles, is a flat open plain region broken by groups of hills and much resembling Nūba country. Here live negroid communities of the Hamaj, Ingessana, Tornasi, Burūn (Mabān), Berta, Uduk, and Koma.

The *Hamaj* of the Funj Hills are a mixed population of arabicized Negroids (as the Arabic name *hamaj*, 'rabble', shows), using Arabic as a lingua franca, but retaining their old languages and pagan customs. They became nominal Muslims during the Funj period and suffered severely during the Mahdiyya. East of Roseires is a small negroid group called the Gumus who emigrated recently from Abyssinian territory, speak Arabic, and profess Islam. The prosperity of the Berta was broken during the Mahdiyya and some hills depopulated; but Arab cultural influence is superficial.

The *Ingessana* are the inhabitants of the Tabi hills who have remained pagan for they were never under Funj rule. Some groups, e.g. the people of Jabal Kukur, have always been in contact with Arab nomads who had no influence upon them for they were never in need of protection, but are now coming under stronger Islamic influence and are said to be adopting Arab names. The recessed grave and the Ramaḍān and Bairām feasts have been incorporated into the Kukur ceremonial system.[2] The majority of the Ingessana are entirely uninfluenced.

The inhabitants of the Tornasi group of hills are pagan, but suffered severely from dervish attacks which caused a breaking down of tribal sanctions.

The *Burūn* (*Mabān*), south of these, adjacent to the Nuer, acknowledge the suzerainty of the *Mānjil* of Dār Funj. They are cultivators, use bows and arrows, and paint themselves with a red paint from the *talḥa*. Their numbers have been considerably reduced by slave-raiding by Abyssinians from the east and Baqqāra from the west. Some are inclined to Islam, but few of them can speak Arabic.

The Arab influence upon all these southern negroid groups was very limited and the Rufā'a themselves were often raided by the

[1] There are Arabic-speaking Malakiyya settlements still farther south, at Waw.

[2] Seligman, *Pagan Tribes*, p. 437.

Ingessana, Burūn, and Dinka. In both physical characteristics and cultures these peoples show affinities with Nūba groups rather than Nilotics. Agriculture is the basis of their economic life, they keep pigs, and have secular and spiritual chiefs.

(*b*) *The Nubas and Islamic Penetration*

The tribes who occupy the Nūba Mountains area offer a very different problem from the Dinka for example. The influence of Islam upon the Nūba is no recent development, but goes far back into the past. This must be stressed if we are to understand the problem.

Before the sixteenth century the Nūba inhabited the whole of Kordofān. Early in the sixteenth century certain Muslim tribes, indigenous to the Sudan, though they may claim to-day an Arab ancestry (Ghodiāt, Bedairiyya, Jawām'a, Jim'a, Jilaidāt, and Shuwaiḥāt),[1] settled in Kordofān and intermarried with Nūba tribes.[2] No extensive raiding was done during the Funj (or Fūr) periods and the Nūba cultivated large tracts of land in the plains surrounding their hills. Jebel Taqalī, whose conversion began with the arrival of a Ja'alī missionary, was overrun in Bruce's time from Dārfūr and Jebel Daier from Sennār, which kingdom it furnished with a large garrison. Bruce mentions meeting pagan Kujūrs at Sennār from both these hill groups.[3]

The Baqqāra drifted eastwards 150 years ago, occupied all the plains and villages and drove the Nūba up into the hills which they then terraced for cultivation and became fossilized primitive hill cultures. During the Egyptian occupation some northern hill groups were attacked and their Nūba population completely decimated;[4] other hills (Dilling, Kadero, Kudr, and Ghulfān) paid slave-tribute and supplied army recruits; whilst others were left to the Baqqāra who were given a free hand in return for slaves.

[1] Cf. MacMichael, *Tribes*, p. 6; and fictitious genealogical tree, p. 71.

[2] Cf. MacMichael (*Hist.* i. 34): 'In the sixteenth and seventeenth centuries the Arab element entered the country from two sides. In the first place the nomads came in from the direction of Dongola and soon obtained a predominance in the plains north of the latitude of Kāga. Here at the present day the so-called Nūba, whose type ranges from the negroid to the debased Arab, and a smattering of Danāgla, hold only the largest hills. . . . In the second place, in the sixteenth century the allied forces of Funj and Arab, having taken Sōba and Ḳerri from the 'Anag or Nūba and founded the Kingdom of Sennār, began to push northwards and westwards. By the middle of the following century they had begun definitely to assert themselves in central Kordofan. The population there in all probability was still essentially Nūba.'

[3] Bruce, op. cit. vi. 373 and 391.

[4] Cf. Pallme (*Travels in Kordofan*, pp. 306 ff.) who was in El-Obeyd 1838–9, describes the extent of the slave-hunts. The slave-raiders in the hills were called *nahhāda*, those based on the river, *baḥḥāra*.

During the Mahdiyya most of the hills were attacked by dervish armies. Some (such as the Nyamang who were well supplied with rifles acquired from the Baqqāra) held out in the caves of their rocky fastnesses; others (Ghulfān) were conquered by force; and others (Miri) were taken by treachery. The whole populations of Ghulfān, Debri, and parts of Kadero were taken to Omdurman and returned back as Muslims in the main after the battle of Omdurman.

Political domination and slave-raiding during these periods materially assisted the spread of Islam; for whilst, on the one hand, it tended to solidify group resistance, so that a people like the Nyamang are most impervious to Islamic and foreign influences, yet other groups were wiped out or scattered or absorbed as detribalized collections. All slaves adopted Islam and if they returned to the tribe did not necessarily give up their nominal Islam.

The gradually stabilizing conditions which have ensued since the advent of the present government have accelerated the arabization or islamization of the Nūba,[1] though now the process is a peaceful one, for the resistance of the Nūba is being weakened by other factors. The increase of public security has brought the Nūba out of their hills to cultivate in the plains. Migration in search of work and recruiting for the army has carried large numbers for some years into a purely Muslim environment. Roads have been opened up along which the camels of the Arab or the lorries of the Ja'aliyyīn do all the carrying trade and regular markets are held throughout the area. The diversity of the Nūba languages has caused Arabic to become the lingua franca. The whole area is linked up economically and administratively with the Muslim north. Nūba and Arab have become mutually dependent, the Nūba being the producer and the Arab the carrier. These are potent factors which cannot be ignored.

Here is the present position. There are a number of hills with a Nūba population in northern Kordofān district.[2] These Nūba are

[1] The official tendency to regard these as two processes is misleading. It is a cultural process and every pagan area that becomes permanently arabicized becomes permanently islamized.

[2] The Nūba of Jebels Al-Ḥarāza, Umm Durrāq, Abu Ḥadīd, Kutūl, and Kāqa. Browne (*Travels in Africa*, App. II) wrote in 1799: 'The inhabitants of Harraza are idolaters of mixed complexion, but mostly of a reddish hue . . . neither Arabs nor Mohammedans.' They were converted by Danāqla (Rikābiyya) who settled there and are now quite arabicized and through intermarriage with Danāqla, especially those of J. Harāza, are distinct from the Nūbas of southern Kordofan (cf. D. Newbold, *S.N.R.* vii. 38). They are still only Muslim in the Sudan Government official sense of profession and Arabic names. They have lost the qualities which endear the pagan Nūba to those who have lived amongst them, and become debased. H. A. MacMichael says of them (*Hist.* i. 34): 'in a few generations they seem likely

completely arabicized except for the usual superstitions and are quite distinct from the southern Nūba. Until recently they had a *nāẓir* of their own, but are now under the Kabābīsh. This is an indication of what might happen in time in the Nūba Mountains proper.

The towns (Dilling, Kaduqli, Talōdi, Dalāmi, Rashad), with their colonies of non-Nūba, Hamitic-Negroid officials, traders, ginnery workers, and others, are Muslim in complexion and largely so in population. The hills of these towns are semi-islamized. The plains are filled with the wandering Baqqāra and some settled arabicized Nūba. At the bases of some southern hills (Elīri, Talōdi) are detribalized groups of Nūba, calling themselves Arab with no claim to the title except that they have taken the name of the tribes (Ḥawāzma and Kawāḥla) they once served as slaves. The hills of Daier, Tukum, Taqali, Kaderu, Tajoi, Dāqo, Qadīr, and Miri are Muslim or semi-Muslim, their customs are changing, taking on an Islamic bias while tribal sanctions are weakening.

The extent of the islamization of these communities varies considerably. On the one hand, there is Taqali, which has been completely islamized; and on the other, Kaderu, with the minimum of Islamic observances, and full retention of tribal sanctions;[1] and the Dāqo 'half clad and wholly immoral, heir to all vices and none of the virtues of the Arab'. Some chiefs profess an allegiance to Islam whilst their people remain wholly pagan. It should, however, be clearly understood that the mass of the Nūba communities remain pagan.

(*c*) *The Pagan Nilotic Tribes*

The great Nilotic tribes, the Dinka, Shilluk, and Nuēr, are a determining factor in the future of the Sudan. They are pastoral peoples, possessing pride of race and impervious to external influences. A large part of the area they inhabit is swampy and inaccessible for some six months during the rainy season. Owing to these two factors they were able to withstand the attacks of the dervishes and although

to be indistinguishable from the sedentary inhabitants of central Kordofān.' Prof. Seligman (*Pagan Tribes*, p. 448) remarks of the inhabitants of Jebel Kāqa: 'although it was stated that rain was from Allah, a ceremony was held in honour of and to propitiate Abu Ali, a great ancestor and rain-maker who did not die but disappeared and whose spirit still possesses participants in the ceremony. Abu Ali is also a great snake; indeed, in some villages of the Kaja massif he is known only in that form, and although he has not been seen since the Mahdiia a yearly ceremony is performed in and before a special hut, built beside the crevasse on the sacred hill, which was his place. A goat is killed, its blood smeared upon the rocks, and its flesh cooked at a fire newly made with fire-sticks and eaten by those concerned in the ceremony, who become possessed by Abu Ali and who described him as "riding" them.'

[1] Cf. S. F. Nadel, 'The Hill Tribes of Kadero' (*S.N.R.* xxv. 37 ff.).

they suffered severely, were not subject to tribal disintegration and maintained their social system intact.

The *Dinka* (750,000) are divided into a number of separate tribes covering a wide area. They are to be found on the White Nile as far north as Renk and extend as far south as Bor and Malek. A large branch occupies the basin of the Baḥr al-ʿArab where they come into contact with the Baqqāra-Rizaiqāt and Habbāniyya. Their settlements are near the river in the dry season and they live inland, often in pile dwellings, during the rainy season. Many were forced to join Islam during the Mahdiyya, but relapsed when Mahdism fell. The Selīm Baqqāra mix closely with the Dinka upon whom they are dependent for grain but have no Islamic influence upon them. Seligman mentions that 'many of the Reik now circumcise, having learnt the practice from the Arabs during the last few years'.[1] Very few of those who have travelled north as slaves, or in the army, show any signs that they once made a profession of Islam.

The *Shilluk* (40,000) live along a narrow fringe of thickly-populated country on the west bank of the Nile from Kaka to Lake No, and for a short stretch on the east bank to Tawfikiyya and eighteen miles up the Sōbat.[2] They have a king who is the temporal and spiritual head of all the Shilluk, belonging to the class of ruler known as 'divine kings'. They resisted the dervishes more fiercely than any other people and though they often defeated them suffered so severely that whole districts became depopulated. They have not yet forgotten those days, nor that the Donqolāwī trader brought syphilis to them through his habit of trading in prostitutes.

The *Nuēr* (430,000) are widely scattered in the country along the Upper Sōbat, the Pibor, and the Zerāf region. There are three main divisions, (1) Zeraf Nuēr, (2) Rill Nuēr, west of the Baḥr al-Jabal, (3) Dok Nuēr.

They are a warlike, independent, and self-reliant people and have been persistent raiders of the riverain Dinkas. In the east of their area is the trading-post of Nāṣir where there is a colony of northern Muslims, called locally 'Arabs', who scrupulously perform their

[1] *Pagan Tribes*, p. 172.

[2] In Browne's time (1798) they extended down the river as far north as the present-day Kawa (*Travels in Africa*, pp. 452–3). They were driven from Dueim by the Egyptian tribe of Jaʿfra during the Funj period. They suffered most severely in 1861 when their lands were overrun by the Selīm Baqqāra under the feki Muḥammad Khair. In 1865 a camp of 1,000 men was formed at Fashoda by Sir Samuel Baker for the suppression of the slave-trade and their country was finally occupied by the Egyptians in 1871. In 1869 Schweinfurth (*The Heart of Africa*, i. 9–10) gives Kawa as the most northerly place they inhabited.

prayers and tell their *sibḥas*. These have some effect upon the local Nuēr, but the natural conservatism and naïve pride of this people render them peculiarly impervious to external influence.

A few members of the Nilotic tribes who go north into a Muslim environment for work, or as army recruits, are circumcised and become Muslims in name, but when they return to their tribe their mental and social environment claims them wholly, though tribal sanctions may not mean so much to them.

In contrast to the Funj-Nūba tribes which have been discussed, Islam has not the protective and social advantages which could attract these Nilotic tribes into its system. In the same way they present a different missionary problem to the tribes farther south amongst whom the work of Christian missions is concentrated.

2. MUSLIM PROPAGANDA AMONGST PAGANS

We have shown how the process of islamization of pagan tribes is active in the region from lat. 12° to 10° amongst small tribes speaking many languages which have been subject to influence for a long time. The great Nilotic tribes and tribes farther south are almost completely uninfluenced. Islam then has not passed beyond certain general boundaries and we must inquire why it is not pressing southwards with greater rapidity.

The most important reason is the natural pride and conservatism of the Nilotes and the nature of their social system with its tribal sanctions, which oppose a firm bulwark to anything external which would break up the system and leave them no longer clan-members but weak individuals at the mercy of unknown dangers. Safe in their own system, that of Islam is not attractive. The bulwark of this system is the 'medicine men' who represent in themselves the traditions of the tribe and resist the foreign encroachments. The protective policy of the Government also has considerable effect since it keeps out itinerant *jallābas* and *fekis* and such institutions as the *khalwa*, whilst its language policy prevented the adoption of Arabic as the official language. Again the experience of these tribes with Muslims has not been happy. The slave-raiding and cruelties of the Egyptians and Mahdists and the treacheries of the Muslim traders have not been forgotten. No doubt with time memory of these things will fade, but it will be long before tribal sanctions cease to rule the people, and Islam can only advance through tribal disintegration.

The small tribal groups between lat. 10° and 12° who mainly

occupy the hills inland, east and west of the Nile, offer a different picture. We have shown how they are coming under persistent Islamic pressure and unless some totally unexpected factor comes into play, such as a 'total' missionary occupation of these areas, nothing can prevent their ultimate absorption into the fold of Islam.

Let us now look briefly at the process. We have shown in Chapter III how Islam has been carried in pagan Africa, not by the true Arabs, but by the Hamitic peoples of Africa whose allegiance it first claimed. Further, it came to negroid peoples through these Hamitic conquerors or merchants, not as a religion, but as the civilization of aristocratic African peoples who, possessing no race-discrimination, were able to intermarry with them and live a common social life and become as black as themselves. African Islam is different from Asiatic Islam where it was super-imposed as a barbaric religion upon ancient civilizations and into which it was absorbed, Muslim saints replacing other gods. This is true in Africa only in the north. It is found in the Sudan, in Donqola, where the saints' tombs are often on ancient Nubian or Christian sites. But it is not so in pagan Africa. To pagans Islam came, not as a religion, but as a cultural system which imposed itself upon African cultures, or rather there was a gradual transference and fusion of culture which produced a new unit. The new civilization, Islam, was assimilated and became indigenous, the religious factor being secondary. The moral demands of Islam are not high and anyway are never involved in its acceptance, for Islam is established for generations before the African learns what it does or does not sanction.

Islam's spread amongst blacks is due, less to the personal missionary work of trader and feki which has been overstressed by writers such as T. W. Arnold, as to the cultural and commercial contact of the black with an Islam which has adapted its social life to that of the African. The character of African Islam is such that its acceptance causes little internal disturbance to the natural man and his social life and customs, for Islam takes over the central features of paganism through syncretism. The pagan customs are retained whilst the spirit of the custom is lost.

Further, where Islam is in competition with Christian missions run by Europeans, even when the rulers are Christians, it still spreads, because it offers more understandable religious, social, and economic values than Western Christianity which only allows its adherents religious and not social equality. On the borderland areas the social and economic values of joining Islam are so obvious because the state is Muslim, ruled as such by British and Muslim officials.

Cultural and commercial contact is the strongest factor in its actual spread. Islam always spreads along the trade-routes, that is to say, wherever the black finds himself in contact with nomads, traders, and fekis; and it claims first the detribalized and any nomadic black tribes. The sedentary tribes do not have the same needs, nor the same customs as these, and strongly resist islamization as long as the group remains intact. But when tribal institutions become undermined, as in the past by conquest or slave-raiding and to-day by infiltration, the higher social prestige of the Muslim African, who has little else to recommend him, begins to attract.

Islam is affecting many Nūba chiefs whose chief ambition is to attain the higher social status of the Muslim, and that is a sufficient introduction. Added to that is the attraction of alliance with the official religion, for the District Commissioner is identified with his staff who are all Muslims. There are Muslim clerks to the *meks* of certain Nūba hills.

Islam and trade are closely allied and it is the transformation of commercial possibilities under the present régime which has opened up new routes of penetration. It is to the interest of the Muslim trader to proselytize, and propaganda by example is easy at the *sūqs*, and in villages, through points of contact with odd Muslims there. Inevitably then, all the new centres that have developed have been islamized and their influence has spread out and embraced the surrounding hills.[1]

The purely Islamic religious factor only exists in the background and does not come into evidence until Islam has been long established. There is a propaganda, it is true, less direct, but slow and continuous, based less on beliefs than on example and imitation of ritual gestures. Wherever a small group of Muslims is gained a primitive *zarība* praying-place is marked out and a feki appears to run a *khalwa* under the village tree. The dervish orders have little real influence upon blacks except when they are in permanent contact. They are effective

[1] Here is an example of penetration in the Nūba area. Muḥammad Tūtū, the chief active *mek* of the Moro, is Muslim and holds a feast after Ramaḍān which attracts his people. There are four authorized *jallābas* amongst the Moro and three amongst the Krongo. There are two definite *sūqs* and four days a week the *jallābas* are allowed to go to other specified places. The indirect method of propaganda is employed when they spread out their prayer-mats before perhaps some 400 people. Only one *jallāba* does direct proselytizing. The Baqqāra come to these *sūqs* and some members will stay, living on the tribe. They do not proselytize, but will sell amulets. Fekis roam the hills. They are prohibited, but are difficult to find and remove, since the chiefs often invite them and will conceal their presence.

An example of the direct method is that of a former *Ma'mūr* of Delāmi who went on pilgrimage and returned keen to propagate his religion and build a mosque. He used to collect the Nūba for *dhikrs* and feasts and converted some chiefs (Delāmi and Kuderi) who now make their people keep Ramaḍān and have the boys circumcised.

only in the urban centres where they give a religious club to the lost.[1]

The religious factor, however, is present and African Islam can exert a strong religious influence. The very belief in Allāh, which is assimilated rather than taught, is reachable and attractive. But it is the African conception of Allāh as the great Power who can bestow magical powers stronger than the powers of the indigenous spirits safeguarding the convert when tribal sanctions have weakened. The idea of a future life also attracts since it is a recognizable, because material, bliss; and the convert's mind becomes saturated with new eschatological hopes; that is why the Mahdī-idea has permeated so deeply amongst African Muslims.

Islam while possessing the strength of its utter certainty of being the true faith, is not revolutionary; it does not conquer the animist soul because it accommodates itself to the animist spirit-life. The result of this accommodating character of Islam is that it has not helped the higher religious development of the African.

Islam spreads only through the breakdown of the extreme clan system and tends in general to create new groups which stand out as independent aristocratic groups. Pride of race is involved though the so-called 'Arab' often entirely resembles a Nūba. Muslim groups such as the Miri Nūba have remained intact, but the breakdown of tribal sanctions does not guarantee that they will remain so.

Islamization in the Eastern Sudan has usually meant eventual absorption into the Arab tribal-system. The broken-up groupings and the detribalized always join some 'Arab' tribe either as clients or actual members. Thus most of the sedentary tribes in the Jezīra, Kordofān, and Dārfūr, with little Arab blood, claim it. The process is natural since it offers protection. It can be seen in progress in the Nūba Mountains where the Messīriyya claim suzerainty over some of the eastern hills, and the Ḥawāzma Rawawqa over the Kaduqli area.[2]

The result then of this peaceful penetration is that the Nūba and certain groups east of the Nile are being more rapidly islamized than in the days when they were raided, when resistance helped to maintain group solidarity. The process of change shows no signs of being a fast one, but it is sure.

[1] At Dilling for instance there are found the Mirghaniyya, Qādiriyya, Ismā'īliyya, and a few Tijāniyya.

[2] It should be pointed out that African racial elements predominate in the Ḥawāzma who are of mixed Arab, Bedairiyya, Nūba, and Takārīr (cf. MacMichael, *Hist.* i. 280–4).

8

The Influence of Westernism on the Sudan

I. THE EFFECT OF BRITISH OCCUPATION

WE are concerned with the cultural life of the Sudanese and our aim in this chapter is to try to see some of the cultural changes that have been brought about in their lives by the impact of modern civilization and the repercussion of advanced Muslim life and thought elsewhere.

When the British had firmly established their rule in the Sudan it was the first time in its history that the country had experienced one organized system of government which cared for the welfare of peoples who, when ruled by other powers, had always been exploited for luxury articles such as slaves, ivory, and gold. Secure from warring factions within and aggression and exploitation from without, the country, through contact with Western civilization, began to make adaptations in the economic, intellectual, and social spheres of life.

The Westernizing forces at work in the Sudan have been much the same as in other Muslim countries, and, on a broad view, the process of change resultant on adaptations appears to be uniform. Yet we can distinguish important differences in detail between the Sudan and other countries, derived from the differing racial material and the environment in which these forces have been working.

Since the days of barbarism lasted until this century there has been a lag in development compared with other Islamic countries. Only after the Battle of Omdurman did the transition from the anarchy of the Mahdiyya to ordered government begin, carrying with it the development of an organized economic life and adaptation to certain aspects of Western civilization. The pace of such development was determined by the unfavourable geographical situation of the country and the poverty of its natural resources. This also determined the form, extent, and sphere of Western influence and the degree to which the masses were modified. The character of the people themselves was an important factor, for Westernism means training in discipline and initiative, and the response varied between different races and between cultivators and nomads, therefore some sections of the population (e.g. Danāqla-Ja'aliyyīn) outstripped others (e.g. Jezīra-Kordofān cultivators). All these factors have to be taken into account.

The attitude of the British from the first had been to regard the Sudanese as dependent peoples who were backward rather than inferior, and as their rulers they sought primarily to institute a just rule, to develop economic life, and to stimulate them as far as possible within the framework of their existing institutions. The theoretical aim of 'indirect rule' as interpreted in the Sudan was not so much the preservation of the communities in their old form, as the adaptation of existing tribal institutions to the changing circumstances and the regulation of the rate and direction of change. But, in practice in Muslim Sudan, indirect rule tended towards preservation and consolidation, because the rulers after the Mahdiyya were no longer faced with any further break-up of indigenous institutions, as compared with that of pagan communities in contact with Westernism in other parts of Africa. Today, however, a network of rural district, municipal, and central councils is transforming the former system of native administration and indirect rule by tribal chiefs into local government on a territorial and democratic basis; thus giving the ordinary Sudanese a share in the management of their own affairs.

The two most important factors brought to the Sudan by the Arabs, the conception of Islamic solidarity and the Arab tribal system, were bolstered up by the new rulers. Below these was the pre-Islamic heritage which had survived both and upon which Westernism has had little effect. These things put a severe brake upon social and cultural change, what has been effected being superficial adaptations caused by the changing economic environment.

The contemporary British government official, being brought up in a social environment in which the material side of life is overstressed, gets a distorted view of social change and seems to think that the diffusion of Western material technique over the Sudanese means their conversion to his own Western civilization. But in spite of such diffusion the inner life of the Sudanese is as true as ever. The effect of Westernism upon the Sudanese has been to force a lop-sided development. Their moral nature, already petrified by Islam, remained on a primitive level; but material developments and intellectual forms were easily communicable and consequently they were rapidly absorbed, for in the intellectual sphere it has always been the form and not the essence that has been accepted.[1] The Sudanese, confronted by

[1] This is shown clearly in the speech of Ibrāhīm Aḥmad Ibrāhīm at the opening of Gordon College as an institution for higher studies on 20. 2. 45, when he said 'the culture which will fill our needs is a blending of Eastern culture, drawing its spirit from *the* true religion, and Western culture which will help us towards scientific thought and practical achievement'. The significant word *the* is omitted in the English translation.

a secular system which, since it came through Egypt, had from the first an Islamic tinge, eagerly accepted whatever they felt would be useful and yet neither disturb the religious *status quo*, nor harm the system. The result is that the educated, in trying to inherit two irreconcilable worlds, have achieved both mental and spiritual dislocation.

2. THE DEVELOPMENT OF EDUCATION

The small group of early political officers exercised a purely personal autocratic rule and the Sudanese at first made no distinction between the English and the *Turuk*. Advance in administration was necessarily slow. There were no educated Sudanese and the general administrative and other needs of the country were provided for by the employment of Egyptians and Syrians. These were gradually supplemented by Sudanese as they were trained by the educational system and so the Sudanese *effendiyya* began to appear.

In a state like the Sudan, given the conditions which prevailed at the end of the last century, there was little incentive to the Government to consider any development in the education of the masses, nor to take any great interest in the economic development of the country through the energies of the Sudanese. The development of education was a purely administrative necessity to provide Sudanese functionaries and so reduce the costly imported staff. One of Lord Kitchener's first actions was to make an appeal for funds to found Gordon College and this was opened in 1902.

Education started at the higher end of the scale and its aim was purely imperialistic. Its purpose was defined in the early days as:

(1) The creation of a competent artisan class.
(2) The diffusion among the masses of the people of education sufficient to enable them to understand the machinery of Government, particularly with reference to the equitable and impartial administration of justice.
(3) The creation of a small administrative class, capable of filling many government posts, some of an administrative, some of a technical nature.[1]

The demand for functionaries increased with the decision to develop the Jezīra and this was followed by the post-war boom. Consequently all the students of the College were absorbed into the administrative or other services and education had become synonymous with the attain-

[1] Sir James Currie, 'The Educational Experiment in the Anglo-Egyptian Sudan, 1900–33', *J. Afr. Soc.*, 1934, p. 364.

ment of a government post. The Education Department was in fact part of the political service and its officers trained in it. But from 1930 the Government could no longer find work for more than a percentage of the boys and had to try to get a balance between production and consumption.

Hindered by the early establishment of Gordon College, the educational authorities had given little thought to the years of education leading to it and laid down only the very elements of a system of elementary education merely to feed the higher schools. Until the 1914–18 war 'one guiding principle had been adhered to throughout—all educational endeavour was co-ordinated with the carrying out of a definite, large-scale economic programme, embodying a collective Government policy, and ancillary to it'.[1]

The Milner Commission Report (1920) had stated that it was not the desire of the Government 'to repeat the mistake which has been made in Egypt of introducing a system which fits pupils for little else than employment in clerical and minor administrative posts, and creates an overgrown body of aspirants to Government employment'. However, no attempt was made to adapt the system which had been designed especially for the object condemned until necessity forced such adaptation upon the Government.

One of the results of the assassination of Sir Lee Stack in 1924 was the withdrawal of many Egyptian functionaries who were replaced by Sudanese, so that the output of Gordon College and the intermediate schools was absorbed for some time. But in 1930 came the economic crisis and retrenchment, together with the development of indirect rule with the result that the output of Gordon College, even though it decreased, was greater than the demand.

In 1932 a Committee was appointed to study the problem of education. This Committee recommended 'a broadening of the base of elementary education and more careful adjustment of secondary education to the present conditions of the country and the opportunities for profitable employment'.[2] This led to significant changes in Sudan education, including the establishment in 1934 of the elementary teachers' training establishment at Ba<u>kh</u>t ar-Ruda near Dueim, and a closer liaison between the Education Department and the provincial authorities who so often disagree about the aims of education.

In 1937 the De La Warr Educational Commission visited the Sudan and made a report upon which educational progress for the

[1] Ibid., p. 368.

[2] *Sudan Annual Report*, 1933, p. 11.

period 1938–46 has been largely based. The chief recommendations were:

(1) The provision of greatly increased funds for education;
(2) The acceleration of the expansion, together with the continued improvement, of elementary education for boys;
(3) The acceleration of the expansion of elementary education for girls;
(4) The improvement and extension of boys' intermediate schools;
(5) The improvement of the secondary school; and
(6) The recognition that a University in Khartoum was the ultimate goal of higher educational policy.[1]

The war hindered the full development of the programme, but still considerable progress has been made. The problem has been the difficulty of producing sufficient trained teachers, for, rightly enough, the Bakht-ar-Ruda centre has concentrated upon quality rather than quantity. This centre has, however, grown from an Elementary Teachers' Training College into an Institute of Education with the same aim extended to all stages—the reform of education—so that it may be related to the pupil's everyday life and the training of teachers in the new method. The day is still far distant when the Sudanese themselves will come to regard education as a training for rural life.

In 1945 the various detached schools for Higher Education (Law, Arts, Science, Engineering, Agriculture, and Veterinary Science) were merged to form the nucleus of a future University College and the name 'Gordon Memorial College', by which the secondary school had been known, was transferred to the new institution. During this eight-year period the annual recurrent overall expenditure on education rose from £E.150,000 in 1938 to an estimate of £E.450,000 for 1946.

The war period, with its growth of nationalistic feeling, gave a further impetus to the demands of the Sudanese for greater educational facilities, and in April 1946 the Director of Education put forward an important plan of development for the next ten-year period which should go far to satisfy those demands. The Director writes: 'it is the avowed intention of Government to make the country's advance along the road leading to self-government as rapid as possible and, for this purpose, to train Sudanese as quickly as possible to fill the more responsible posts in the local and central services.' Consequently

[1] See 'Note by the Director of Education on the Government Plan for Educational Development in the Northern Sudan for the Next Ten Years', presented to the Fifth Session of the Northern Sudan Advisory Council in April 1946.

considerable attention is to be given to the consolidation of secondary and intermediate education and the training of teachers and professional men, whilst stress is laid upon the preparation of boys for further vocational training fitting them at the same time to play their part in Sudanese communal life.

An additional training establishment for elementary school teachers is proposed, and it is calculated that at the end of the ten-year period 56 per cent. of the boys in urban areas and 29 per cent. of those in rural areas will have facilities for education at sub-grade (the barest literacy) and elementary schools. An important feature of the programme is the proposal to follow up these boys through adult education and after-care work, the development of rural community centres, and the formation of a Publications Bureau. This latter will provide a cheap and plentiful supply of good, but simple, Arabic literature, so helping to save them from relapsing into illiteracy.

3. INTELLECTUAL AND SOCIAL CHANGE

The geographical position and the desert character of the Sudan cut it off from any direct cultural and economic contact with Europe. This has meant that its contact with Egypt has been most important, whence were derived all the new cultural elements in the development of an 'Arab' country. Egypt in some way bridges the gap between the intellectual and social penury which is the inheritance of the Sudanese Muslim and the life of Europe.

The Sudan is a country in which a degree of westernization has resulted in the formation of an 'intellectual proletariat' (the *effendiyya*)[1] and the beginnings of a struggle for participation in the direction of the State. It is not correct to call the effendiyya a 'class'. They are rather a 'tendency', for they have no place in the traditional social scheme, and cut across all the natural classes. No really significant change in social life can yet be identified, the effendi has not broken away from the family, but this tendency or change of cultural direction and economic life must lead to social change.

The effendiyya are those Sudanese who have acquired a modern education, an occidental wardrobe, and a disrupted cultural and religious life. They are very largely drawn from the riverain Danāqla–Ja'aliyyīn tribes, who have a higher standard of intelligence, a more vivid spirit of independence, through the absence of a slave class, and

[1] Sing. *afandī*, plur. *afandiyya*. We use the popular transcription.

a more highly developed communal spirit, as contrasted with the individualistic spirit of the Arab.

The effendiyya are alike in training and occupation. They have all been educated in the Sudan, either at an intermediate school or a secondary school. The method and content of training, except for religion, is Western; and its effect is disruptive rather than integrative. It has exposed their minds to greater ephemeral distraction, but left their spirits hungry. They are taught how to do clerical or technical work, but not how to live.

The effendi's social environment enchains him wholly, yet he is drawn to a wider outlook which makes him recognize it as enchaining and leaves him subject to conflicting loyalties and purposes. A former Warden of Gordon College (as a secondary school) classed the boys who left the school into three intellectual types:

(1) those who reject modern ideas and ways of life and become hard fanatical Muslims;

(2) those few who become secret unbelievers, who stick to the social system, but over whose lives religion has no influence;

(3) the majority who keep their modern ideas and religion in separate water-tight compartments, which results in a split-personality.

Account should be taken of the fact that the school is but one of the educative influences on the Sudanese. Other factors are the press, cinema, radio, and above all employment in government offices, workshops, farms, and hospitals, which, employing a different standard of values from that of his normal environment, influence him unconsciously.

We tend to designate all who have learnt the elements of reading and writing as literate, but are they really so? All the products of the elementary schools can only be called semi-literate, because such is the nature of Arabic and training in it that they cannot read a newspaper easily, and since there is no graded literature or adult-education classes the majority never read again. But we must go further. Those who cannot read significant material with intelligence and understanding are *functionally* illiterate. This applies to most 'graduates' of intermediate and secondary schools, amongst whom exists social, political, and religious illiteracy. In this case the difficulty is not so much of the language as of the Muslim mentality and the foreignness of their intellectual current slavishly derived from Muslim Egypt.

Cairo we have said is the intellectual mecca of the Sudan. It pours out a flood of newspapers, magazines, and modern and religious literature. In the coffee-houses of Omdurman we can feel the clashes of currents of thought and the intellectual disintegration and adjustments caused by the impact of Western intellectual, social, and political ideas upon Islam. The life of Muḥammad by Haikal, the works of Ṭāhā Ḥusain and other modernists are eagerly read. Many are drifting away from their traditional moorings of belief and are like sheep without a shepherd.

The secularism of the effendi, however, does not go very deep and in times of crisis he shows the influence of his early formative years lived in a *ḥōsh* impregnated with superstition. He will seek modern medical treatment, but will not long resist his family's persuasions to visit a feki. He will show an attitude of agnosticism with his special friends one day and be a defender of Islam with the crowd the next. One week he will be listening to a lecture in the Cultural Club on the position of women and the next he will be a bedecked *dihn*-smeared bridegroom. He has a European furnished room for his friends, but his women live in the usual squalor. He is an intellectual coward, only daring to criticize the old ways within his own circle, for he is afraid of the censure of his elders. Because of this fear he never acquires a scientific attitude of mind to Islam as a faith or a social system. He cannot fit his faith into his new scheme of life, yet he clings to the system desperately as an attitude towards the Western world, to which Islam is *eo ipso* opposed, feeling it to be his only means of security. His moral instability arises from the fact that his early religious training did not teach him that religion has anything to do with the ethics of everyday life. Wrong to him, as to any villager, is what the *sharīʿa* forbids, and right is whatever he can get away with.

Further, the effendiyya are alike in occupation. The purpose of education to them, and their only ambition in life, is to become a government servant with a pension to look forward to. Education means to the effendi a kind of apprenticeship to a trade; it is a means to be among the olympians, so that any culture they acquire is only apparent and superficial. Therein lies the danger in that the Western training he receives, being divorced from ethical teaching, does not lead to integrity of character or the development of the spirit of service. That is the reason why he cannot learn responsibility and European supervision is always necessary if Western standards are to be maintained. His brain works like that of the peasant. He can imitate, he will do all his superior tells him to do, but is quite incapable of relating knowledge. He cannot see things as a whole. The more dangerous are those who have had too little education to get a good post. The administration and commerce not being able to absorb them all, the least fitted are thrown out and live a precarious existence as parasites on their family or on a low-salaried job. These have a bleak social existence and their struggle to live at a raised standard of life on a low salary is pathetic. These tend to make up the ranks of the disaffected.

Nothing can stop the spread of the effendiyya spirit. The Government originally wanted clerks and, having set the process of production in motion, now finds itself in the quandary of Qāsim Bābā in the tale of *ʿAlī Bābā and the Forty Thieves* who knew the formula for entering the cave, but not the complementary one for letting himself out. The bitterest complaint of the effendiyya is the Government's attempt to limit higher education, the key to wealth and honour. If the Government will not provide it they intend to provide it for themselves, supposing that if there are the trained men the Government will create the office stools.[1]

The effendiyya may be mistaken in their conception of the aims and ideals of education, but they cannot be ignored because so much depends upon them for the future of the country. The future before them without a profound spiritual reorientation is bleak. They need guiding to an integration of the new world of science and technics with ethics and religion, which will restore to their distorted spirits such serenity as will satisfy the whole man.

No very profound reactions can yet be seen in the way of social change. The little there is, although it impresses the administrator, seems to be superficial. Westernism in a Muslim country, because of the nature of the social system of Islam, does not have the disruptive effect on social life that it has on pagan African communities. Islam is quite literally immune from any danger to the system from Western civilization, chiefly because that civilization is presented to the Muslim deprived of those spiritual elements which alone give it validity and to which he is unappeasably opposed. On the other hand, Islam itself cannot change its social form for it does not admit of free social application. It may almost be said to have no principles because it is committed to fixed rules. Therefore any conformity to Western social standards by the effendi is only superficial and not real.

The effendi, we have shown, like Muslims everywhere, still leads his life in two water-tight compartments. His family life is quite

[1] *Ahliyya* (national) intermediate schools, administered by a board of Sudanese, have been started in Omdurman and El Obeyd, whilst another is projected for Al-Fāshir. Another well-known school is that of Shaikh Bābikr Badrī, himself a self-educated man. All these schools in Omdurman started secondary classes in 1943–4.

separate from the life he leads in his office and with his friends at the coffee-houses or clubs. Social differentiation based on race has always existed, but there is yet little sign of its extension on a basis of occupation, culture, and property. The effendi may show pride and arrogance, but he is still one with the family.

From much that has been said before we shall not expect to find any true sense of nationality in the Northern Sudan, though there is a common cultural and religious heritage.[1] Patriotism, too, in any sense in which we know it, is unknown; its place being taken by that vague feeling of the unity of believers over against the Western world.

The masses, having always been in subjection, did not feel any actual political change under the early direct administration of the present régime, except that they felt secure from famine and hostile neighbours. Since then there has been a gradual devolution of authority through local administrations under their old tribal or patriarchal heads. The masses are contented with their political lot. At the same time the present régime produced the effendiyya who, through their training under a Western system of education and their occupation in one administration, developed a feeling of Sudanese solidarity and became welded together by common interests and aspirations which they find in conflict with the devolutionary policy of the Government with its bolstering up of local authority which they do not favour. This has led to the nascent expressions of nationalism by a 'Congress' (*mu'tamar*) of the Graduates' Club which, although it was growing from 1924, first took expression at the beginning of the war in 1940. It has led to negative criticism of what the Government does or does not do. It is still weak because it has not succeeded in winning over either the best-informed Sudanese or the rural population. It is an expression of the awakening individualism of the intelligentsia whose minds, overshadowed by the Western system, stimulated by the Cairo press to criticize and mimic talk about ideals of freedom which they have not the background to feel, are stirred to a political reaction in favour of their own class. At the same time they are awakening more and more to the significance of external political events, especially any, such as the relationship between the Sudan and Egypt, the Italo-Abyssinian War, the present war, and the Atlantic Charter, which can be related to their own future.

The political scene in the Sudan like everything else cannot be

[1] When you ask anyone, 'What are you?' (*jinsak shinu?*) he will reply Ja'ali or Sukkōtī or Bishārī or Shā'iqī as the case may be, but not Sūdānī. Only the effendiyya have adopted this wider concept from British officials and use it now to express their political aspirations.

understood without taking religion into account. The Graduates' Club, which was started originally as a club of effendiyya who had received an intermediate school education, split in 1932 into the two factions of Mahdists and Mirghanists over the election of a president. These two factions are now the two chief political parties—the *Umma* (nationalists) who are Mahdists and the *Ashiqqa* (separatists) who are the Mirghanists. This 'nationalist movement' is a step towards their coming-of-age and the Government is wisely guiding it along channels which may lead to progress, and preparing the way through local government and regional councils for a higher degree of self-determination.

The result of the change in the *muzāriʿīn* is that the villages have gradually, and especially since the development of motor transport, been learning a wider outlook. New possibilities have entered into their lives and they are gaining a wider conception of the world. The cultivators are in closer touch with the large centres. A few large villages have elementary schools and some children go to school or work in towns. The cafés and other 'excitements' have not yet invaded the villages except those on trade-routes, though Western types of gambling are spreading; and the feki is still respected as schoolmaster and oracle. Certain tastes are being modernized through greater prosperity and access to new amenities like tea and sugar, which have become life-necessities. Old customs which are out of gear with new economic facts cause some tension in village life, but there are no signs of this leading to the development of a new social order. The Government medical service, dispensaries, and midwives have effected an improvement in health. Bilharzia, the plague of Egypt, and other diseases have been checked. The Government is well aware of the importance of preventive medicine and has prepared schemes for its further development after the war. The appalling conditions under which children are reared, and widespread diseases such as syphilis and malaria, seriously reduce the energy and efficiency of the individual whilst at the same time permitting him to live. The problem is that remedial treatment is merely palliative unless the environment can be changed, and the root weakness is the state of Muslim family life. It seems useless, for instance, to treat venereal diseases when the patient returns after a few weeks in a worse condition than before.

Some change of attitude towards laws and anti-social acts is evident. Formerly no Sudanese had any conception of law as a thing of inherent value and consequently a thing to be obeyed by all. They regarded laws as arbitrary regulations imposed by those in authority.

Consequently they would try to evade the law by any possible means, such as bribing the ruler. With the development of native courts responsible to the central government for the administration of justice and the maintenance of peace, and their increasing imposition of deterrent sentences, instead of following *'āda*, a new sense of law is being introduced. At the same time it should be stressed that tribal and village councils still base their decisions largely on the old customs and the change to the individual is little more than an increasing confidence in the possibility of obtaining justice.

The rhythm of the life of the agriculturalist cannot be said to have been modified. It is true that 'no one bathes twice in the same river', yet for the practical purpose of bathing it remains the same river. So the 'spirit' of village life is unchanged though the flow may be faster and strange new objects are seen floating down. The changes brought by Westernism are irrelevant to the essential spirit of village society. This is not the fault of poverty, the agriculturalist is better off than ever before and fear of famine has gone; the fault may be partly due to the problem of teaching the language of the Book, which even when a man knows how to read, leaves him a stranger to the exchange of ideas; but the main cause is the inertia of the villager determined by the mental and geographical environment he inherits, which makes him cling desperately to the life he knows.

The root of the problem for those who plan for the future of the sedentary Sudanese is that of keeping all that is basically consistent with the life of a people who must remain agricultural, and yet filling them with something new and vital which will so influence their inner lives that they will be not static but dynamic. So far as the administrators are concerned the agriculturalists need more far-sighted rural finances, directed towards enduring values, as contrasted with urban finance and immediate gains. Real progress among them will come from a freedom, an unloosening in the original sense of the term *e-ducere*, so that, though still enchained by their physical environment, their mental life and personality may be vital.

The effect upon the nomads of a settled government has been towards consolidation or settlement. Many nomads are always ready to seize any opportunity of escaping from their insecurity either by joining larger tribes or changing to semi-nomadism. So in the Sudan we find nomads in every stage of transition. The living conditions of the Baqqāra, for instance, have been modified through the introduction of cotton, though the profits still go into cattle. Among the Beja 'the process of unification under native rulers is advancing fast. Tribal gatherings attract, by sports, race meetings, and feasting, more persons than ever from distant fastnesses. On these occasions a quite new desire to settle feuds and replace dissension by unity is apparent.'[1]

4. ECONOMIC CHANGE

The Sudan is in a most unfavourable economic position. The extent of desert, the nature of the soil, the necessity for irrigation for which certain regions only are suitable, and the difficulties of transport, prevent any wide development. Yet in no sphere of life have there been greater changes than in economic life. The influence of a Western government, bringing a new security, administrative reform, and transport facilities, has been such that there has been an economic penetration to a greater or lesser degree into every section of peasant and nomad life and economic activity has a far-reaching effect upon the life of a people.

Three types of economic organization prevail in the Sudan out of the five mentioned by Lord Hailey in his *African Survey*:[2]

(1) Where the European supplies the capital, technical management, transportation, and marketing; the native being responsible, under some supervision, for primary production. This is found in the Jezīra scheme of the Sudan Plantations Syndicate which is a tripartite collaboration between cultivator, private enterprise, and the State.[3] The State took a lease of the land; the control of cultivation and marketing was given to the Syndicate; and the tenants, who are mostly the original right-holders of the land, cultivate and pick the cotton and receive a fixed share of proceeds. They also have land for ordinary subsistence cultivation.

(2) Where 'the native population undertakes and finances the primary production without any consistent non-native supervision and the non-native's functions are confined to the marketing and transportation of his products', as in cotton cultivation in the Nūba Mountains and communal pumping-schemes in Donqola.

(3) A primitive subsistence economy which prevails over the greater part of the Sudan.

Many cultivators in the Jezīra, Gash, and Tokār cotton-growing

[1] Governor-General's Report on the Sudan, 1930. [2] Cf. *African Survey*, p. 1360.

[3] Op. cit., pp. 1053–5. The Sudan Government announced in August 1944 that the Jezīra Concessions Agreement will be allowed to expire in 1950 and the scheme become nationalized.

regions have become tied to the European economy and therefore dependent upon factors which lie beyond their control. The dangers of having a large district such as the Jezīra dependent upon one product, because of fall in prices, are provided against by the scheme. The cultivators' insecurity is made as little as possible whilst full provision is made for the cultivation of *dura*, thus stabilizing the food supply of the whole country. New Beja village communities have grown up along the canal banks of the cotton-producing area of the Gash and Baraka whose prosperity affects the life of the nomad tribes.

Under the present régime the Sudan has suffered comparatively little shifting of population compared with that which took place during the Mahdiyya, but there has been a great increase in the employment of seasonal labour. Westerners (Dārfūrian and Fallāta) and Nūba migrate eastwards to work in the Jezīra. Attempts made to improve the primitive methods employed in subsistence cultivation have had little success, even though at the same time the cultivators may be working on products like cotton under new conditions.

Native industries have decayed, but Western influence cannot be blamed for that, for they had decayed before the reoccupation, but it has not lent itself to their revival. Native cloth (*dammūr*), for instance, was being squeezed out by the importation of cheap fabrics. The war, however, has led the Government to encourage the revival of spinning and weaving.

Economic revolution in rural areas centres around the *sūqs*. Formerly owing to the risk of travel the tribesmen were confined to their tribal limits. Now the construction of railways and roads, the development of lorry transport, and the safety of travel have developed rural *sūqs* and linked them more closely with the towns. Former great markets have passed and once insignificant weekly *sūqs* owing to their position on roads have developed into market towns. The Sudan has been made commercially independent of Egypt by building a railway to Port Sudan. Trade has been centralized in Khartoum, Omdurman, and Port Sudan. The result has been a decay of the old market centres (Berber, Dāmar, Shendī, and Metemmah) and a growth of new ones (Omdurman, Atbara, Wādī Ḥalfa, Kareima, Wad Medanī).

Whilst the greater part of the population lives on the land, the growth of commerce based on towns has drawn many into an economic dependence not based on the land. Life in the cities is faster, more absorbing, pleasures and social prestige can be bought, therefore new economic motives, based on these new desires, have taken hold of many, and the way has been opened for satisfying them.

One thing should be stressed, that, whilst the economic centre of gravity for so many lies outside the community in which they were born, it has not led to individuals attempting to free themselves of family ties. The family holds as strongly as ever and those who become destitute will be cared for.

It is natural that a wide disparity should exist between the economic conditions of the rural and urban populations. There are, however, few wealthy land-owners (except religious heads) as in Egypt, who live directly on the labour of the cultivators. Further, the groups who sell the products of the peasant (other than cotton) to foreign markets, and import manufactured goods in return, are mainly foreigners, Greeks, Syrians, and Armenians. The disparity in wealth amongst the Sudanese themselves is mainly between the primary producer and the effendi, who cannot yet be said to be a member of a new class because his link with his village is unbroken and he may be found there during his holiday living a peasant life.

In general, it may be said that the Sudanese producer is given a fair chance; training, supervision, and a market for his produce, so that his economic future within the narrow limits imposed by his environment, is safeguarded.

5. WOMEN AND SOCIAL CHANGE

We have already shown that whilst social life is governed by *'āda*, family relationships are governed by the *sharī'a*, therefore the possibilities of the development of women in an environment like that of the Sudan are strictly limited. Yet it is clear that the training of girls, because of the contribution which they alone can make to the welfare of the home and community, is most vital. The training of the future mother is especially important in a land where the social order is based on the selfishness of men, where the woman has no place in the established order, and her link with the past is based on custom and superstition. Her round of customary observances, whilst it relieves the monotony of life, cannot enrich it.

Missions were pioneers in the education of women, Government schools followed with the opening in 1921 of a Teachers' Training College in Omdurman. In 1933 there were 22 elementary schools with 2,203 pupils, and in 1938, 35 schools with 3,411 pupils. In them the girls are given a groundwork of the three Rs and Qur'ān reading, the rest of the work being designed to be of value to home life, such as hygiene, mother-craft, needlework, and cooking. A girls' intermediate school was opened in Omdurman in 1939. The De La

Warr Commission in 1938 stressed the need for the expansion of girls' education, lengthening the school period, and making more provision for teacher-training.

Progress has been very slow, most of these schools being in the towns, and but a minute percentage of the women have been touched. Many parents withdraw their daughters from school at the age of 11 or 12 to be immured in the *ḥōsh* until marriage. But the prejudices against women's education, which missions had to overcome in their pioneer work, are fast disappearing and even nomad tribes are asking for teachers for their girls. The Governor-General's Report for 1930 contained the following statement:

> At a recent assembly of the Amarar section of the Beja people, the Nazir was found to be a stout advocate of female education. His reasons in support are interesting. 'Are not girls,' he said, 'at the bottom of most tribal affrays and murders? And how, unless our girls know how to read and write, can an absent husband communicate with the sharer of his secrets at home?'[1]

The development of medical treatment has had to face the opposition of the *ḥabōbāt* and the *fuqarā'*, and even to-day in the cities women patients are often brought to the hospitals only when feki-treatment has failed. In 1921 a Midwives' Training School was opened in Omdurman and to-day there are certified midwives in the remote rural districts. The general effect of school and medical work in the towns is that many of the children are cleaner and better cared for, and the women are learning the wisdom of visiting dispensaries, welfare centres, and hospitals. The training of the village girl is a totally neglected field. There is no woman's movement as in Egypt and other Near Eastern countries.

The roots of life have not been affected at all, and there has been no lightening of the bonds of custom and superstition. Even educated men show no signs of realizing the position and needs of women. In regard to seeking educated women as wives, the effendi is pulled two ways. He has little choice, of course, in the matter of a wife, but he is afraid that an educated wife might demand a new kind of life and be freer than is desirable. At the same time he would like a wife who could talk of something other than *ḥōsh*-gossip, and alternately coax and scream about new trinkets or leave to visit. The educated wife suffers the same immurement as others. She has possibilities, it is true, of enriching woman's life, but only if stimulation comes from outside through after-care work of the kind that missionaries especially can give. In general, all the effendi seeks is a plaything and childbearer,

[1] *Report on the Sudan*, 1930, pp. 12–13.

his ideals of companionship being satisfied by romantic homosexual friendships with members of his own sex, a particular form of vice normal and natural in any Islamic society.

6. THE PRESS

The Press is too important a current in the modern life of a Muslim community to be ignored in this survey, for it is but one more proof of the solidarity of the Islamic system.

The dominant editorial thinking is Islamic. This is natural because the two daily newspapers (*An-Nīl* and *Ṣōṭ as-Sūdān*) are owned by the two leading religious heads (Mahdist and Mirghanist) and reflect their bias; but at bottom, since the same is evident in other Islamic countries with secular owners, the Islamic bias is due to the domination of Islam over all departments of life. This ownership, however, has resulted in the newspapers being still less free than in other Islamic countries. At the same time the newspapers do bring in a flood of new ideas that have no place in the traditional scheme, though any discussion on, for example, the position of women is carefully edited.

The newspaper by no means holds the place in the Sudan that it does in other Muslim lands. The proportion of genuine literacy is not more than 2 per cent., and few even of these will spend P.T. 1 a day on a newspaper.[1] There is little reading aloud in cafés.[2] On the other hand, the newspaper is an index to currents of thought passing through cafés and clubs, though the Sudan Press is slavishly dependent upon Egypt for news and thought-direction.

[1] The daily circulation figures are *An-Nīl*, 1,200; *Ṣōṭ as-Sūdān*, 800 (1945). The Government literacy figures are: 1937, 2·2 per cent., 1942, 4 per cent.

[2] A recent war-time development, the broadcasting of news by public radio, has been much more effective.

INDEX

Arabic names to which the definite article *al-* is prefixed will be found under the initial letter, e.g. -Ghazālī for al-Ghazālī. The letter *b.* between two names stands for *ibn* (son of . . .). Arabic words and titles of books cited are printed in italic.

Aahmes I, Pharaoh, 40.
Aba Island, 93, 94, 160, 201.
ʿAbābda (T), 12, 15, 37, 68, 144.
ʿAbbāsids, 106, 188.
ʿAbd Allāh b. ʿAlī al-Ḥalanqī, 16, 133.
ʿAbd Allāh b. Dafaʿ Allah al-ʿArakī, 196, 198, 219, 240.
ʿAbd Allāh al-Ḥammāl, 219.
ʿAbd Allāh Jammāʿ, 74 n., 85, 196.
ʿAbd Allāh al-Mirghanī, 232.
ʿAbd Allāh b. Saʿd, 60–2, 67 n., 75.
ʿAbd Allāh b. Salīm al-Aswānī, *see* Ibn Salīm.
ʿAbd Allāh b. Sanbu, 70.
ʿAbd Allāh ash-Sharqāwī, 226 n.
ʿAbd Allāh at-Taʿaishī, al-Khalīfa, 4, 94–6, 104, 122, 147, 154, 157, 162, 170, 227–8.
ʿAbd al-Karīm al-Jāmiʿ, 90.
ʿAbd al-Maḥmūd b. Nūr ad-Dā'im, 228 n.
ʿAbd al-Mājid b. Ḥamad, 130.
ʿAbd al-Maʿrūf, 145.
ʿAbd al-Mutaʿāl b. Aḥmad b. Idrīs, 229.
ʿAbd al-Qādir I, Funj King, 86.
ʿAbd al-Qādir b. Idrīs, 138.
ʿAbd al-Qādir al-Jīlānī, 16, 130, 175, 192, 193, 198, 201, 202, 217–18, 220, 221, 222.
ʿAbd ar-Raḥmān b. Asīd, 119–20.
ʿAbd ar-Raḥmān b. Jābir, 131.
ʿAbd ar -Raḥmān b. al-Mahdī, 33, 158, 160.
ʿAbd ar-Raḥmān ar-Rashīd, 90.
ʿAbd ar-Rāziq Abū Qurūn, 130.
ʿAbd ar-Rāziq wad ʿIwaiḍa, 133.
ʿAbd al-Wahhāb, 155.
ʿAbd al-Wahhāb at-Tāzī, 229.
ʿAbdullāb (T), 81, 85, 87, 88, 89, 196, 219.
Abī ʿUmar, 116 n.
ʿAbīd, 19; *see* Slavery.
Abū'l-ʿAbbās al-Mursī, 222.
Abū ʿAbd Allah M. b. Sulaimān, *see* al-Jazūlī.
Abū Bakr, 192.
Abū Dilaiq, 132.
Abū'l-Faḍl ʿAllāmī, 194.
Abū Ḥamad, 144.
Abū Ḥanīfa, 115.
Abū'l-Ḥasan ʿAlī ash-Shādhilī, 193, 213 n., 222, 224.
Abū Jarīd, 240–1.
Abukr Ismāʿīl, Sultan of Maṣālīṭ, 33.
Abū Kabbās, 173.
Abū Makarram Hibat Allah, 68.
Abū Naṣr as-Sarrāj, 214.
Abū'l-Qāsim, *see* al-Qushairi.
Abū'l-Qāsim Aḥmad Hāshim, 121.
Abū Ṣāliḥ, 53 n., 64 n., 66, 68, 69, 73, 76 n., 87 n.
Abū Sharīʿa, 157.
Abū Surūr al-Faḍlī, 101 n.
Abū Yazīd al-Bistāmī, 193.
Abū Zaid, 101 n.
Abyssinia, 49 n., 59 n., 75, 79, 85, 174, 243.
Abyssinians, 6, 15, 57, 59 n., 74, 88, 181.
ʿĀda (customary observance), 26 n., 107, 114, 122, 182, 184, 263, 266.
Ādam Muḥammad al-Barqāwī, 158.
ʿAdlān II, Funj King, 168.
Aedesius, 49 n.
Aeizanes, (ʿEzānā), 45, 46, 48, 49 n., 55 n.
Aḥamda (T), 29.
ʿAhd, 205, 221, 224; *see* Initiation.
Ahl adh-Dhimma, 61, 70 n., 113, 187.
Ahl Ibl (camel nomads), 25–8, 110.
Ahl Sawāqī (cultivators by means of water-wheel), 19, 20.
Aḥmad al-Azharī, 235.
Aḥmad al-Badawī, 175, 193, 200, 213 n., 228 n.
Aḥmad Bokkor, 90.
Aḥmad al-Hajūnī al-Ghafrūnī, 200.
Aḥmad al-Huda, 132.
Aḥmad b. Idrīs al-Fāsī, 102, 199, 208 n., 225, 228–32.
Aḥmad b. Khōjālī, 223.
Aḥmad al-Maʿqūr, 90.
Aḥmad b. M. b. al-Mukhtār at-Tijānī, 236.
Aḥmad ar-Rifāʿī, 193, 213 n.
Aḥmad wad at-Taraifī, 145.
Aḥmad aṭ-Ṭayyib b. al-Bashīr, 199, 226–7, 228 n.
Aḥmadiyya *ṭarīqa*, 147, 228, 241.
ʿAidhāb, 58, 68 n., 84.
A'isha bint Abū Dilaiq, 132 n.
Aitikiya (Itika), 57.
ʿAjīb al-Mānjilak, or al-Kāfūtī, 74 n., 115, 196, 218–19.
— Awlād, *see* ʿAbdullāb, Wadʿ Ajīb.
-Akhḍari, 120.
ʿAlawiyya al-Mirghanī, 141, 234.
Alfa Hāshim, 160 n., 238.
ʿAlī b. Abī Ṭālib, 192.
ʿAlī Dīnār ibn Zakariyya, Sultan of Dārfūr, 33 n., 91, 97, 238, 239.
ʿAlī Wad Ḥilu, Khalīfa of Mahdī, 94, 154.
ʿAlī al-Hujwīrī, 127.
ʿAlī wad ʿIshaib, 139.
ʿAlī al-Labadī, 137.
ʿAlī al-Mirghanī, Sir, 234–5.

ʿAlī wad Mōj, 130.
ʿAlī Mubārak, 200.
ʿAlī an-Nīl, 197–8, 219.
ʿAlī b. Yaʿqūb b. al-Murshidī, 208 n.
Aliāb, section of Bishārīn, 12.
ʿĀlim, 122; see *ʿUlamā*.
-ʿAllāqī, 63, 67, 73 n.
Alodaei, 47 n., 55, 56–8.
Alodia, 49, 54, 55–8.
Alvarez, F., *Narrative of the Portuguese Embassy to Abyssinia*, cited, 77.
ʿAlwa, 45, 61, 63, 65, 72–5, 77, 79, 99, 196.
ʿAmal, 168, 175 n.
Amāna (a trust), 12.
ʿAmāra Dūnqas, *see* ʿUmāra.
Ammar'ar (T), 11, 12–13, 37, 221, 267.
Amon, 41, 42.
Amon Tarit, Candace of Ethiopia, 44.
ʿAmr ibn al-ʿĀṣī, 59–60.
Amrāb (section of Bishārīn), 12.
Amulets, 169–70, 180; see *Ḥijāb*.
Animism in Sudanese Islam, 32, 33, 101, 107, 108–9, 111, 163 ff., 249.
Annoubádes, 46.
ʿAnqarīb (rope bedstead), 21, 38 n., 117, 183.
Anṣār, 152, 154, 158, 161, 201.
Appion, Bishop of Syene, 46.
ʿAqīqa, 180–1.
Arabic Language, 37–8, 83, 243, 245, 248, 258.
Arabic-speaking Sudanese, 16–30, 82.
Arabs, 5, 6, 7, 16–19, 59–61, 68, 71, 106, 179, 180, 182, 184, 185, 242, 244, 245, 247, 251, 258.
— emigration into Sudan, 10, 17–18, 36, 67–72, 74, 81 ff., 98 ff.
— tribal organization, 19–20, 26, 79, 82, 97, 99, 115, 251, 253.
ʿArakiyyīn, 145, 196, 220.
Arbāb (*Arābīb*), 88.
Arbaʿjī, 74, 75, 87, 218.
ʿĀrif (gnostic), 189.
Arius, 209 n.
Arkell, A. J., 74.
Arnold, Sir T. W., 99 n., 249.
Arteiqa (Beja tribe), 15.
-Aʿsar, Shaikh, 146.
Aṣḥābāb ʿAbābda, 12.
-Ashʿarī, 118.
ʿĀshiq, 207, 208.
Ashiqqa Party, 262.
Al-ʿAshmāwī, 120.
Asshurbanipal, 41.
Atbai Umm Naji (section of Bishārīn), 12.
Athanasius, 50.
Aurelian, 44.
Awarfiūla, King of Nobadae, 55.
Awlād Ḥamaid (T), 29, 30, 82.
Awliyā, see *Walī*.
Awqāf, see *Waqf*.
Awrād (pl. of *wird*), 124, 169, 181, 199, 203, 204, 205, 206, 207, 208, 213, 222, 224, 225, 228, 231, 238.
ʿAwūdo b. ʿUmar, 128.
Axum, Kingdom of, 45, 47, 49 n., 58 n., 59.
Ayyām al-arbaʿīn, 173, 181.
Ayyām al-furāsh (*bikāʿ*), 184.
Ayyūbids, 68.
Azande, 35.
-Azhar, 116 n.
ʿAzīma, 135, 136, 167.
ʿAzmiyya *ṭarīqa*, 147 n., 239–40.

Baʿāti, 173.
Babikr Badrī, 260.
Badana (sub-section of tribe), 11, 12, 13.
Badawī b. Abū Dalaiq, 220.
Badawī, Shaikh, 103.
Badawiyya *ṭarīqa*, 193, 200, 228 n., 241.
Bādi II Abū Diqn, Funj King, 86.
Bādi IV, Funj King, 88.
Bādi b. Rubāṭ, 196.
Bādiya (nomads), 25.
Badōb (cotton soil), 3.
Badrāb, 220.
Baḥrite Mamlūks, 69, 79.
Baiʿa, 94, 153, 205, 221.
Baibars, Rukn-ad-Dīn, 69, 70, 79.
-Baiḍāwī, 149.
Baiqo (T), 34.
Bait al-māl, 154–5.
Baker, Sir Samuel, 92, 247 n.
Bakhra, 167–8.
-Bakrī, Shaikh, 194, 200.
Bakrī b. ʿAbd Allah, 143.
Bakrī wad Idrīs, 143.
Bakharās, 63 n., 64 n.
Bakht ar-Ruḍa, 255–6.
-Balādhurī, 60 n.
Balal ash-Shaib b. aṭ-Ṭālib, 134.
Balaña, 59.
Balaw, Eritrean tribe, 14, 59 n., 77 n.
Balīyūn, 59 n.
Bān an-Naqā, 136, 146, 196, 219.
Banjaman, Patriarch of Alexandria, 60.
Banī ʿĀmir (T), 11, 14–15, 37, 182, 233.
Banū Ḥalba (T), 29.
Banī Hilāl, 90, 98.
Banū Jaʿd, 70.
Banū Kanz, 68, 70, 71, 72, 79, 83–4; *see* Kanūz.
Banī Sulaim, 98.
Baqirmi, 91, 160.
Baqqāra, 3, 17, 20, 24, 25, 28–30, 37 n., 81, 83, 94, 96, 110, 122, 153, 154, 158, 160, 182, 242, 243, 244, 246, 263.
Baqṭ, 61, 63, 67, 69, 70, 76.
Barābra, 5, 7, 34, 84.
Baraka, 109, 110, 111, 118, 124, 127, 128, 129, 131, 135, 138, 139, 141, 142, 143,

161, 164, 165, 169, 173, 195, 196, 197, 203, 206, 212, 226.
Bāri (T), 35, 104.
-Barzanjī, 147 n., 221, 224.
-Bashīr Aḥmad Jalāl ad-Dīn, 202.
Bashīr b. Marwān, 10, 12.
Baṭāḥīn (T), 2, 17, 18.
Baṭn al-Ḥajar, 15.
Baṭn al-Manāṣir, 179.
Bayān, 139, 143, 233.
Bayūmiyya, 147 n., 241.
Beaton, A. C., 185–6.
Becker, C. H., 62 n., 99 n.
Bedairiyya (T), 17, 82, 84, 235, 244.
Beḍawi (Beja language), 10, 13, 14, 15, 37.
Bedāyāt (T), 32, 239.
Beja, 5, 6, 10–16, 24, 37, 38 n., 39, 41, 48, 49 n., 58–9, 63, 67, 68, 71, 81, 83, 85, 101, 110, 153, 171, 178, 179, 181, 183, 184, 185, 199, 221, 226, 233, 263, 265.
Berta (T), 29, 32, 243.
Bertī (Dārfūr tribe), 34, 160.
Bint Iblīs, 172.
Birqed (T), 34, 36 n.
Birth customs, 180–1.
Bishārīn (T), 11, 12, 37, 144, 146, 170, 178, 226, 261 n.
Blemmyes, 15, 44, 45, 46, 47, 49 n., 50, 56, 58 n.
Blood-money, 12, 27.
Bonet-Maury, G., 49 n.
Bornu, 91, 99, 100, 160.
Borqu, 31, 101.
Browne, W. G., 182, 245 n., 247 n.
Bruce, James, cited, 75, 86, 87, 88 n., 101 n., 244.
Budge, E. A. Wallis, 45 n., 46 n., 47 n.
-Bukhārī (traditionalist), 132, 149, 163.
Burckhardt, *Travels in Nubia*, 84 n., 120, 142 n., 222 n., 225.
Burhāmiyya, 200.
Burjī Mamluks, 84.
Burton, Sir R. F., 203 n.
Burūn (T), 32, 101, 243, 244.
-Būṣīrī, *Burda*, 147 n.
Buṭāna, 2, 11, 12, 17, 18, 26, 81.
Buwaihids, 193 n.

Caetani, Prince, 62 n.
Candace, 44.
Chatelier, A. le, 200.
Christianity among the Beja, 58–9.
— in Egypt, 49–50, 58, 76.
— in North Africa, 50.
— in Sudan, 9, 36, 47 n., 48–80.
Chronique de Michel le Syrien, 49 n., 60, 62–3 n.
Churchill, Winston, 154.
Circumcision, 180, 181–2.
Clement of Alexandria, 50.
Climate of Sudan, 3–4, 22.
Constantine the Great, 49 n., 50.
Coptic, 49–50, 66, 72.
Cosmas Indicopleustes, 50–1.
Cotton cultivation, 11, 13, 263, 264–5.
Cromer, Lord, 104 n., 117.
Crowfoot, J. W., 66–7, 73 n., 83, 182 n.

Dafa'-Allāh 'al-Gharqān', 139.
Dafa'-Allāh (al-'Arakī) b. M. Abū Idrīs, 131, 134, 198.
Dahara (rain cultivation), 20.
-Dairābī, 177.
-Dajjāl, 148–9, 158–9.
Dājo (T), 32, 33, 89, 178, 246.
Dāli (Dalīl Baḥr), King of Dārfūr, 90.
Damāliq, 33.
Damar (Arab nomads' summer settlement), 27.
Danāqla, 2, 5, 7, 8–9, 17, 19, 20, 48 n., 84, 89, 96, 100, 102, 153, 180, 182, 233, 244 n., 245 n., 247.
Danāqla-Ja'aliyyīn, 8 n., 17, 89, 92, 252, 257.
Dār Fartīt, 84.
Dār Funj, 31–2, 109, 165, 177, 178, 185, 242, 243.
Dārfūr, 3, 29, 30, 31, 32, 33, 81, 83, 84, 89–91, 99, 101, 102, 109, 110, 118, 160, 165, 177, 178, 182, 185, 200, 242, 251.
— Kingdom of, 89–91, 97, 100, 101–2.
Dār Ḥāmid (T), 16, 17.
Dār al-Ḥarb, 113.
Dār al-Islām, 113.
Dār Misairiyya, 33.
Dār Muḥārib (T), 29, 81.
Dār Runga, 84.
Darat (harvest season), 4.
Ḍarb al-mandal, 177.
Ḍarb al-raml, 177.
Ḍarb al-wada', 177.
Darqāwiyya, 200, 222.
Darwīsh (pl. *darāwīsh*), 152, 175, 192, 194, 204, 206, 223.
Da'ud b. 'Abd al-Jalīl, 218.
David, King of Maqurra, 69, 70.
Daw, 71.
Da'wa, 167, 173.
Dawālīb (T), 17.
De La Warr Commission, 255, 266–7.
Dervish, 132, 139, 192, 194.
Dervish Orders, 102, 111, 112, 123, 124, 126, 139, 141, 153, 187–241, 250–1.
Devolution in Sudan, 11, 20, 26, 97, 253, 261.
Dhikr, 16, 110, 123, 124, 146, 147, 162, 180, 181, 194, 195, 204, 205, 206, 207, 209, 211, 212–17, 221–2, 228, 230, 236, 238–9, 240, 241.
Dhimmīs, 61, 70 n., 113, 187.
Dhū'l-Nūn al-Maṣrī, 188.
Diglāl, chief of Banī 'Āmir, 14.

Dinka, 3, 35, 88 n., 104, 242–4, 246–7.
Diocletian, Emperor, 44 n., 51.
Dīra (*dā'ira* grazing range), 27.
Disūkiyya *ṭarīqa*, 200, 241.
Divorce, 9, 24, 176.
Dīya' (blood-money), 12, 27.
Ḍiyā' ad-Dīn Suhrawardi, 193.
Dodekaschoinos, 44.
Doughty, Charles, *Arabia Deserta*, cited, 28, 146 n., 165.
Dūdū, 173.
Dukhn (Pennissetum typhoideum), 32.
Dura (*Sorghum vulgare*), 2, 8, 18, 21 n., 32, 73, 117, 265.
Dushain, Qāḍī, 115 n., 116 n.

Economic change, 11, 21, 97–8, 250, 253, 255, 263, 264–6.
Education in Sudan, 116–22, 254–7.
Effendiyya, 112, 123, 129, 162, 169, 254 ff.
Egypt, 39, 49, 59–60, 67, 69, 70, 71, 76, 194, 200, 201, 255, 267.
— Christianity in, 49–50, 58, 76.
— Relations with Sudan, 39–47, 51, 60, 67–71, 83–4, 89, 91 ff., 96–7, 103–4, 226, 238, 241, 244, 254, 257, 258–9, 261.
Endoka, Sultan of Maṣālīṭ, 33 n.
Environment, adaption to, ix–x, 6–7, 18, 22, 27.
Eratosthenes, 43.
Ergamene, King of Meroë, 43.
Ethiopia, 39, 43, 44, 49 n.
Eusebius of Caesarea, 49 n., 58 n.
Eutycheus, 64.
Evil eye (*'ain ḥārra*), 25, 170–1, 174, 181.
'Ēzānā, King of Axum, 45, 46, 48, 55 n.

Fairaqi son of Zakariyya, Prince of Maqurra, 62 n.
Fanā' (dying to self), 132, 134 n., 208.
Fanaticism, 15, 30, 94, 157, 161, 163, 202.
Faqīh, 140 n.
Faqīr, *see* feki.
Faraḥ wad Taktōk, 158.
Faras, 53, 59, 63.
Fartīt, 84, 103.
Fasting, 25, 124.
Fatḥ al-kitāb (Bibliomancy), 177.
Fātiḥa, 128, 144, 184, 216, 217, 221, 224, 240.
Fāṭimid Dynasty, 62, 68, 147 n., 150, 193.
Fatra, 118.
Fatwa, 120.
Feki (pl. *fuqahā* or *fuqarā*), 8, 15, 16, 30, 31, 32, 90–1, 100, 101, 103, 108, 110, 117, 118, 119, 123, 129 ff., 140, 165, 167, 173, 195, 197, 241, 248, 249, 259, 262, 267.
Fellāḥīn, 83, 241.
Fellāta, 29, 31, 34, 159, 160, 172, 177, 238, 265.
Fellāta Melle of Kasala, 6.
Farīq (nomad encampment), 21, 30.
Fezāra, 72.
Fezzān, 57 n.
Fidaykiyya (T), 7.
Fiqh (jurisprudence), 114, 115, 116, 118, 119, 122, 130.
Firāsa, 128.
Frumentius, missionary to Axum, 49 n.
Fulāni, 31 n., 102.
Fulbe, 31.
Funj, 31–2, 79, 81, 82, 84, 85, 100, 110, 115, 196.
Funj régime, 16, 32, 74–5, 83, 85–9, 91, 100, 101, 108, 116, 195, 197–8, 219, 221, 243, 244.
Fuqahā, *see* feki.
Fuqarā, *see* feki.
Fuqarā' l-'ilm, 118.
Fuqarā'l-Qur'ān, 118.
Fūr (T), 32–3, 90–1, 118, 173 n., 177, 178, 185–6, 244.

Garamantes, 50–1, 56, 57 n.
Ge'ez, 37.
George, King of Maqurra, 61 n.
Ghafrūniyya, 200.
Gharbiyya Berbers, 85.
Ghazāla, 172.
-Ghazālī, 116, 130, 134, 190, 192.
Ghodiāt (T), 17, 82, 178, 244.
Ghūl, 173.
Ghulām Allāh b. 'Aid, 100.
Ghuzz, 84, 85.
Goldziher, I., 107.
Gordon, General, 92–3, 95, 96.
Gordon College, 253 n., 254–6, 258.
Greek influence on Sudan, 66, 72, 73, 76.
Gregory the Great, Pope, 58 n.
Griffith, F. Ll., 44, 64 n., 65 n., 72 n.
Gumus, 243.

Ḥabāb (T), 14, 37, 233.
Habbāniyya (T), 29, 247.
Ḥabīb Allāh al-'Ajamī, 198, 219 n.
Ḥabōba (grandmother), 23, 25, 111, 112, 182, 267.
Habūb (dust-storms), 3, 4.
Ḥadāreb, 10, 59 n.
Hadendiwa (T), 6, 11, 13–14, 15, 16, 20, 37, 59 n., 96, 172, 179, 222 n., 226, 234.
Ḥadīth, 115, 119, 156.
Ḥaḍra, 206, 215.
Ḥafnawiyya *ṭarīqa*, 226 n.
Haikal Pasha, Muḥammad, 259.
Hailey, Lord, 264.
Hajā b. 'Abd al-Laṭīf, 137.
Ḥajj, *see* Pilgrimage.
Ḥājju 'Abd al-Qādir al-Māsi', 139, 221 n.

-Ḥākim, Fāṭimid Khalīfa, 68, 76.
Ḥakkāma (Baqqāra tribal poetess), 30.
Ḥāl (mystical term), 132, 237.
Ḥalanqa (T), 15, 16, 37, 233.
Ḥalāwiyyin, 199, 227.
-Ḥallāj, 134, 190, 209 n.
Ḥalqa (*dhikr* circle), 212.
Ḥamad Abū Dunāna, 196, 223.
Ḥamad b. M. al-Majdhūb, 197, 198, 202, 224–5.
Ḥamad an-Naḥlān, 150.
Ḥamad b. Shaikh Idrīs, 220.
Ḥamad wad at-Turābī, 219.
Ḥamadorāb (section of Bishārīn), 12.
Hamaj, 6, 32, 85, 86, 88, 178, 243.
Ḥamar (T), 17, 18, 26, 81, 227.
Ḥanafī Madhhab, 121, 148.
Ḥannek (third cataract), 39, 84.
Ḥaqīqa, 207.
-Ḥaqīqat al-Muḥammadiyya, 209–10.
Ḥaqq ash-Sharāfa, 117.
-Ḥarāza, 180 n.
Ḥārith b. Asad al-Muḥāsibī, 188.
Ḥasan wad Ḥasūna, 87 n., 131, 134 n., 135, 136, 138, 144.
Ḥasan b. Muḥammad ʿUthmān al-Mirghanī, 143, 202, 233.
Ḥasaniyya (T), 18, 225.
Hausa, 31, 101 n.
Ḥawāzma (T), 20, 29, 246, 251.
Ḥayūt, 241.
Heraclius, Emperor, 60, 76 n.
Herodotus, 182 n.
Hicks, General, 95, 153, 154.
Ḥijāb (amulet), 129, 169–70, 172, 175 n., 179.
Ḥijāz, 100, 101, 108, 124, 195, 198, 219, 229.
-Ḥijāzī b. Abī Zaid, 168.
Hillelson, S., 34 n., 36 n., 37 n., 45 n., 48 n., 129 n., 134 n., 158, 178.
Hishām b. ʿAbd al-Malik, 64.
Ḥizb, 205, 213, 217.
Ḥōliyya, 146, 208 n., 215, 230.
Homburger, L., 37.
Ḥōsh (compound), 23, 117, 172, 174, 179, 215, 259.
Howāra Berbers, 84.
Hrihor, High Priest of Amon, 41 n.
Hulūl (incarnation), 190.
Ḥumr (Baqqāra tribe), 29.
Ḥunain b. Isḥāq, 189.
Ḥuqūq aṭ-ṭarīq (rules of a *ṭarīqa*), 207.
Ḥūr, 174.
Hurgronje, Snouck, cited, 164, 174 n.
Ḥuwār (student disciple), 117.
Hyksos, 40.

ʿ*Ibāḍī*, 15 n.
ʿIbba (T), 31.
Ibn ʿAbd al-Ḥakam, 60, 61 n., 62 n., 67 n.
Ibn Abī Zaid of Qairawān, 119.
Ibn al-ʿArabī, 190, 209, 216.
Ibn Baṭūṭa, 10, 59 n., 71 n., 194, 222 n.
Ibn al-Fāriḍ, 208 n.
Ibn Ḥanbal, 209 n.
Ibn Janbalān, 84.
Ibn Khaldūn, ʿ*Ibar*, cited, 59 n., 71–2, 74.
Ibn Khaldūn, *Muqaddama*, cited, 28, 116–17, 120, 149, 188.
Ibn Masarrah, 189.
Ibn Saʿad, 209 n.
Ibn Saʿīd, 59 n.
Ibn Salīm al-Aswānī, 10, 61, 63, 64, 65, 71 n., 72, 73, 78, 88 n., 99–100, 182 n.
Ibn Saʿūd, 230.
Ibn Sīrīn, 177.
Ibn Ṭūlūn, 63 n., 67.
Ibn Tūmart, 150.
Ibrāhīm, Sultan of Dārfūr, 91.
Ibrāhīm b. Adham, 193.
Ibrāhīm al-Bulād, 116.
Ibrāhīm ad-Disūkī, 200, 213 n.
Ibrāhīm Pasha, 84 n.
Ibrāhīm ar-Rashīd, 199, 208 n., 229, 231.
Ibrāhīm b. Umm Rābʿa, 131.
Ibrāhīmiyya, 241.
Ibrīm (Primis), 44, 46, 64, 68.
ʿ*Īd al-fiṭr* (or ʿ*Īd aṣ-ṣaghīr*), 118, 124.
ʿ*Īd al-kabīr* (*-qurbān, -aḍḥā*), 15, 124.
ʿ*Idda*, 115 n.
Idrīs b. al-Arbāb, 101 n., 116 n., 131, 196, 197, 219, 220.
Idrīs al-Majdhūb, 142 n.
-Idrīsī, 59 n., 64 n., 65.
Idrīsids of ʿAsīr, the, 230.
Idrīsiyya *ṭarīqa*, 9, 93, 151, 199, 212, 228–31, 234.
Ijāza (licence), 131, 203, 228.
Ijmāʿ, 113, 114, 190.
Iḥsān (righteousness), 123.
ʿIkka, 31.
ʿIkrīma, 70, 72.
ʿ*Ilm at-Tawḥīd*, 116, 118, 119.
Imām, 118, 122, 123, 186.
Īmān (faith), 123.
ʿ*Imma*, 87, 221, 228.
Infibulation of women, 9, 17, 23, 83, 181–2.
Ingessana (T), 32, 101, 243, 244.
Initiation, 133–4, 185, 200, 203, 205–6.
-Insān al-Kāmil, 209–11.
ʿĪsā, *-Nabī*, 112, 148–9, 158–60, 161.
Ishrāqī, 189, 222.
Isis, Temple of, at Philae, 46, 47, 50, 51.
Islām, among the Beja, 15–16, 59 n.
— animism in, 32, 33, 101, 107, 108–9, 111, 163 ff., 242, 249–51.
— as a social system, 4, 102, 106 ff., 260.
— conception of God in, 109, 164, 165, 209, 251.
— contrast between African and Asiatic, 249.

Islām, education in, 116–22.
— eschatology in, 108, 148 ff.
— holiness in, *see* saints, *walī*, *baraka*.
— influence of Manichaeanism on, 189 n.
— legal system of, 107 ff.; see also *Sharī'a*.
— Logos conception in, 209–11.
— mysticism in, *see* Ṣūfism.
— orthodox, 109, 112 ff.
— spread in the Sudan, 75–6, 79, 86, 90–1, 98–104, 248 ff.
— syncretism in, 106–7.
Islamic law, 104, 105, 165, 180, 190, 208; see *Sharī'a*.
Ismā'īl b. 'Abd Allāh, founder of Ismā'īliyya, 141, 147 n., 200, 202, 235.
Ismā'īl b. 'Abd al-Qādir, 157.
Ismā'īl b. Makki 'd-Daqalāshī, 135 n.
Ismā'īl Pasha, 91, 92, 93, 225.
Ismā'īliyya *ṭarīqa*, 141, 147, 200, 202, 235–6.
Isnād, 192.
-Istakhrī, Abū Isḥāq, 59 n.
Istiḥyā, 179.
Istikhāra, 177.

Ja'aliyyīn, 17, 18 n., 19, 81, 82, 84, 96, 180, 182, 198, 224–6, 237, 245, 261 n.
Ja'aliyyīn-Danāqla, 8 n., 17, 96, 110, 180.
Jabalāwīn, 32.
Jabal Barkal, 41.
Jabal Gūle, 32, 178.
Jabal Marra, 3, 32, 89.
Jabal Māssa, 150, 151.
Jabal Mīdōb, 34, 36 n.
Jabal Mōya, 32, 42, 86.
Jabal Sagadi, 67, 73, 86.
Jābar al-Anṣarī, 84.
Jadhb or *Jadhba*, 132, 151, 213.
Ja'far al-Mirghanī, 211, 215.
Ja'farā, 241, 247 n.
-Jāḥiẓ, 117, 187.
Jalāl ad-Dīn ar-Rūmī, 193.
Jallāba (petty traders), 8, 248, 250.
Jamā'a, 113, 174 n.
Jamā'at Abū Jarīd, 240–1.
Jammāla (camel people), 25.
Jāmi' (congregational mosque), 123, 147.
Jām'i (T), 16 n.
Jamū'iyya (T), 16 n., 17, 18 n., 59 n., 81, 199, 227.
Jawābra (T), 17, 84.
Jawām'a (T), 16 n., 17, 18 n., 82, 244.
-Jazarī, 120.
Jazīra, 3, 17, 19, 31, 45, 81, 85, 86.
-Jazūlī, 196, 213 n., 223.
Jazūliyya *ṭarīqa*, 222.
Jihād, 70 n., 85, 94, 99, 149, 154, 156, 157, 159, 187.
Jilaidāt (T), 244.
-Jīlānī, *see* 'Abd al-Qādir.
Jim' (T), 29, 30, 244.
Jimī'āb (T), 10 n.
Jinn, 25, 128 n., 132, 152, 163, 164, 167, 171–2, 181.
Jirtiq, 17, 180, 181, 182–3.
Jizya, 70 n.
John, Abbot of Biclarum, 51, 56, 57.
John, Bishop of Ephesus, 49, 51–8.
Juhaina, 17, 28, 29, 67, 68 n., 72, 74, 82 n.
Julian, missionary to Nubia, 51–4.
Julianus of Halicarnassus, 57.
Julius Aemilianus, 44.
-Junaid, 191.
Junaidiyya *ṭarīqa*, 232.
Justin II, Emperor, 51 n., 54, 56.
Justinian I, Emperor, 46, 47, 51–2, 56, 57.

Ka'ba, 130, 165.
Kabābīsh (T), 17, 27, 38, 81, 180 n., 246.
Kabūshiyya, 41, 55, 72.
Kakar, 87, 198, 219, 221.
Kalām (dogmatic theology), 116, 119, 130, 224.
Kānem, 80, 99.
Kāno, 102.
Kanz ad-Dawla, 68, 70.
Kanūn, chief of Beja tribe, 67.
Kanūrī, 31.
Kanūz (T), 5, 7, 68, 182; *see also* Ban Kanz.
Karāma, 22 n., 127, 128, 135, 172, 184, 232.
Kash (Kush), 39, 40, 41.
Kashta, King of Kash, 41.
Kāsū (Meroë), 45.
Katsena, 102.
Kawāhla, 10, 16 n., 25, 27, 83, 199, 227, 246.
Keith, Sir Arthur, cited, 16.
Kēra Dynasty in Dārfūr, 90.
Kerembes, King of Maqurra, 70.
Kerma, 40.
Khalīfa (of a *ṭarīqa*), 123, 131, 139, 143, 145, 192, 194, 195, 196, 197, 202, 203–4, 215, 217, 241.
Khalīfa 'Abd Allāh, *see* 'Abd Allāh.
Khalīl b. Isḥāq, 119.
'Khalīl', manual of jurisprudence, 116, 120, 130–1, 134, 224.
Khalwa, 16, 93, 100, 112, 115 n., 117, 123, 133, 134, 137, 138, 141, 191, 205, 212, 223, 227, 248, 250.
Khalwatiyya, 147 n., 226, 236.
-Khāmsiyya, 162 n., 240.
Khānqāh, 191, 193–4.
Kharāj, 70 n.
-Kharāzī, 120.
Kharīf (rainy season), 4, 18, 20, 25.
Kharqa, 206.
Khasa, *see* Tigrē language.
Khasham bait (section of tribe), 26.
Khaṭīb (preacher), 123.

Khatmiyya, 16, 147, 199, 202, 217, 231, 234; *see* Mirghaniyya.
Khawālda (T), 81.
-Khiḍr, 95, 127 n., 135, 152.
Khōjalī b. ʿAbd ar-Raḥmān, 130, 136, 137, 143, 145, 197, 204, 220, 223.
Khōma, 32, 101, 243.
Khurāfāt (legends), 172.
Khuṭba, 70 n., 125.
Kihāna, 163.
Kināna (T), 25, 83.
Kirwan, L. P., 56 n., 63 n.
Kisra (millet bread), 21 n., 73, 173, 204.
Kitchener, Lord, 158, 177, 254.
Koldāji, 102.
Korosko, 68.
Kraus, P., 49 n., 56 n.
Kresh, 103.
Kubrā b. Surūr, King of Maqurra, 65.
Kūdiya, 175–6.
Kujūr, 34, 86, 165, 178, 244.
Kukur (Tabi hills), 32, 243.
Kumeilāb (T), 15.
Kungāra, 32–33.
Kurbāj (hippo-hide whip), 9.
Kushshāf, 7, 84.

Lailat al-Qadr, 145.
Lailiyya, 214–17, 221.
Lake Chad, 29, 80, 99.
Lampen, E., cited, 178.
Lampen, G. D., cited, 30.
Lane, E. W., cited, 140, 174 n., 213.
Languages of Islamic Sudan, 35–8.
Lauture, d'E. de, 38, 140.
Letronne, 64 n.
Libyans, 40, 41, 44.
Littmann, E., 45 n.
Logos conception in Islam, 209–11.
Lōḥ, 136 n.
Longinus, Bishop of Nubia, 54–8.

Maʿāliyya (T), 29.
Mabān, 242, 243; *see* Burūn.
Mai Aḥmad, 31, 160.
Mai Wurno, 31, 160, 238.
Macdonald, D. B., 127 n., 190, 191 n., 234 n.
MacMichael, H. A., *History of the Arabs in the Sudan*, 1922, cited, 6, 16 n., 17, 32–3, 46 n., 48 n., 74 n., 89–90 n., 129, 144, 159 n., 165, 173 n., 242 n., 244 n., 245 n.
Madhhab (plur. *madhāhib*), 114–15, 118, 153, 162.
Ma'dhūn, 122.
Magic, 109, 110, 163 ff.
-Maʿhad al-ʿilmī, 121, 122.
Maḥaī, 7.
Maḥas (T), 5, 7, 19, 35, 65, 84, 101, 182.
Mahdī, 102, 132, 148 ff., 251; *see* Muḥammad Aḥmad b. ʿAbd Allāh, Ibn Tūmart, -Sanūsī, Muḥammad ʿUbaid Allāh.
-Mahdī al-Muntaẓar, 94.
Mahdism, modern, 33, 147, 157–63, 227, 262, 268.
Mahdiyya, 4, 15, 18, 19, 29, 33 n., 93–6, 103, 104, 108, 121, 123, 147, 150–7, 162, 200, 233–4, 243, 245, 247, 265.
Maḥmūd Abū Shaiba, 143.
Maḥmūd al-ʿArakī, 100, 115.
Maḥmūd al-Miṣrī, 116.
Majādhīb, *see* Majdhūbiyya *ṭarīqa*.
Majdhūb, 151, 211, 213.
Majdhūbiyya *ṭarīqa*, 16, 153, 197, 199, 201, 202, 222, 223, 224–6, 234.
Makk (pl. *mukūk*), 84, 87.
Makoritae, 47 n., 51 n., 56, 57.
Mala'ikat al-Baḥr, 174.
Malāmatiyya, 135, 150, 211.
Malakiyya, 243.
Mālik b. Anas, 115, 118.
Mālikiyya *madhhab*, 108, 115, 120, 121, 182, 232 n.
Malle (Māli), 99.
Mamlūks, 67–8, 69, 70, 71, 74, 76, 79, 88, 89, 99.
-Ma'mūn, Khalīfa, 67 n.
Manāḥa, 183.
Manichaeanism, 189 n.
Mānjil, 32, 87, 178, 243.
Maqāmāt, 208.
Maqdūm, 33.
Maqurra, Christian Kingdom of, 49, 59–71, 73, 79, 99.
-Maqrīzī, 10 n., 59 n., 60 n., 61 n., 62 n., 63 n., 64 n., 67 n., 68 n., 69 n., 70 n., 100 n., 147 n., 179, 193.
Marabbaʿ (rectangular mud building), 23.
Margoliouth, D. S., 148.
Maʿrifa (gnosis), 189.
Marīs, 64, 65, 68, 69.
Marīsī, language of Maḥas, 7.
Marriage customs, 30, 156 n., 165, 179, 180, 182–3.
Maʿrūf al-Karkhī, 188.
Maryam al-Mirghanī, 141, 234.
Maṣālīt (T), 32, 33, 159, 160, 177.
Maṣawwaʿ (Masawa), 85, 200.
Masjid, 123; *see* Mosque.
Maspero, J., 49 n., 54 n.
Massignon, L., 190.
-Masʿūdī, *Les Prairies d'Or*, cited, 10 n., 59 n., 65, 71 n., 72, 173 n.
Matokiyya (T), 7.
Matrilinear system, 71–2, 179–80.
Mawālid; see *Mūlid* (recitation).
Mawlāwiyya *ṭarīqa*, 193.
Maximinus, General, 46.
Medanī an-Nāṭiq, 146.
Meinhof, C., 36.

Meleikāb (s-tribe of ʿAbābda), 15.
Melkites, 52 n., 54, 55, 57, 58, 60, 64.
Merīsa (millet beer), 21, 73, 124.
Meroë, 36, 41–6, 48.
Meroitic Language, 36, 45.
Merowe, 84.
Messīriyya (T), 29.
Metamorphosis, 33, 137, 177.
Meyer, E., 41 n.
Michael the Syrian; see *Chronique de Michel le Syrien.*
Mīdōb (T), 34, 36 n., 178, 180.
Miḥāya, 168.
Milk taboos, 15, 185.
Milner Commission Report, 255.
Mīma (T), 34.
Miracles, 135–9, 145; see *Karāma.*
Miʿrāj, 132.
Mirghaniyya *ṭarīqa*, 9, 16, 143, 147, 158, 199, 201, 202, 203, 204, 205, 207, 213, 214–17, 220, 223, 230, 231–5, 262, 268.
Misairiyya (T), 33, 182, 251.
Mittu, 104.
Monophysite Christianity in Abyssinia, 49 n., 57, 75, 78.
— in Eastern Sudan, 48–59, 66–7, 73, 75–80.
— in Egypt, 49–50, 52 n., 58, 60, 64, 76.
Mosque, 105, 115, 118, 122 ff.
Mourning customs, 183–4.
Muʾadhdhin (muezzin), 122, 123.
-Muḍawwī, 100 n., 119.
Muftī, 121.
Muhājirīn, 118.
Muḥammad, the prophet, 59, 105, 149, 152, 163, 184, 209, 210, 259.
Muḥammad b. ʿAbd al-Karīm as-Sammānī, 199, 226 n.
Muḥammad b. ʿAbd aṣ-Ṣādiq, 196.
Muḥammad Abū Likailik Kamtūr, 88, 227.
Muḥammad b. ʿAdlān, 101 n., 119.
Muḥammad Aḥmad b. ʿAbd Allāh, the Mahdī, 18, 93–6, 122, 132, 148, 150 ff., 201, 226, 227, 228, 239.
Muḥammad b. ʿAli b. M. b. Aḥmad Idrīs, 230.
Muḥammad ʿAli Pasha, 89, 91–2, 103, 200.
Muḥammad ibn ʿAlī as-Sanūsī, 199, 229, 233, 239.
Muḥammad al-Badawī, 121, 139, 237.
Muḥammad Badr, 220.
Muḥammad Baḥr ad-Dīn, Sultan of Maṣālīṭ, 33.
Muḥammad Bey the Daftardār, 91, 92.
Muḥammad b. Dāʾūd al-Agharr, 221.
Muḥammad al-Hamīm, 115, 116 n., 135, 219.
Muḥammad al-Ḥasan as-Sammānī, 226 n.
Muḥammad wad ʿIsa ʿSuwār adh-Dhahab,' 116, 197.
Muḥammad Khair, 247.
Muḥammad Māḍī Abū'l-ʿAzāʾim, 239–40.
Muḥammad al-Mahdī as-Sanūsī, 150, 154, 239.
Muḥammad al-Majdhūb aṣ-Ṣughayyir, 199, 225.
Muḥammad b. M. b. Masʿūd b. ʿAbd ar-Raḥmān, 200.
Muḥammad b. al-Mukhtār, 132, 134 n., 147 n., 200, 237.
Muḥammad an-Naqshabandī, 193.
Muḥammad an-Nāṣirī'sh-Shādhilī, 197, 223.
Muḥammad b. Qadam, 116.
Muḥammad Qaili, 137.
Muḥammad b. ar-Raida, 119.
Muḥammad b. Salīm al-Hafnīsī, 226 n.
Muḥammad Sharif b. Nūr ad-Dāʾim, 93, 94, 227, 228.
Muḥammad Sharīf, Khalīfa of Mahdī, 154.
Muḥammad Sirr al-Khatm, 216, 233.
Muḥammad at-Tiwaim, 157.
Muḥammad ʿUthmān Abū Jirja, 154.
Muḥammad ʿUthmān al-Mirghanī, 14 n., 147, 199, 200, 210, 211, 216, 229, 231 ff.
Muḥammad Ẓāhir al-Madanī, 225.
Muʿizz, Fāṭimid Khalīfa, 61 n.
Muʿjizāt, 127 n.
Mukāshafāt, 136.
Mūlid (recitation of Prophet's birth story), 146, 210, 213, 221, 236.
Mūlid an-Nabī, 125, 146, 216, 226 n., 228.
Munshid, 215, 216, 217.
Muqaddam, 194, 203, 221, 236, 238, 241.
Murābiṭīn, 99.
Murāqabāt, 144.
Murīd, 193, 194, 203, 206, 211, 221, 224, 228, 238.
Mūsā b. Ibrāhīm, 13.
Mūsā b. Yaʿqūb, 131.
Murray, G. W., 36, 41 n., 144, 146, 171, 178.
Murshid, 133, 193, 194, 228.
Muṣabaʿāt, 88, 92.
Muṣāfaḥa, 206, 238.
-Musallamī'ṣ-Ṣaghīr, 134, 136.
Musallamiyya, 220.
Mushāhara, 171, 180, 181.
Muslim (traditionalist), 148, 163 n.
Muṣṭafa b. Kamāl ad-Dīn al-Bakrī, 226 n.
Muṭahhar b. Ṭāhīr al-Maqdisī, 59 n.
Muʿtaṣim, Khalīfa, 62 n.
-Mutawakkil, Khalīfa, 67 n.
Muttaḥidīn, 155.
Muwalladīn, 241.
Muzāriʿīn (cultivators), 19–25, 123, 124, 153, 196, 262–3.
Mysticism, *see* Ṣūfism.

Nabtāb, 14–15.
Nadī'n-Nūbiyyīn (Guild of Nubians), 7 n.

Naḥās (tribal drums), 26 n., 87.
Nā'ib (of *ṭarīqa*), 194.
Napata, 41–2, 43, 44.
Naqīb, 194, 240.
Naqshabandiyya *ṭarīqa*, 193, 232, 241.
Narses, 44.
-Nāṣir Muḥammad b. Qalā'un, 70.
Nationalism, 18, 151, 261–2.
Nāẓir (tribal chief), 18, 20, 26, 29, 32.
Negroids, 5, 35, 39–40, 45, 48, 99, 103–4, 179, 242–51.
— Muslim, 31–4, 243, 245–6, 248 ff.; *see* Funj, Fellāta, Fūr.
Neoplatonism, 189, 209 n.
Nero, 44.
Nicholson, R. A., cited, 134 n., 135 n., 208, 209, 211 n.
-*Nīl* (newspaper), 182 n., 268.
-*Nīl al-Azraq*, 85 n.
Nilotic tribes, 35, 99, 103–4, 242, 246–8.
Nitria, monastery, 52 n.
Nōba, 45, 46.
Nobadae, 47, 52, 54, 55, 56, 57, 59, 64.
Nomadism in Sudan, 11, 18 n., 79, 97, 263–4.
Noubai, 43–6.
Nūba, 3, 6, 16 n., 36 n., 40, 42, 44, 45, 46, 48, 61, 64, 81, 82, 83, 84, 86, 87, 89, 101, 102, 103, 104, 115, 178, 186, 232, 242, 244–6, 250, 265.
Nubia, 5, 39, 40, 44, 46, 49, 50, 51, 54, 55, 59 n., 63, 64, 68, 69, 76, 79, 81, 83–4, 99, 101.
Nubian Language, 35–7, 45, 48, 49, 59, 65–6.
Nubians, 2, 7–10, 12, 21, 44, 47, 48, 50, 51, 53, 54, 60, 65, 67, 68, 71, 76, 78, 83, 102, 110, 179, 232.
Nuēr, 3, 35, 104, 246–7.
Nūr al-Muḥammadiyya, 209–10.
Nushūgh (tribal dispersal during rains), 27.
Nyamang, 104, 245.

Olympiodorus, 46 n.
Omdurman, 31, 96, 139, 142 n., 143, 147, 154, 174, 180, 230, 245.
Origen, 49 n., 50.
'Osmān ('Uthmān) Diqna, , 153, 226.

Palestine Pilgrims' Text Society, 66.
Pallme, L., *Travels in Kordofan*, cited, 102, 103, 244 n.
Palmer, Sir R., cited, 80.
Pa-smun, son of Paesi, 44 n.
Petronius, Prefect of Egypt, 44.
Philae, 42, 46, 47, 54, 64 n.
Piankhi, King of Kash, 41.
Pilgrimage (*ḥajj*), 25, 31, 100, 124, 156, 160, 195.
Plotinus, 189 n.
Pregnancy, 180.
Press, 268.
Primis (Ibrīm), 44, 46 n., 47.
Priscus, 46 n., 51.
Procopius of Caesarea, *De Bello Persico*, cited, 44 n., 47, 51.
Proverbs, Sudanese, 22, 135, 137, 140, 142, 181, 219 n.
Ptolemaic Dynasty, 43.
Ptolemy, geographer, 57 n.

Qāḍi, 121, 122, 140.
Qādiriyya, 101, 139, 147 n., 160 n., 192, 193, 196, 197, 199, 202, 204, 212, 217–22, 223, 232.
Qalā'ūn, Sultan, 70.
Qalīdūrūn, King of Maqurra, 61.
-Qalqashandī, *Ṣubḥ al-A'shā*, 84 n.
Qarīb Allāh, 139, 228.
Qarībiyya, 228.
Qarīna, 167, 172.
-Qaṣr, 64, 65.
Qaṭī' (store-room), 218.
Qawāsma, section of Rufā'a, 74.
Qerri, 74 n., 81, 85, 196, 244 n.
Qibla, 133.
Qirā'āt (variant readings), 116, 119.
Qiyās, 113, 114.
Quatremère, 69 n.
Qubba, 105, 136, 139, 141–6, 196, 204.
-Qumait, 209 n.
Qura'ān (T), 32, 98, 239.
Qur'ān, 33, 105, 106, 107, 109, 111, 112, 113, 114, 115, 116, 117, 118, 119, 124, 126, 130, 140, 141, 144, 148, 156, 163, 169, 172, 184, 185, 187, 190, 212, 228, 229.
-Qurashī, Shaikh al-, 94, 227.
-Qurtabī, 151 n.
-Qushairī, 187 n., 188 n., 190 n.
Quṭb, 95, 127, 131, 135, 152, 211.
Quṭṭiyya (pl. *qaṭāṭī*), grass hut, 23 n.

Rabī'a (T), 10, 67, 68, 82 n.
Rābi'a al-'Adawiyya, 188.
Raḥmāniyya, 200.
-Raḥrāḥ, Governor of al-Abwāb, 72.
Rākūba, 23 n., 117, 122, 133.
Rakwa, 136, 228.
Ramaḍān, 32 n., 124, 184, 243.
Rashā'ida (tribe), 25, 226, 231.
Rashīdiyya *ṭarīqa*, 199, 230–1.
Rashāsh (sowing season), 4.
Rātib, 156, 162, 213, 236.
Ra'ūf Pasha, 94, 235.
Reincarnation, 173.
Reinsch, 37.
Reisner, G. A., 41, 42 n., 43, 47.
Ribāṭ, 73, 191, 193, 217.
Riḍā (quietism), 188.
Rifā'iyya *ṭarīqa*, 147, 193, 200, 213 n., 241.
-*rīḥ al-aḥmar*, 174–7.

Rinn, L., 218.
'Risāla', 116, 119, 134, 224.
-*Risālat as-sādisa*, 132, 134 n., 237–8.
Rites de passage, 166, 180 ff.
Rizaiqāt (T), 29, 247.
Romans, 43, 44, 50.
Rosary, see *sibḥa*.
Rubāṭāb (T), 18, 180.
Rufāʿa (T), 17, 19, 74, 81, 85, 242, 243.
Rufinus, 49 n.

Ṣadaqāt, 124, 184.
Ṣādiqāb, 196, 219.
Saʿdiyya *ṭarīqa*, 200.
Sāḥir, 168, 170–1, 177.
Saidokki (T), *see* Maḥas.
Saʿīd Pasha, Khedive of Egypt, 92, 237.
Ṣaif (hot, dry season), 3, 4, 20, 25.
Saints, 25, 100, 101, 102, 108, 109, 110. 126 ff., 191, 195 ff., 200, 204, 249.
Saïtes, (26th) dynasty of Egypt, 41.
Sakali, 183.
Ṣalāḥ ad-Dīn (Saladin), 68, 193.
Ṣalāt, 114, 122, 123, 124, 156, 212, 228.
Ṣāliḥ b. Bān an-Nāqa, 134 n., 198, 219, 220.
Salīm I, Sultan of Turkey, 84, 85.
Salmān aṭ-Ṭawwālī, 128 n.
-*Salṭana'z-Zarqā'*, 85 n.; *see* Funj régime.
-Samarkandī, 85.
Sammāniyya, 93, 139, 147, 151, 196, 199, 201, 220, 221, 223, 226–8.
Samory, 104 n.
Sanders, G. E. R., 13.
-Sanūsī, *Muqaddama*, 119.
Sanūsiyya *ṭarīqa*, 201, 230, 239.
Sāqiya (water-wheel), x, 8, 20, 144.
Sārī Saqatī, 191.
Sawālif, 11, 180 n., 184.
Ṣawm (fast), 25, 124.
Selaim (T), 29, 81, 227, 242, 247.
Seligman, Prof. C. G., 5, 10, 32, 35, 41 n., 48 n., 88 n., 186 n., 246 n., 247.
Selūka (foreshore cultivation), 20.
Sennār, 31, 40, 85, 86, 87, 101, 244.
Sennār Confederation, *see* Funj régime.
Senusret III, Pharaoh of Egypt, 40.
Shabaka, Pharaoh, 41.
S͟hād͟hiliyya *ṭarīqa*, 101, 193, 196, 197, 208, 213, 222–4, 229, 231, 232, 236, 240.
S͟hadūf, 8.
-S͟hāfiʿī, 115, 116, 182 n.
S͟hāfiʿiyya mad͟hhab, 115, 120.
S͟hahāda, 53 n., 78, 100, 155.
S͟haik͟h al-Bakrī, 194, 200.
S͟haik͟h as-Sijjāda, 202, 203, 228.
S͟haik͟h aṭ-Ṭuruq, 200.
S͟haik͟h al-ʿUlamā, 121, 139.
S͟haik͟hiyya *ṭarīqa*, 222.
S͟hā'iqiyya (T), 17, 18, 83, 84, 88–9, 100, 182, 225, 231, 233, 261 n.
S͟haiāb (T), 15.
S͟hakalōta, 173.
S͟hakanda, 69.
S͟hamamūn, King of Maqurra, 70.
S͟hams ad-Dawla Ṭūrān S͟hāh, 68.
S͟hank͟hāb (T), 29.
S͟hantirāb (section of Bis͟hārīn), 12.
S͟haraf ad-Dīn wad Burrī, 133–4, 139.
-S͟haʿrānī, 129, 187.
S͟harḥ, 119.
S͟harqāwiyya *ṭarīqa*, 226 n.
S͟harīʿa, 9, 11, 12, 26 n., 107, 109, 113–14, 116, 121, 122, 123, 124, 134–5, 179, 180, 182, 184, 185, 190, 207, 259, 266.
S͟harṭā'i, 33.
Shashank, King of Nubia, 41.
S͟haṭḥāt, 134 n., 215, 241.
-S͟hātibī, 120.
Shāu Dors͟hīd, Tunjur ruler of Dārfūr, 90.
S͟hihāb ad-Dīn Suhrawardī, 193.
Shilluk (T), 3, 35, 48, 75, 86, 88, 101, 104, 241, 242, 246–7.
S͟hita (winter), 4.
S͟hukriyya (T), 2, 17, 18, 20, 182, 233, 234.
S͟huqair, Naʿūm, *Ta'rīk͟h as-Sūdān*, 84 n., 85 n., 87, 94 n., 151 n., 152 n., 154 n., 170.
S͟huwaiḥāt (T), 17, 82, 244.
Sibḥa (rosary), 25, 198, 212 n., 222 n., 228, 248.
Sibr, 180.
Sīd al-qōm, 86, 88.
Siḥr, 163, 165, 168.
Sijjāda, 198, 221.
Siʿlāt, 173.
Silko, King of Nobades, 46 n., 47, 55 n.
Silsila, 192, 207, 208.
Simāya (naming ceremony), 180, 215.
Slatin, *Fire and Sword*, 91, 94 n., 156, 170.
Slavery, 23 n., 29, 63, 78, 93, 103, 104, 244–5, 248.
Sōba, capital of ʿAlwa, 54, 63, 72, 73, 77, 79, 244.
Sōba stone, 165, 178.
Songhai, 99.
Ṣōṭ as-Sūdān, 268.
Stack, Sir Lee, 255.
Strabo, 43, 44, 182 n.
Sudan, Arab invasion of, 36, 60–2, 81–3.
— Christianity in, *see under* Christianity.
— devolutionary method in, 11, 20, 26, 97, 253, 261.
— French, 1, 29, 81, 160, 242.
— Funj regime in, 75, 85–9, 100–1.
— Greek influence on, 43, 66, 72.
— languages of, 35–8.
— nationalism in, 18, 151, 261–2.
— nomadism in, 11, 18 n., 79, 97, 263–4.
— peoples of, 4–38.
— relations with Egypt, 40 ff., 83–5, 89, 96.
— religious orders in, *see* Dervish Orders.

Sudan, slavery in, 23 n., 29, 84–5, 93, 103, 104, 244–5, 248.
— southern, 5, 35, 43, 72, 73.
— spread of Islam in, 75–6, 79, 86, 90–1, 98–104, 248–51.
— western, 1, 29, 81, 99, 104, 160, 242, 265.
— western influence on, 20, 21, 97–8, 252–68.
— women in, 9, 16, 23–5, 30, 179, 266–8.
Sudd (Ar. *sadd* block), 1, 3, 42, 44, 99.
Ṣūfī, 94, 116, 120, 134–5, 151, 191 ff.
Ṣūfī Doctrine, 188–90, 206–12.
Ṣūfism, 101, 108, 112, 116, 130, 187 ff.
Sufraji (house boy), 141.
Suhrawardiyya *ṭarīqa*, 193.
Sukkōt (T), 5, 84, 182, 261 n.
Sulaimān Solong, King of Dārfūr, 90, 91, 102.
Suʿluwwa, 173.
Sunkāb, 183.
Sunna, 113.
Sūq (market), 18, 21, 117, 146, 169, 250, 265.
Syene, 44–7.

Taʿai<u>sh</u>a (T), 29, 160.
Ṭabaqāt, *see* Wad Ḍaif Allāh.
Tafsīr, 119, 156.
Ṭāḥā Ḥusain, 259.
Ṭahūr, *see* Circumcision.
Tāj ad-Dīn al-Bahārī, 196, 218–19.
Tajwīd (methods of Qur'ān recitation), 116, 119.
Takārīr (sing. Takrūrī), 31 n.
Takkāzē (Atbara), 45.
Talmis, 47.
Talqīn, 203.
Tamīma, 169.
Tamīm ad-Dārī, 187.
Tanutamon, 41.
Tāqiyya, 205, 219.
Tāqiyya umm qarnain, 87.
Ṭarīqa, 94, 133, 144, 147, 153, 162, 191, 192 ff.
Taṣawwuf, 116, 130, 187; *see* Ṣūfism.
Tawḥīd, 189; see *ʿilm at-tawḥīd*.
Ṭayyibiyya *ṭarīqa*, 222.
Teherāb, Sultan of Dārfūr, 102.
Teqalī (Nūba people and Kingdom), 20, 83, 86, 87, 100, 219, 244, 246.
Tereramani, King of Blemmyes, 44 n.
<u>Th</u>aqalān, 152.
Thebaid, 44, 50, 51, 52.
Thebes, 40, 41.
Theodora, Empress, wife of Justinian I, 51–2, 53, 54, 56.
Theodore, Bishop of the Thebaid, 54.
Theodore, Monophysite Patriarch of Alexandria, 56.
Theodosius I, the Great, 51.
Theodosius II, Emperor, 46.
Theodosius, Patriarch of Alexandria, 51–2, 53, 54.
Tibbu (Tubu), 32, 81, 239.
Tigrē (serfs of Banī ʿĀmir), 14.
— language, 37.
Tiffa (fuzzy-head), 6, 13.
Tijāniyya (*ṭarīqa*), 33 n., 104 n., 132, 147, 160 n., 193, 200, 201, 212, 236–9.
-Tilimsānī, 116, 197.
Tilmī<u>dh</u>, 195, 204.
Timbuktoo, 102.
Tirhāka, 41.
Tombs, see *qubba*.
Tornasi, 243.
Tribal Court, 26 n., 122, 185.
Tukl (pl. *takala*, grass hut adjoining *quṭṭiyya*), 23, 142, 143.
-Tūnīsī, *Voyage au Darfour*, cited, 33, 91 n., 118 n., 177 n., 182, 220–1.
Tunjur, 89–90, 101.
Turko-Egyptian rule, 18, 19, 91–3, 102–3, 200.

ʿUbaid Allāh b. al-Ḥabḥāb, 67.
Uduk (T), 243.
ʿUlamā, 114, 115, 116, 120 ff., 132, 190, 202, 207, 208 n., 222, 229, 233.
ʿUmar, al-ḥājj, 104 n.
ʿUmar Ganbo, 200, 238.
ʿUmar al-<u>Kh</u>alwatī, 226 n.
ʿUmar b. al-<u>Kh</u>aṭṭāb, 64.
ʿUmāra Dūnqas, 74 n., 85, 115.
-ʿUmarī, Ibn Faḍl Allāh al-, 69, 70 n., 71 n.
Umayyads, 106, 188.
ʿUmda (head of tribal section or group of villages), 20, 21, 29.
Umm al-Barāhīn, 119.
Umm Buʿullū, 173.
Umm Durmān, *see* Omdurman.
Umm aṣ-Ṣubyān, 167, 172, 173.
Umma, 113.
Umma Party, 262.
ʿUqba ibn Nāfiʿ, 60, 98.
ʿUqda, 169–70.

Valerian, 51.
Van Gannep, 166.

Wad (i.e. walad) ʿAjīb, 75, 86, 87.
Wad Ḍaif Allāh, *Ṭabaqāt*, cited, 75, 87 n., 88 n., 100 n., 115, 116 n., 119–20, 128 n., 129, 130–9, 146, 196, 197, 198, 218–21, 224.
Wad Umm Maryūm, 139 n.
Wadā'i, 32, 90, 91, 99, 100, 101, 160, 161.
Waddān, 57 n.
Waḥdat al-wujūd, 209.

Wahhābism, 102, 103, 155, 198, 199, 228, 229, 230, 240.
Wajd, 212.
Walī, 126, 128, 131, 139, 140, 169, 175 n., 194, 203, 215, 226.
Waqf, 194, 201.
Warsh, 116.
Waẓīfa, 213.
Wensinck, A. J., 119.
Were-wolf, 33; *see* metamorphosis.
West Africans, 31, 99, 124, 158, 160, 161, 171, 200, 238, 265; *see* Fellāta.
Westermann, D., 36.
Westernism, influence of, 20, 21, 97–8, 252–68.
Wingate, Sir Reginald, 4, 104 n., 152, 156, 157.
Wird, 203, 205, 213 n., 222 n., 231, 236.
Women in Sudan, 9, 16, 23–5, 30, 179, 266–8.
Wüstenfeld, F., 64 n.

Yaʿqubāb, 123 n., 139, 196, 219, 220, 221, 227.
-Yaʿqūbī, 58 n., 60 n., 63, 73 n.
Yāqūṭ, 59 n.
Yemenites, 147 n.
Yūsuf Abū Shara, 145.
Yūsuf al-Hindī, 147 n., 227.

-Zabālʿa, 240.
Zaghārīṭ, 183 n.
Zaghāwa (T), 32, 122, 160, 178.
Zāhid, 189.
Zailaʿīn, 15 n.
-Zain b. Ṣaghairūn, 130.
Zakarias, Patriarch of Alexandria, 76.
Zakāt, 124, 155.
Zalangei, 33.
Zanāfaj, 59 n., 88 n.
Zanātiyya, 84 n.
Zande (T), 3, 104.
Zār (pl. *zairān*), 171, 174–7.
Zāwiya, 16, 100, 101, 118, 123, 193, 197, 200, 205, 206, 215, 222, 229, 233, 236.
Zenkovsky, S., 182 n.
Zindīq, 189, 207.
Zinj, 6, 72.
Zinzīr, Shaikh, 145.
Zīr (large water-pot), 137.
Ziyāra, 25, 144.
Zubair Pasha, 91, 92, 94, 95.
Zuhd (asceticism), 188.
Zyhlarz, 36, 45 n., 48.